Triumph Toledo & Dolomite 1300 Owners Workshop Manual

by J H Haynes

Member of the Guild of Motoring Writers

and A J H Phelps

Models covered:
Triumph Toledo. 1296 cc
Triumph Dolomite 1300. 1296 cc

ISBN 0 900550 86 4

Printed in England

ABCDE 086 · 8D2
FGHIJ
KLMNO
PQRST

HAYNES PUBLISHING GROUP
SPARKFORD YEOVIL SOMERSET ENGLAND
distributed in the USA by
HAYNES PUBLICATIONS INC
861 LAWRENCE DRIVE
NEWBURY PARK
CALIFORNIA 91320
USA

D1789458

Acknowledgements

Thanks are due to BL Cars (Triumph Division) for technical information and for certain illustrations. Wadham Stringer Ltd of Wellington Road, Taunton, Somerset were also of great help, in particular Mr Hackney, with the supply of further technical information. Castrol Ltd supplied further details on lubrication and the Champion Sparking Plug Company Limited supplied the illustrations showing the various spark plug conditions. The bodywork repair photographs used in this manual were provided by Lloyds Industries Limited who supply 'Turtle Wax', 'Dupli-color Holts', and other Holts range products.

Last, but not least, thanks must go to all those people at Sparkford who assisted in the production of this manual, particularly Stanley Randolph, Trevor Hosie, Ian Robson, John Rose and Peter Ward.

About this manual

Its aim

The aim of this Manual is to help you get the best value from your car. It can do so in several ways. It can help you decide what work must be done (even should you choose to get it done by a garage), provide information on routine maintenance and servicing, and give a logical course of action and diagnosis when random faults occur. However, it is hoped that you will make full use of the Manual by tackling the work yourself. On simpler jobs it may even be quicker than booking the car into a garage, and having to go there twice, to leave and collect it. Perhaps most important, a lot of money can be saved by avoiding the costs the garage must charge to cover its labour and overheads.

The Manual has drawings and descriptions to show the function of the various components so that their layout can be understood. Then the tasks are described and photographed in a step-by-step sequence so that even a novice can do the work.

Its arrangement

The manual is divided into thirteen Chapters, each covering a logical sub-division of the vehicle. The Chapters are each divided into consecutively numbered Sections and the Sections into paragraphs (or sub-sections), with decimal numbers following on from the Section they are in, eg 5.1, 5.2, 5.3 etc.

It is freely illustrated, especially in those parts where there is a detailed sequence of operations to be carried out. There are two forms of illustration: figures and photographs. The figures are numbered in sequence with decimal numbers, according to their position in the Chapter: eg Fig. 6.4 is the 4th drawing/illustration in Chapter 6. Photographs are numbered (either individually or in related groups) the same as the Section or sub-section of the text where the operation they show is described.

There is an alphabetical index at the back of the manual as well as a contents list at the front.

References to the 'left' or 'right' of the vehicle are in the sense of a person facing forwards in the driver's seat.

Whilst every care is taken to ensure that the information in this manual is correct no liability can be accepted by the authors or publishers for loss, damage or injury caused by any errors in, or omissions from, the information given.

Contents

Chapter	Section	Page	Section	Page
	Lubrication chart	6	Ordering spare parts	8
	Recommended lubricants	7	Routine maintenance	9
1 Engine	Removal	15	Reassembly	30
	Dismantling	18	Final assembly	40
	Decarbonisation	30	Fault diagnosis	41
2 Cooling system	Draining	43	Thermostat	45
	Flushing	43	Water pump	45
	Filling	43	Fan belt adjustment	48
	Radiator	43	Fault diagnosis	49
3 Fuel system and carburation	Air cleaner	50	Fuel tank	60
	Fuel pump	50	Fuel pipe lines	60
	Carburettor	54	Fault diagnosis	63
4 Ignition system	Contact breaker points	66	Ignition timing	69
	Condenser	66	Spark plugs	70
	Distributor	66	Fault diagnosis	71
5 Clutch and actuating mechanism	Bleeding	74	Removal and replacement	77
	Slave cylinder	75	Release mechanism	78
	Master cylinder	75	Fault diagnosis	80
6 Gearbox	Removal and replacement	83	Reassembly	90
	Dismantling	83	Cover extension	94
	Mainshaft	85	Top cover	94
	Input shaft	88	Fault diagnosis	97
7 Propeller shaft and universal joints	Propeller shaft removal and replacement	98	Universal joints	100
			Centre bearing	100
8 Rear axle	Half shafts	101	Pinion oil seal	104
	Differential assembly	104	Removal and replacement	104
9 Braking system	Bleeding	108	Handbrake	116
	Adjustment	108	Front disc brakes	118
	Master cylinder	112	Servo unit	121
	Wheel cylinder	116	Fault diagnosis	122
10 Electrical system	Battery	124	Horns	134
	Alternator	125	Headlight units	134
	Starter motor	129	Fuses	136
	Windscreen wiper	130	Fault diagnosis	142
11 Suspension and steering	Front hub bearings	146	Steering wheel	154
	Front suspension	147	Rack and pinion	154
	Rear hub assembly	152	Wheel alignment	160
	Rear suspension	153	Fault diagnosis	160
12 Bodywork and underframe	Maintenance	161	Seats	170
	Repairs	163	Heater	170
	Doors	163	Bonnet	172
	Windscreen	170	Boot	172
13 Supplement	Introduction	175	Propeller shaft	190
	Fuel system and manifolds	178	Braking system	193
	Ignition system	180	Electrical system	195
	Gearbox (single rail)	183		
Index				204

Introduction to the Triumph Toledo

The Triumph Toledo was introduced to the English market in August 1970 as Triumph's new small car (even before the last Herald 13/60 was made!) At the same time they introduced the Triumph 1500 and this together with the Toledo superseded the Triumph 1300. They, therefore, had two new models both a little 'grander' than the two models they replaced; the Toledo for the 13/60 Herald and the 1500/1300.

The mechanical layout of the Toledo differs from all the other models and does not in fact follow either the 1300 type front wheel drive nor the Herald rear wheel drive. It is front engined and rear wheel drive but has non-independent rear suspension and the engine it uses is that of the 13/60 Herald. It does however, bear a striking resemblance to both the 1300 and the 1500.

It is designed for a market which would appreciate the quality of a Triumph, but below the cost of a 1300/1500, and yet have its space at the price of the 13/60 Herald. It is a straightforward simple small family saloon with an air of refinement. It succeeds by having well tried and successful mechanical components in a pleasant yet uncomplicated bodyshell of conventional construction.

The models described in this manual are those for the English market in that they are fitted with the 1296 cc engine with either 2 or 4 door bodyshells. Both drum and disc front brake models are covered. Some markets are supplied with a 1500 version of the Toledo; whilst this model is not dealt with here specifically it will be very similar.

General dimensions and weights

Wheelbase	8 ft. 0.5/8 in.	2460 mm.
Track (Four up)		
Front	4 ft. 5 in.	1348 mm.
Rear	4 ft. 2 in.	1270 mm.
Ground clearance (Four up)	4¼ in.	108 mm.
Turning circle	34 ft.	10.4 m.
Overall dimensions		
Length	13 ft. 0.1/8 in.	3970 mm.
Width	5 ft. 1¾ in.	1572 mm.
Height (unladen)	4 ft. 6 in.	1372 mm.
Weights (approx.)		
Dry (ex extra equipment)	16½ cwt.	840 kg.
Basic kerb (inc. tools, fuel oil and water)	17½ cwt.	890 kg.
Gross vehicle weight (max.)	24 cwt.	1220 kg.
Interior dimensions (Seats empty)		
Front	in.	mm.
Width - door to door	51	1300
Seat width (each)	20	508
Seat height (floor to cushion)	13	330
Seat depth	19	483
Headroom (from seat cushion)	34	864
Squab to clutch pedal (Max.)	37½	952
(Min.)	31½	800
Steering wheel clearance from seat squab (Max.)	18½	470
(Min.)	12½	292
Steering wheel clearance from seat cushion	7	178
Rear		
Rear seat effective width	47½	1208
Rear seat height - floor to cushion	13	330
Rear seat depth	17½	445
Rear head room - from seat cushion	33½	852
Rear squab to back of front seat (Max.)	31½	800
(Min.)	25½	658
Luggage compartment		
Height (Max.)	17	432
(Min.)	13½	343
Depth (Max.)	33	837
(Min.)	26	660
Width (Max.)	52½	1335
Width between wheel arches	39½	1005
Effective opening width	40	1018
Capacity	10.7 cu.ft.	.29 cu.m.
Capacities		
Petrol tank	10½ gal.	48 litres
Engine sump	7 pints	4.0 litres
Engine oil filter	1 pint	0.56 litres
Gearbox - from dry	1½ pints	0.85 litres
Rear axle - from dry	1½ pints	0.85 litres
Cooling system with heater	8½ pints	4.8 litres

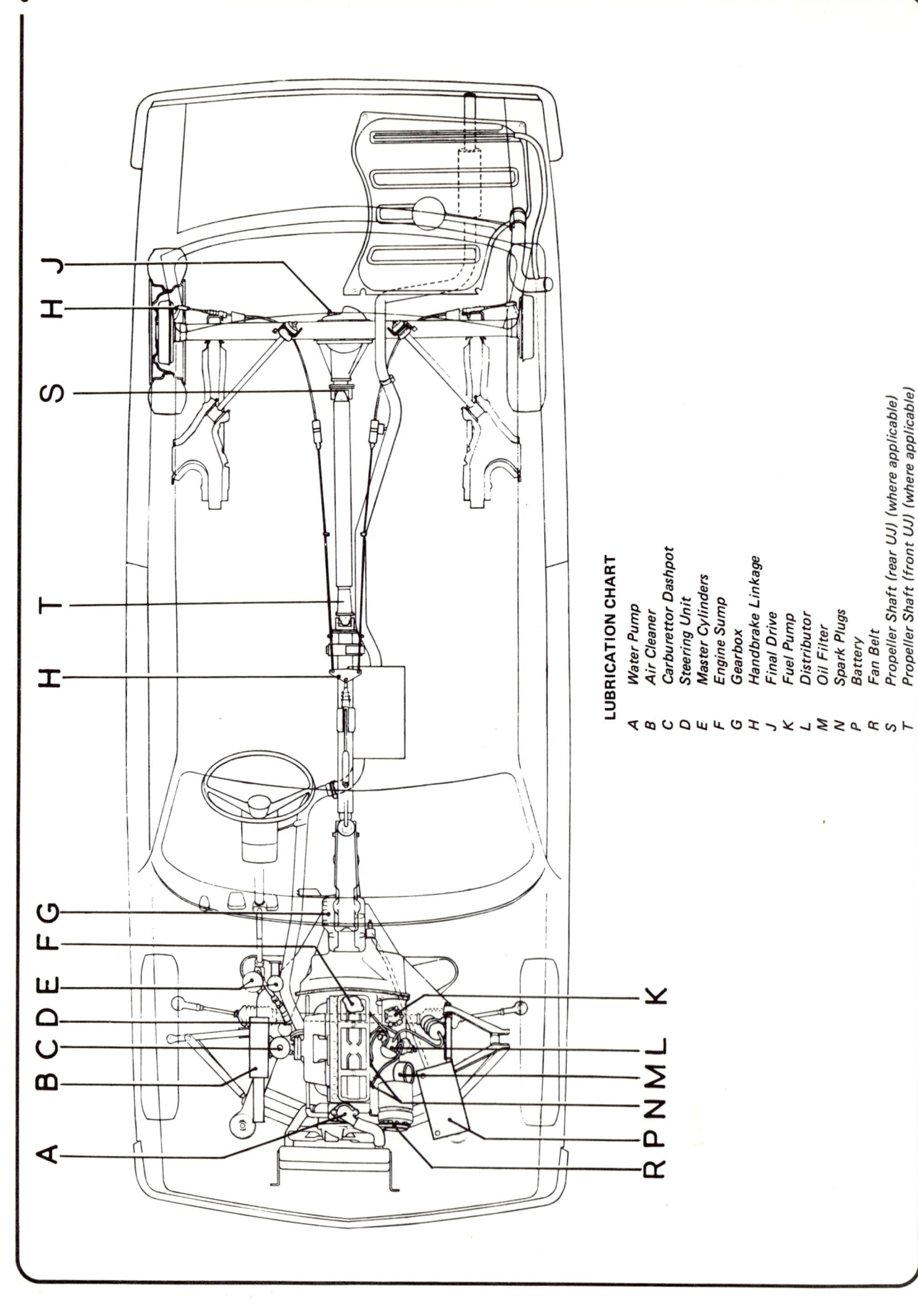

LUBRICATION CHART

A Water Pump
B Air Cleaner
C Carburettor Dashpot
D Steering Unit
E Master Cylinders
F Engine Sump
G Gearbox
H Handbrake Linkage
J Final Drive
K Fuel Pump
L Distributor
M Oil Filter
N Spark Plugs
P Battery
R Fan Belt
S Propeller Shaft (rear UJ) (where applicable)
T Propeller Shaft (front UJ) (where applicable)

Recommended lubricants and fluids

Component	Type of lubricant or fluid	Correct Castrol Products
ENGINE	20W/50 multigrade engine oil to exceed the latest API SE specification	CASTROL GTX
GEARBOX	90 EP hypoid extreme pressure gear oil to meet MIL—L—2105 and API Service GL4 specifications ...	CASTROL HYPOY
REAR AXLE	As for the gearbox	CASTROL HYPOY
ALL CHASSIS, STEERING AND SUSPENSION GREASING POINTS ...	Multi-purpose high melting point lithium based grease	CASTROL LM GREASE
CLUTCH AND BRAKE SYSTEM RESERVOIRS	Special high performance brake and clutch fluid with a minimum boiling point of 550F, meeting SAE specification J1703c	CASTROL GIRLING UNIVERSAL BRAKE AND CLUTCH FLUID
APPROVED ANTI-FREEZE SOLUTION	Solution with anti-corrosion additives with ethylene glycol	CASTROL ANTI-FREEZE

Ordering spare parts

Always order genuine Triumph spare parts from your local British Leyland agency. Authorised dealers carry a comprehensive stock of genuine parts and can supply most items 'over the counter'. Orders can be placed through local garages but this is not as desirable.

When ordering new parts it is essential to give full details of your car to the storeman. He will want to know the car model and details found on the engine identification plate, and chassis type. The location of the plate is shown in the illustration. Year of manufacture is necessary too. If at all possible take along the part to be replaced.

If you want to re-touch the paintwork you can obtain an exact match (providing the original paint has not faded) by quoting the paint colour in conjunction with the model details.

The Commission Number (chassis number) is stamped on a plate affixed to the top of the left-hand front wing valance.

The Engine Number is stamped on a flange on the left-hand side of the cylinder block.

The Gearbox Number is stamped on the top right-hand face of the gearbox casing.

The Rear Axle Number is stamped on the bottom flange of the axle casing.

Paint and Trim Numbers are included on the Commission Number plate.

When obtaining new parts remember that many assemblies can be exchanged. This is very much cheaper than buying them outright and throwing the old part away.

Commission number plate

L034

Routine maintenance

The maintenance instructions listed are basically those recommended by the manufacturer. They are supplemented by additional maintenance tasks which practical experience has shown, should be carried out at the intervals suggested.

The service intervals are given in a summary table at the end of the tasks.

1 Check thickness of disc pads (if fitted): if less than 1/8 inch (3 mm) they must be renewed.

2 Check that all tyres, including the spare, have at least 1 mm depth of tread across ¾ of their width, and are free from cuts, ruptures, and severe abrasions on their sidewalls.

3 Check exhaust system for leaks, and that hangers and brackets are intact and firmly fixed.

4 Lubricate between windscreen wiper shafts and rubber bushes with 1 - 2 drops of glycerine. No NOT use oil. Renew blades if they leave an absolutely clean windscreen streaky.

5 Change engine oil. Place container of 1.25 gallons (5.7 litres) capacity under warm engine: remove and clean sump plug. Clean filler cap in petrol or paraffin: allow to dry before replacing. Refit sump plug and washer securely and refill with 7 pints (4 litres) of Castrol GTX. Run engine and check for leaks. When cool, recheck dipstick level.

6 Top up gearbox with Castrol Hypoy.

7 Top up rear axle with Castrol Hypoy.

8 Clean inside of distributor cap and check carbon brush moves freely in recess. Remove rotor arm. Inspect contact breaker points and renew if pitted: adjust gap to 0.015 inch/0.38 mm. Add 2 drops of Castrol GTX to cam retaining screw and spindle, and 7 - 8 drops through central hole in contact breaker plate; and 1 drop to pivot post. Smear contact breaker cam lightly with Castrol LM Grease. Replace rotor arm and cap. Clean coil and all leads between distributor, coil and plugs, and inspect for cracking and deterioration. Check ignition timing and reset if necessary. Road test the car and make final adjustments with the vernier control on the distributor if necessary.

9 Clean out all ventilating slots in alternator: no lubrication is needed.

10 Hold each side of jacked up front wheel and rock firmly. If steering wheel does not immediately respond in both directions, the steering system ball joints are worn and must be replaced. Check boot-type gaiters or bellows of steering system. If damaged, renew them. Lubricate steering rack with 5 strokes only of a gun filled with Castrol LM Grease.

11 Lubricate with Castrol GTX all linkages, pin and moving parts of the controls of the carburettor, clutch and footbrake. Apply Castrol LM Grease to handbrake linkage.

12 Check cooling system hoses and clips: look for cracking walls and splits starting, and renew before bursting occurs.

13 Remove top of air cleaner. Remove single element and clean by tapping lightly. Clean inside of container and cover before reassembling; replace the breather pipe.

14 Clean off any corrosion around battery terminals and clamps, and smear these areas with a trace of petroleum jelly, such as vaseline. Check earth connection is firm.

15 Top up carburettor dashpot with Castrol GTX to within about 0.5 inch (13 mm) of the top of the tube. Check engine idling, at normal working temperature. If uneven, or if it tends to stop, adjust with jet adjusting nut and throttle stop screw.

16 Adjust fan belt and renew if there are signs of cracking or fraying. Check tension, which should permit a 0.75 inch (19 mm) depression midway along the longest run.

17 Clean spark plugs and reset gaps to 0.025 inch (0.6 mm).

18 Check brake wear. Remove brake drums, clean out dust, and

Drain engine oil and refill with Castrol GTX

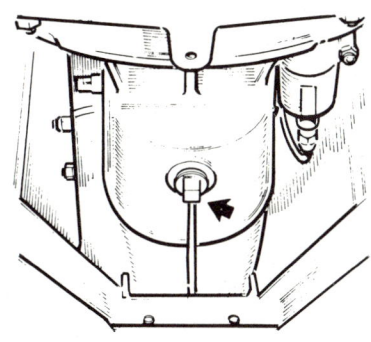

Top up gearbox with Castrol Hypoy

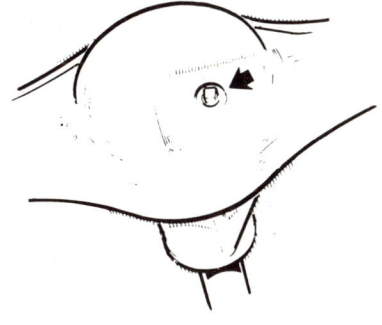

Top up rear axle with Castrol Hypoy

check that no fluid is present. If brake shoes are less than 1/32 inch (0.8 mm) above the rivet heads, they must be renewed.

19 Adjust brakes using bottom square headed adjuster on front wheels and top adjuster on rear wheels (four wheel drum brake models). Handbrake should be off and wheels chocked in turn. Rotate each adjuster clockwise until jacked up wheel locks, then back a notch at a time until wheel just frees. On front disc brake models all brakes are self-adjusting. Use of handbrake adjusts rear brakes, so if handbrake travel becomes excessive, check brake shoe wear before considering adjustment.

20 Inspect hydraulic master cylinder and all rigid and flexible pipes for leaks, chafing, damage and corrosion. Check fuel system and pipes similarly.

21 Lightly lubricate with Castrol Everyman all hinges, locks, lock cylinders, courtesy light plungers, heater controls. Lightly grease door striker plates with Castrol LM Grease.

22 Check security of fixing of the following: starter motor, front and rear suspension mountings, suspension arms, steering column clamp, steering rack mounting, carburettor flange and manifold, exhaust manifold and downpipe, wheel nuts, alternator fixing bolts, steering universal joint bolts.

23 Check front wheel balance and alignments. This requires special equipment and is best dealt with by your British Leyland dealer.

24 Change engine oil filter when changing engine oil as in Operation 5. Unscrew filter unit and discard: clean joint face and lightly oil both it and new sealing ring before screwing in new filter unit firmly.
Note: refill quantity with filter change is increased to 8 pints (4.6 litres) of Castrol GTX.

25 Remove plug on water pump, fit screwed nipple, and apply grease gun filled with Castrol LM Grease.

26 Hold top and bottom of each jacked up front wheel and rock firmly. If slack is felt, adjust bearings to correct running clearance.

27 Check engine rubber mountings for damage or deterioration.

28 Unscrew top nut on fuel pump. Remove bowl, clean bowl, filter screen and sediment chamber with petrol. Check gasket is sound; then reassemble.

29 Check valve clearances and adjust the specified settings.

30 Check propeller shaft universal joints for wear, and for tightness of locknuts. Apply grease gun filled with Castrol LM Grease to nipple on sliding joint at gearbox (or axle, if applicable) end of shaft.

31 Clean areas around springs, and shock absorbers and inspect for damage and fluid leaks. If empty car is not level on level ground, suspect weak or broken spring. Bounce each corner: if bouncing is not quenched immediately, the shock absorbers need attention. Check for rust, where suspensions are attached. Check rubber bushes for play or deterioration.

32 Check seat belts for fraying, especially at clips and clamps, and that anchor bolts are secure.

33 Fit new set of spark plugs set to gap of 0.025 inch (6 mm).

34 Remove top of air cleaner and discard single element. Clean container and cover before fitting new element, and replace the breather pipe correctly at summer or winter setting.

35 Remove top of carburettor and clean out float chamber. When reassembling, take special care not to damage float needle and valve.

Special note:
1 OIL CHANGES
   Your car manufacturer recommends more frequent oil and oil filter changes when the following adverse motoring conditions apply:

1 Stop/start motoring with prolonged engine idling.
2 Regular short journey use.
3 Frequent cold weather starting.

   The inspection of all oil and fluid should be made with the car standing on a level surface.

2 Undertake the following weekly checks no matter what

mileage the car covers and in addition to the Routine Maintenance tasks just described.

   Check engine oil level and top up as necessary with Castrol GTX.

   Check level of battery electrolyte and top up with distilled water.

   Top up windscreen washer reservoir.

   Check tyre pressures (when cold).

   Check level of radiator coolant (NOT while hot, it can be dangerous). Correct level is halfway up the expansion chamber.

   If filled with Castrol Anti-freeze, top up with mixture in same proportions.

   Top up brake and clutch reservoirs to levels indicated with Castrol Girling Universal Brake and Clutch Fluid. Check breathing hole in cap is clear.

   Check the horn and all lights, including brake lights, direction indicators, and headlight alignment.

3 Road test the car after each service to check that the operations have been carried out satisfactorily.

Interval summary

Every 3000 miles or three months

---

1 Check brake pad wear.
2 Check tyres.
3 Check exhaust system.
4 Lubricate windscreen wiper shafts.

Every 6000 miles or six months

---

5 Change engine oil and filter.
6 Top up gearbox.
7 Top up rear axle.
8 Lubricate and adjust carburettor.
9 Service alternator.
10 Check wear in steering system.
11 Lubricate driver's controls.
12 Check cooling system.
13 Service air cleaner.
14 Service battery.
15 Tune carburettor.
16 Adjust fan belt.
17 Adjust spark plugs.
18 Check brake shoe wear.
19 Adjust brakes.
20 Inspect hydraulic brake system.
21 Lubricate bodywork fittings.
22 Check mountings.
23 Check wheel alignment.

Every 12000 miles or twelve months

---

24 Change engine oil filter.
25 Lubricate water pump.
26 Adjust front wheel bearings.
27 Check engine mountings.
28 Clean fuel pump.
29 Adjust valve clearances.
30 Check transmission.
31 Check suspension system.
32 Check seat belts.
33 Renew spark plugs.
34 Renew air cleaner element.
35 Clean carburettor.

Every 36000 miles or 3 year intervals renew the brake servo air filter (if fitted) and renew all hydraulic brake seals, hoses and fluid.

Chapter 1 Engine

Contents

General description 1	Timing gears and chain - examination and renovation ... 33
Major operations with engine in place... 2	Timing chain tensioner - examination and renovation ... 34
Major operations with engine removed 3	Rockers and rocker shaft - examination and renovation ... 35
Methods of engine removal 4	Tappets - examination and renovation 36
Engine removal with gearbox 5	Flywheel starter ring - examination and renovation ... 37
Dismantling the engine - general 6	Flywheel - examination and renovation 38
Removing ancillary engine components 7	Oil pump - examination and renovation 39
Cylinder head removal - engine on bench 8	Cylinder head - decarbonisation 40
Cylinder head removal - engine in car 9	Valve guides - examination and renovation 41
Valve - removal 10	Sump - examination and renovation 42
Valve guide - removal 11	Engine reassembly - general 43
Dismantling the rocker assembly 12	Crankshaft - replacement 44
Timing cover, gears and chain - removal 13	Piston and connecting rod - reassembly 45
Camshaft - removal 14	Piston ring - replacement 46
Distributor drive - removal 15	Piston - replacement 47
Sump, piston, connecting rod and big end bearing - removal 16	Connecting rod to crankshaft - reassembly 48
Gudgeon pin - removal 17	Camshaft and front endplate - replacement 49
Piston ring - removal 18	Timing gears - chain tensioner and cover - replacement ... 50
Flywheel and engine endplate - removal 19	Valve and valve spring - reassembly 51
Crankshaft and main bearing - removal 20	Rocker shaft and tappet - reassembly 52
Lubrication and crankcase ventilation systems - description.. 21	Cylinder head - replacement 53
Oil filter - removal and replacement 22	Rocker arm/valve - adjustment... 54
Oil pressure relief valve - removal and replacement ... 23	Crankshaft rear seal, housing, endplate and flywheel - re-
Oil pump - removal and dismantling 24	placement 55
Timing chain tensioner - removal and replacement 25	Oil pump - replacement 56
Examination and renovation - general... 26	Sump - replacement 57
Crankshaft examination and renovation 27	Distributor and distributor drive - replacement 58
Big end and main bearings - examination and renovation ... 28	Final assembly 59
Cylinder bores - examination and renovation 29	Engine - replacement 60
Pistons and piston rings - examination and renovation ... 30	Engine - initial start-up after overhaul or major repair ... 61
Camshaft and camshaft bearings - examination and renovation 31	Fault diagnosis 62
Valves and valve seats - examination and renovation 32	

Specifications

Type ... ... 4 cylinder in-line, ohv, water-cooled

Cylinder bore ... ... 2.90 in (73.70 mm)

Stroke, ... 2.99 in (76.00 mm)

Capacity, ... 1296 cc

Compression ratio ... ... 8.5 : 1

Firing order ... ... 1 - 3 - 4 - 2

Maximum power, ... 58 bhp net at 5300 rev/min

Ventilation ... ... Closed circuit breathing from rocker cover to depression side of carburettor

Crankshaft ... ... Three main journals, integral balance weights

Main journal diameter ... ... 2.3115 to 2.3120 in (58.713 to 58.725 mm)

Regrind undersizes ... ... −.010 in (−.25 mm), −.020 in (−.51 mm), −.030 in (−.76 mm) stamped on crankshaft web

Crankpin diameter ... ... 1.8750 to 1.8755 in (47.625 to 47.638 mm)

Regrind undersizes ... ... As main journals

Endfloat ... ... .004 to .008 in (.10 to .20 mm)

Thrust washer oversizes ... ... .005 in (.13 mm)

Maximum run-out of centre journal (with front and rear supported) .003 in (.076 mm)

Maximum out of balance with key and dowel fitted ... ... .3 oz/inch (3.36 g/cm)

Main and big end bearings ... ... Steel backed, lead-bronze with lead-indium overlay

Undersizes available	−.010 in (−.25 mm), −.020 in (−.51 mm), −.030 in (−.76 mm) stamped on undersize of shell

Cylinder block ...   .   Chromium iron
    Original size bore, Grade F ...   .   2.8995 to 2.9000 in (73.64 to 73.66 mm)
                    Grade G ...   .   2.9001 to 2.9005 in (73.66 to 73.77 mm)
    Maximum rebore size   ...   .   + .020 in (+ .51 mm)

Camshaft ...   .   Chilled cast iron, 4 bearing, chain driver
    Journal diameter   ...   .   1.9649 to 1.9654 in (49.91 to 49.92 mm)
    Endfloat   ...   .   .0042 to .0085 in (.110 to .216 mm)
    Bore in block...   ...   .   1.9680 to 1.9695 in (49.980 to 50.025 mm)
    Timing chain ...   .   .375 in (9.52 mm) pitch x 62 pitches

Pistons ...   .   Aluminium alloy, solid skirt
    Diameter, top, Grade F   ...   .   2.875 to 2.880 in (73.03 to 73.15 mm)
             bottom, Grade F   ...   .   2.8976 to 2.8981 in (73.59 to 73.61 mm)
             top, Grade G   ...   .   2.875 to 2.880 in (73.03 to 73.15 mm)
             bottom, Grade G   ...   .   2.8982 to 2.8987 in (73.617 to 73.620 mm)
    Oversizes   ...   .   + .020 in (+.52 mm)
    Groove width, bottom   ...   .   .1578 to .1588 in (3.99 to 4.01 mm)
             centre and top   ...   .   .064 to .065 in (1.625 to 1.650 mm)

Piston rings
    Width, centre and top compression   ...   .   .0620 to .0625 in (1.575 to 1.5787 mm)
             oil control (3 part) ...   .   .1540 to .1560 in (3.90 to 3.96 mm)
    Oversizes   ...   .   + .010 in (+.25 mm),+ .020 in (+.51 mm), +.030 in (+.76 mm)
    Gaps ...   .   .012 to .020 in (.30 to .50 mm)

Connecting rods ...   .   Obliquely split big end, solid small end
    Small end bush diameter (fitted)   ...   .   .8126 to .8129 in (20.64 to 20.65 mm)
    Maximum rod bend ...   .   .0015 in (.04 mm)
    Maximum rod twist ...   .   .0045 in (.114 mm)

Gudgeon pins ...   .   Fully floating
    Diameter   ...   .   .8123 to .8125 in (20.63 to 20.64 mm)

Connecting rod and piston assemblies
    Weight variation between heaviest and lightest assembly   ...   Maximum 4 drams

Cylinder head ...   .   Cast iron, individual ports

Valves
    Head diameter, inlet   ...   .   1.304 to 1.308 in (33.12 to 33.22 mm)
                exhaust   ...   .   1.168 to 1.172 in (29.66 to 29.76 mm)
    Stem diameter, inlet   ...   .   .3107 to .3112 in (7.87 to 7.90 mm)
                exhaust   ...   .   .3100 to .3105 in (7.874 to 7.887 mm)
    Seat face angle   ...   .   90 deg. total inclusive angle
    Stem to guide clearance, inlet   ...   .   .0008 to .0023 in (.02 to .06 mm)
                exhaust ...   .   .0015 to .0030 in (.03 to .07 mm)

Valve guides
    Length   ...   .   2.0625 in (52.387 mm)
    Bore   ...   .   .312 to .313 in (7.92 to 7.95 mm)
    Outside diameter   ...   .   .501 to .502 in (12.72 to 12.75 mm)
    Height above cylinder head   ...   .   .749 to .751 in (19.025 to 19.075 mm)

Valve springs
    Working coils, ...   3¼
    Length at 27 to 30 lb (12¼ to 13½ kg) load   ...   .   1.36 in (34.54 mm)
    Free length ...   .   1.61 in (40.89 mm)
    Solid length, ...93 in (23.62 mm)

Valve timing
    Inlet opens, ...   18 deg. BTDC
    Inlet closes, ...   58 deg. ABDC
    Exhaust opens, ...   58 deg. BBDC
    Exhaust closes, ...   18 deg. ATDC

Rocker gear clearances
    Standard, cold   ...   .   .010 in (.25 mm)
    Valve timing only, No.7 and 8   ...   .   .050 in (1.27 mm)

Lubrication

Oil pump	High capacity rotor type
Clearance between inner and outer rotor	.010 in (.25 mm) maximum
Clearance between outer rotor and body	.008 in (.20 mm) maximum
Rotor endfloat	.004 in (.10 mm) maximum
Oil filter	Full flow replaceable element
Warning light goes outat	3 to 5 lb/sq inch (.21 to .35 kg/sq cm) oil pressure

Torque wrench settings

	lb ft	kg m
Air cleaner to carburettor	7 to 9	1.0 to 1.2
Alternator to mounting bracket and front engine plate	16 to 20	2.2 to 2.8
Alternator to adjusting link...	16 to 20	2.2 to 2.8
Cylinder block oil gallery	11 to 14	1.5 to 2.0
Cylinder block oil gallery seals	16 to 20	2.2 to 2.8
Cylinder block drain plug	30 to 37	4.1 to 5.1
Crankshaft pulley to crankshaft	90 to 110	12.4 to 15.2
Connecting rod bolt	38 to 45	5.2. to 6.2
Camshaft chainwheel locking plate	20 to 24	2.8 to 3.3
Cylinder head to block	38 to 45	5.2 to 6.2
Carburettor to manifold	11 to 14	1.5 to 2.0
Clutch to flywheel	16 to 20	2.2 to 2.8
Distributor pedestal to block	11 to 14	1.5 to 2.0
Distributor to pedestal	16 to 20	2.2 to 2.8
Dynamo mounting bracket to cylinder block	16 to 20	2.2 to 2.8
Flywheel to crankshaft	38 to 45	5.2 to 6.2
Front engine plate to cylinder block	16 to 20	2.2 to 2.8
Front engine plate and camshaft	16 to 20	2.2 to 2.8
Fuel pump to cylinder block	11 to 14	1.5 to 2.0
Fan to pulley	7 to 9	1.0 to 1.2
Gearbox and rear engine plate to block	11 to 14	1.5 to 2.0
Inlet manifold to exhaust manifold	11 to 14	1.5 to 2.0
Lifting eye bracket to cylinder block	38 to 45	5.2 to 6.2
Manifold inner to head	20 to 24	2.8 to 3.3
Manifold outer to head	20 to 24	2.8 to 3.3
Oil filters attachment	16 to 20	2.2 to 2.7
Oil pump attachment	7 to 9	1.0 to 1.2
Oil sump drain plug	20 to 24	2.7 to 3.3
Oil sump to block	16 to 20	2.2 to 2.8
Oil pressure switch	11 to 14	1.5 to 2.0
Plug to cylinder head	20 to 24	2.8 to 3.3
Rocker pedestal to cylinder head	26 to 32	3.6 to 4.4
Rocker oil feed to block	16 to 20	2.2 to 2.8
Main bearing cap bolts	50 to 65	7 to 9
Rear crankshaft seal	16 to 20	2.2 to 2.8
Rear engined plate to cylinder block	16 to 20	2.2 to 2.8
Rocker shaft locating screw	3 to 4	.4 to .6
Rocker cover to head	1 to 2	.14 to .3
Sealing block to engine plate	16 to 20	2.0 to 3.0
Sealing block to cylinder block	11 to 14	1.5 to 2.0
Spark plug to head	16 to 20	2.2 to 2.7
Timing cover and front engine plate to cylinder block	16 to 20	2.2 to 2.7
Timing cover and front engine plate to block	11 to 14	1.5 to 2.0
Timing cover to front engine plate...	7 to 9	1.0 to 1.2
Throttle relay lever to mounting bracket	16 to 20	2.2 to 2.8
Throttle relay mounting bracket assembly attachment	11 to 14	1.5 to 2.0

1 General description

The engine is of the four cylinder overhead valve type and is conventional in most details. It is derived from the Triumph Herald 13/60 Series and only minor changes have been made.

The cylinders each have an inlet and exhaust valve mounted vertically in the cast iron cylinder head and run in pressed-in valve guides. They are operated by rocker arms, pushrod and tappets from the camshaft which is located at the base of the cylinder bores in the left hand side of the engine. The correct valve stem to rocker arm pad clearance can be obtained by adjusting screws in the ends of the rocker arms.

The cylinder block and the upper half of the crankcase are cast together. The bottom half of the crankcase consists of a pressed steel sump.

The flat-top pistons are of aluminium alloy with solid skirts.

Two compression rings and a slotted oil control ring are fitted. The gudgeon pin is retained in the little end of the connecting rod by circlips.

Renewable - shell type bearings are fitted to the big ends.

At the front of the engine a single chain drives the camshaft via the camshaft and crankshaft gear wheels which are enclosed in a pressed steel cover.

The chain is tensioned automatically by a spring blade which presses against the non-driving side of the chain so avoiding any lash or rattle.

The camshaft runs in four housings bored directly into the cylinder block. Bearings are not fitted on this model; only on the 1500 Export model which is not covered in this Manual. End-float is controlled by a forked locating plate positioned on the engine front plate.

The statically and dynamically balanced forged steel crankshaft is supported by three renewable thinwall shell main

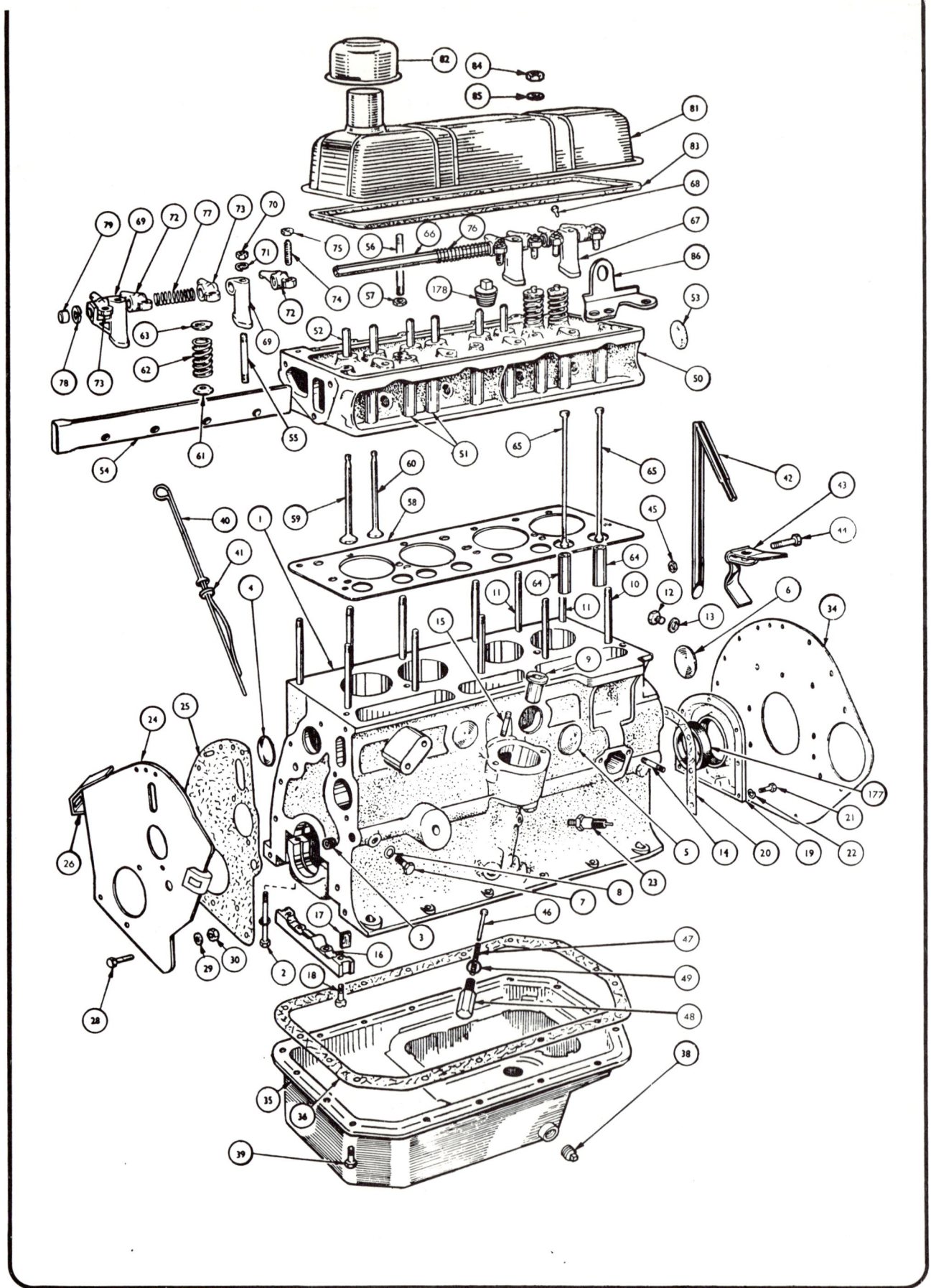

bearings which are in turn supported by substantial webs which form part of the crankcase. Crankshaft endfloat is controlled by semi-circular thrust washers located on each side of the rear main bearing.

The centrifugal water pump and radiator cooling fan are driven, together with the alternator, from the crankshaft pulley wheel by a rubber/fabric belt. The distributor is mounted in the middle of the left-hand side of the cylinder block and advances and retards the ignition timing by mechanical and vacuum means. The distributor is driven at half crankshaft speed by a short shaft and skew gear from a skew gear on the camshaft located between the second and third journals.

The oil pump is located in the crankcase and is driven by a short shaft from the skew gear on the camshaft.

The flywheel is secured to crankshaft end flange by four bolts and carries the starter ring and the clutch assembly. The clutch bellhousing is bolted to a removable engine endplate.

The engine is supported by two rubber mountings.

2 Major operations with engine in place

The following major operations can be carried out to the engine with it in place in the body frame:-
1 Removal and replacement of the cylinder head assembly.
2 Removal and replacement of the sump.
3 Removal and replacement of the big end bearings.
4 Removal and replacement of the pistons and connecting rods.
5 Removal and replacement of the timing chain and gears and the timing cover oil seal.
6 Removal and replacement of the camshaft.
7 Removal and replacement of the oil pump.

3 Major operations with engine removed

The following major operations can be carried out with the engine out of the body frame and on the bench or floor:-
1 Removal and replacement of the main bearings.
2 Removal and replacement of the crankshaft.
3 Removal and replacement of the flywheel.

4 Methods of engine removal

There are two methods of engine removal: The engine can either be removed complete with gearbox, or the engine can be removed without the gearbox by separation at the gearbox bellhousing.

If one is carrying out a major engine overhaul, then we recommend that the gearbox be removed at the same time, since very little extra work is involved, and it does give one a chance to inspect the gearbox and anticipate any future problems in that area.

If, for some reason, the engine alone is to be removed then the instructions given in Section 5 can be followed with the exception that paragraphs 16 to 23 inclusive should be ignored.

In their place it is necessary to:
1 Remove the two bolts that secure the starter motor to the engine end plate, and remove it together with any packing or shims; these should be preserved along with the bolts and spring washers. The cable should have been disconnected previously.
2 Remove the nuts and bolts that secure the engine endplate to the bellhousing; most of these are accessible from beneath the car but the remainder are more easily released if the gearbox tunnel cover is removed: they can then be got at from inside the car. Note the clip that secures the clutch hydraulic pipe to the top centre stud. These operations are detailed in Chapter 6.

5 Engine and gearbox - removal and refitting

The following sequence of operations is in the order that we recommend, but strict adherence to the sequence is not critical; where an operation must be performed prior to another operation, we will state this.
1 Remove the bonnet by unscrewing the two setscrews from each of the front hinges, and withdrawing the split pin from the clevis pin securing the bonnet stays. (photos)
2 Disconnect and remove the battery. Do not tilt it when lifting out of the car or some electrolyte may be spilled on the paintwork or your clothes. (photos)
3 Drain the cooling system (Chapter 2). (photos)
4 Place a suitable receptacle, with a capacity of at least 7 pints, beneath the engine sump. Remove the drain plug and allow the oil to drain for several minutes. Refit the plug when draining is complete; ensure the washer is on the plug. (photo)
5 Remove the top and bottom hoses from the engine and the smaller bore hose from the expansion tank. When pulling these hoses off their pipes, do not lever them about too much since it is quite easy to fracture the joint where the stub pipes are connected to the radiator. Open the clips fully and ease the hoses off gradually. (photos)
6 Remove the radiator by releasing the four bolts either side; this will leave the mounting brackets, with horns attached, in the car. (photo)
7 Loosen the clips securing the two heater hoses to the engine rear; these are small bore hoses and can easily be pulled off the stub pipes. (photo)
8 Disconnect the throttle cable linkage from the single or twin carburettors. With a single carburettor, simply unscrew the inner cable clamp bolt from the linkage, then squeeze the ferrule retaining the outer cable to the linkage. Tie the inner and outer cable, complete, away from the engine. When twin carburettors are fitted it will be necessary to withdraw the split pin from the clevis pin on the linkage, and then slacken the adjuster nuts securing the outer cable to the bracket. Lift the complete cable away from the linkage and tie back. (photo)
9 Disconnect the choke cable by releasing the screw securing the cable inner to the choke cam, first loosening the locknut; then pulling on the choke control knob until the inner cable is withdrawn sufficiently to separate the cable outer at the rocker box connector. The inner cable will be left hanging and should be tied out of the way. (photo)

FIG. 1.1. EXPLODED VIEW OF THE CYLINDER BLOCK, CYLINDER HEAD, SUMP, AND ENGINE MOUNTINGS

1 Cylinder block. 2 Bolt and lock washer. 3 Oil gallery end plug. 4 Welch plug. 5 Welch plug for rear face and L.H. side of block. 6 Welch plug for rear of camshaft. 7 Oil gallery bolt. 8 Washer. 9 Oil pump shaft bush. 10 Cylinder head stud. 11 Cylinder head/ lifting eye bracket studs. 12 Water drain plug. 13 Fibre washer. 14 Petrol pump attachment stud. 15 Distributor mounting stud. 16 Front sealing block. 17 Filler piece. 18 Screw. 19 Oil retaining cover. 20 Gasket. 21 Bolt. 22 Spring washer. 23 Oil pressure indicator switch. 24 Front engine plate. 25 Gasket. 26 Engine mounting foot. 28 Bolt. 29 Spring washer. 30 Nut. 34 Rear engine plate. 35 Sump. 36 Gasket. 38 Oil drain plug. 39 Bolt. 40 Dipstick. 41 Felt washer. 42 Breather pipe. 43 Deflector. 44 Bolt. 45 Nut. 46 Oil pressure relief valve piston. 47 Piston spring. 48 Retaining plug. 49 Washer. 50 Cylinder head. 51 Pushrod tubes. 52 Valve guide. 53 Core plug. 54 Water delivery tube. 55 Rocker pedestal stud. 56 Rocker pedestal stud. 57 Nut. 58 Gasket. 59 Inlet valve. 60 Exhaust valve. 61 Lower collar. 62 Valve spring. 63 Valve spring upper collar. 64 Tappet. 65 Pushrods. 66 Rocker shaft. 67 Rocker pedestal drilled. 68 Bolt/shakeproof washer. 69 Plain rocker pedestal. 70 Nut. 71 Lock washer. 72 Rocker No. 1. 73 Rocker No. 2. 74 Ball pin. 75 Locking nut. 76 Centre rocker spring (1). 77 Intermediate rocker springs (2). 78 Outer rocker springs (2). 79 Collar. 81 Rocker cover. 82 Oil filler cap/breather. 83 Rocker cover gasket. 84 Nut. 85 Plain/ fibre washers. 86 Support bracket. 177 Oil seal. 178 Plug.

5.1a Removing the bonnet stays and hinge bolts before lifting off bonnet

5.1b Removing the bonnet stays and hinge bolts before lifting off bonnet

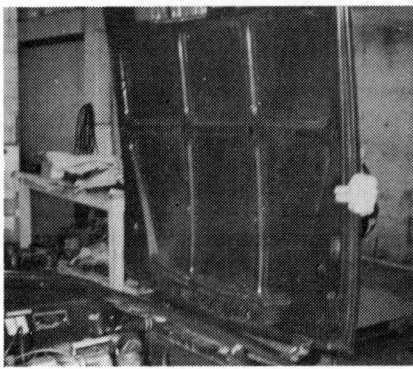

5.1c Removing the bonnet stays and hinge bolts before lifting off bonnet

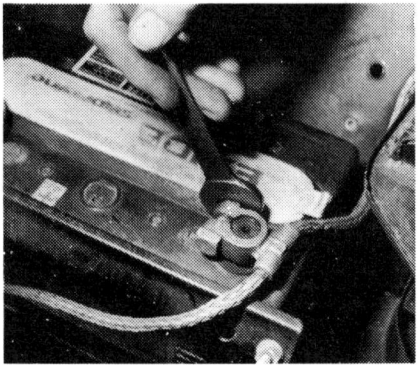

5.2a Disconnecting and removing the battery

5.2b Disconnecting and removing the battery

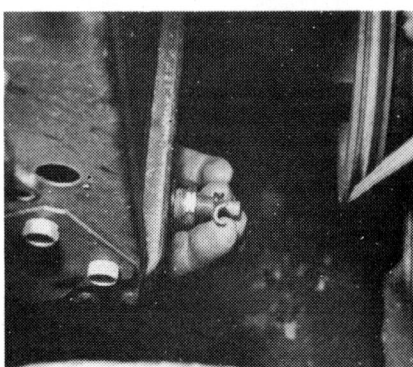

5.3a Draining the radiator

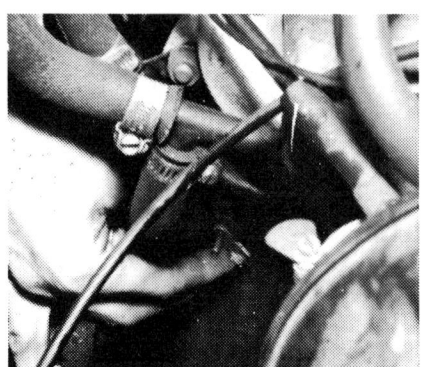

5.3b Draining the cylinder block

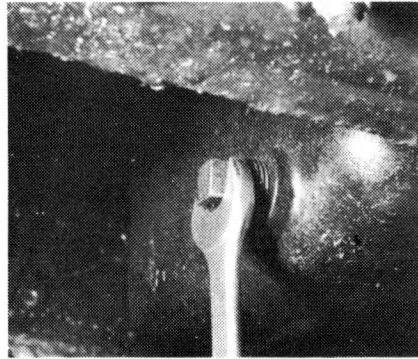

5.4 Removing the engine sump drain plug

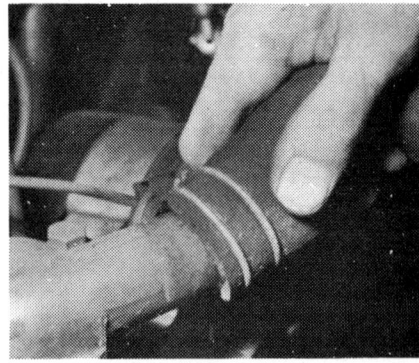

5.5a Releasing the top hose

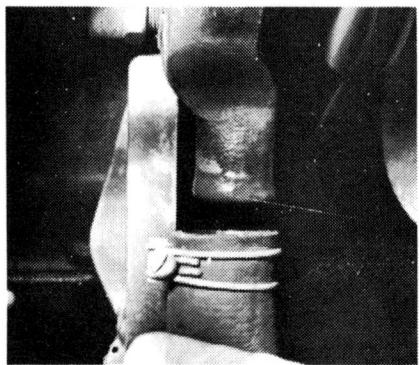

5.5b Releasing the bottom and expansion tank hoses

5.5c Releasing the bottom and expansion tank hoses

5.6 Removing the radiator

5.7 Releasing the two rear heater hoses

5.8 Disconnecting the throttle cable

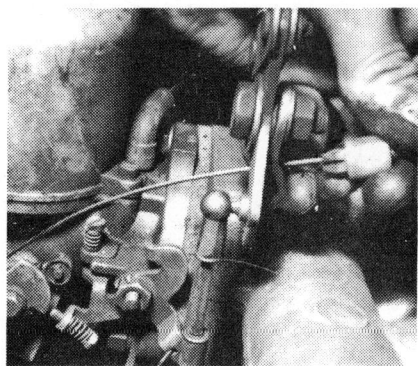

5.9 Disconnecting the choke cable

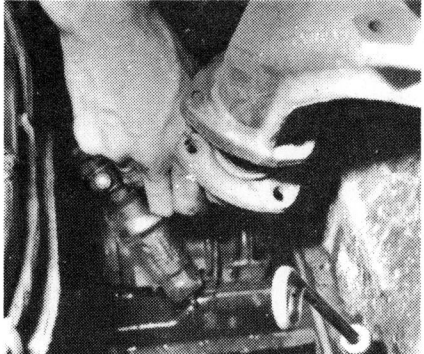

5.10 Releasing exhaust pipe from manifold

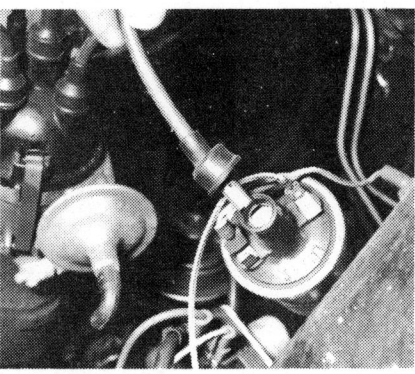

5.11a Disconnecting the HT lead (A) and LT leads (B) from the coil. Only one LT lead is shown for clarity

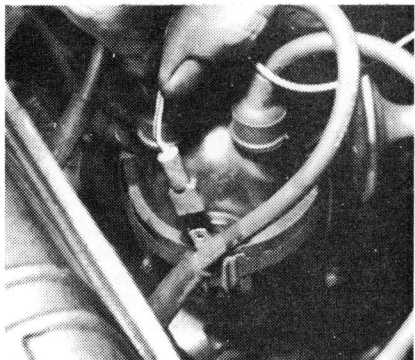

5.11b Disconnecting the HT lead (A) and LT leads (B) from the coil. Only one LT lead is shown for clarity

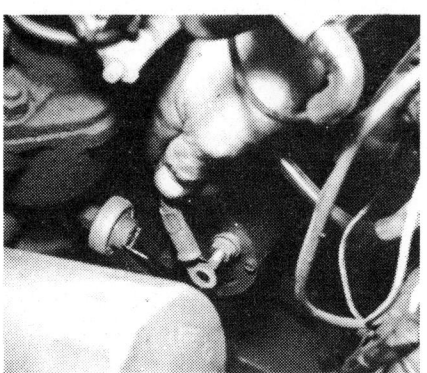

5.12 Releasing starter motor lead

5.13 Disconnecting multi-socket connector from alternator

5.14a Releasing the oil pressure switch wire

5.14b Releasing the water temperature transmitter wire

5.15 Removing fuel pump inlet pipe

5.16 Disconnecting the propeller shaft

10 Remove the three nuts and washers securing the exhaust front pipe to the manifold. Retain the gasket released by this operation. (photo)

11 Release the HT and LT leads from the distributor. Identify each lead. (photos)

12 Disconnect the starter cable by removing the nut and washer that secures it to the terminal post. (photo)

13 Withdraw the multi-socket connector from the alternator. (photo)

14 Disconnect the oil pressure switch wire, the water temperature transmitter wire, and the battery earth lead from the alternator mounting bracket. Identify each wire with some form of tag and carefully tie back out of the way of the engine. (photos)

15 Remove the fuel feed pipe to the fuel pump inlet and plug the end of the pipe to prevent the ingress of dirt or fuel syphoning out. (photo)

16 Working underneath the car, disconnect the propeller shaft from the gearbox drive flange by removing the four bolts and locknuts. Mark a line across the flange-to-shaft joint before breaking the joint. It may be necessary to jack a rear wheel off the ground and turn the wheel in order to gain access to all the retaining bolts. (photo)

17 Disconnect the gear lever from the gearbox extension by, working from beneath the vehicle, unscrewing the nut connecting the lever to the extension rod and withdrawing the bolt and washer. (photo)

18 Remove the nut and washer securing the gearbox rear mounting to the sub-frame; it is advisable to support the gearbox extension with a jack or blocks before disconnecting the mounting. This will leave the mounting attached to the gearbox when it is removed from the car. (photo)

19 Remove the nut and bolt securing the exhaust pipe clip to the gearbox support arm. (photo)

20 Disconnect the speedometer drive cable from the gearbox extension by undoing the knurled nut and pulling the cable out. (photo)

21 Remove the clamp bolt securing the clutch slave cylinder to its housing; ease the cylinder away from the gearbox and lift it into the engine compartment. Tie the cylinder out of the way of the engine. (photos)

22 Working inside the car, remove the gear lever knob and locknut, gearbox carpet, and the four screws securing the clamp ring to the grommet. Lift the grommet and clamp ring away from the gear lever. (photos)

23 Release the gear lever cap by twisting anticlockwise and thus releasing it from the two projections on the extension boss. Withdraw the steel and nylon cups over the gear lever and then remove the circlip and spring. Pull the gear lever out of the extension; the nylon half-sphere will remain on the bottom of the lever. (photo)

24 Attach the lifting equipment to the engine lifting eyes and take the weight of the engine on the sling. (photo)

25 Remove the two nuts and bolts securing each front mounting to the sub-frame. Lift the engine slightly to raise the sump above the sub-frame and make a final check to ensure that all connections are free of the engine. Raise the hoist slowly and manoeuvre the engine and gearbox clear of the vehicle. It is sound practice to place some form of padding over the perimeter of the engine compartment in case the paintwork or chrome is damaged when removing the assembly. (photos)

26 With the combined engine/gearbox safely on the workshop floor it is necessary to remove the gearbox before work can commence on the engine. Remove the bolts and washers securing the bellhousing to the engine rear plate. Pull the gearbox and bellhousing away from the engine, endeavouring to keep the input shaft central as it is withdrawn from the splines. The weight of the gearbox should never be allowed to hang on the clutch splines.

6 Dismantling the engine - general

1 It is best to mount the engine on a dismantling stand, but if one is not available, stand the engine on a strong bench to be at a comfortable working height.

2 During the dismantling process the greatest care should be taken to keep the exposed parts free from dirt. As an aid to achieving this, thoroughly clean down the outside of the engine, removing all traces of oil and congealed dirt.

3 Use paraffin or Gunk. The latter compound will make the job much easier for, after the solvent has been applied and allowed to stand for a time, a vigorous jet of water will wash off the solvent with all the grease and filth. If the dirt is thick and deeply embedded, work the solvent into it with a wire brush.

4 Finally, wipe down the exterior of the engine with a rag and only then, when it is quite clean, should the dismantling process begin. As the engine is stripped, clean each part in a bath of paraffin or petrol.

5 Never immerse parts with oilways in paraffin, ie the crankshaft, but to clean, wipe down carefully with a petrol dampened rag. Oilways can be cleaned out with pipe cleaners. If an air line is present, all parts can be blown dry and the oilways blown through as an added precaution.

6 Re-use of old engine gaskets is false economy and can give rise to oil and water leaks, if nothing worse. Always use new gaskets throughout.

7 Do not throw the old gaskets away, for it sometimes happens that an immediate replacement cannot be found and the old gasket is then very useful as a template. Hang up the old gaskets as they are removed on a suitable hook or nail.

5.17 Removing the gear lever-to-extension rod securing bolt

5.18 Removing gearbox rear mounting nut

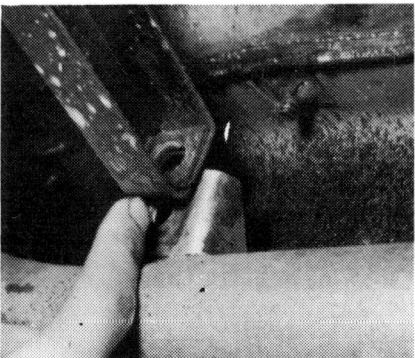
5.19 Disconnecting exhaust pipe from the support arm

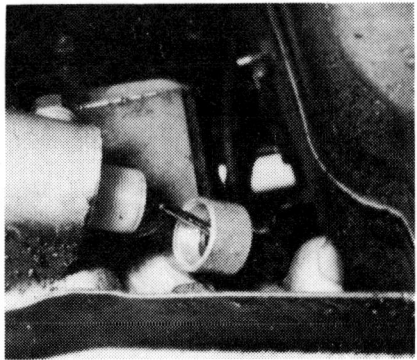
5.20 Releasing speedometer drive cable

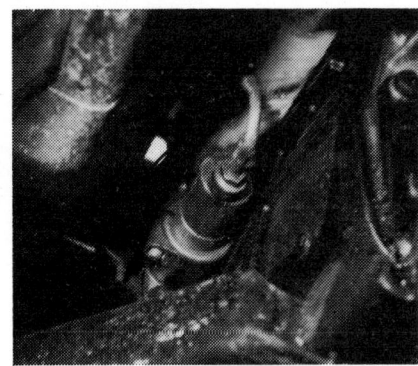
5.21a Loosening the clamp bolt securing the clutch slave cylinder

5.21b Easing the cylinder away from its housing

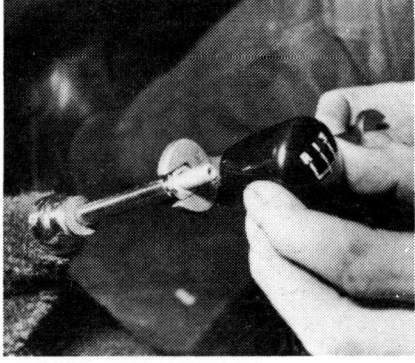
5.22a Removing the gear lever knob.....

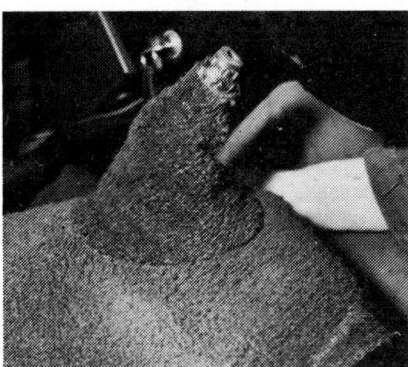
5.22b.....and carpet then.....

5.22c.....remove the rubber boot holding screws and.....

5.22d.....lift off the rubber boot

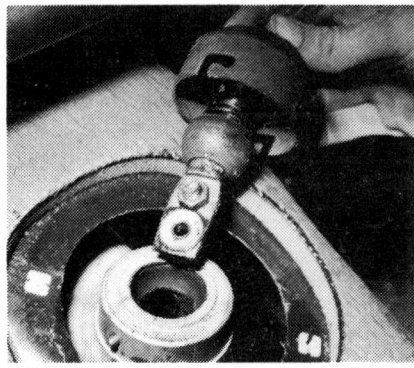
5.23 Removing the gear lever

5.24 Lifting sling attached to engine. This photo shows the rocker cover removed and a lifting eye attached to a cylinder head bolt

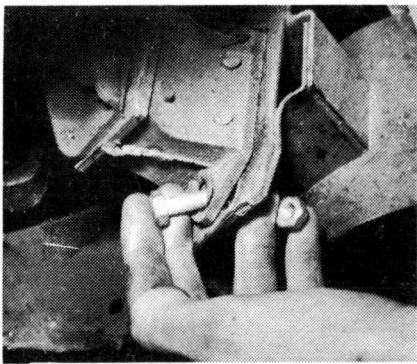
5.25a Removing engine mounting bolts...

5.25b.....and easing the combined engine and gearbox out of the vehicle

8   To strip the engine it is best to work from the top down. The sump provides a firm base on which the engine can be supported in an upright position. When the stage where the sump must be removed is reached, the engine can be turned on its side and all other work carried out with it in this position.

9   Wherever possible, replace nuts, bolts and washers finger-tight from where they were removed. This helps avoid later loss and muddle. If they cannot be replaced then lay them out in such a fashion that it is clear from where they came.

7   Removing ancillary engine components

1   Before basic engine dismantling can begin, the engine should be stripped of all its ancillary components. These items should also be removed if a factory exchange reconditioned unit is being purchased. The items comprise:

Alternator and alternator brackets
Water pump and thermostat housing
Starter motor
Distributor and spark plugs
Inlet and exhaust manifold and carburettor
Fuel pump and fuel pipes
Oil filter and dipstick
Oil filler cap
Clutch assembly

2   All these items can be removed with the engine in the car, if it is merely an individual item which requires attention. It is easy to renew the clutch with engine and gearbox still in the car.

3   Starting work on the lefthand side of the engine, slacken off the alternator retaining bolts and remove the unit and then the support brackets. (photos)

4   Take off the distributor and housing, after undoing the two nuts and washers which hold the bottom flange of the distributor housing to the cylinder block. Retain and note the shims between the housing and the block. Do not loosen the square nut on the clamp at the base of the distributor body, or the timing will be lost. Undo the spark plugs. (photo)

5   Note that the fuel pump is held in place by two studs. A nut fits on the stud on the left, and a special screw over the stud on the right.

6   Undo the nut and screw and lift off the fuel pump. (photo)

7   Undo and remove the low oil pressure warning sender unit located beneath the distributor mounting. (photo)

8   Undo and remove the oil filter. The complete body screws off anticlockwise (photo).

9   Moving to the front of the engine, undo the two thermostat housing cover securing bolts. Lift away the cover and the thermostat. (photo)

10 Undo the nuts and washers which hold the inlet and exhaust manifolds to the cylinder head. The inner nuts are very difficult to get at and are best loosened with a thin ring spanner.

11 Lift off the inlet and exhaust manifolds together with the carburettor. If stiff, tap the manifolds gently with a piece of wood.

12 Undo the bolts which hold the water pump in place on the front face of the block (photo).

13 Undo a quarter of a turn at a time, the six bolts which hold the clutch pressure plate assembly to the flywheel.

14 Lift off the pressure plate together with the loose friction plate.

15 Undo the two bolts holding the starter motor in place and lift off the motor. Note and retain the distance piece and any shims that are fitted. (photo).

8   Cylinder head removal - engine on bench

1   With the engine out of the car and standing on the bench or floor, remove the cylinder head as follows:

2   Unscrew the two rocker cover nuts and lift away the nuts, plain washers, rocker cover and cork gasket.

3   Unscrew the four rocker pedestal nuts, and lift away the nuts and washers. Carefully lift the rocker assembly from the top of the cylinder head.

4   Undo the ten cylinder head nuts half a turn at a time. When all the nuts are no longer under tension they may be screwed off the cylinder head retaining studs, one at a time. Lift away the lifting bracket from the two rear right hand studs. The cylinder head nuts should be removed in the reverse order to that given in Fig. 1.6.

5   Remove the pushrods keeping them in the relative order in which they were removed. The easiest way to do this is to push them through a sheet of thin card in the correct sequence. Make sure the tappets remain in their bores.

6   The cylinder head can now be removed by lifting upwards. If the head is jammed, try to rock it to break the seal. Under no circumstances try to prise it apart from the cylinder block with a screwdriver or cold chisel, as damage may be done to the faces of the head or block. If the head will not free readily, turn the engine over by the flywheel or starter ring gear carrier, as the compression in the cylinders will often break the cylinder head joint. If this fails to work, strike the head sharply with a plastic headed hammer or wooden hammer, or with a metal hammer with an interposed piece of wood to cushion the blows. Under no circumstances hit the head directly with a metal hammer, as this may cause the iron casting to fracture. Several sharp taps with the hammer, at the same time pulling upwards, should free the head. Lift the head off and place on one side. Recover the cylinder head gasket.

9   Cylinder head removal - engine in car

To remove the cylinder head with the engine still in the car, the following additional procedure should be carried out before that listed in Section 8.

1   Disconnect the battery earth terminal for safety reasons.

2   Drain the water by turning on the taps at the base of the radiator and the rear of the cylinder block.

3   Loosen the clip at the thermostat housing end on the top water hose and pull the hose from the thermostat housing pipe.

4   Slacken the alternator securing bolts and move alternator inwards towards the cylinder head. Remove the fan belt.

5   Undo and remove the alternator mounting bolts and nuts and lift away the alternator. Unscrew the two bolts and spring washers securing the alternator mounting bracket to the side of the cylinder head. Lift away the bolts, spring washers and the alternator mounting bracket.

6   Disconnect the fuel line at the carburettor installation end. Also detach the vacuum advance/retard pipe at the distributor vacuum unit.

7   Mark the HT leads to the spark plugs for correct identification and detach the leads from the spark plugs. Release the HT lead from the centre of the ignition coil.

8   Undo and remove the two nuts and spring washers securing the distributor clamping plate to the cylinder block and lift away the distributor.

9   Disconnect the choke and throttle controls at the carburettor installation.

10 Undo and remove all securing nuts and washers holding the inlet and exhaust manifolds to the cylinder head. Detach the exhaust manifold connection from the exhaust system down pipe and lift away the inlet and exhaust manifolds. Recover the gaskets.

12 Disconnect the rubber hose connection at the thermostat housing by slackening the clip and drawing off the hose.

13 Undo the heater pipe connection union nut at the rear of the water pump body. Detach the temperature gauge sender unit cable terminal from the unit on the thermostat housing.

14 Slacken the bottom radiator hose clip at the water pump and detach the hose from the water pump.

15 Undo and remove the three bolts securing the water pump to the front of the cylinder head and lift away the water pump. Recover the paper gasket.

7.3a Removing the alternator

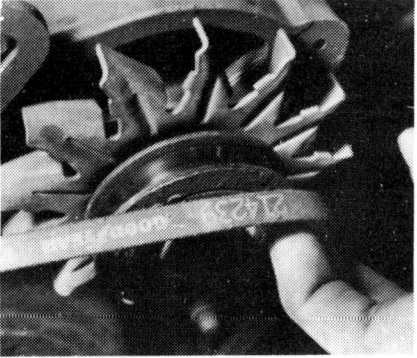
7.3b Removing the alternator

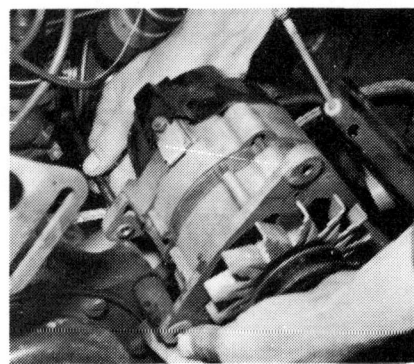
7.3c Removing the alternator

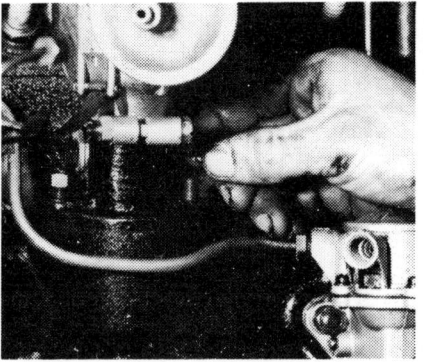
7.4 Removing the distributor

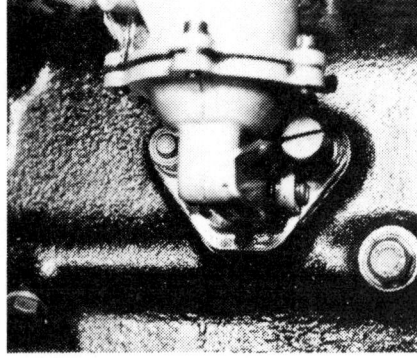
7.5 Method of securing fuel pump

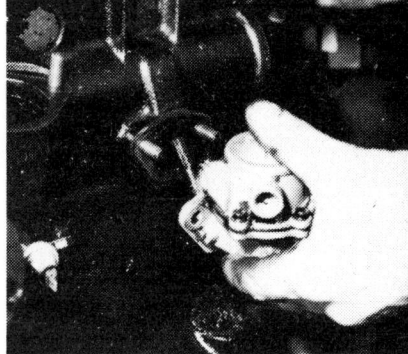
7.6 Removing fuel pump

7.7 Removing oil pressure sender

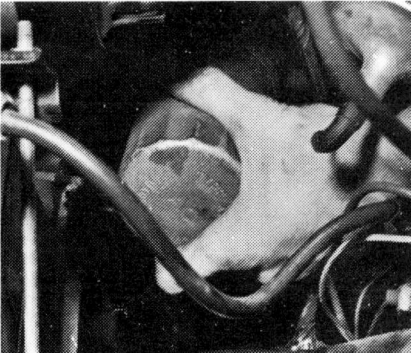
7.8 Unscrewing the oil filter

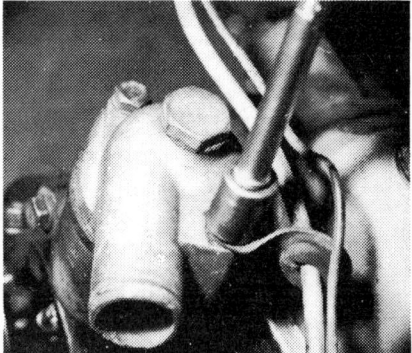
7.9 Releasing thermostat bolts

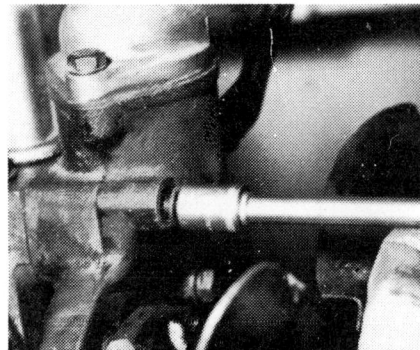
7.12 Removing water pump bolts

7.15 Removing the starter motor and distance piece

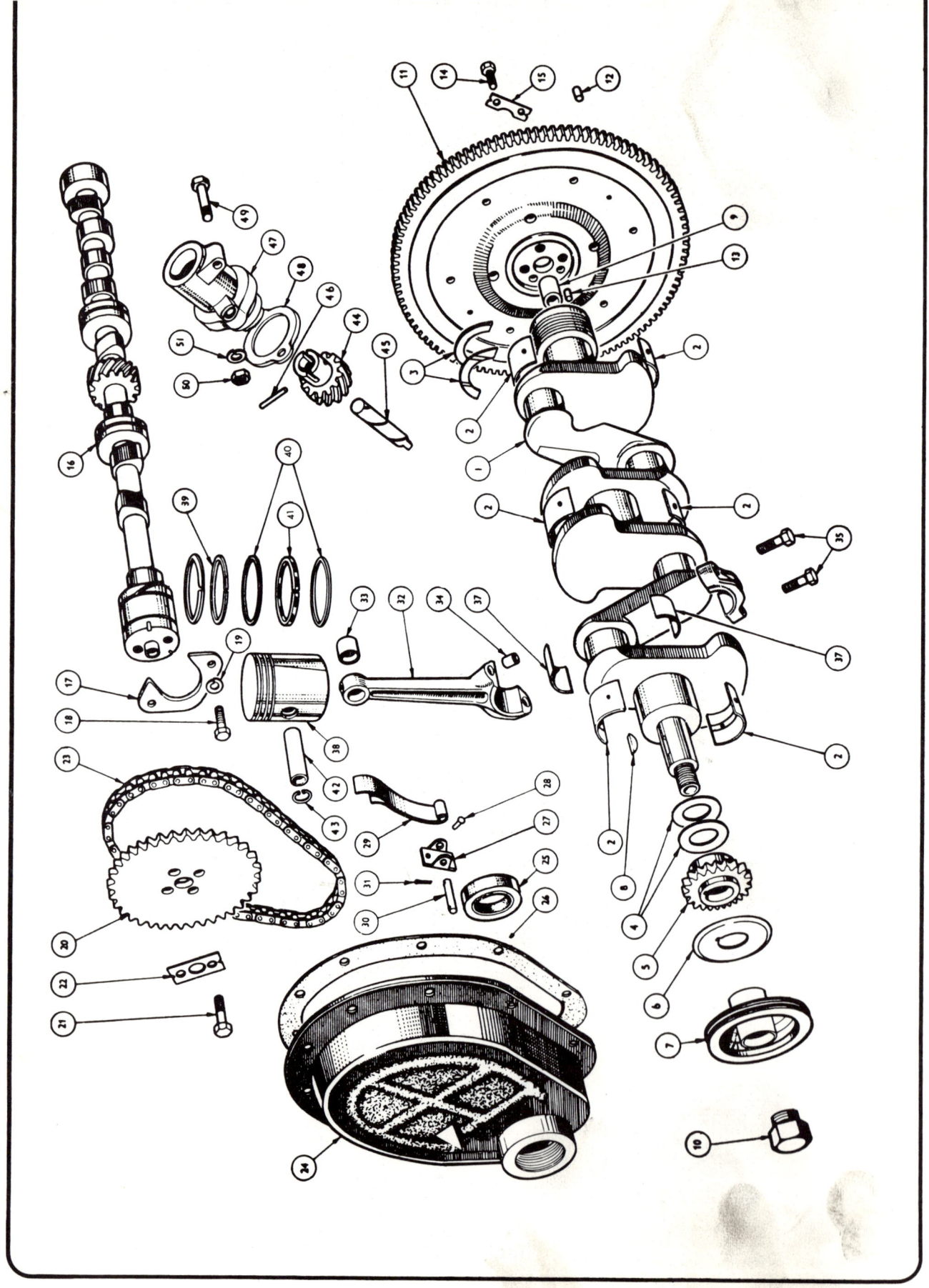

FIG. 1.2. EXPLODED VIEW OF THE MAIN MOVING ENGINE COMPONENTS

1 Crankshaft
2 Main bearings
3 Thrust washers
4 Shims
5 Crankshaft chain wheel
6 Oil slinger
7 Pulley wheel
8 Woodruff key
9 Bush for nose of gearbox input shaft
10 Pulley wheel securing nut
11 Flywheel
12 Dowel
13 Flywheel to crankshaft dowel
14 Bolt
15 Bolt locking plate
16 Crankshaft
17 Camshaft locating plate
18 Bolt
19 Spring washer
20 Camshaft chain wheel
21 Bolt
22 Bolt locking plate
23 Timing chain
24 Timing chain cover
25 Oil seal
26 Gasket
27 Timing chain tensioner anchor plate
28 Rivet
29 Spring tensioner
30 Tensioner spring anchor pin
31 Cotter pin
32 Connecting rod
33 Small end bush
34 Hollow dowel
35 Big end bolts
37 Big end bearings
38 Piston
39 Chrome plated top compression ring
40 Plain compression ring
41 Oil control ring
42 Gudgeon pin
43 Circlip
44 Distributor and oil pump drive gear
45 Oil pump drive shaft
46 Gear to shaft
attaching pin
47 Distributor mounting
48 Gasket (2 thicknesses available .006 in and .020 in)
49 Bolt
50 Nut
51 Spring washer

16 The procedure is now the same as for removing the cylinder head when the engine is on the bench or floor. One tip worth noting is that should the cylinder refuse to free easily, the battery can be reconnected and the engine turned over on the solenoid switch. Under no circumstances turn the ignition on, and ensure that the fuel inlet pipe is disconnected from the mechanical fuel pump.

10 Valves - removal

It is essential that the valves are kept in their correct sequence unless they are so badly worn that they are to be renewed. If they are going to be kept and used again, place them in a sheet of card having eight holes numbered 1 to 8 corresponding with the relative positions the valves were in when fitted. Also keep the springs and collets in the correct order.

Two types of valve spring retainers are used; one type has twin holes in its face while the other uses the conventional collet method. Proceed as follows for the twin-hole type:
1 Place a block of wood within the combustion chamber area of the cylinder head to support the valve head.
2 Push the valve collar down and then move sideways to allow the larger diameter to move up the valve stem. Lift away the collar, valve spring, spring locating collar and the valve itself.
3 To remove the conventional valve spring retainer, compress each spring in turn with a valve spring compressor until the two halves of the collets can be removed. Release the compressor and remove the cap, spring, shroud and valve.
4 If, when the valve spring compressor is screwed down, the valve spring retaining cap refuses to free and expose the split collet, do not continue to screw down on the compressor as there is a likelihood of damaging it.
5 Gently tap the top of the tool directly over the cap with a light hammer. This will free the cap. To avoid the compressor jumping off the valve spring retaining cap when it is tapped, hold the compressor firmly in position with one hand. Drop each valve out through the combustion chamber.

11 Valve guide - removal

If it is wished to remove the valve guides they can be removed from the cylinder head in the following manner.
Place the cylinder head with the gasket face on the bench and with a suitable hard steel punch, drift the guides out of the cylinder head.

12 Dismantling the rocker assembly

1 To dismantle the rocker assembly release the rocker shaft locating screw, remove the split pin from the front of the shaft, and slide the shaft from the pedestals, rocker arms and rocker spacing springs. The rear pedestal is secured to the shaft by a Phillips screw.
2 From the end of the shaft, undo the plug which gives access to the inside of the rocker, which can now be cleaned of sludge etc. Ensure the rocker arm lubricating holes are clear.

13 Timing cover, gears and chain - removal

The timing cover, gears, and chain can be removed with the engine in the car providing the radiator and fan blades and belt are removed. The procedure for removing the timing cover, gears and chain is otherwise the same irrespective of whether the engine is in the car or on the bench, and is as follows:-
1 Bend back the locking tab of the crankshaft pulley locking washer under the crankshaft pulley retaining nut and remove the nut and washer. If the engine is still in the car it will be necessary to work from underneath the car, in order to gain access to the crankshaft nut.

2 The crankshaft pulley wheel may pull off quite easily. If not, place two large screwdrivers behind the camshaft pulley wheel at 180° to each other, and carefully lever off the wheel. It is preferable to use a proper pulley extractor if this is available, but large screwdrivers or tyre levers are quite suitable, providing care is taken not to damage the pulley flange.

3 Unscrew the bolts holding the timing cover to the block. Note the special short screw adjacent to the crankshaft nose.

4 Pull off the timing cover and gasket. Check the chain for wear by measuring how much the chain can be depressed. More than ½ in (12.7 mm) means a new chain must be fitted on reassembly. (photo)

5 With the timing cover off, take off the oil thrower. NOTE that the dished periphery faces the timing chain cover.

6 With a drift or screwdriver, tap back the tabs on the lockwasher under the two camshaft gearwheel retaining bolts and undo the bolts. (photo)

7 To remove the camshaft and crankshaft timing gears complete with chain, ease each gear forward a little at a time levering behind each gearwheel in turn with two large screwdrivers at 180° to each other. If the gears are locked solid then it will be necessary to use a proper gearwheel and pulley extractor, and if one is available this should be used anyway in preference

to screwdrivers. With both gears safely off, remove the woodruff key from the crankshaft with a pair of pliers and place in a container for safe keeping. Note the number of very thin packing washers behind the crankshaft gear and remove them very carefully.

14 Camshaft - removal

The camshaft can be removed with the engine in place in the car, or with the engine on the bench. If the camshaft is to be removed with the engine in the car, the radiator, fan blades and belt, and the radiator left-hand grille should be removed after the cooling system has been drained. The inlet and exhaust manifolds, rocker gear, pushrods and tappets, and fuel pump must also be removed. The timing cover, gears and chain, must be removed as described in Section 13. It is also necessary to remove the distributor drive gear as described in Section 15. With the drive gear out of the way, proceed in the following manner:-

1 First measure the camshaft endfloat with a feeler gauge placed between the keeper plate and the flange. If endfloat exceeds .008 in. it will be necessary to fit a new plate. Then

13.4 Removing the timing cover and gasket

13.6 Easing back the lockwasher tabs

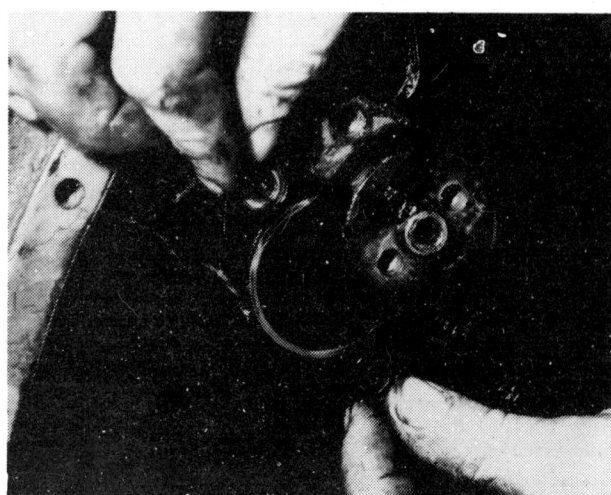
14.2 Removing the camshaft end plate

15.2 Lifting out distributor drive shaft

remove the two bolts and spring washers which hold the camshaft locating plate to the block. The bolts are normally covered by the camshaft gearwheel.

2 Remove the plate (photo). The camshaft can now be withdrawn. Take great care to remove the camshaft gently. It may be necessary to remove the engine mountings and jack-up the engine sufficiently to enable the camshaft to be withdrawn through the radiator grille. (photo)

15 Distributor drive - removal

1 To remove the distributor drive with the sump still in position first undo the two nuts which hold the distributor housing in place.

2 Lift off the distributor, distributor housing and the associated gasket, which should be stored for possible re-use. Then with a pair of long nosed pliers lift out the drive shaft. As the shaft is removed turn it slightly to allow the shaft skew gears to disengage with the camshaft skew gear. (photo)

16 Sump, piston, connecting rod and big end bearing - removal

1 The sump, pistons and connecting rods can be removed with the engine still in the car or with the engine on the bench. If in the car, proceed as for removing the cylinder head with the engine in the car, as described in Section 9. If on the bench proceed as for removing the cylinder head with the engine in this position, as described in Section 8. The pistons and connecting rods are drawn up out of the top of the cylinder bores.

2 If the engine is in the car it will be necessary to drain the sump oil, remove the engine mountings and raise the engine sufficiently to lower the sump, turn it 90° and withdraw. The sump itself is removed by releasing the sixteen bolts that secure it to the crankcase. Retrieve the sump gasket. Note the longer bolts fitted at the rear of the sump.

3 Remove the oil pump strainer by releasing the locknut and unscrewing the strainer.

4 Knock back with a cold chisel the locking tabs on the big end retaining bolts, and remove the bolts and locking tabs.

5 Remove the big end caps one at a time, taking care to keep them in the right order and the correct way round. Also ensure that the shell bearings are kept with their correct connecting rods and caps unless they are renewed. Normally, the numbers 1 to 4 are stamped on adjacent sides of the big end caps and connecting rods, indicating which cap fits on which rod and which way round the cap fits. If no numbers or lines can be found, then with a sharp screwdriver or file scratch mating marks across the joint from the rod to the cap. One line for connecting rod No 1, two for connecting rod No 2, and so on. This will ensure there is no confustion later as it is most important that the caps go back in the correct position on the connecting rods from which they were removed.

6 If the big end caps are difficult to remove they may be gently tapped with a soft hammer.

7 To remove the shell bearings, press the bearing opposite the groove in both the connecting rod, and the connecting rod caps and the bearings will slide out easily.

8 Withdraw the pistons and connecting rods upwards and ensure they are kept in the correct order for replacement in the same bore. Refit the connecting rod caps and bearings to the rods, if the bearings do not require renewal, to minimise the risk of getting the caps and rods in the wrong order.

17 Gudgeon pin - removal

1 To remove the gudgeon pin and free the piston from the connecting rod, remove one of the circlips at either end of the pin with a pair of circlip pliers.

2 Press out the pin from the rod and piston with your fingers.

3 If the pin shows reluctance to move, then on no account force it out, as this could damage the piston. Immerse the piston in a pan of boiling water for three minutes. On removal the expansion of the aluminium should allow the gudgeon pin to slide out easily.

4 Make sure the pins are kept with the same piston for ease of refitting.

18 Piston ring - removal

1 To remove the piston rings, slide them carefully over the top of the piston, taking care not to scratch the aluminium alloy. Never slide them off the bottom of the piston skirt. It is very easy to break the iron piston rings if they are pulled off roughly, so this operation should be done with extreme caution. It is helpful to make use of an old hacksaw blade with the teeth ground off, or better still, an old 0.020 in. feeler gauge.

2 Lift one end of the piston ring to be removed, out of its groove, and insert the end of the feeler gauge under it.

3 Turn the feeler gauge slowly round the piston and, as the ring comes out of its groove, apply slight upward pressure so that it rests on the land above. It can then be eased off the piston with the feeler gauge stopping it from slipping into any empty groove, if it is any but the top piston ring that is being removed.

19 Flywheel and engine end plate - removal

Having removed the clutch (see Chapter 5), the flywheel and engine end plate can be removed. It is only possible for this operation to be carried out with the engine out of the car.

1 Bend back the locking tabs from the four bolts which hold the flywheel to the flywheel flange on the rear of the crankshaft.

2 Unscrew the bolts and remove them, complete with the locking plates if fitted. (photo)

3 Lift the flywheel away from the crankshaft flange in order to clear the locating dowel. NOTE: Some difficulty may be experienced in removing the bolts by the rotation of the crankshaft every time pressure is put on the spanner. To lock the crankshaft in position while the bolts are removed, use a screwdriver as a wedge between a backplate stud and the ring gear. Alternatively a wooden wedge can be inserted between the crankshaft and the side of the block inside the crankcase. (photo)

4 The engine endplate is held in position by a number of bolts and spring washers of varying sizes. Release the bolts noting where different sizes fit and place them together to ensure none of them become lost. Lift away the endplate from the block. (photo)

5 The front engine endplate is removed in identical fashion.

20 Crankshaft and main bearing - removal

With the engine out of the car, remove the timing gears, sump, oil pump, and the big end bearings, pistons, flywheel and engine endplates as has already been described in Sections 13, 16 and 19. Removal of the crankshaft can only be attempted with the engine on the bench or floor. Take off the front sealing block and the packing pieces.

1 Undo by one turn, the bolts which hold the three main bearing caps in place.

2 Unscrew the bolts and remove them, together with the washers.

3 At the rear of the engine, remove the seven bolts which hold the rear oil seal housing in place and remove the housing and its gasket. (photo)

4 Remove the main bearing caps and the bottom half of each bearing shell, taking care to keep the bearing shells in the right caps.

5 When removing the rear bearing cap, NOTE the bottom semi-circular halves of the thrust washers, one half lying on either side of the main bearing. Lay them with the centre bearing

19.2 Releasing flywheel bolts

19.3 Lifting flywheel away from engine end plate

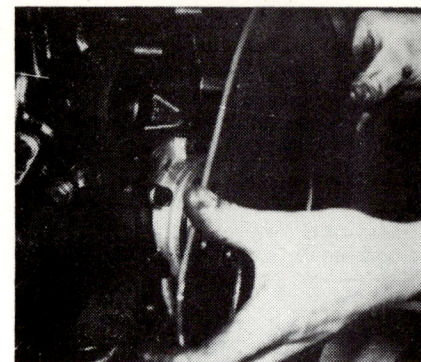
19.4 Removing engine end plate

20.3 Releasing bolts that retain the rear oil seal housing

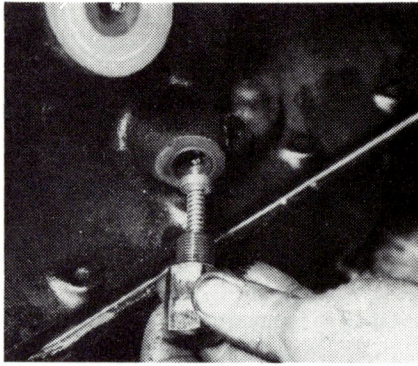
23.2 Withdrawing oil pressure relief valve

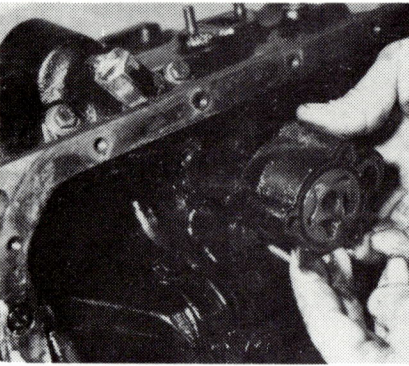
24.2 Removing the oil pump

25.1 Excessive wear on timing chain tensioner

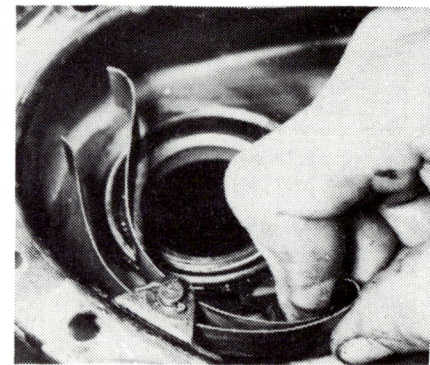
25.2 Removing the timing chain tensioner

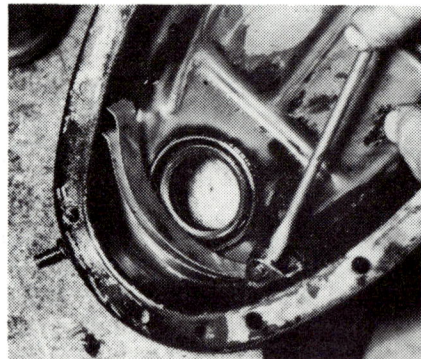
25.3 Removing the timing chain tensioner

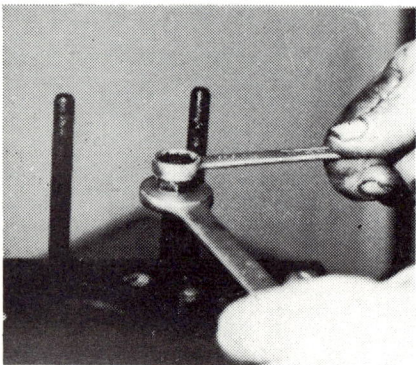
29.5 Method of removing cylinder head studs

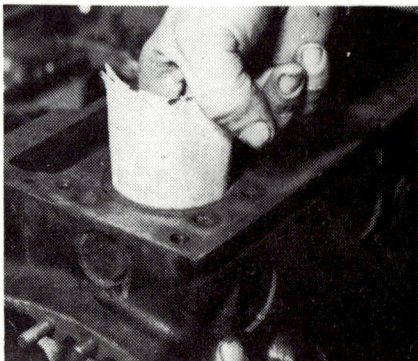
29.6 Rubbing down the glaze on the sides of the bores

32.2 Valve re-grinding

along the correct side.

6 Slightly rotate the crankshaft to free the upper halves of the bearing shells and thrust washers which should now be extracted and placed over the correct bearing cap.

7 Remove the crankshaft by lifting it away from the crankcase.

21 Lubrication and crankcase ventilation systems - description

1 A forced feed system of lubrication is fitted, with oil circulated round the engine from the sump below the block. The level of engine oil in the sump is indicated on the dipstick which is fitted on the right-hand side of the engine. It is marked to indicate the optimum level which is the maximum mark.

2 The level of the oil in the sump, ideally, should not be above or below this line. Oil is replenished via the filler cap on the rocker cover.

3 The eccentric rotor-type oil pump is bolted in the left-hand side of the crankcase and is driven by s short shaft from the skew gear on the camshaft which also drives the distributor shaft.

4 The pump is the non-draining variety to allow rapid pressure build-up when starting from cold.

5 Oil is drawn from the sump via the pick-up strainer. From the oil pump the lubricant passes through a non-adjustable relief valve to the full flow filter. Filtered oil enters the main gallery which runs the length of the engine on the left-hand side. Drillings from the main gallery carry the oil to the crankshaft and camshaft journals.

6 The crankshaft is drilled so that oil under pressure reached the crankpins from the crankshaft journals. The cylinder bores, pistons and gudgeon pins are all lubricated by splash and oil mist.

7 Oil is fed to the valve gear via the hollow rocker shaft at a reduced pressure by means of a scroll and two flats on the camshaft rear journal.

8 Drillings and grooves in the camshaft front journal lubricate the camshaft thrust plate, and the timing chain and gearwheels. Oil returns to the sump by gravity, the pushrods and cam followers being lubricated by oil returning via the pushrod drillings in the block.

9 The crankcase ventilation is of the closed-circuit type, with a pipe connecting the rocker cover to the air intake filter. This reduces the possibility of crankcase fumes entering the interior of the car.

22 Oil filter - removal and replacement

1 The oil filter on all models is readily accessible and can be replaced very quickly. It is located on the left-hand side of the engine towards the front. Unscrew the complete filter unit by grasping it firmly and turning it anticlockwise.

2 Throw the complete filter unit away. clean the mating faces on a new filter and the crankcase, and ensure the sealing ring on the new filter is undamaged.

3 Smear oil round the sealing ring and screw the new filter on tightly.

23 Oil pressure relief valve - removal and replacement

1 To prevent excessive oil pressure, for example when the engine is cold, an oil pressure relief valve is built into the left-hand side of the engine immediately above the crankcase flange and in line vertically with the distributor.

2 The relief valve assembly is dismantled by undoing the large hexagonal headed bolt which holds the relief valve piston and spring in place. (photo)

3 Always renew the spring at a major overhaul. To replace the assembly, fit the valve piston into its orifice in the block, then the spring followed by the bolt, ensuring that the sealing washer is in place on the latter.

24 Oil pump - removal and dismantling

1 Undo the three bolts and spring washers which hold the pump to the underside of the cylinder block.

2 Removal of these bolts also releases the end cover so the pump can be taken from the engine and the outer and inner rotors pulled off, together with the pump and strainer. (photo)

25 Timing chain tensioner - removal and replacement

1 With time, the spring bladed timing chain tensioner will become worn and it should be renewed at the same time as the timing chain. Wear can be clearly seen at two grooves on the face of the tensioner where it presses against the chain. (photo)

2 To remove the tensioner, bend it back and then pull it out from its securing pins. (photo)

3 On replacement, fit the open end of the tensioner over the pin and press the blade with the aid of a screwdriver until it snaps into place. (photo)

26 Examination and renovation - general

With the engine stripped down and all parts thoroughly cleaned, it is now time to examine everything for wear. The following items should be checked and, where necessary, renewed or renovated as described in the following sections.

27 Crankshaft - examination and renovation

Examine the crankpins and main journal surfaces for signs of scoring or scratches. Check the ovality of the crankpins at different positions with a micrometer. If more than 0.001 in. (0.025 mm) out of round, the crankpins will have to be reground. They will also have to be reground if there are any scores or scratches present. Also check the journals in the same fashion. If it is necessary to regrind the crankshaft and fit new bearings your local Triumph garage or engineering works will be able to decide how much metal to grind off and the correct undersize shells to fit.

28 Big end and main bearings - examination and renovation

Big end bearing failure is often accompanied by a noisy knocking from the crankcase, and a slight drop in oil pressure. Main bearing failure is accompanied by vibration, which can be quite severe as the engine speed rises and falls, and a drop in oil pressure.

Bearings which have not broken up, but are badly worn will give rise to low oil pressure and some vibration. Inspect the big ends, main bearings and thrust washers for signs of general wear, scoring, pitting and scratches. The bearings should be matt grey in colour. With lead-indium bearings, should a trace of copper colour be noticed, the bearings are badly worn as the lead bearing material has worn away to expose the indium underlay. Renew the bearings if they are in this condition, or if there is any sign of scoring or pitting.

The undersizes available are designed to correspond with the regrind sizes, ie -0.010 in. (0.254 mm) bearings are correct for a crankshaft reground -0.010 in. (0.254 mm) undersize. The bearings are in fact, slightly more than thhe stated undersize, as running clearances have been allowed for during their manufacture.

Very long engine life can be achieved by changing big end bearings at intervals of 30000 miles and main bearings at intervals of 50000 miles, irrespective of bearing wear. Normally, crankshaft wear is infinitesimal and a change of bearings will ensure mileages of between 100000 to 120000 miles before crankshaft regrinding becomes necessary. Crankshafts normally have to be reground because of scoring due to bearing failure.

29 Cylinder bores - examination and renovation

1   The cylinder bores must be examined for taper, scoring and scratches. Start by carefully examining the top of the cylinder bores. If they are at all worn, a very slight ridge will be found on the thrust side. This marks the top of the piston ring travel. The owner will have a good indication of the bore wear prior to dismantling the engine, or removing the cylinder head. Excessive oil consumption, accompanied by blue smoke from the exhaust, is a sure sign of worn cylinder bores and piston rings.
2   Measure the bore diameter just under the ridge with a micrometer, and compare it with the diameter at the bottom of the bore, which is not subject to wear. If the difference between the two measurements is more than 0.006 in, then it will be necessary to fit special pistons and rings or to have the cylinders rebored and to fit oversize pistons. If no micrometer is available, remove the rings from a piston and place the piston in each bore in turn about ¾in below the top of the bore. If an 0.010 feeler gauge can be slid between the piston and the cylinder wall on the thrust side of the bore, then remedial action must be taken.
3   Pistons are available in an oversize of 0.020 in. (0.52 mm). These are accurately machined to just below these measurements to provide correct running clearances in bores bored out to the exact oversize dimensions.
4   If the bores are slightly worn but not so badly worn as to justify reboring them, then special oil control rings and pistons can be fitted which will restore compression and stop the engine burning oil. Several different types are available, and the manufacturer's instructions concerning their fitting must be followed closely.
5   If the block is to be sent away for reboring, it is essential to remove the cylinder head studs. Lock two nuts together on a stud and then wind the stud out by turning the bottom nut anticlockwise. (photo)
6   If new pistons are being fitted and the bores have not been reground, it is essential to slightly roughen the hard glaze on the sides of the bores with fine glass paper so the new piston rings will have a chance to bed in properly. (photo)

30 Pistons and piston rings - examination and renovation

If the old pistons are to be refitted, carefully remove the piston rings and then thoroughly clean them. Take particular care to clean out the piston ring grooves. At the same time do not scratch the aluminium in any way. If new rings are to be fitted to the old pistons, then the top ring should be stepped so as to clear the ridge left above the previous top ring. If a normal but oversize new ring is fitted, it will hit the ridge and break, because the new ring will not have worn in the same way as the old, which will have worn in unison with the ridge.

Before fitting the rings on the pistons, each should be inserted approximately 3 in. (76 mm) down the cylinder bore and the gap measured with a feeler gauge. This should be between 0.015 and 0.038 in. (0.381 and 0.965 mm). It is essential that the gap should be measured at the bottom of the ring travel, as if it is measured at the top of a worn bore and gives a perfect fit, it could easily seize at the bottom. If the ring cap is too small, rub down the ends of the ring with a very fine file until the cap, when fitted, is correct. To keep the rings square in the bore for measurement, line up each in turn by inserting an old piston in the bore upside down and using the piston to push the ring down about 3 in. Remove the piston and measure the piston ring gap.

When fitting new pistons and rings to a rebored engine, the piston ring gap can be measured at the top of the bore as the bore will not taper. It is not necessary to measure the side clearance in the piston ring grooves with the rings fitted, as the groove dimensions are accurately machined during manufacture. When fitting new oil control rings to old pistons, it may be

necessary to have the grooves widened by machining to accept the new wider rings.

31 Camshaft and camshaft bearings - examination and renovation

In the majority of engines the camshaft runs direct in the cylinder block, and wear of the journals and bearings is negligible. If pre-formed camshaft bearings are fitted, it is possible for these to be replaced, but it is an operation for the local Triumph garage or the local engineering works as it demands the use of specialised equipment. The bearings are removed with a special drift, after which new bearings are pressed in, care being taken to ensure the oil holes in the bearings line up with those in the block. On no account can the bearings be reamed in position.

The camshaft itself should show no signs of wear, but, if very slight scoring on the cams is evident, the score marks can be removed by very gentle rubbing down with a very fine emery cloth. The greatest care should be taken to keep cam profiles smooth.

32 Valves and valve seats - examination and renovation

1   Examine the heads of the valves for pitting and burning, especially the heads of the exhaust valves. The valve seatings should be examined at the same time. If the pitting on valve and seat is very slight, the marks can be removed by grinding the seats and valves together with coarse, and then fine, grinding paste. Where bad pitting has occured to the valve seats, it will be necessary to recut them and fit new valves. If the valve seats are so worn that they cannot be recut, then it will be necessary to fit new valve seat inserts. These latter two jobs should be entrusted to the local Triumph garage or engineering works. In practice, it is very seldom that the seats are so badly worn that they require renewal. Normally, it is the exhaust valve that is too badly worn for replacement, and the owner can easily purchase a new set of valves and match them to the seats by valve grinding.
2   Valve grinding is carried out as follows:
Smear a trace of coarse carborundum paste on the seat face and apply a suction grinder tool to the valve head. With semi-rotary motion, grind the valve head to its seat, lifting the valve occasionally to redistribute the grinding paste. When a dull matt even surface finish is produced on both the valve seat and the valve, then wipe off the paste and repeat the process with fine carborundum paste, lifting and turning the valve to redistribute the paste as before. A light spring placed under the valve head will greatly ease this operation. When a smooth unbroken ring of light grey matt finish is produced, on both valve and valve seat faces, the grinding operation is completed. (photo)
3   Scrape away all carbon from the valve head and the valve stem. Carefully clean away every trace of grinding compound, taking care to leave none in the ports or in the valve guides. Clean the valves and valve seats with a paraffin soaked rag, then with a clean rag, and finally, if an air line is available, blow the valves, valve guides and valve ports clean.

33 Timing gears and chain - examination and renovation

Examine the teeth on both the crankshaft gearwheel and the camshaft gearwheel for wear. Each tooth forms an inverted V with the gearwheel periphery, and if worn, the side of each tooth, ie one side of the inverted V will be concave when compared with the other. If any sign of wear is present the gearwheels must be renewed.

Examine the links of the chain for side slackness, and renew the chain if any slackness is noticeable when compared with a new chain. It is a sensible precaution to renew the chain at about 30000 miles and at a lesser mileage if the engine is stripped down for a major overhaul. The actual rollers on a very badly worn chain may be slightly grooved.

34 Timing chain tensioner - examination and renovation

1 If the timing chain is badly worn it is more than likely that the tensioner will be too.
2 Examine the side of the tensioner which bears against the chain and renew it if it is grooved or ridged. See Section 25 for details.

35 Rockers and rocker shaft - examination and renovation

Remove the threaded plug from the end of the rocker shaft with a screwdriver and thoroughly clean out the shaft. As it acts as the oil passage for the valve gear also, ensure the oil holes in it are quite clear after having cleaned them out. Check the shaft for straightness by rolling it on the bench. It is most unlikely that it will deviate from normal, but if it does, then a judicious attempt must be made to straighten it. If this is not successful, purchase a new shaft. The surface of the shaft should be free from any worn ridges caused by the rocker arms. If any wear is present, renew the shaft. Wear is only likely to have occured if the rocker shaft oil holes have become blocked.

Check the rocker arms for wear of the rocker bushes, for wear at the rocker arm face which bears on the valve stem, and for wear of the adjusting ball ended screws. Wear in the rocker arm bush can be checked by gripping the rocker arm tip and holding the rocker arm in place on the shaft, noting if there is any lateral rocker arm shake. If shake is present, and the arms are very loose on the shaft, a new bush or rocker arm must be fitted.

Check the tip of the rocker arm where it bears on the valve head for cracking or serious wear on the case hardening. If none is present, re-use the rocker arm. Check the lower half of the ball on the end of the rocker arm adjusting screw. On high performance engines, wear on the ball and top of the pushrod is easily noted by the unworn 'pip' which fits in the small central oil hole on the ball. The larger this 'pip' the more wear has taken place to both the ball and the pushrod. Check the pushrods for straightness by rolling them on the bench. Renew any that are bent.

36 Tappets - examination and renovation

Examine the bearing surface of the tappets which lie on the camshaft. Any indentation in this surface, or any cracks, indicate serious wear and the tappets should be renewed. Thoroughly clean them out, removing all traces of sludge. It is most unlikely that the sides of the tappets will prove worn, but, if they are a very loose fit in their bores and can be rocked readily, they should be exchanged for new units. It is very unusual to find any wear in the tappets, and any wear present is likely to occur only at very high mileages.

37 Flywheel starter ring - examination and renovation

If the teeth on the flywheel starter ring are badly worn, or if some are missing, then it will be necessary to remove the ring. This is achieved by splitting the ring with a cold chisel. The greatest care should be taken not to damage the flywheel during this process. It is sometimes advantageous to drill a ¼ inch hole at the intersection point of two teeth, and to strike this point with the cold chisel.

To fit a new ring heat it gently and evenly with an oxy-acetylene flame until a temperature of 200° C maximum is reached. This is indicated by a light metallic blue surface colour. With the ring at this temperature, fit it to the flywheel with the front of the teeth facing the flywheel register. The ring should be tapped gently down onto its register and left to cool naturally when the shrinkage of the metal on cooling will ensure that it is a secure and permanent fit. Great care must be taken not to overheat the ring, as if this happens the temper of the ring will be lost. A safer method is to place the ring in an oil bath and heat the oil to 200° C maximum. A maximum gap of 0.025 in (0.635 mm) is tolerable between the ring gear and the flywheel face around the circumference. Ring gear eccentricity must not exceed 0.010 in (0.254 mm)

38 Flywheel - examination and renovation

If the flywheel clutch face is deeply scored, a new flywheel should be obtained. It is possible for the surface to be skimmed using a lathe. The maximum allowable flywheel face run-out relative to the spigot face is 0.002 in. (0.051 mm) at a radius of 3 ins. (76.2 mm)

39 Oil pump - examination and renovation

Thoroughly clean all the component parts in petrol and then check the rotor end float and lobe clearances in the following manner:
1 Position the rotors in the pump and place the straight edge of a steel ruler across the joint face of the pump. Measure the gap between the bottom of the straight edge and the top of the rotors with a feeler gauge. If the measurement exceeds 0.004 in. (0.102 mm) then check the lobe clearances as described in the following paragraphs. If the lobe clearances are correct, then lap the joint face on a sheet of plate glass. Methods of measuring are given in Fig. 1.3.
2 Measure with a feeler gauge the gap between the inner and outer rotors. It should not be more than 0.010 in (0.254 mm).
3 Then measure the gap between the outer rotor and the side of the pump body which should not exceed 0.008 in. (0.203 mm). It is essential to renew the pump if the measurements are outside these figures. It can be safely assumed that at any major reconditioning the pump will need renewal.

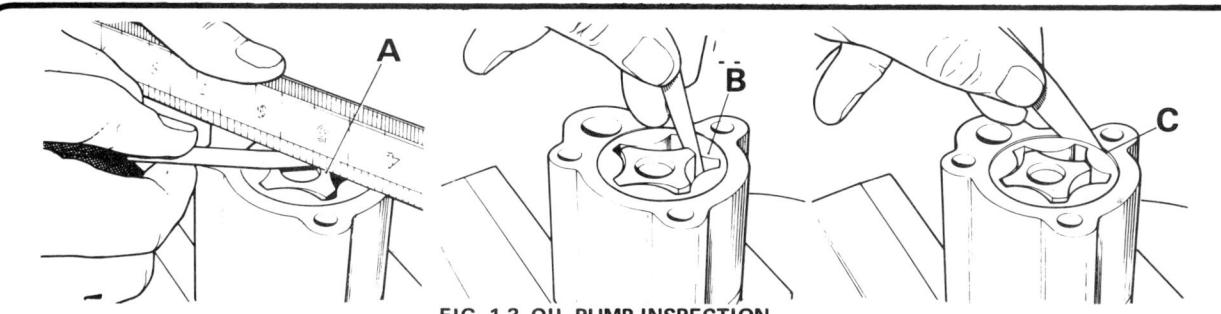

FIG. 1.3. OIL PUMP INSPECTION

A Measuring rotor end float   B Measuring lobe clearance between inner and outer rotors   C Measuring lobe clearance between the outer rotor and side of the body pump

40 Cylinder head - decarbonisation

With the cylinder head off, carefully remove with a wire brush and blunt scraper all traces of carbon deposits from the combustion spaces and the ports. The valve head stems and valve guides should also be freed from any carbon deposits. Wash the combustion spaces and ports down with petrol and scrape the cylinder head surface free of any foreign matter with the side of a steel rule, or a similar article.

Clean the pistons and top of the cylinder bores. If the pistons are still in the block, then it is essential that great care is taken to ensure that no carbon gets into the cylinder bores as this could scratch the cylinder walls or cause damage to the piston and rings. To ensure this does not happen, first turn the crankshaft so that two of the pistons are at the top of their bores. Stuff rag into the other two bores, or seal them off with paper and masking tape. The waterways should also be covered with small pieces of masking tape to prevent particles of carbon entering the cooling system and damaging the water pump.

There are two schools of thought as to how much carbon should be removed from the piston crown. One school recommends that a ring of carbon should be left around the edge of the piston and on the cylinder bore wall as an aid to low oil consumption. Although this is probably true for early engines with worn bores, on later engines the thought of the second school can be applied, which is that for effective decarbonisation, all traces of carbon should be removed.

If all traces of carbon are to be removed, press a little grease into the gap between the cylinder walls and the two pistons which are to be worked on. With a blunt scraper, carefully scrape away the carbon from the piston crown, taking great care not to scratch the aluminium. Also scrape away the carbon from the surrounding lip of the cylinder wall. When all carbon has been removed, scrape away all the grease which will now be contaminated with carbon particles, taking care not to press any into the bores. To assist prevention of carbon build-up, the piston crown can be polished with a metal polish such as Brasso. Remove the rags or masking tape from the other two cylinders, and turn the crankshaft so that the two pistons which were at the bottom are now at the top. Place rag or masking tape in the cylinders which have been decarbonised and proceed as just described.

If a ring of carbon is going to be left round the piston, this can be helped by inserting an old piston ring into the top of the bore to rest on the piston and ensure that carbon is not accidentally removed. Check that there are no particles of carbon in the cylinder bores. Decarbonising is now complete.

41 Valve guides - examination and renovation

Examine the valve guides internally for wear. If the valves are a very loose fit in the guides and there is the slightest suspicion of lateral rocking using a new valve, then new guides will have to be fitted. If the valve guides have been removed compare them internally by visual inspection with a new guide as well as testing them for rocking with a new valve: The valve guide height above the cylinder head should be 0.75 inches (19.05 mm).

42 Sump - examination and renovation

1   It is essential to thoroughly wash out the sump with petrol and this can only be done properly with the gauze removed.
2   With a screwdriver and a pair of pliers carefully pull back the tags which hold the gauze in place.
3   The gauze can then be lifted out and the inside cleaned out properly. Scrape all traces of the old sump gasket from the flange.

43 Engine reassembly - general

1   To ensure maximum life with minimum trouble from a rebuilt engine, not only must everything be correctly assembled, but all the parts must be spotlessly clean, all the oilways must be clear, locking washers and spring washers must always be fitted where indicated, and all bearing and other working surfaces must be thoroughly lubricated during assembly. Before assembly begins, renew any bolts or studs the threads of which are in any way damaged, and whenever possible, use new spring washers.
2   Check the core plugs for signs of weeping and always renew the plug at the front of the engine as it is normally covered by the engine end plate.
3   Drive a punch through the centre of the core plug.
4   Using the punch as a lever, lift out the old core plug.
5   Thoroughly clean the core plug orifice and, using a small diameter headed hammer as an expander, firmly tap a new core plug in place, convex side facing out.
6   Apart from normal tools, a supply of clean rag, an oil can filled with engine oil (an empty plastic detergent bottle thoroughly cleaned and washed out, will invariable do just as well), a new supply of assorted spring washers, a set of new gaskets and preferably a torque wrench, should be collected together.

44 Crankshaft - replacement

Ensure that the crankcase is thoroughly clean and that all oilways are clear. A thin twist drill or a nylon pipe cleaner is useful for cleaning them out. If possible, blow them out with compressed air.

Treat the crankshaft in the same manner and then inject engine oil into the crankshaft oilways.

Commence work on rebuilding the engine by replacing the crankshaft and main bearings:
1   If the old main bearing shells are to be replaced (it is false economy not to do so unless they are virtually new), fit the three upper halves of the main bearing shells to their location in the crankcase, after wiping the locations clean. (photo)
2   Note that at the back of each bearing is a tab which engages in the locating grooves in either the crankcase or the main bearing cap housings.
3   If new bearings are being fitted, carefully clean away all traces of the protective grease with which they are coated.
4   With the three upper bearing shells securely in place, wipe the lower bearing cap housings and fit the three lower shell bearings to their caps, ensuring that the right shell goes into the right cap if the old bearings are being refitted. (photo)
5   Wipe the recesses either side of the rear main bearing which locates the thrust washers. Smear some grease onto the thrust washers and place the upper halves in position. (photo)
6   Note the milled faces of the thrust washers face outwards as shown in this photo.
7   Generously lubricate the crankshaft journals and the upper and lower main bearing shells. (photo)
8   Carefully lower the crankshaft into position.
9   Fit the main bearing caps in position ensuring they locate correctly. The mating surfaces must be spotlessly clean or the caps will not seat correctly. As the bearing caps were assembled to the cylinder block and then line bored during manufacture, it is essential that they are returned to the same positions from which they were removed.
10   Refit the main bearing cap bolts and washers and tighten the bolts to a torque wrench setting of 50 to 65 lb ft (7 to 9 kg m). (photo)
11   Test the crankshaft for freedom of rotation. Should it be stiff to turn or possess high spots, a most careful inspection must be made, preferably by a qualified mechanic, with a micrometer to get to the root of the trouble. It is very seldom that any trouble of this nature will be experienced when fitting the crankshaft.
12   Check the crankshaft end float with a feeler gauge measuring the longitudinal movement between the crankshaft and the rear

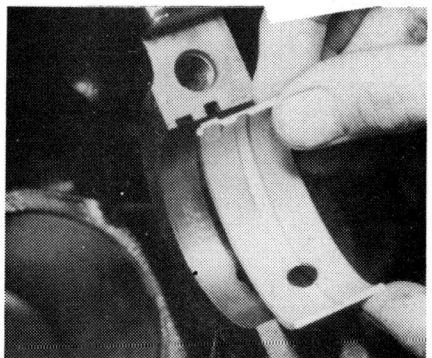

44.1 Fitting main bearing shells to crank-case

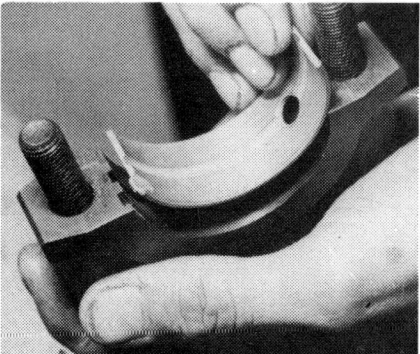

44.4 ... and their associated caps. Note that the oil holes and locating tabs are correctly positioned

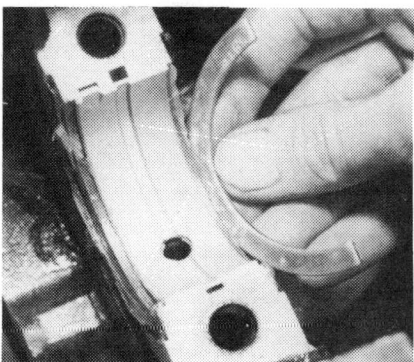

44.5 Greasing the thrust washers

44.6 Placing thrust washers in position with oil grooves outside

44.7 Lubricating the bearing shells

44.10 Tightening main bearing cap bolts

44.12 Checking crankshaft end float

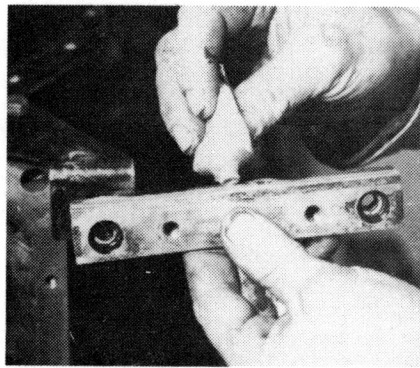

44.13 Applying jointing compound to sealing block

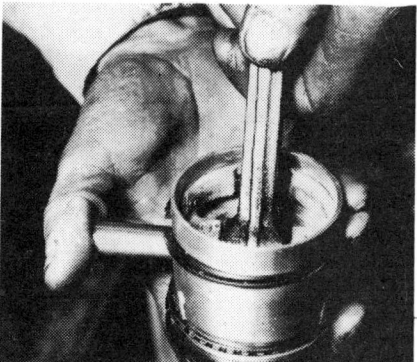

45.6 Fitting gudgeon pin to piston

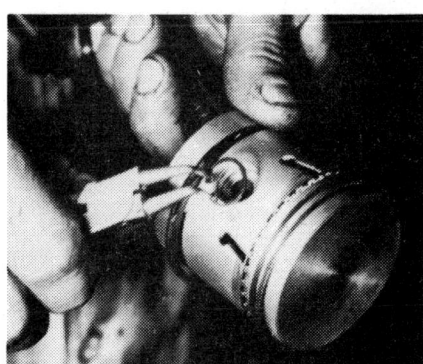

45.7 Fitting circlip to secure gudgeon pin

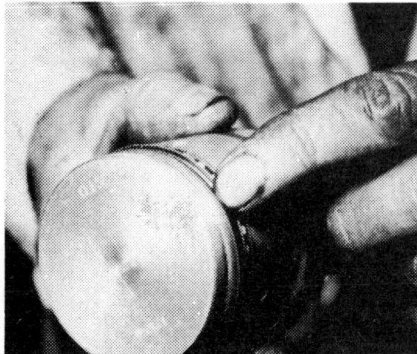

45.8 Checking for groove on new oil control pistons top ring

47.3 Showing the piston ring gaps apart from each other

main bearing cap. End float should be between 0.004 to 0.008 in. (0.102 to 0.203 mm). If end float is excessive, oversize thrust washers can be fitted. (photo)

13 The sealing block may next be fitted over the front main bearing cap. Smear the ends of the block with jointing compound and fit the block in place. Fit the securing screws but do not tighten fully. Fit new wooden wedge seals at each end and line up the front face of the block with the front of the cylinder block. Tighten the screws fully and cut the wedge seals flush with the crankcase flange. The method of refitting the sealing block is shown in Fig. 1.4. (photo)

45 Piston and connecting rod - reassembly

1 If the same pistons are being used, then they must be mated to the same connecting rod with the same gudgeon pin. If new pistons are being fitted, it does not matter which connecting rod they are used with, but the gudgeon pins should be fitted on the basis of selective assembly.

2 Because aluminium alloy, when hot, expands more than steel, the gudgeon pin may be a very tight fit in the piston when cold. To avoid damage to the piston, it is best to heat it in boiling water when the pin will slide in easily.

3 Lay the correct piston adjacent to each connecting rod and remember that the same rod and piston must go back into the same bore. If new pistons are being used, it is only necessary to ensure that the right connecting rod is placed in each bore.

4 Fit a gudgeon pin circlip in position at one end of the gudgeon pin hole in the piston.

5 Locate the connecting rod in the piston with the arrow on the piston crown towards the front of the engine, ie the timing cover end, and the connecting rod cap towards the camshaft side of the engine.

6 Slide the gudgeon pin in through the hole in the piston and through the connecting rod little end, until it rests against the previously fitted circlip. NOTE that the pin should be a push fit. (photo)

7 Fit the second circlip in position. Repeat this procedure for all four pistons and connecting rods. (photo)

8 Where special oil control pistons are being fitted, should the position of the top ring be the same as the position of the top ring on the old piston, ensure that a groove has been machined on the top of the new ring so no fouling occurs between the unworn portion at the top of the bore and the piston ring, when the latter is at the top of its stroke. (photo)

46 Piston ring - replacement

1 Check that the piston ring grooves and oilways are thoroughly clean and unblocked. Piston rings must always be fitted over the head of the piston and never from the bottom.

2 The easiest method to use when fitting rings, is to wrap a 0.020 feeler gauge round the top of the piston and place the rings one at a time, starting with the bottom oil control ring over the feeler gauge.

3 The feeler gauge, complete with ring, can then be slid down the piston over the other piston ring grooves until the correct groove is reached. The piston ring is then slid gently off the feeler gauge into the groove.

4 An alternative method is to fit the rings by holding them slightly open with the thumbs and both index fingers. This method requires a steady hand and great care as it is easy to open the ring too much and break it.

47 Piston - replacement

The pistons, complete with connecting rods can be fitted to the cylinder bore in the following manner:

1 With a wad of clean rag, wipe the cylinder bores clean.

2 The pistons, complete with connecting rods, are fitted to their bores from the top of the cylinder block.

3 Before each piston is inserted make sure that the piston rings gaps are apart from each other to ensure a gas tight joint. Endeavour to avoid a gap on the thrust side of the cylinder bore. (photo)

4 As each piston is inserted into its bore, ensure that it is the correct piston/connecting rod assembly for that particular bore, that the connecting rod is the correct way round, and also that the front of the piston is towards the front of the bore, ie towards the front of the engine. An arrow (thus Δ) points to the front of the piston. The con-rod cap should be towards the camshaft side of the engine.

5 Lubricate the piston before inserting into the bore (photo).

6 The piston will only slide into the bore as far as the oil control ring. It is then necessary to compress the piston rings using a clamp. (photo)

7 Gently push the piston into the bore with the wooden handle of a hammer. (photo)

48 Connecting rod to crankshaft - reassembly

1 Wipe clean the connecting rod half of the big end bearing cap and the underside of the shell bearing and fit the shell bearing in position with its locating tongue engaged with the corresponding rod. (photo)

2 If the bearings are nearly new and are being refitted, then ensure they are replaced in their correct locations on the correct rods.

3 Generously lubricate the crankpin journals with engine oil, and turn the crankshaft so that the crankpin is in the most advantageous position for the connecting rod to be drawn onto it. (photo)

4 Wipe clean the connecting rod bearing cap and back of the shell bearings and fit the shell bearing in position, ensuring that the locating tongue at the back of the bearing engages with the locating groove in the connecting rod cap.

5 Generously lubricate the shell bearing and offer up the connecting rod bearing cap to the connecting rod. Ensure that the connecting rod bolt bushes are correctly located. (photo)

6 Fit the connecting rod bolts and tighten them to a torque wrench setting of 38 to 45 lb ft (5.2 to 6.2 kg m). (photo)

7 When all the connecting rods have been fitted, rotate the crankshaft to check that everything is free and that there are no high spots causing binding.

49 Camshaft and front end plate - replacement

1 Wipe the camshaft bearing journals clean and lubricate them generously with engine oil. (photo)

2 Insert the camshaft into the crankcase gently, taking care not to damage the camshaft bearings with the cams. (photo)

3 Fit a new gasket over the front of the cylinder block using the dowel to locate it correctly. (photo)

4 Carefully fit the front end plate aligning it with the dowel. (photo)

5 Fit the one securing bolt located immediately above the crankshaft nose. (photo)

6 Replace the camshaft locating plate. (photo)

7 Tighten the two camshaft locating plate securing bolts and spring washers. (photo)

50 Timing gears, chain tensioner and cover - replacement

1 Place the gearwheel in position without the timing chain, and place the straight edge of a steel ruler from the side of the camshaft gear teeth to the crankshaft gearwheel, and measure the gap (if any) between the steel rule and the crankshaft gearwheel. If a gap exists, a suitable number of packing washers must be placed on the crankshaft nose to bring the crankshaft gearwheel onto the same plane as the camshaft gearwheel. (photo)

47.5 Lubricating the piston before refitting

47,6 Easing the piston in the bore with clamp compressing the rings

47.7 Completing piston entry into bore

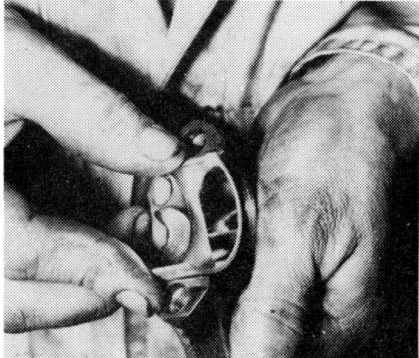

48.1 Fitting bearing shell to connecting rod cap

48.3 Lubricating crankpin journals

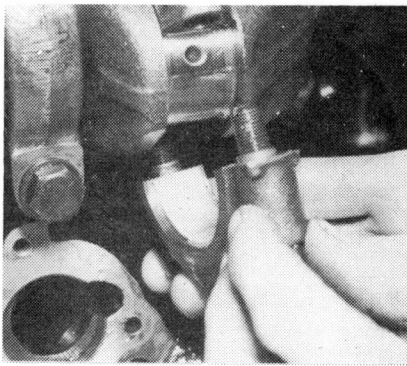

48.5 Fitting connecting rod bearing caps

48.6 Tightening the connecting rod bolts

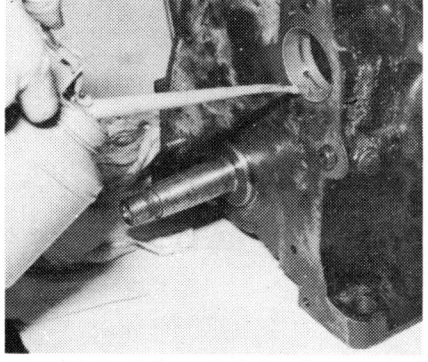

49.1 Lubricating camshaft housings

49.2 Inserting camshaft

49.3 Mating new gasket to front of cylinder block

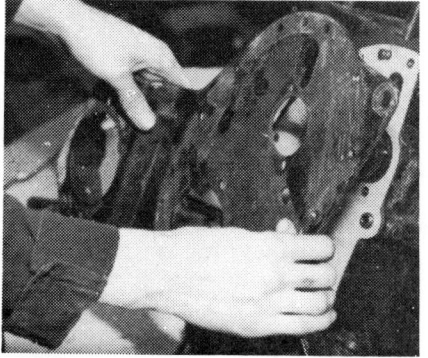

49.4 Fitting front plate over locating dowels

49.5 Tightening front plate bolt

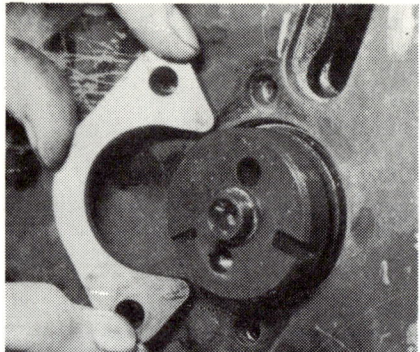
49.6 Replacing camshaft end plate

49.7 ... and tightening the retaining bolts

50.1 Replacing timing wheels to check if they are on the same level

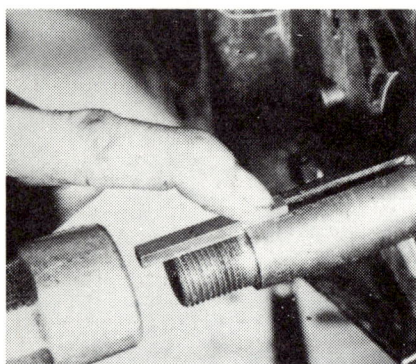
50.2 Fitting Woodruff key

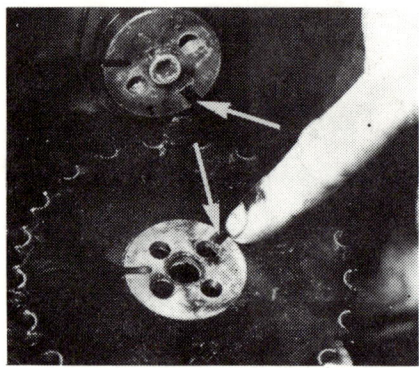
50.3 Checking that camshaft timing gear is refitted with the slots (arrowed) adjacent to each other

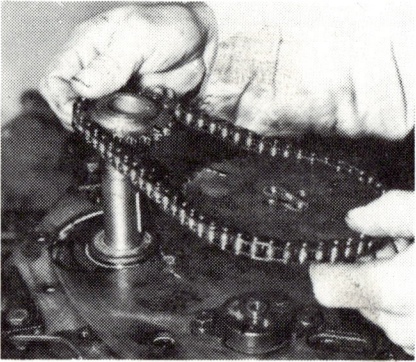
50.5 Replacing the complete timing chain and gears assembly

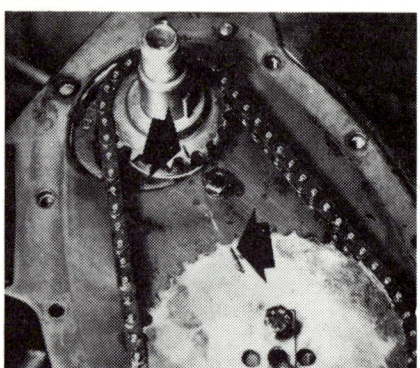
50.6 When fitted, the marks on the gear-wheels (arrowed) should be aligned

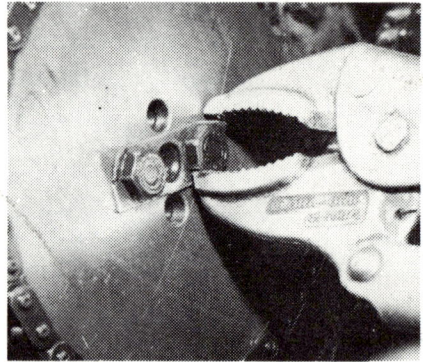
50.8 Bending over the lockwasher tabs

50.9 Removing oil seal from timing cover

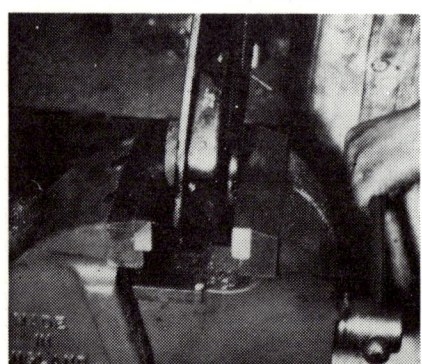
50.10 Fitting new oil to timing cover with the aid of a vice

50.11 Assembling oil thrower to the nose of the crankshaft with the dished edge towards the cover

50.12 Mating new gaskets to front plate

2 Fit the woodruff key to the slot in the crankshaft nose. (photo)

3 It is all too easy to fit the sprocket wheel 180° out on the camshaft. The best way of ensuring that the wheel is fitted the right way round is to make certain the two different slot marks on the back of the wheel correspond with the slots on the front of the camshaft. (photo)

4 Lay the camshaft gearwheels on a clean surface so that the two timing marks are adjacent to each other. Slip the timing chain over them and pull the gearwheels back into mesh with the chain so that the timing marks, although further apart, are still adjacent to each other. A special point to note is that should the chain have a removable link, always position it so that the spring clip faces forwards.

5 With the timing marks adjacent to each other, hold the gearwheels above the crankshaft and camshaft. Turn the camshaft and crankshaft so that the woodruff key will enter the slot in the crankshaft gearwheel, and the camshaft gearwheel is in the correct position relative to the camshaft (see paragraph 3). (photo)

6 Fit the timing chain and gearwheel assembly onto the camshaft and crankshaft, keeping the timing marks adjacent. (photo)

7 Fit a new double tab washer in place on the camshaft gearwheel and fit the two retaining bolts to a torque wrench setting of 24 to 26 lb ft (3.32 to 3.59 kg m).

8 Bend up the tabs on the lockwasher. (photo)

9 The oil seal in the front of the timing cover should be renewed. To remove it, carefully prise it out with a screwdriver taking care not to damage the timing cover in the process. (photo)

10 Evenly press a new seal into the cover using a vice ensuring that the seal lip is towards the crankshaft sprocket wheel. (photo)

11 Fit the oil thrower in place on the nose of the crankshaft making sure that the dished periphery is towards the cover. (photo)

12 Lubricate the front cover oil seal, fit a new gasket in place on the end plate and fit the cover at an angle so as to catch the spring tensioner against the side of the chain. Alternatively, it can be hooked back using a piece of bent rod. (photo)

13 Swing the cover into its correct position and insert one or two screws finger tight. (photo)

14 Replace the five screws, six bolts and one nut that secure the cover. Fig. 1.4. gives the position of these items. Do not tighten at this stage.

15 Insert the crankshaft pulley over the woodruff key and through the seal.

16 Replace the pulley securing nut and tighten to a torque of 90 to 100 ft lb (12.4 to 13.8 kg m).

17 Tighten the screws, bolts and nut that secure the timing cover. NOTE: The camshaft timing sprocket is provided with four holes which are equally spaced but are offset from a tooth centre. A half-tooth adjustment is obtained by turning the sprocket 90° from its position. A quarter-tooth adjustment is obtained by turning the sprocket 'back to front' and a three-quarter-tooth variation by turning it on the bolt locations by 90° in this reverse position.

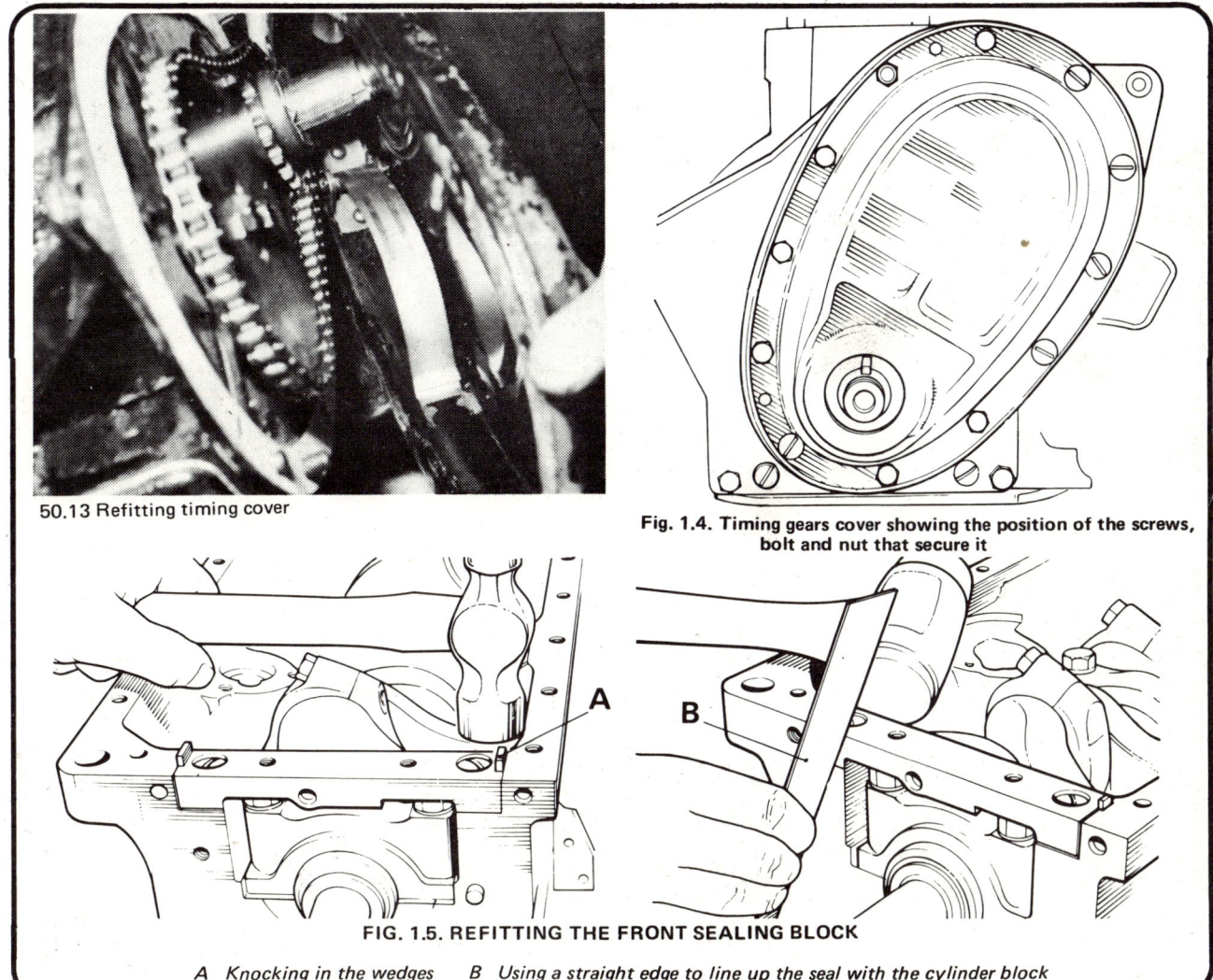

50.13 Refitting timing cover

Fig. 1.4. Timing gears cover showing the position of the screws, bolt and nut that secure it

FIG. 1.5. REFITTING THE FRONT SEALING BLOCK

A Knocking in the wedges   B Using a straight edge to line up the seal with the cylinder block

51 Valve and valve spring - reassembly

To refit the valves and valve springs to the cylinder head proceed as follows:

1 Rest the cylinder head on its side.

2 Fit each valve and valve spring in turn, wiping down and lubricating each stem as it is inserted into the same valve guide from which it was removed. (photo)

3 Build up each valve assembly by first fitting the lower collar. (photo)

4 Fit the valve spring so that the closely coiled portion of the spring is adjacent to the cylinder head. (photo)

5 On engines which use the double hole spring retaining collar, press the valve in firmly with one hand, and with the other fit the collar over the valve stem by means of the offset hole. (photo)

6 Press down hard on the collar to compress the spring and, as soon as the collar is in line with the groove in the valve stem, push the collar across into the smaller hole so the spring is securely retained. (photo)

7 On engines which use split collets to retain the upper retaining collar, move the cylinder head towards the edge of the work bench if it is facing downwards and slide it partially over the edge of the bench so as to fit the bottom half of a valve spring compressor to the valve head. Slide the spring and upper collar over the valve stem.

8 With the base of the valve compressor on the valve head, compress the valve spring until the collets can be slipped into place in the collet grooves. Gently release the compressor. (photo)

9 Repeat this procedure until all eight valves and valve springs are fitted.

52 Rocker shaft and tappet - reassembly

1 Fit the rear pedestal over the rocker shaft with its associated rocker; secure in position with a Phillips screw, ensuring that it engages with the rocker shaft.

2 Slide the rockers, pedestals, springs and spacers over the front end of the shaft.

3 When all is correctly assembled, fit the split pin to the front of the shaft and oil the components thoroughly.

4 Generously lubricate the tappets internally and externally and insert them in the bores from which they were removed. (photo)

53 Cylinder head - replacement

1 Thoroughly clean the cylinder head block face and then refit the cylinder head studs using the double nut method. (photo)

2 Note that the two slightly longer studs must be fitted to the last two holes towards the rear of the block on the right-hand side. (photo)

3 Apply a little jointing compound around the one hole shown in this photo.

4 Fit a new gasket in place. If one side of the gasket is marked TOP it must naturally be fitted with this side facing upwards. (photo)

5 Generously lubricate each cylinder with engine oil.

6 Ensure that the cylinder head face is perfectly clean and then lower the cylinder head into place, keeping it parallel to the block to avoid binding on any of the studs. (photo)

7 With the head in place, lift the lifting eye over the two rear right hand studs (photo).

8 Fit the cylinder head nuts and washers and tighten down the nuts half a turn at a time in order shown in Fig. 1.6. to a torque wrench setting of 38 to 45 lb ft (5.2 to 6.2 kg m). (photo)

9 Insert the pushrods into the block so the ball end rests in the tappet. Ensure the pushrods are replaced in the same order in which they were removed. (photo)

10 Then refit the rocker shaft assembly ensuring that the rocker arm ball joints seal in the pushrod cups. (photo)

11 Replace the four rocker pedestal nuts and plain washers and tighten them down evenly. (photo)

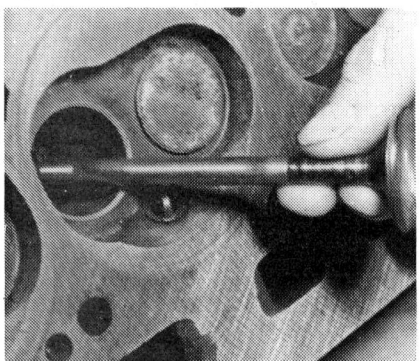

51.2 Inserting valve into its guide after lubricating its stem

51.3 Fitting valve lower collar

51.4 ... and spring with closer coils at the bottom

51.5 Method of refitting double-hole collars

51.6 Method of refitting double-hole collars

51.8 Using a valve spring compressor and fitting the collets to the valve stem

52.4 Inserting tappets after lubrication internally and externally

53.1 Refitting cylinder head studs

53.2 Showing the position of the two longer studs

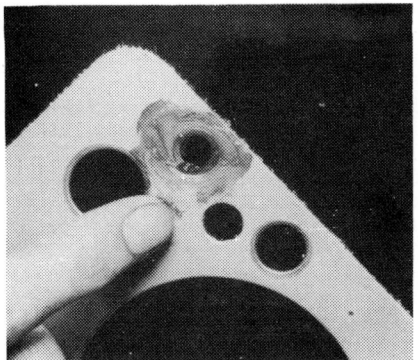

53.3 Apply a little jointing compound around this hole in the gasket

53.4 Refit gasket to cylinder head

53.6 Easing cylinder head over the studs

53.7 Assembling lifting eye to the two rear righthand studs

53.8 ... and tightening the head nuts

53.9 Inserting pushrods into tappets

53.10 Refitting rocker shaft over the oedestal studs

53.11 ... and tightening the retaining nuts

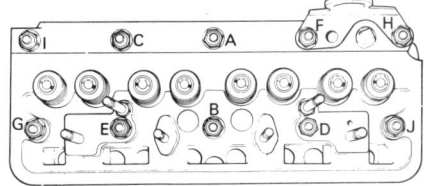

Fig. 1.6. Cylinder head nuts tightening sequence

54 Rocker arm/valve - adjustment

1   The valve adjustments should be made with the engine cold. The importance of correct rocker arm/valve stem clearances cannot be overstressed as they vitally affect the performance of the engine.

2   If the clearances are set too open, the efficiency of the engine is reduced as the valves open late and close earlier than was intended. If, on the other hand, the clearances are set too close, there is a danger that the stems will expand upon heating and not allow the valves to close properly. This will cause burning of the valve head and seat, and possible warping.

3   If the engine is in the car, to get at the rockers it is merely necessary to remove the two holding down studs from the rocker cover, and then to lift the rocker cover and gasket away.

4   It is important that the clearance is set when the tappet of the valve being adjusted, is on the heel of the cam (ie opposite the peak). This can be done by carrying out the adjustments in the following order, which also avoids turning the crankshaft more than necessary:

Adjust valves	Valves fully open
1 and 3	8 and 6
5 and 2	4 and 7
8 and 6	1 and 3
4 and 7	5 and 2

5   The correct valve clearance of 0.010 in. is obtained by slackening the hexagonal locknut with a spanner while holding the ball pin against rotation with the screwdriver. Then, still pressing down with the screwdriver, insert a feeler gauge in the gap between the valve stem head and the rocker arm and adjust the ball pin until the feeler gauge will just move in and out without nipping. Still holding the ball pin in the correct position, tighten the locknut. (photo)

6   An alternative method is to set the gaps with the engine running, and although this may be faster it is no more reliable.

55 Crankshaft rear seal, housing, end plate and flywheel - replacement

1   A lip type crankshaft rear oil seal is used and is located in the rear seal housing.

2   Coat both sides of a new gasket with jointing compound and position the gasket on the crankcase joint face. (photo)

3   Press a new seal into the oil seal housing with the lip of the seal facing the crankshaft. Oil the seal and carefully fit the housing, making sure that the lip of the seal is not turned over. (photo)

4   Replace the housing bolts finger tight, turn the crankshaft over several times to centralise the seal and tighten the bolts down firmly. (photo)

5   Fit a new input shaft bush into the hole in the centre of the crankshaft rear journal.

6   No gasket is fitted between the end plate and the cylinder block. Fit the end plate in position and tighten down the securing bolts and washers.

7   Make certain that the flange of the flywheel and crankshaft are perfectly clean, and offer up the flywheel to the end of the crankshaft. Ensure that the dowel enters the locating hole in the flywheel.

8   Refit the four bolts and lockwashers (if fitted). Tighten down the four retaining bolts in a diagonal manner to a torque wrench setting of 38 to 45 lb ft (5.2 to 6.2 kg m). Bend over the lockwasher tabs.

9   Smear the crankshaft spigot bush with a small quantity of zinc oxide grease.

56 Oil pump - replacement

1   Wipe the mating faces of the oil pump and crankcase and fit the pump and drive shaft. If the drive gear shaft is fitted, ensure the oil pump drive shaft engages it correctly.

2   Prime the pump to preclude any possibility of oil starvation when the engine starts.

3   Refit the cover to the pump and tighten down the three securing bolts and washers. (Fig.1.7)

4   Fit the pick-up strainer to the pump, if not previously fitted, and ensure the locknut is secure.

57 Sump - replacement

1   After the sump has been thoroughly cleaned, scrape all traces of the old sump gasket from the sump and crankcase flanges, fit a new gasket in place and then refit the sump.

2   Insert and tighten down the sump bolts and washers remembering to fit the longer bolts at the rear of the sump, where they mate with the holes in the oil seal housing.

58 Distributor and distributor drive - replacement

It is important to set the distributor drive correctly as otherwise the ignition timing will be totally incorrect. It is easy to set the distributor drive in apparently the right position, but in fact exactly 180° out, by omitting to select the correct cylinder which must not only be at TDC but must also be on its firing stroke with both valves closed. The distributor should, therefore, not be fitted until the cylinder head is in position and the valves can be observed. Alternatively, if the timing cover has not been replaced, the distributor drive can be replaced when the marks on the timing wheels are adjacent to each other.

1   Rotate the crankshaft so that No 1 piston is at TDC and on its firing stroke (the marks on the timing gears will be adjacent to each other). When No 1 piston is at TDC the inlet valve on No 4 cylinder is just opening and the exhaust valve closing. The notch on the pulley hub should be aligned with the 9 degree BEFORE graduation on the timing cover scale.

2   Insert the distributor drive into its housing so that when fully home, the slot in the top of the drive shaft is positioned with the larger segment facing downwards. Ensure that the slot is in line with the threaded hole for oil filter attachment. The end of the shaft engages with a slot in the top of the oil pump rotor shaft. It may be necessary to turn the pump rotor shaft to allow the distributor drive to engage fully. Fig.1.8 shows the distributor drive shaft in position.

3   It is essential that between 0.003 and 0.007 in. (0.076 and 0.178 mm) end float exists between the top side of the gear driven by the skew gear on the camshaft and the underside of the pedestal boss. If the same components are being used, it will be safe to assume that the end float is correct, but ensure the same number of packing washers are used (if any) and always fit a new gasket.

4   If the drive gears are assembled without end float, wear on the crankshaft gearwheels, chain and distributor drive gear, will be very heavy. If new components are being fitted then cut a small notch in the outer edge of the distributor housing flange gasket and bolt the housing down firmly. Measure the thickness of the gasket with a feeler gauge placed in the notch. Then remove the distributor housing and gasket and replace the housing without the gasket. Measure the gap between the underside of the housing flange and the block and subtract this latter figure from the former to determine the end float with the standard gasket.

5   Turn the distributor so that the rotor arm is pointing to the terminal in the cap which carries the lead to No 1 cylinder, and fit the distributor to the distributor housing. The lip on the distributor should mate perfectly with the slot in the distributor drive shaft. Fit the bolt which holds the distributor clamp plate

54.5 Adjusting valve clearances

55.2 Mating new gaskets to rear seal housing position on the block

55.3 Assembling the seal housing to the block

55.4 ... and tightening the retaining bolts

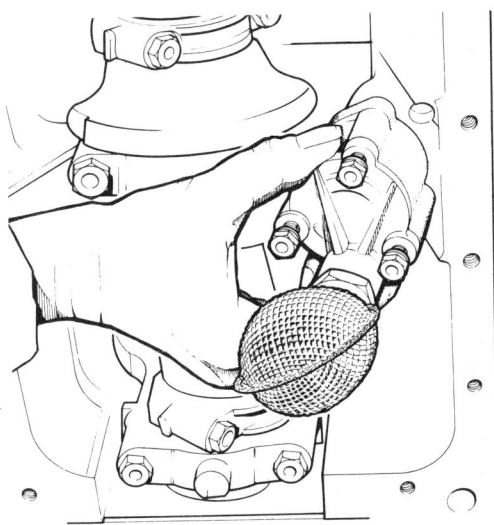
Fig. 1.7. Replacing the oil pump and strainer

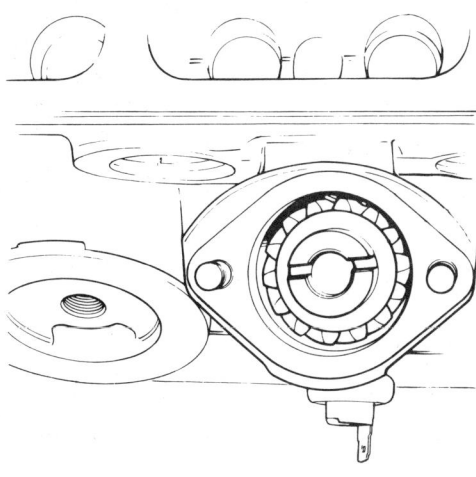
Fig. 1.8. The distributor drive shaft in the correct position before replacing the distributor

to the housing.

6 Tighten down the two nuts and washers which hold the distributor housing in place.

7 If the clamp bolt on the clamping plate was not previously loosened and the distributor body was not turned in the clamping plate, then the ignition timing will be as before. If the clamping bolt has been loosened, then it will be necessary to re-time the ignition as described in Chapter 4.

59 Engine - final assembly

1 Fit a new rocker cover gasket and carefully fit the cover in place. (photo)

2 Replace the washers over the rocker cover holding down studs, ensuring that the sealing washer lies under the flat steel washer. Replace the rocker cover nuts. Do not forget to refit the choke cable support under the forward nut. (photo)

3 Make sure the mating faces of the water pump body and cylinder head are clean and fit a new gasket holding it in position with a little jointing compound. (photo)

4 Place the water pump body in position on the cylinder head face.

5 Secure the water pump body with the three securing bolts. Note that the fuel pipe bracket is retained by the top right bolt. These bolts are of different lengths and their positions should have been noted when dismantling. (See also Chapter 2).

6 Make sure that the mating faces of the water pump and body are clean and fit a new gasket to the water pump body.

7 Refit the water pump over the three studs.

8 Replace the three nuts and spring washers and tighten fully.

9 Refit the starter motor into its aperture; replace the identical packing and shims that were removed on dismantling. Note the terminal at the rear is away from the crankcase.

10 Secure the starter motor with the two nuts, bolts and spring washers.

11 The alternator should be refitted next. Position the alternator and fit the main mounting bolt assembly to the block.

12 Fit the alternator adjustment bracket to the head.

13 Swing the alternator towards the head and fit the adjustment bolt assembly through the bracket and alternator.

14 Refit the fan belt. Adjust the tension until there is ¾ in. (19 mm) of lateral movement at the mid-point position of the belt between the alternator pulley wheel and the crankshaft pulley wheel. Tighten the nuts.

15 Refit the fuel pump using a new joint gasket, easing the rocker arm to the outside of the cam.

16 Secure the fuel pump with the one nut, shaped nut and spring washers.

17 Refer to Chapter 3 and refit the carburettor and inlet manifold. Reconnect the fuel line from the fuel pump to the carburettor installation.

18 Smear a little engine oil onto the threads of a new oil filter

and screw in the filter.

19 Fit new spark plugs and the complete unit is now ready for refitting to the car.

60 Engine - replacement

Although the engine, or engine and gearbox, can be replaced by one man and a suitable winch, it is easier if two are present. One to lower the unit into the engine compartment, and the other to guide the unit into position and to ensure that it does not foul anything. Generally speaking engine replacement is a reversal of the procedures used when removing the engine (See sections 4 and 5) but one or two added tips may come in useful.

1 Ensure all the loose leads, cables etc., are tucked out of the way. If not, it is easy to trap one and cause much additional work after the engine is replaced.

2 Carefully lower the unit into position (photo) and then refit the following:

a) Engine mountings and gearbox mounting
b) Propeller shaft to gearbox
c) Refit the clutch slave cylinder to its housing and tighten the clamp bolt
d) Speedometer cable
e) Gear change lever and linkage
f) Multi-socket connector to alternator
g) Oil pressure switch and cable
h) Wires to coil and distributor
i) Carburettor controls
j) Air cleaner
k) Exhaust manifold to downpipe
l) Earth and starter motor cables
m) Radiator and hoses
n) Heater hoses
o) Water temperature cable
p) Vacuum advance and retard pipe
q) Battery

3 Finally check that the drain taps are closed and refill the cooling system with water and the engine with the correct grade of oil.

61 Engine - initial start up after overhaul or major repair

1 Make sure the battery is fully charged and that all lubricants, coolants and fuel are replenished.

2 If the fuel system has been dismantled, it will require several revolutions of the engine on the starter motor to get the petrol up to the carburettor. An initial 'prime' of about 1/3 cupful of petrol poured down the in tube to the carburettor will help the engine to fire quickly, thus relieving the load on the battery. Do

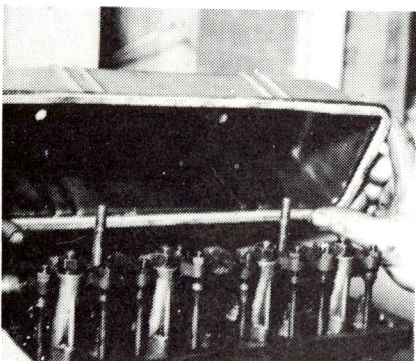
59.1 Fitting rocker cover and new gasket

59.2 ... and securing with sealing washer, steel washer and nut

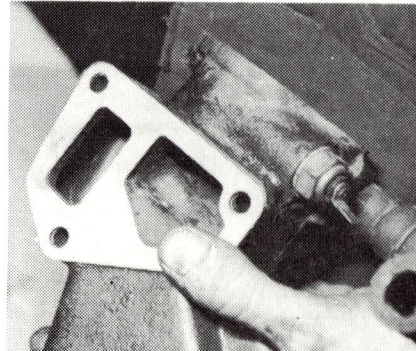
59.3 Assembling new gasket to water pump body

not overdo this however, as flooding may result.
3 As soon as the engine fires and runs, keep it going at a fast tickover only (no faster) and bring it up to normal working temperature.
4 As the engine warms up, there will be odd smells and some smoke from parts getting hot and burning off oil deposits. Look for leaks of oil or water, which will be obvious if serious. Check also the clamp connections of the exhaust pipes to the manifolds as these do not always 'find' their exact gas tight position until the warmth and vibration have acted on them, and it is almost certain that they will need tightening further. This should be

done, of course, with the engine stopped.
5 When running temperature has been reached, adjust the idling speed as described in Chapter 3.
6 Stop the engine and wait a few minutes to see if any lubricant or coolant is driping out when the engine is stationary.
7 Road test the car to check that the timing is correct and giving the necessary smoothness and power. Do not race the engine - if new bearings and/or pistons and rings have been fitted, it should be treated as a new engine and run in at reduced revolutions for 500 miles.

62 Fault diagnosis

Symptom	Reason/s	Remedy
Engine will not turn over when starter switch is operated	Flat battery Bad battery connections Bad connections at solenoid switch and/or starter motor	Check that battery is fully charged and that all connections are clean and tight.
	Starter motor jammed	Rock car back and forth with a gear engaged. If ineffective remove starter (not automatic).
	Defective solenoid	Remove and check solenoid.
	Starter motor defective	Remove starter and overhaul.
Engine turns over normally but fails to fire and run	No spark at plugs	Check ignition system according to procedures given in Chapter 4.
	No fuel reaching engine	Check fuel system according to procedures given in Chapter 3.
	Too much fuel reaching the engine (flooding)	Check fuel system if necessary as described in Chapter 3.
Engine starts but runs unevenly and misfires	Ignition and/or fuel system faults	Check the ignition and fuel systems as though the engine had failed to start.
	Incorrect valve clearances	Check and reset clearances.
	Burnt out valves	Remove cylinder head and examine and overhaul as necessary.
Lack of power	Ignition and/or fuel system faults	Check the ignition and fuel systems for correct ignition timing and carburettor settings.
	Incorrect valve clearances	Check and reset the clearances.
	Burnt out valves	Remove cylinder head and examine and overhaul as necessary.
	Worn out piston or cylinder bores	Remove cylinder head and examine pistons and cylinder bores. Overhaul as necessary.
Excessive oil consumption	Oil leaks from crankshaft oil seal, rocker cover gasket, drain plug gasket, sump plug washer	Identify source of leak and repair as appropriate.
	Worn piston rings or cylinder bores resulting in oil being burnt by engine (smoky exhaust is an indication)	Fit new rings or rebore cylinders and fit new pistons, depending on degree of wear.
	Worn valve guides and/or defective valve stem seals	Remove cylinder head and recondition valve guides and valves and seals as necessary.
Excessive mechanical noise from engine	Wrong valve to rocker clearances Worn crankshaft bearings Worn cylinders (piston slap)	Adjust valve clearances. Inspect and overhaul where necessary.
Unusual vibration	Misfiring on one or more cylinders Loose mounting bolts	Check ignition system. Check tightness of bolts and condition of flexible mountings.

NOTE: When investigating starting and uneven running faults do not be tempted into snap diagnosis. Start from the beginning of the check procedure and follow it through. It will take less time in the long run. Poor performance from an engine in terms of power and economy is not normally diagnosed quickly. In any event the ignition and fuel systems must be checked first before assuming any further investigation needs to be made.

Chapter 2 Cooling system

Contents

General description 1	Water pump - dismantling and reassembly 8
Cooling system - draining 2	Anti-freeze mixture 9
Cooling system - flushing 3	Temperature gauge - fault diagnosis and rectification ... 10
Cooling system - filling 4	Temperature gauge and sender unit - removal and replacement 11
Radiator and expansion tank - removal, inspection, cleaning and replacement ... 5	Fan belt - adjustment 12
Thermostat - removal, testing and replacement 6	Fan belt - removal and replacement 13
Water pump - removal and replacement 7	Fault diagnosis 14

Specifications

Type of system	Pressurised no-loss system incorporating pump impeller, and expansion tank. Fan assisted
Thermostat type	Wax-filled
Thermostat setting	82°C
Expansion tank	
Filler cap - type	AC
Filler cap pressure	13 lb sq in
Fan blades	
Number	7
Diameter	11½ in (29.2 cm)
Temperature gauge operation	Electrical transmitter and 10V stabiliser

Torque wrench settings	lb ft	kg m
Water elbow to water pump attachment	18 - 20	2.489 - 2.765
Water pump attachment (bolt)	18 - 20	2.489 - 2.765
Water pump attachment (stud)	12 - 14	1.659 - 1.936
Water drain plug	30 - 35	4.148 - 4.839
Radiator to body	6 - 8	0.830 - 1.106

1 General description

The engine coolant is circulated in a pressurised thermo-syphon, water pump assisted system. It is effectively a sealed system, increasing the boiling point to approximately 225°F.

The cooling system comprises the radiator, top and bottom hoses, heater hoses, expansion (or overflow) tank and hoses, the impeller, water pump, the thermostat, the two drain taps, and seven-bladed fan mounted on the front of the water pump spindle. The expansion tank collects excess coolant from the radiator as the coolant expands on becoming hot. A partial vacuum, created as the system cools, causes the coolant to flow back to the radiator from the expansion tank.

If the coolant temperature exceeds 225° F, pressure in the system forces the internal part of the expansion tank filler cap off its seat to expose the overflow pipe. Steam from the boiling coolant passes down the overflow pipe and condenses, thus relieving the pressure. It is, therefore, important to check that the filler cap is in good condition and that the spring behind the sealing washers has not weakened. If in doubt renew the cap, its the only sure way.

The system functions in the following manner: Cold water in the bottom of the radiator is drawn up the lower radiator hose to the water pump, where it is pressured through the water passages in the cylinder block, helping to keep the cylinder bores and pistons cool.

The water then flows into the cylinder head and circulates round the combustion spaces and valve seats absorbing more heat, and then when the engine is at its proper operating temperature, flows out of the cylinder head, past the open thermostat into the upper radiator hose and so onto the radiator header tank.

The water travels down the radiator where it is rapidly cooled by the in-rush of cold air through the radiator core, which is created by both the fan and the motion of the car. The water, now cold, reaches the bottom of the radiator, when the cycle is repeated.

When the engine is cold the thermostat (which is a valve opening and closing according to the temperature of the water) maintains the circulation of the water through the engine, without diverting it to the radiator for cooling. In this way a more rapid warm-up of the engine is achieved.

2 Cooling system - draining

1 With the car on level ground drain the system as follows:

2 If the engine is cold, remove both the radiator filler plug and the expansion tank filler cap by turning them anticlockwise. If the engine is hot, turn the expansion tank filler cap slightly, to relieve pressure in the system, but use a rag over the cap for protection against any escaping steam. If the engine is very hot the sudden release of the cap (causing a drop in pressure) can result in the water boiling. After relieving the system pressure, remove the filler plug and the filler cap.

3 If antifreeze is in the radiator, drain it into a clean bowl for re-use.

4 Open the radiator drain tap (when fitted) and the cylinder block drain tap, see Figs. 2.1.and 2.2. Ensure the heater control knob is in the 'HOT' position. Where a radiator drain tap is not fitted disconnect the bottom hose.

5 When the water has finished running, probe the drain tap orifices with a short piece of wire to dislodge any particles of rust or sediment which may be blocking the taps and preventing all the water draining out.

3 Cooling system - flushing

1 With the passing of time, the cooling system will gradually lose its efficiency as the radiator becomes choked with rust scales, deposits from water and other sediment. To clear the system out, remove the radiator plug and drain taps, and leave a hose running in the radiator plug orifice for ten to fifteen minutes.

2 Then close the drain taps and refill with water and a proprietary cleansing compound. Run the engine for ten to fifteen minutes. All sediment and sludge should now have been removed.

3 If the cooling system is very dirty, reverse flush the radiator as follows: Close the cylinder block tap and fit a water hose over the open radiator tap to force water up through the radiator and out through the filler plug orifice. When clean water flows from the orifice, remove the hose and insert it through the filler plug orifice to flush out the radiator in the usual way.

4 Cooling system - filling

1 Close the two drain taps.

2 Half fill the expansion tank with soft water, (rain water) then completely fill the radiator through the filler plug orifice.

3 Refit the filler plug and expansion tank cap.

4 Run the engine at a fast idling speed for three minutes.

5 Top up the system by filling the expansion tank to within ½ in. (12 mm) of the filler orifice. Overfilling will result in spilling over, which obviously should be avoided if anti-freeze is being used.

6 Use anti-freeze only if it has a glycerine or ethylene glycol base, such as Castrol Anti-freeze.

7 Allowing anti-freeze to remain in the system throughout summer provides protection against corrosion. The anti-freeze should, however, be renewed at the start of each winter as it becomes exhausted.

5 Radiator and expansion tank - removal, inspection, cleaning and replacement

1 Refer to Section 2 and drain the cooling system.

2 Slacken off the clips at the radiator end which secure the top radiator hose, bottom radiator hose and radiator/expansion tank hose, then pull off the hoses. Refer to Fig. 2.3.

3 Remove the electrical lead from each horn.

4 Support the radiator then remove the four mounting bolts and washers and VERY carefully lift the radiator, complete with mounting brackets and horns, out of the engine compartment. Unless great care is taken, damage could result to the radiator matrix, possibly distortion or even perforation (Fig. 2.4.)

5 With the radiator out of the car, any leaks can be soldered up or repaired with a compound such as Cataloy. Clean out the inside of the radiator by flushing as detailed in Section 3.

6 When the radiator is out of the car, it is advantageous to turn it upside down for reverse flushing. Clean the exterior of the radiator by hosing down the radiator matrix with a strong jet of water to clean away road dirt, dead flies etc.

7 Inspect the radiator hoses for cracks, internal or external perishing and damage caused by overtightening of the securing clips. Replace the hoses as necessary. Examine the radiator hose

Fig. 2.1. Cylinder block drain tap

Fig. 2.2. Radiator drain tap

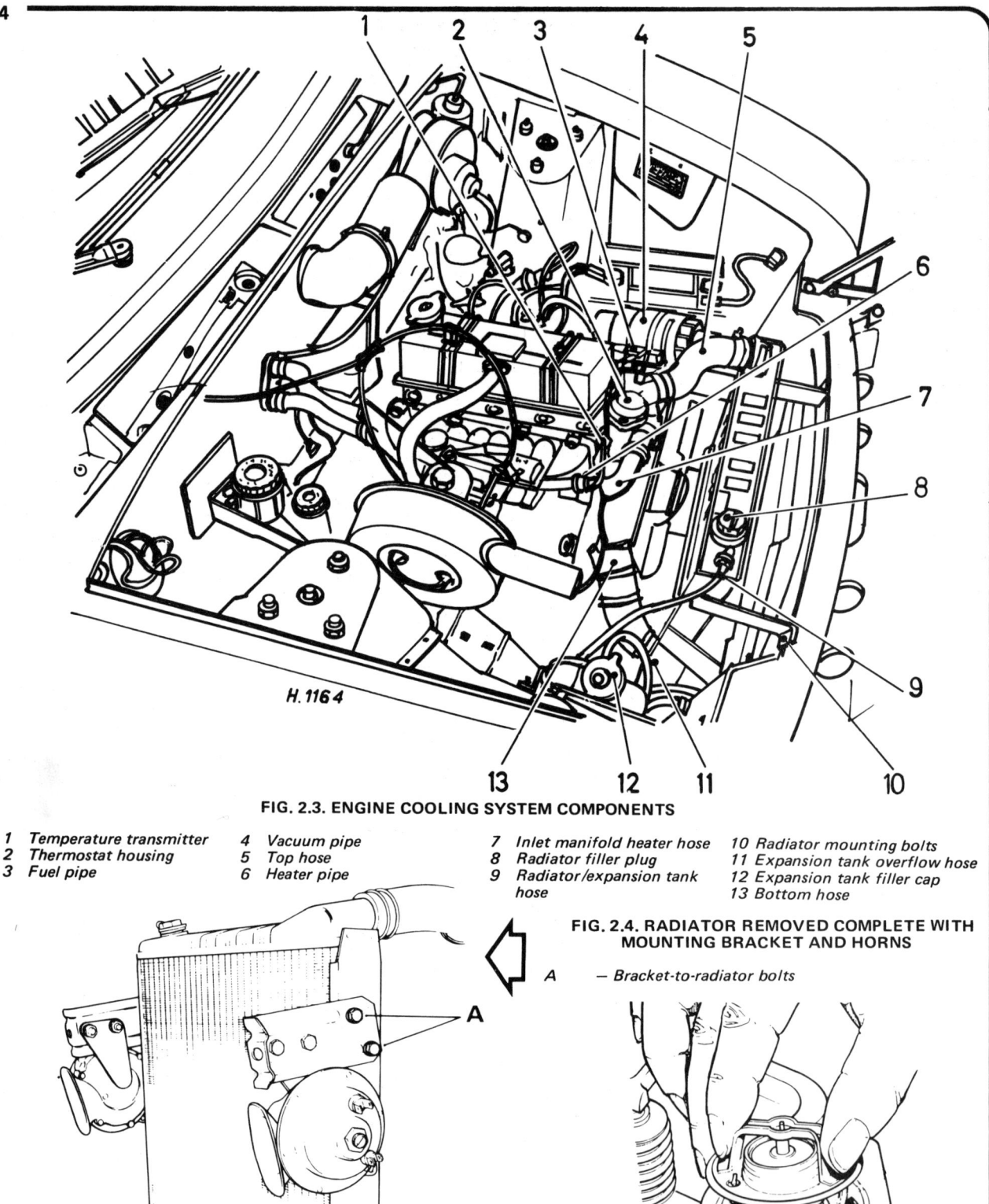

H. 1164

FIG. 2.3. ENGINE COOLING SYSTEM COMPONENTS

1 Temperature transmitter	4 Vacuum pipe	7 Inlet manifold heater hose	10 Radiator mounting bolts
2 Thermostat housing	5 Top hose	8 Radiator filler plug	11 Expansion tank overflow hose
3 Fuel pipe	6 Heater pipe	9 Radiator/expansion tank hose	12 Expansion tank filler cap
			13 Bottom hose

FIG. 2.4. RADIATOR REMOVED COMPLETE WITH MOUNTING BRACKET AND HORNS

A — Bracket-to-radiator bolts

Fig. 2.5. Removal of thermostat

securing clips and renew them if they are rusted or distorted. The drain taps should be renewed if leaking, but ensure the leak is not resulting from a faulty washer behind the tap. If the tap is suspected, try a new washer to see if this clears the trouble first.

8 Replacement is a straightforward reversal of the removal procedure.

9 Disconnect the radiator/expansion tank hose.

10 Remove the two mounting bolts, retaining strap and rubber packing, then lift the expansion tank out of the engine compartment.

11 Drain and flush out the expansion tank.

12 Refitting the radiator and expansion tank is a straightforward reversal of their removal procedure.

6 Thermostat - removal, testing and replacement

1 Partially drain the cooling system (4 pints is enough) before removing the thermostat. Slacken off the clip, at the thermostat elbow end of the radiator hose, then pull the hose off the elbow.

2 Unscrew the two set bolts and spring washers from the thermostat housing and lift the housing and paper gasket away. Take out the thermostat. (Fig. 2.5).

3 Test the thermostat for correct functioning by dangling it by a length of string in a saucepan of cold water together with a thermometer (Fig. 2.6.).

4 Heat the water and note when the thermostat begins to open. This temperature is stamped on the flange of the thermostat and is also given in the specifications.

5 Discard the thermostat if it opens too early. Continue heating the water until the thermostat is fully open, then let it cool down naturally. If the thermostat will not open fully in boiling water, or does not close down as the water cools, then it must be renewed.

6 If the thermostat is stuck open when cold, this will be apparent when removing it from the housing.

7 Replacing the thermostat is a reversal of the removal procedure. Remember to use a new paper gasket between the thermostat housing elbow and the thermostat. Renew the thermostat elbow if it is badly eroded.

7 Water pump - removal and replacement

1 If the water pump is badly worn the only remedy is to fit a reconditioned unit. Drain the cooling system as described in Section 2 and slacken the two alternator mounting bolts so the fan belt can be removed.

2 Disconnect the positive terminal from the battery.

3 Undo the union at the end of the heater pipe (6) (Fig. 2.3.) from the rear of the water pump body.

4 Slacken the top and bottom hose clips and completely remove the two hoses (5, 13).

5 Disconnect the inlet manifold heater hose (7) from the thermostat housing.

6 Pull off the Lucar connector from the temperature indicator transmitter (1).

7 Disconnect the fuel feed pipe (3) from the carburettor and the vacuum pipe (4) at the carburettor end.

8 Refer to Fig. 2.7. and remove the three bolts and washers (A) which clamp the pump housing to the front of the cylinder block. Note the three bolts differ in length.

9 Pull the fuel and vacuum pipes clear of the water pump and lift the water pump, with blades still attached, away from the front of the engine. Remove the gasket.

10 Remove the four bolts securing the fan blades to the pulley and lift away the fan blades. The old pump can now be discarded.

11 Replacement is a straightforward reversal of the removal sequence. Note that the fan belt tension must be correct when all is reassembled. If the belt is too tight it will place undue strain on the water pump and alternator bearings, and if the belt is too loose, it will slip and wear rapidly as well as giving rise to low output from the alternator.

12 If the vehicle is one of the later models, i.e. from engine No. DG1605, the water pump and pulley are an integral unit and can only be replaced as a complete assembly (Fig. 2.9.)

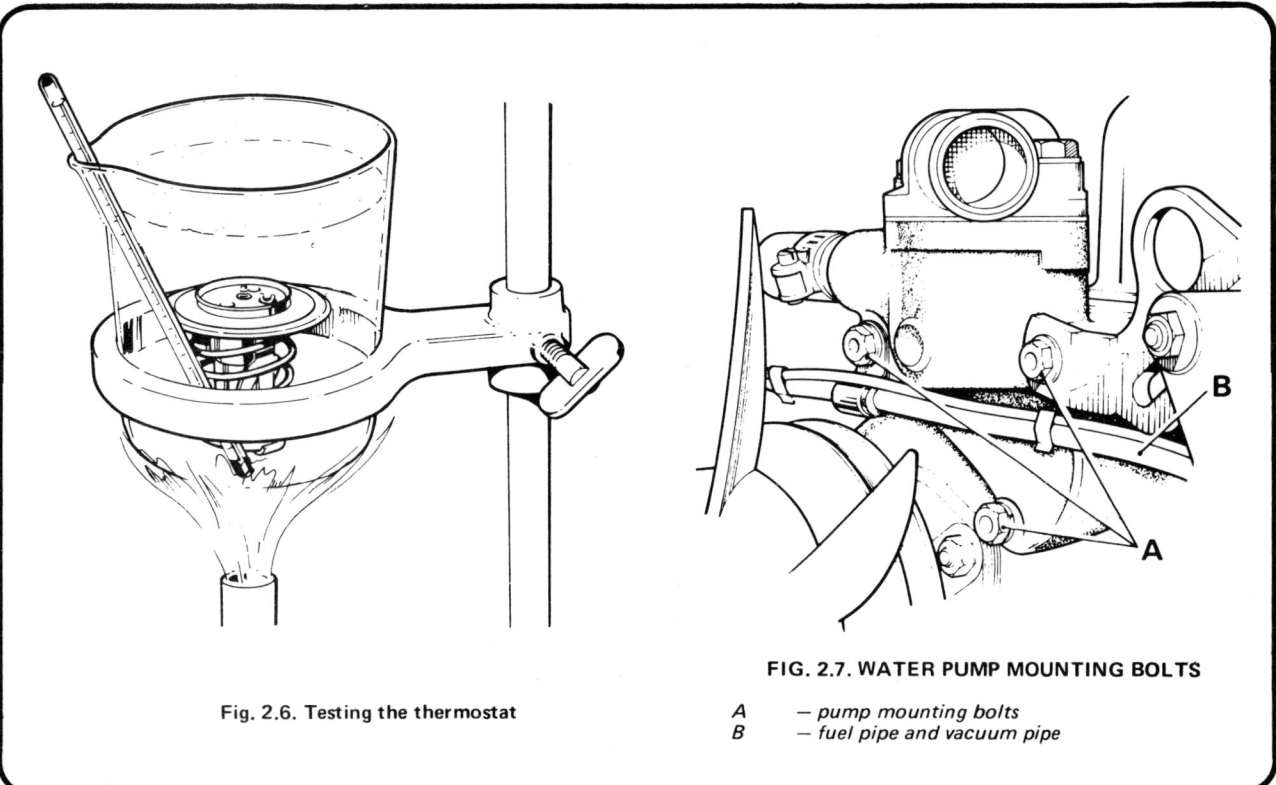

Fig. 2.6. Testing the thermostat

FIG. 2.7. WATER PUMP MOUNTING BOLTS

A — pump mounting bolts
B — fuel pipe and vacuum pipe

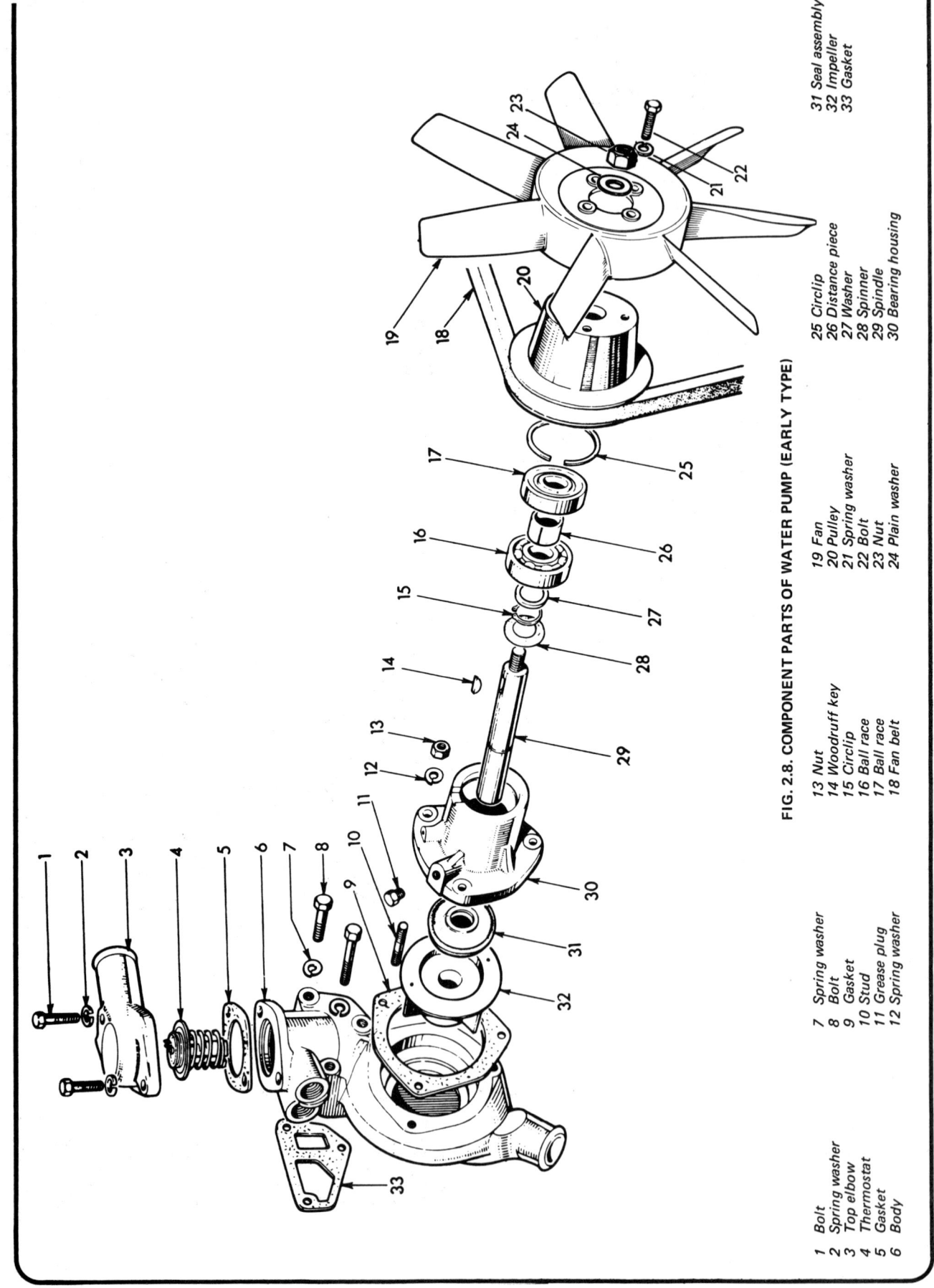

FIG. 2.8. COMPONENT PARTS OF WATER PUMP (EARLY TYPE)

1 Bolt	7 Spring washer	13 Nut	19 Fan	25 Circlip	31 Seal assembly
2 Spring washer	8 Bolt	14 Woodruff key	20 Pulley	26 Distance piece	32 Impeller
3 Top elbow	9 Gasket	15 Circlip	21 Spring washer	27 Washer	33 Gasket
4 Thermostat	10 Stud	16 Ball race	22 Bolt	28 Spinner	
5 Gasket	11 Grease plug	17 Ball race	23 Nut	29 Spindle	
6 Body	12 Spring washer	18 Fan belt	24 Plain washer	30 Bearing housing	

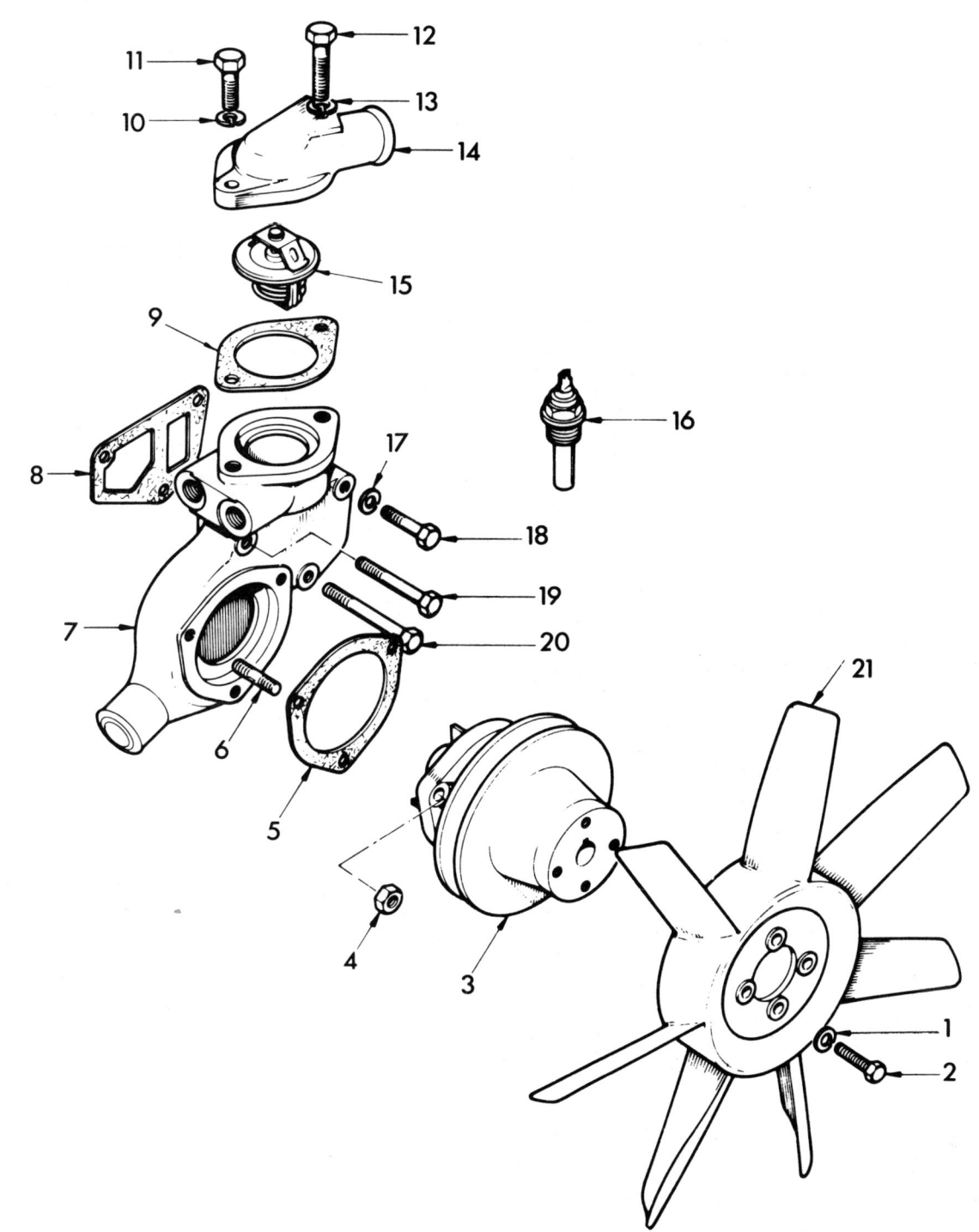

FIG. 2.9. COMPONENT PARTS OF WATER PUMP (LATER TYPE)

1 Spring washer (3)
2 Bolt (4)
3 Bearing housing assembly complete with pulley
4 Nut (3)
5 Gasket
6 Pump body stud (3)
7 Pump body
8 Pump body-to-block gasket
9 Thermostat gasket
10 Spring washer
11 Bolt
12 Bolt
13 Spring washer
14 Water elbow
15 Thermostat
16 Temperature transmitter
17 Spring washers (3)
18 Pump body retaining bolts. Note the different lengths
19 Pump body retaining bolts. Note the different lengths
20 Pump body retaining bolts. Note the different lengths
21 Fan assembly

8 Water pump - dismantling and reassembly

1 If it is wished to repair the pump, first ascertain that spare parts are available. It should be remembered that after engine No. DG1605, the water pump and pulley are an integral unit and can only be replaced as a complete assembly. If an early model pump is fitted the following instructions are valid and relate to Fig. 2.8.

2 Remove the four bolts and spring washers which hold the fan blade (19) in place. Undo the nut and washer (23, 24) which hold the fan pulley (20) in place and with the aid of an extractor pull off the pulley wheel and prise out the woodruff key (14).

3 Undo the three nuts and spring washer (12, 13) which hold the bearing housing (30) to the pump body (6) and pull out the bearing housing.

4 With the aid of a vice and an extractor, pull the impeller (32) off the spindle (29). Remove the sealing gland (31) from the back of the impeller (32).

5 Remove the bearing retaining circlip (25) from the bore of the housing and pull out the spindle complete with bearing. The bearing (17), distance piece (26), bearing (16), washer (27), circlip (15) and bearing seal (28) can now all be removed.

6 If the pump is badly worn the bearing will require renewal and the gland face on the housing, recut. (This is a job for your local Triumph garage or engineering works).

7 Reassembly of the water pump is a reversal of the above sequence. The following additional points should be noted:

8 Position the bearings so that their unshielded sides are adjacent to the distance piece, and the grease seal faces outwards. Pack the bearings, and area around the distance piece with grease.

9 The shaft and bearings are fitted to the housing with the aid of a drift made from a piece of tubing.

10 Press the impeller onto the spindle until a 0.030 in (0.762 mm) clearance, measured with a feeler gauge, exists between the flat face of the spindle and the housing. The impeller should then be soldered to the shaft to prevent water seepage down the spindle.

11 When fitting the pulley wheel, fan and balance weight, note if a small alignment hole has been drilled in these units. If so, line the components up with the aid of a 1/16 in. drill, or similar, while the securing bolts are being done up.

12 Regrease the water pump on completion of the assembling operation.

9 Anti-freeze mixture

1 Prior to anticipated freezing conditions, it is essential that some of the water is drained and an adequate amount of ethylene glycol anti-freeze, such as that manufactured by Castrol, is added to the cooling system.

2 If Castrol Anti-freeze is not available, any anti-freeze which conforms with specification BS 3151 or BS 3152 can be used. Never use an anti-freeze with an alcohol base as evaporation is too high.

3 Castrol Anti-freeze with an anti-corrosion additive can be left in the cooling system for up to two years, but after six months it is advisable to have the specific gravity of the coolant checked at your local garage and thereafter, every three months.

4 Listed below are the amounts of anti-freeze which should be added to ensure adequate protection down to the temperature given:

Amount of anti-freeze	Protection to:
1.7 pints (1 litre)	−17.8°C (0°F)
2.0 pints (1.3 litres)	−28.9°C (−20°F)
2.3 pints (1.43 litres)	−34.5°C (−30°F)
3.0 pints (1.7 litres)	−40.0°C (−40°F)

10 Temperature gauge - fault diagnosis and rectification

For further information on this subject refer to Chapter 10, as, due to circuit design, a set sequence of diagnosis is necessary to eliminate the fault, which could be in another circuit.

11 Temperature gauge and sender unit - removal and replacement

1 For details of how to remove and replace the temperature gauge see Chapter 10.

2 To remove the sender unit, disconnect the battery, pull off the wire at the snap connector on the unit, and undo the unit with a spanner. On replacement, renew the fibre washer to prevent the possibility of leaking.

12 Fan belt - adjustment

1 It is important to keep the fan belt correctly adjusted, and it is considered that this should be a regular maintenance task performed every 6000 miles (10,000 km).

2 The fan belt tension is correct when there is 0.75 to 1.0 inch (20 to 25 mm) of lateral movement at the midpoint position of the belt between the alternator pulley wheel and the crankshaft pulley wheel.

3 To adjust the fan belt, slacken the alternator securing bolts

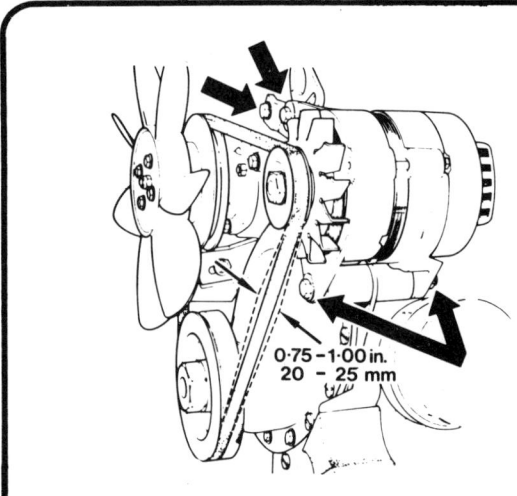

0·75 - 1·00 in.
20 - 25 mm

Fig. 2.10. Fan belt adjustment. The arrows indicate alternator securing points

and move the alternator either in or out until the correct tension is obtained. It is easier if the alternator bolts are only slackened a little, so it requires some force to move the alternator. In this way the tension of the belt can be arrived at quicker than by making frequent adjustments (Fig. 2.10.).

4 With the alternator bolts only slightly loosened, difficulty may be experienced in moving the alternator away from the engine. A long spanner placed behind the alternator and resting against the block serves as a very good lever, and can be held in this position while the alternator bolts are tightened. On no account overtighten the fan belt.

13 Fan belt - removal and replacement

1 If the fan belt is worn or has stretched unduly, it should be replaced. The most usual reason for replacement is that the belt has broken in service. It is, therefore, recommended that a spare belt is always carried. Replacement is a reversal of the removal procedure, but as replacement due to breakage is the most usual operation, it is described below.

2 Loosen the alternator pivot bolt and the nut on the adjusting link, and push the alternator in towards the engine.

3 Slip the belt over the crankshaft, alternator and water pump pulleys.

4 Adjust the belt as described in the previous Section and tighten the alternator mounting nuts. NOTE after fitting a new belt it will require adjustment 250 miles (400 km) later.

14 Fault diagnosis

Symptom	Reason/s	Remedy
Heat generated in cylinder not being successfully disposed of by radiator	Insufficient water in cooling system	Top up expansion tank.
	Fan belt slipping (accompanied by a shrieking noise on rapid engine acceleration)	Tighten fan belt to recommended tension or replace if worn.
	Radiator core blocked or radiator grille restricted	Reverse flush radiator, remove obstructions.
	Bottom water hose collapsed, impeding flow	Remove and fit new hose.
	Thermostat not opening properly	Remove and fit new thermostat.
	Ignition advance and retard incorrectly set (accompanied by loss of power and perhaps, misfiring)	Check and reset ignition timing.
	Carburettor incorrectly adjusted (mixture too weak)	Tune carburettor.
	Exhaust system partially blocked	Check exhaust pipe for constrictive dents and blockages.
	Oil level in sump too low	Top up sump to full mark on dipstick.
	Blown cylinder head gasket (water/steam being forced down the expansion tank overflow pipe under pressure)	Remove cylinder head, fit new gasket.
	Engine not yet run-in	Run-in slowly and carefully.
	Brakes binding	Check and adjust brakes if necessary.
Too much heat being dispersed by radiator	Thermostat jammed open	Remove and renew thermostat.
	Incorrect grade of thermostat fitted allowing premature opening of valve	Remove and replace with new thermostat which opens at a higher temperature.
	Thermostat missing	Check and fit correct thermostat.
Leaks in system	Loose clips on water hoses	Check and tighten clips if necessary.
	Top, bottom or expansion tank water hoses perished and leaking	Check and replace any faulty hoses.
	Radiator core leaking	Remove radiator and repair.
	Thermostat gasket leaking	Inspect and renew gasket.
	Pressure cap spring worn or seal ineffective	Renew pressure cap.
	Blown cylinder head gasket (pressure in system forcing water/steam down overflow pipe)	Remove cylinder head and fit new gasket.
	Cylinder wall or head cracked	Dismantle engine, dispatch to engineering works for repair.
	Expansion tank leaking	Repair or replace expansion tank.

Chapter 3 Fuel system and carburation

Contents

General description 1	Carburettor - water or dirt in the carburettor 14
Air cleaner - removal and replacement 2	Carburettor - jet centering 15
Fuel pump - general description 3	Carburettor - float chamber fuel level adjustment ... 16
Fuel pump - removal and replacement 4	Carburettor - needle replacement 17
Fuel pump - testing 5	Carburettor - adjustment and tuning 18
Fuel pump - dismantling, overhaul and reassembly 6	Fuel tank - removal and replacement 19
Carburettor - general description 7	Fuel tank - cleaning 20
Carburettor installation - removal and refitting 8	Fuel tank sender unit - removal and refitting... ... 21
Carburettor - dismantling and reassembly 9	Throttle pedal and cable - removal and replacement 22
Carburettor - examination and repair 10	Choke cable - removal and replacement 23
Carburettor - piston sticking 11	Fuel pipe lines - inspection and replacement 24
Carburettor - float needle sticking 12	Fault diagnosis 25
Carburettor - float chamber flooding 13	

Specifications

Air cleaner

Type ... ... Replaceable paper element. Combined air cleaner and silencer

Carburettor

Type ... ... S.U. HS4 side draught
Needle size ... ... AAK
Main jet ... ... 0.090 in (2.286 mm)
Venturi ... ... 1.50 in (38.10 mm)

Fuel pump

Make and type ... ... AC mechanically-operated diaphragm
Pressure ... ... 2.5 to 3.5 lb in^2 (0.175 to 0.245 kg cm^2)

Fuel gauging unit

Type ... ... Incorporated with tank unit and 10 volt stabiliser

Fuel tank

Type ... ... Flat tank in luggage compartment floor, vented via filler cap
Capacity ... ... 10½ gallons (48 litres)

1 General description

The fuel system fitted to the Toledo comprises a fuel tank at the rear of the car; a mechanically-operated fuel pump and a single side-draught SU HS4 carburettor.

A combined air cleaner and silencer is fitted to the carburettor intake and has disposable paper filter elements that should be renewed at the specified mileage.

2 Air cleaner - removal and replacement

1 The air cleaner should be serviced in accordance with the Routine Maintenance detailed in the preliminaries to this manual.
2 Release the two bolts securing the air cleaner to the carburettor intake flange and withdraw the air cleaner from the engine bay. Detach cover plate from the container and remove

the paper element. (photos)
3 Clean between the folds of the element using a low pressure air line or soft brush. Clean the container.
4 Reassemble, in the reverse order to previous operations, ensuring that the sealing rings are correctly positioned and that the carburettor flange gasket is in good condition and correctly positioned.

3 Fuel pump - general description

The mechanically operated AC fuel pump is actuated through a spring loaded rocker arm. One arm of the operating lever (23) bears against an eccentric on the camshaft and the operating fork (19) actuates a diaphragm pull rod (Fig. 3.1.).

As the engine camshaft rotates, the eccentric moves the pivoted rocker arm outwards, which in turn pulls the diaphragm (12) down against the pressure of the diaphragm spring (13).

This creates sufficient vacuum in the pump chamber to draw

2a Removing the air cleaner retaining bolts

2.2b Paper element being removed from air cleaner

petrol in the tank, through the sediment chamber incorporated in the body (6), fuel filter gauze (5) and non-return valve (11 LHS).

The rocker arm is held in constant contact with the eccentric by an anti-rattle spring (26), and as the engine camshaft continues to rotate, the eccentric allows the rocker arm to move inwards. The diaphragm spring (13) is thus free to push the diaphragm assembly (12) upwards, forcing the fuel in the pump chamber out to the carburettor through the non-return outlet valve (11 RHS).

When the float chamber is full, the float chamber needle valve will close so preventing further flow from the fuel pump.

The pressure in the delivery line will hold the diaphragm downwards against the pressure of the diaphragm spring, and it will remain in this position until the needle valve in the float chamber opens to admit more petrol.

4 Fuel pump - removal and replacement

The fuel pump is mounted on the left hand side of the engine on a level with the camshaft. To remove the pump proceed as follows:

1 Wipe the area around the unions, and pull off the rubber connectors securing the petrol inlet and outlet pipes to the pipe stems on the body of the pump.
2 Plug the pipes and the pump stems to stop dirt ingress into the system.
3 Undo and remove the two nuts and spring washers securing the pump to the studs. Lift away the pump and paper gasket from the cylinder block. Note the special nut on the right-hand stud.
4 Refitting the fuel pump is the reverse sequence to removal. Always use a new paper gasket to ensure oil leaks do not occur. Make sure that the mating faces are perfectly clean and, when fitting the rocker arm into position, ensure that it lies on the side of the camshaft eccentric and not behind it.

5 Fuel pump - testing

Assuming that the fuel lines and unions are in good condition and that there are no leaks anywhere, check the performance of the fuel pump in the following manner:

1 Disconnect the fuel pipe at the carburettor inlet union and the high tension lead to the ignition coil. With a suitable large container or large rag in position to catch the ejected fuel, turn the engine over on the starter motor solenoid: a good spurt of petrol should emerge from the end of the pipe every second revolution.
2 If a pressure gauge is available, connect it in the pump-to-carburettor fuel line. Start the engine and observe the pressure: it should be 2.5 to 3.5 lb in^2 (0.175 to 0.245 kg cm^2. If the pressure is too high it can be reduced by fitting extra paper washers between the pump and cylinder block. Where pressure is too low, the pump should be overhauled.

6 Fuel pump - dismantling, overhaul and reassembly

1 Unscrew the securing bolt (1) (Fig. 3.1.) from the centre of the cover (3). Lift the bolt (1), washer (2) and cover (3) with cork joint washer (4) from the top of the pump body (6). (photo)
2 With a knife remove the cork joint washer (4) and place to one side. Lift up the gauze filter using the knife carefully inserted under one of the two metal tags in the centre of the filter. (photo)
3 With a scriber, or file, mark the upper and lower flanges of the pump that are adjacent to each other, so that they may be fitted in their original positions upon reassembly.
4 Unscrew the five screws (7) and lift away the screws and spring washers which hold the two halves of the pump body together. Separate the two halves, with great care, ensuring that the diaphragm does not stick to either of the two flanges.
5 Note which way the valves are fitted and then, using a screwdriver, prise out the valves and their gaskets. These can now be discarded and new valves and gaskets obtained. (Fig. 3.2.)
6 Note the location of the tag of the diaphragm circumference and then rotate the diaphragm through 90° so as to release the pull rod from the operating lever (23). Lift away the diaphragm and pull rod (which is securely fixed to the diaphragm and cannot be removed from it).
7 Lift away the diaphragm spring (13) and the metal and fibre washers (14, 15) under it.
8 Should it be necessary to dismantle the rocker arm assembly, draw out the two retainers from the lower pump body (16) and extract the spindle (20) from the rocker arm lever joint. Note the location of the two washers (22, 25). Recover the return spring (26).
9 Carefully wash the filter gauze (5) and clean all parts using petrol and an old toothbrush. Scrape out any sediment from the sediment chamber.
10 Check the condition of the cork cover sealing washer (4) and

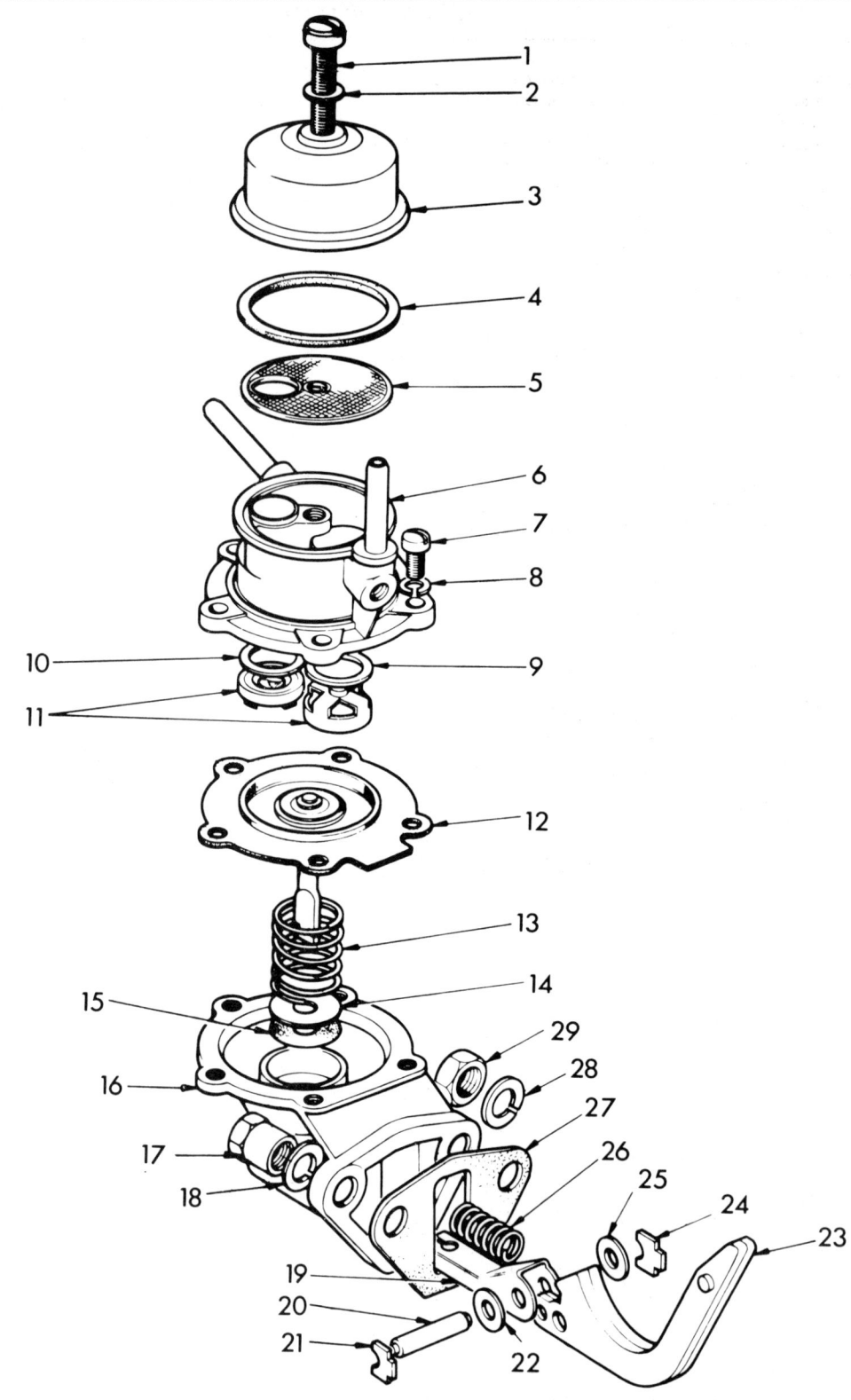

FIG. 3.1. FUEL PUMP COMPONENTS

1 Bolt	8 Spring washer	15 Washer (fibre)	22 Plain washer
2 Fibre washer	9 Valve gasket	16 Lower half of body	23 Operating lever
3 Cover	10 Valve gasket	17 Special nut	24 Retainer
4 Gasket	11 Valves	18 Spring washer	25 Plain washer
5 Filter gauze	12 Diaphragm assembly	19 Operating fork	26 Return spring
6 Upper half of body	13 Spring	20 Spindle	27 Gasket
7 Screw	14 Washer (metal)	21 Retainer	28 Spring washer
			29 Nut

if it is hardened or broken it must be replaced. The diaphragm should be checked for signs of perishing, hardening, or distortion and a new one obtained if necessary.

11 It is unlikely that the pump body will be damaged but check for fractures or cracks. Particularly check the thread in the body (6) for the cover securing bolt as this could be damaged by overtightening.

12 Inspect the cover for signs of distortion caused by over-tightening.

13 To reassemble the pump, first reassemble the rocker operating linkage to the lower half of the body.

14 Renew the valves in the body by pressing them into the casting with a suitable drift, e.g., a piece of steel tubing. Ensure the gaskets are replaced and the valves are correctly positioned:
a) Inlet-to-pump valve: press in so that raised side faces downwards.
b) Outlet-to-engine valve: press in so that concave side faces downwards.

Then stake the casting, around each valve, in six places with a suitable punch (Fig. 3.3.).

15 Position the fibre and steel washers (15, 14) in that order in the base of the pump and place the diaphragm spring (13) over them.

16 Replace the diaphragm and pull rod assembly (12) with the pull rod downwards and the tab 90° from its fitted position as was noted during dismantling.

17 With the body of the pump held so that the rocker arm is facing away from one, press down the centre of the diaphragm so locating the end of the pull rod in the operating rod fork (19), and turn it 90° to the left at the same time keeping the diaphragm depressed. This will engage the slot on the pull rod with the operating lever. The small tab on the diaphragm should now be in its original position.

18 Move the rocker arm (23) until the diaphragm is level with the body flanges and hold the arm in this position. Reassemble the two halves of the pump, ensuring that the previously made marks on the flanges are adjacent to each other.

19 Insert the five screws (7) and spring washers, and tighten them down finger tight.

20 Move the rocker arm up and down several times to centralise the diaphragm and then with the arm held down, tighten the screws securely in a diagonal manner.

21 Refit the gauze filter (5) in position. Fit the cork sealing washer to the cover (3); fit the cover and insert the bolt with the fibre washer under its head. Do not overtighten the bolt but ensure that it is tight enough to preclude all leaks.

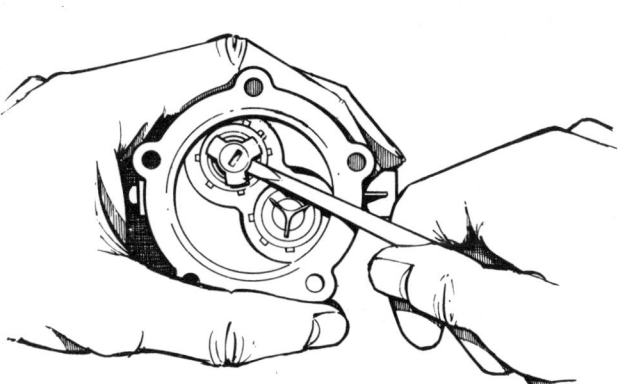

Fig. 3.2. Prising out the valves

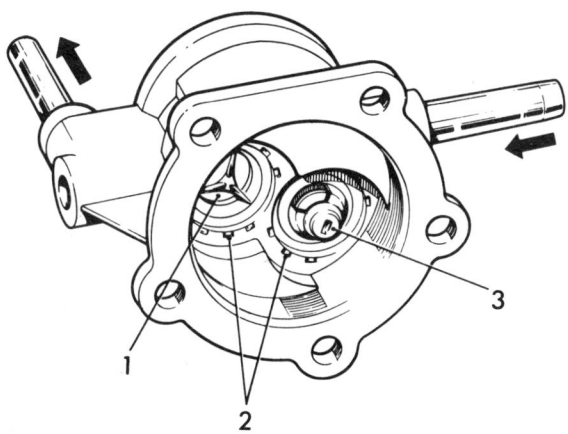

FIG. 3.3. VALVE POSITION IN RELATION TO FUEL FLOW

1 Outlet valve　　2 Stake marks
　　　　　　　　　3 Inlet valve

6.1 Unscrewing the fuel pump cover retaining bolt

6.2 The fuel pump cover with the filter gauge in position

7 Carburettor - general description

1 The variable choke SU carburettor is a relatively simple instrument and is basically the same irrespective of its size and type. It differs from most other carburettors in that instead of having a number of various fixed jets for different conditions, only one variable jet is fitted to deal with all possible conditions. (Fig. 3.4. and 3.5).

2 Air passing rapidly through the carburettor draws petrol from the jet, so forming the petrol/air mixture. The amount of petrol drawn from the jet depends on the position of the tapered carburettor needle, which moves up and down the jet orifice according to the engine load and throttle opening, thus effectively altering the size of jet, so that exactly the right amount of fuel is metered for the prevailing road conditions.

3 The position of the tapered needle in the jet is determined by engine vacuum. The shank of the needle is held at its top end in a piston which slides up and down the dashpot in response to the degree of manifold vacuum. In the past SU carburettors have had needles that were theoretically central in the jet. However, the minor variations that were bound to occur meant fuel/air mixtures in proportions not quite correct, giving unwanted exhaust emissions. Therefore recent SU carburettors, have needles that are biassed to one side. The needle is given the bias by a light spring which holds it in gentle contact with the jet. The needle will therefore always be in the same relationship to the jet, and though not central, will give a consistent fuel/air mixture.

4 With the throttle fully open, the full effect of inlet manifold is felt by the piston which has an air bleed into the choke tube, on the outside of the throttle. This causes the piston to rise fully, bringing the needle with it. With the accelerator partially closed, only slight inlet manifold vacuum is felt by the piston (although of course on the engine side of the throttle the vacuum is greater), and the piston only rises a little, blocking most of the jet orifice with the metering needle.

5 To prevent the piston fluttering, and giving a richer mixture when the accelerator is suddenly depressed, an oil damper and light spring are fitted inside the dashpot.

6 The only portion of the piston assembly to come into contact with the piston chamber or dashpot, is the actual central piston rod. All the other parts of the piston assembly, including the lower choke portion, have sufficient clearance to prevent any direct metal to metal contact which is essential if the carburettor is to function correctly.

7 The correct level of the petrol in the carburettor is determined by the level of the float chamber. When the level is correct, the float rises and by means of a lever resting on top of it, closes the needle valve in the cover of the float chamber. This closes off the supply of fuel from the pump. When the level in the float chamber drops as fuel is used in the carburettor, the float drops. As it does, the float needle is unseated, so allowing more fuel to enter the float chamber and restore the correct level.

8 Carburettor installation - removal and refitting

1 Undo and remove the two bolts and spring washers securing the air cleaner assembly to the carburettor air intake. Lift the air cleaner assembly away from the carburettor. Recover the paper gasket. (photo)

2 Wipe the fuel inlet pipe connection to the carburettor float chamber, and disconnect the pipe from the union. Plug the end of the pipe with a pencil to stop dirt ingress.

3 Disconnect the choke cable accelerator cable and return springs. Pull off the breather pipe and the manifold-to-distributor pipe. Disconnect the throttle linkrod from the manifold bracket by pulling off the spring-loaded socket from the ball on the operating lever. (photos)

4 Undo and remove the two nuts and spring washers securing the carburettor to the inlet manifold.

5 Lift off the carburettor and gasket. (photo)

6 Refitting is the reverse sequence to removal. It is recommended that new gaskets are fitted and that all linkages are lightly oiled. (photo)

9 Carburettor - dismantling and reassembly

1 Unscrew the piston damper and lift it away from the chamber and piston assembly. Using a screwdriver or small file, scratch identification marks (YY) on the suction chamber and carburettor body, so that they may be refitted together in their original position. Remove the three suction chamber retaining screws and lift the suction chamber from the carburettor body leaving the piston in situ. (Fig. 3.5).

2 Lift the piston spring from the piston, noting which way round it is fitted, and remove the piston. Invert it and allow the oil in the damper bore to drain out. Place the piston in a safe place so that the needle will not be touched, or the piston roll onto the floor. It is recommended that the piston be placed on the neck of a narrow jam jar with the needle inside, so acting as a stand.

3 Mark the position of the float chamber lid relative to the body. Unscrew and remove the three screws, spring washers and one identification plate securing the lid to the float chamber body. Remove the lid and withdraw the pin, thereby releasing the float and float lever. Recover the float needle. Using a spanner or socket, remove the needle valve.

4 Disconnect the jet link from the base of the jet and unscrew the nut holding the flexible nylon tube into the base of the float chamber. Carefully withdraw the jet and nylon connection tube.

5 Unscrew the jet adjustment nut and lift away together with its locking spring. Also unscrew the jet locknut and lift away together with the lockwasher and jet bearing.

6 Remove the bolt securing the float chamber to the carburettor body, and separate the two parts.

7 To remove the throttle and actuating spindle undo the lever retaining nut and lift away the tab washer, fork lever and throttle lever from the spindle. Note which way round the parts are fitted for correct reassembly.

8 Straighten the ends of the two throttle disc screws and remove the two screws. Make a note of the tapered edges of the throttle disc by scratching identification marks so that the disc will be fitted the correct way round, and slide it out of the throttle spindle. Finally slide the throttle spindle from the carburettor body.

9 Reassembly is a straight reversal of the dismantling procedure. Do not forget to top up the damper with Castrol "Everyman" oil until the level is a ½ inch (13 mm) above the top of the hollow piston rod, (photo).

10 Carburettor - examination and repair

The SU carburettor generally speaking is most reliable but even so it may develop one of several faults which may not be readily apparent unless a careful inspection is carried out. The common faults the carburettor is prone to are:

1 Piston sticking;
2 Float needle sticking;
3 Float chamber flooding;
4 Water and dirt in the carburettor.

In addition the following parts are susceptible to wear after high mileages and, as they vitally affect the economy of the engine, they should be checked and renewed, where necessary, every 24000 miles (40,000 km):

a) The carburettor needle. If this has been incorrectly fitted at some time so that it is not centrally located in the jet orifice, then the metering needle will have a tiny ridge worn on it. If a ridge can be seen, then the needle must be renewed. SU carburettor needles are made to very fine tolerances and, should a ridge be apparent, no attempt should be made to rub the needle down with fine emery paper. If it is wished to clean the needle, it can be polished lightly with metal polish.

b) The carburettor jet. If the needle is worn, it is likely that the rim of the jet will be damaged where the needle has been striking it. It should be renewed, as otherwise fuel consumption will suffer. The jet can also be badly worn or ridged on the outside where it has been sliding up and down between the jet bearing every time the choke has been pulled out. Removal and renewal is the only answer.

c) Check the edges of the throttle and the choke tube for wear. Renew if worn.

d) The washers fitted to the base of the jet and under the float chamber lid, may leak after a time and can cause a great deal of fuel wastage. It is wisest to renew them automatically when the carburettor is stripped down.

e) After high mileages, the float chamber needle and seat are bound to be ridged. They are not an expensive item to replace and must always be renewed as a set.

11 Carburettor - piston sticking

1 The hardened piston rod which slides in the centre guide tube in the middle of the dashpot, is the only part of the piston assembly (which comprises the jet needle, suction disc, and piston choke) which should make contact with the dashpot. The piston rim and the choke periphery are machined to very fine tolerances so that they will not touch the dashpot or the choke tube walls.

2 After high mileages, wear in the centre guide tube may allow the piston to touch the dashpot wall. This condition is known as sticking.

3 If piston sticking is suspected, or if it is wished to test for this condition, rotate the piston about the centre guide tube at the same time as sliding it up and down inside the dashpot. If any portion of the piston makes contact with the dashpot wall, then

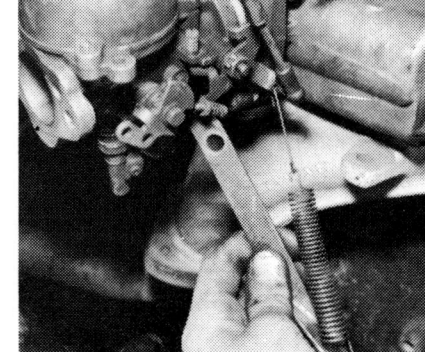
8.1 Pulling off the fuel line from the pump

8.3a Disconnecting the throttle return spring

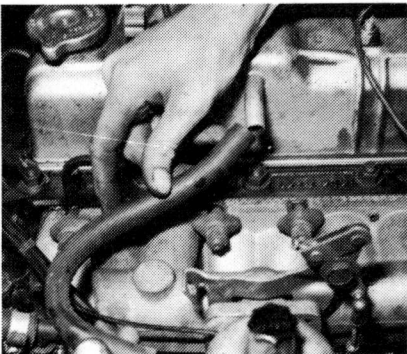
8.3b Pulling off the breather pipe

8.3c Pulling off the vacuum advance pipe

8.3d ... and disconnecting the throttle link

8.5 Lifting the carburettor away from the inlet manifold

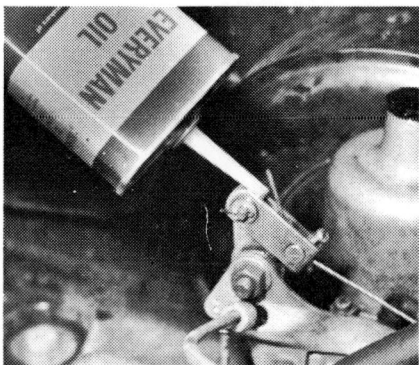
8.6 Oiling the carburettor linkages

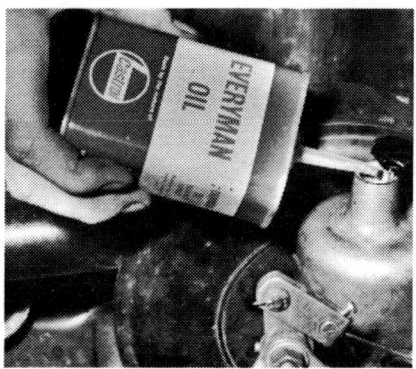
9.9 Topping up the SU carburettor piston damper with oil

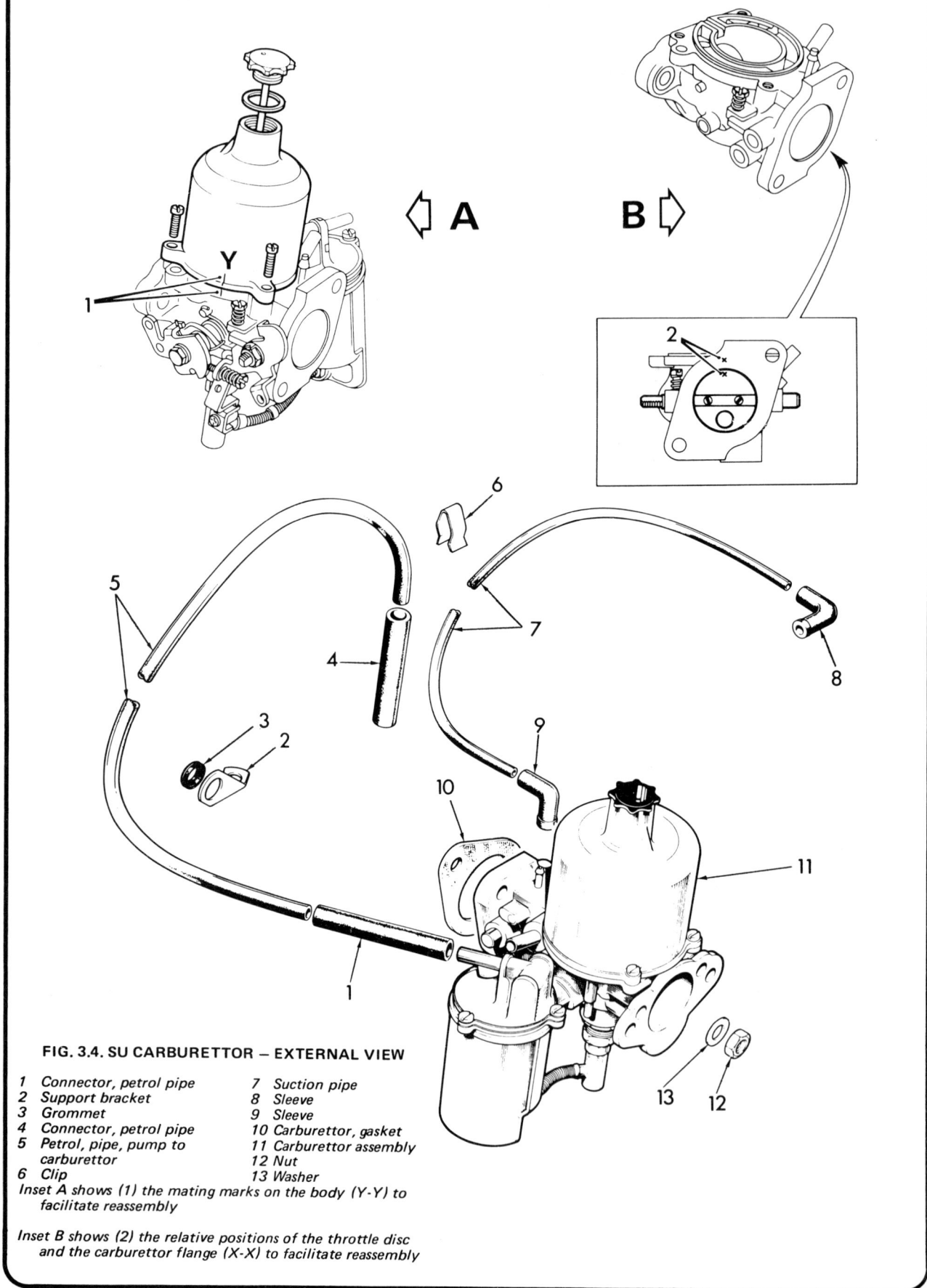

FIG. 3.4. SU CARBURETTOR – EXTERNAL VIEW

1	Connector, petrol pipe	7	Suction pipe
2	Support bracket	8	Sleeve
3	Grommet	9	Sleeve
4	Connector, petrol pipe	10	Carburettor, gasket
5	Petrol, pipe, pump to	11	Carburettor assembly
	carburettor	12	Nut
6	Clip	13	Washer

Inset A shows (1) the mating marks on the body (Y-Y) to
    facilitate reassembly

Inset B shows (2) the relative positions of the throttle disc
    and the carburettor flange (X-X) to facilitate reassembly

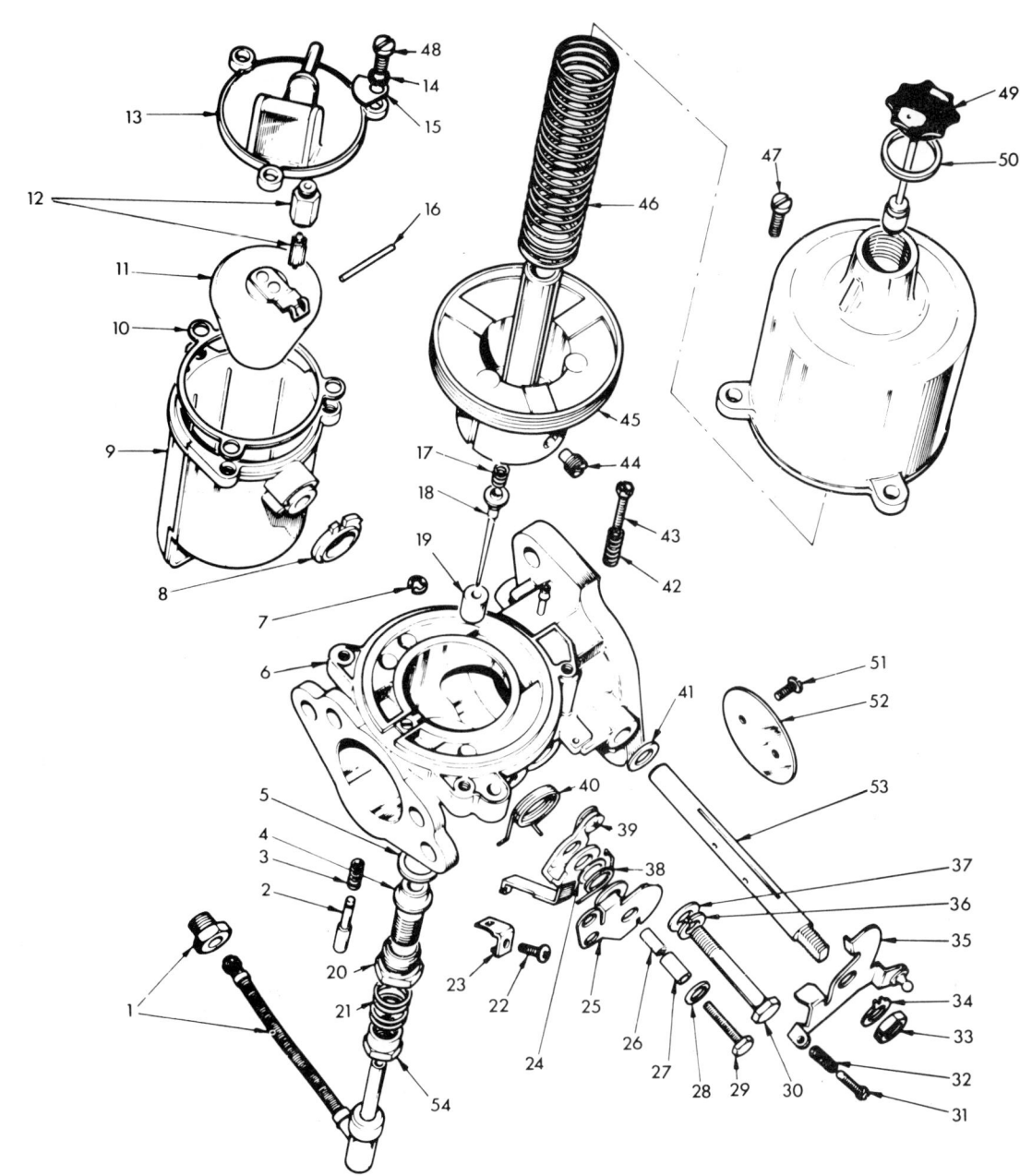

FIG. 3.5. SU CARBURETTOR COMPONENTS

1 Jet assembly
2 Pin
3 Spring
4 Jet bearing
5 Washer
6 Carburettor body
7 Circlip
8 Adaptor
9 Float chamber
10 Gasket
11 Float assembly
12 Needle and seat assembly
13 Float chamber lid
14 Washer
15 Identity label

16 Hinge pin
17 Needle spring
18 Jet needle
19 Needle guide
20 Screw
21 Spring
22 Screw
23 Bracket
24 Skid washer
25 Cam lever
26 Tube
27 Tube
28 Distance washer
29 Pivot bolt
30 Bolt

31 Stop screw
32 Spring
33 Nut
34 Washer, tab
35 Throttle lever assembly
36 Spring washer
37 Plain washer
38 Spring, cam lever
39 Pick up lever and link assembly
40 Return spring
41 Washer
42 Spring
43 Stop screw
44 Needle securing screw
45 Suction chamber and

piston assembly
46 Piston spring
47 Screw
48 Screw
49 Damper assembly
50 Washer
51 Screw
52 Throttle disc
53 Carburettor throttle spindle
54 Jet adjustment nut

that portion of the wall must be polished with a metal polish until clearance exists. In extreme cases, fine emery cloth can be used.

The greatest care should be taken to remove only the minimum amount of metal to provide the clearance, as too large a gap will cause air leakage and will upset the functioning of the carburettor. Clean down the walls of the dashpot and the piston rim, and ensure that there is no oil on them. A trace of oil may be judiciously applied to the piston rod.

4 If the piston is sticking, under no circumstances attempt to clear it by trying to alter the tension of the light return spring.

12 Carburettor - float needle sticking

1 If the float needle sticks, the carburettor will soon run dry and the engine will stop, despite there being fuel in the tank.
2 The easiest way to check a suspected sticking float needle, is to remove the inlet pipe at the carburettor end and then disconnect the HT lead from the centre of the ignition coil. Turn the engine over by pressing the solenoid rubber button. If fuel spurts from the end of the pipe (direct it towards the ground into a wad of cloth or jar) then the fault is almost certain to be a sticking float needle.
3 Remove the float chamber lid. Dismantle the valve and clean the housing and float chamber out thoroughly.

13 Carburettor - float chamber flooding

If fuel emerges from the small breather hole in the cover of the float chamber, this is known as flooding. It is caused by the float chamber needle not seating properly in its housing. Normally, this is because a piece of dirt or foreign matter is jammed between the needle and needle housing. Alternatively, the float may have developed a leak or be maladjusted so that it is holding open the float chamber needle valve even though the chamber is full of petrol. Remove the float chamber cover, clean the needle assembly, then check the fuel level in accordance with Section 16. Shake the float to verify if any petrol has leaked into it.

14 Carburettor - water or dirt in the carburettor

1 Because of the size of the jet orifice, water or dirt in the carburettor is easily cleared. If dirt in the carburettor is suspected, lift the piston assembly and flood the float chamber. The normal level of the fuel should be about 1/16 in. (1.588 mm) below the top of the jet, so that on flooding the carburettor the fuel should flow out of the jet hole.
2 If little or no petrol appears, start the engine (the jet is never completely blocked) and with the throttle fully open, block off the air intake. This will cause a partial vacuum in the choke tube and help suck out any foreign matter from the jet tube. Release the throttle as soon as the engine speed alters considerably. Repeat this procedure several times, stop the engine and then check the carburettor as detailed in the first paragraph of this Section.
3 If this fails to do the trick, then there is no alternative but to remove and blow out the jet.

15 Carburettor - jet centering

1 This operation is always necessary if the carburettor has been dismantled, but to check if this is necessary on a carburettor in service, first screw up the jet adjusting nut as far as it will go without forcing it, and lift the piston and then let it fall under its own weight. It should fall onto the bridge making a soft metallic 'click'. Now repeat the procedure, but this time with the adjusting nut screwed right down. If the soft metallic 'click' is not audible in either of the two tests proceed as follows:

2 Disconnect the jet link from the bottom of the jet, and the nylon flexible tube from the underside of the float chamber. Gently slide the jet and the nylon tube from the underside of the carburettor body. Next unscrew the jet adjusting nut and lift away the nut and the locking spring. Refit the adjusting nut without the locking spring and screw it up as far as possible without forcing. Replace the jet and tube, but there is no need to reconnect the tube.
3 Slacken the jet locking nut so that it may be rotated with the fingers only. Unscrew the piston damper and lift away the damper. Gently press the piston down onto the bridge and tighten the locknut. Lift the piston using the lifting pin and check that it is able to fall freely under its own weight. Now lower the adjusting nut and check once again. If this time there is a difference in the two metallic clicks repeat the centering procedure until the sound is the same for both tests.
4 Gently remove the jet and unscrew the adjusting nut. Refit the locking spring and jet adjusting nut. Top up the damper with oil, if necessary, and replace the damper. Connect the nylon flexible tube to the underside of the float chamber and finally reconnect the jet link.

16 Carburettor - float chamber fuel level adjustment

1 It is essential that the fuel level in the float chamber is always correct as otherwise excessive fuel consumption may occur. Carburettors fitted to later models have non-adjustable floats.
2 (Early models only) with the carburettor fitted to the engine and the float chamber full of petrol remove the piston dashpot assembly.
3 Check that the level of fuel in the jet is about 1/16 inch (1.588 mm) below the top of the jet. If it is above or below this level it may be adjusted by removing the needle and seat from the underside of the float chamber lid and either adding or removing washers so raising or lowering the relative position of the needle valve.

17 Carburettor - needle replacement

1 Should it be necessary to fit a new needle, first remove the piston and suction chamber assembly, marking the chamber for correct reassembly in its original position.
2 Slacken the needle clamping screw and withdraw the needle, guide and spring from the underside of the piston.
3 To refit the needle assembly fit the spring and guide to the needle and insert the assembly into the piston. (Fig. 3.6).
a) The lower edge of the guide is flush with the face of the piston.
b) The guide is positioned so that the etched locating mark on its lower face is adjacent to, and in line with, the centre line between the two piston transfer holes.
NOTE: Alternative needle guides may be fitted which have a flat machined on the guide and must be positioned so that the guide locking screw tightens down on to the flat. If the guide is incorrectly positioned, the locking screw will not tighten down on the flat and will remain proud of the piston resulting in damage to the piston bore.

18 Carburettor - adjustment and tuning

1 To adjust and tune the SU carburettor proceed in the following manner: Check the colour of the exhaust at idling speed with the choke fully in. If the exhaust tends to be black and the tailpipe interior is also black, it is a fair indication that the mixture is too rich. If the exhaust is colourless and the deposit in the exhaust pipe is very light grey it is likely that the mixture is too weak. This condition may also be accompanied by intermittent misfiring, while too rich a mixture will be associated with 'hunting'. Ideally the exhaust should be colourless with a medium grey pipe deposit.

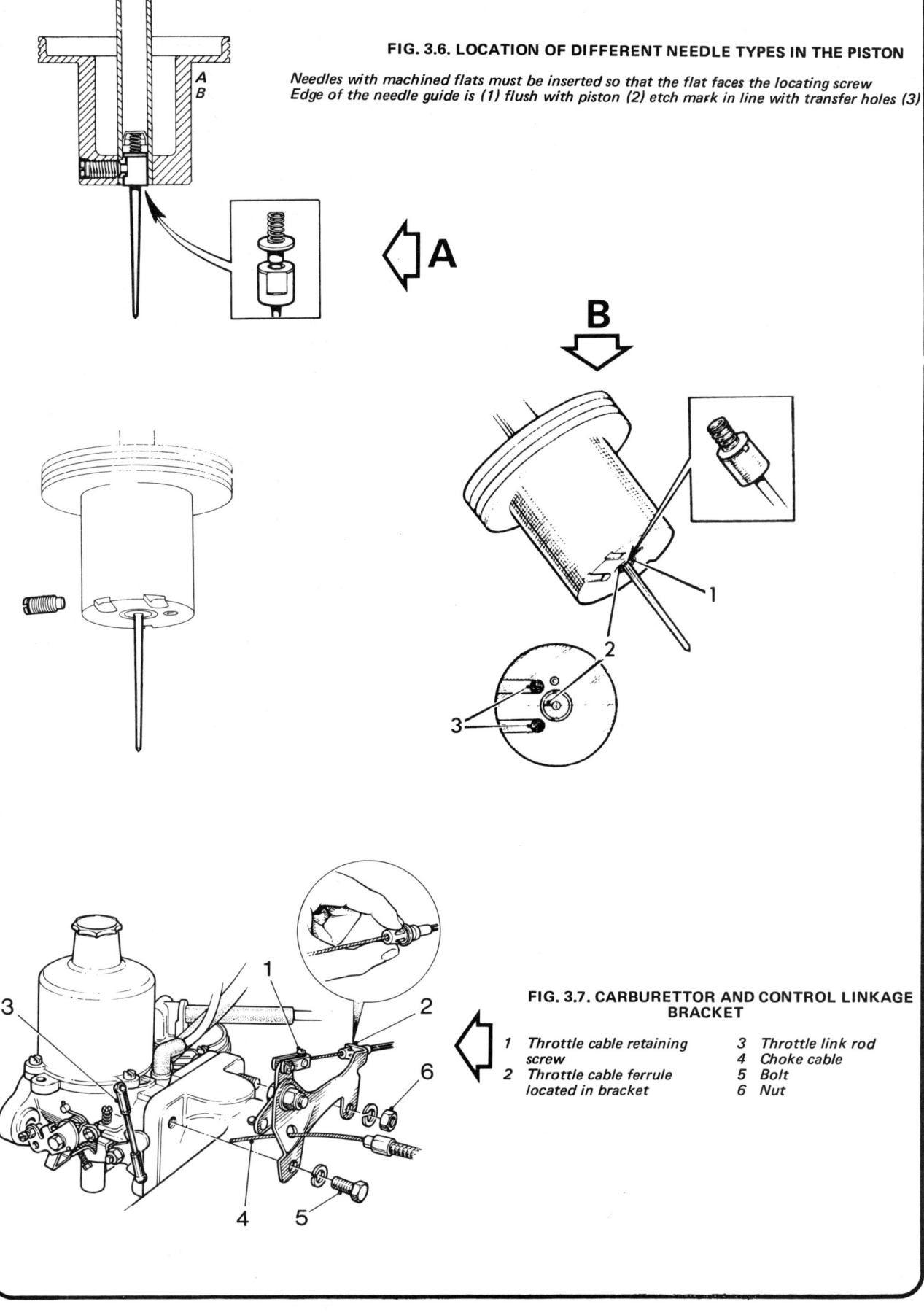

FIG. 3.6. LOCATION OF DIFFERENT NEEDLE TYPES IN THE PISTON

Needles with machined flats must be inserted so that the flat faces the locating screw
Edge of the needle guide is (1) flush with piston (2) etch mark in line with transfer holes (3)

A

B

FIG. 3.7. CARBURETTOR AND CONTROL LINKAGE BRACKET

1 Throttle cable retaining
   screw
2 Throttle cable ferrule
   located in bracket

3 Throttle link rod
4 Choke cable
5 Bolt
6 Nut

2 The exhaust pipe deposit should only be checked after a good run of at least 20 miles (30 km). Idling in city traffic and stop/start motoring is bound to produce excessively dark exhaust pipe deposit.

3 Once the engine has reached its normal operating temperature, detach the carburettor air intake cleaners.

4 Only two adjustments are provided on the SU carburettor. Idling speed is governed by the throttle adjusting screw and the mixture strength by the jet adjusting nut. The SU carburettor is correctly adjusted for the whole of its engine revolution range when the idling mixture strength is correct.

5 To adjust the mixture, set the engine to run at about 1000 rpm by screwing in the throttle adjusting screw.

6 Check the mixture strength by lifting the piston of the carburettor approximately 1/32 in (0.794 mm) with the piston lifting pin, so as to disturb the air flow as little as possible. If:

a) The speed of the engine increases appreciably, the mixture is too rich;

b) The engine speed immediately decreases, the mixture is too weak;

c) The engine speed increases very slightly, the mixture is correct.

To enrich the mixture, rotate the adjusting nut, which is at the bottom of the underside of the carburettor, in an anticlockwise direction, ie downwards. Only turn the adjusting nut a flat at a time and check the mixture strength between each turn. It is likely that there will be a slight increase or decrease in rpm after the mixture adjustment has been made, so that the throttle idling adjusting screw should now be turned so that the engine idles between 600 to 700 rpm.

19 Fuel tank - removal and replacement

1 Disconnect the battery and extinguish all naked lights.

2 Remove the petrol tank drain plug and drain the fuel into a suitably sized container.

3 Disconnect the main line fuel pipe from the tank outlet pipe and clamp the ends of the rubber pipe together to prevent fuel leakage back from the main pipe run.

4 Remove the luggage compartment carpet and spare wheel cover; then the spare wheel.

5 Slacken the two hose clips on the tank-to-filler pipe hose. Push the hose upwards to clear the petrol tank inlet.

6 Carefully squeeze the clip connecting the breather pipe to the tank and pull off the breather pipe.

7 Disconnect the leads to the fuel tank gauge unit after first noting which cables are connected to the respective terminals. On most later models it will be necessary to remove a square guard from the top of the gauging unit before the cables can be disconnected from the Lucar-type connectors. Tuck the harness to one side of the compartment.

8 Remove the four bolts and spring washers securing the tank to the car body.

9 Lift out the tank, taking care not to damage the tank outlet pipe

10 Refitting the tank is the reverse procedure to removal.

20 Fuel tank - cleaning

With time it is likely that sediment will collect in the bottom of the fuel tank. Condensation, resulting in rust and other impurities, will usually be found in the fuel tank of any car more than three or four years old.

When the tank is removed, it should be vigorously flushed out and turned upside down, and if facilities are available, steam cleaned.

21 Fuel tank sender unit - removal and refitting

1 For safety reasons disconnect the battery earth lead.

2 Open the luggage compartment lid and remove the floor carpeting.

3 With a screwdriver, ease up and remove the rubber cover.

4 Make a note of the electrical cable connections on the sender unit and disconnect the cables.

5 Using two screwdrivers on the locking ring undo the locking ring in a counter clockwise direction. Lift away the locking ring.

6 Carefully lift away the tank unit and sealing ring, easing the float arm through the hole so that it is not bent.

7 If the sender unit is suspect, check the circuit, gauge and sender unit.

22 Throttle pedal and cable - removal and replacement

1 Working inside the car, above the throttle pedal pivot point, remove the retaining clip and lift the cable nipple end out of the pedal fork.

2 Transferring your attentions to the engine compartment, remove the two bolts, plain washers and spring washers securing the pedal bracket to the bulkhead.

3 Remove the bracket and pedal assembly from the car to the workbench. Take out the split pin, withdraw the washers both wavy and plain, and pull out the clevis pin. Ease the pedal and return spring out of the bracket.

4 In order to release the cable from the bulkhead it is necessary to squeeze the ears of the ferrule and push it through the bulkhead into the engine compartment.

5 Disconnect the cable from the carburettor linkage by slackening the pinch screws, squeezing the ears of the ferrule and pushing it through the bracket.

6 Refitting is the reverse of the above sequence of operations, but ensure the cable is not kinked, and the snap clip has a secure grip on the cable inner nipple at the pedal fork.

23 Choke cable - removal and replacement

1 Disconnect the inner cable from the carburettor by undoing the screw and locknut on the cam.

2 Separate the inner cable from the outer by pulling the choke control on the instrument panel.

3 Unscrew and remove the ferrule securing the outer cable to the control panel: ease the outer cable away from the back of the instrument panel.

4 Separate the two halves of the outer cable at the rubber connector above the rocker box in the engine bay.

5 From inside the car, pull the outer cable through the bulkhead grommets into the car and remove.

6 To refit the cable, feed the control panel section of the outer cable through the bulkhead into the engine bay; secure the control panel with the ferrule and locknut.

7 Feed the inner cable through the entry in the control panel. In the engine bay, feed the inner cable through the rubber connector and then through the carburettor section of the outer cable. Connect the inner cable to the cam on the carburettor, tighten the securing screw and then the locknut. These should be approx. 1/16 inch (1.6 mm) free movement of the cable before the linkage starts to move the cam.

24 Fuel pipe lines - inspection and replacement

With the vehicle either raised on a ramp or jacked up and supported on axle stands, it is well worth while inspecting the main fuel line that runs from the rear tank to the fuel pump. Ensure that there are no signs of corrosion or cracking, deep scores, or evidence of fouling or chafing the bodywork or components.

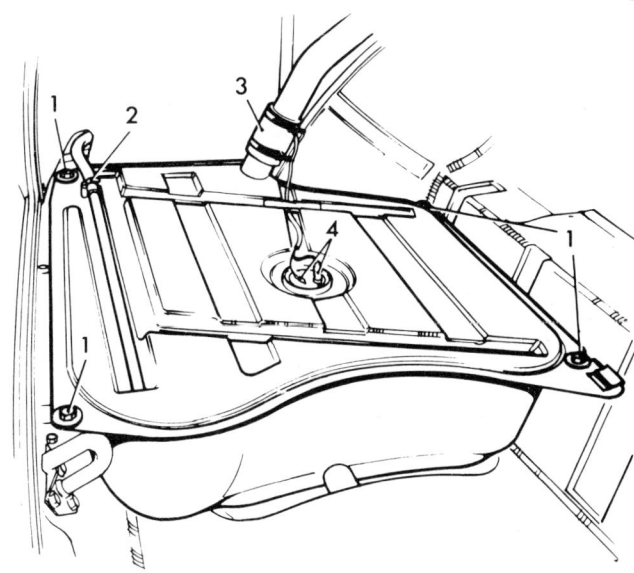

FIG. 3.8. FUEL TANK INSTALLATION

1   Retaining bolts
2   Clip securing breather
    pipe
3   Tank-to-filler pipe hose
4   Cable connections to
    fuel gauging unit

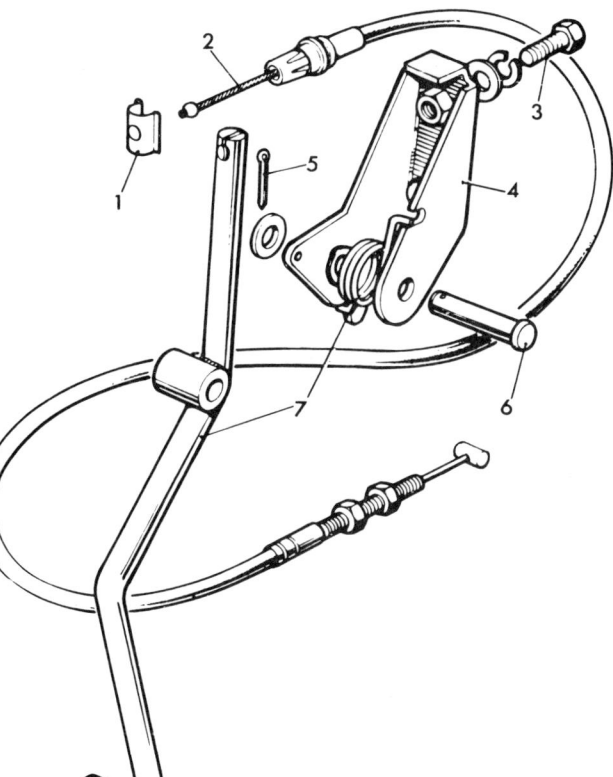

FIG. 3.9. THROTTLE PEDAL AND CABLE ASSEMBLY

1   Retaining clip
2   Throttle cable inner
3   Bracket retaining bolt
4   Pedal bracket
5   Split pin
6   Clevis pin
7   Pedal and return spring

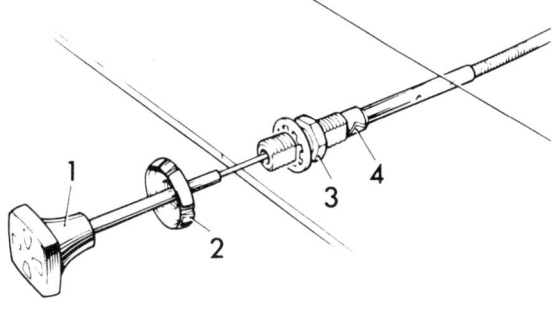

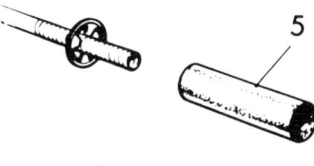

FIG. 3.10. CHOKE CABLE COMPONENTS

1   Choke control knob
2   Ferrule
3   Locknut
4   Cable outer
5   Rubber connector
    in engine bay

Inspect the rubber connectors that link each pipe section and renew if cracked or damaged. Replacement of any pipe section is straightforward since, between each rubber connector, they are only clipped in position on the chassis.

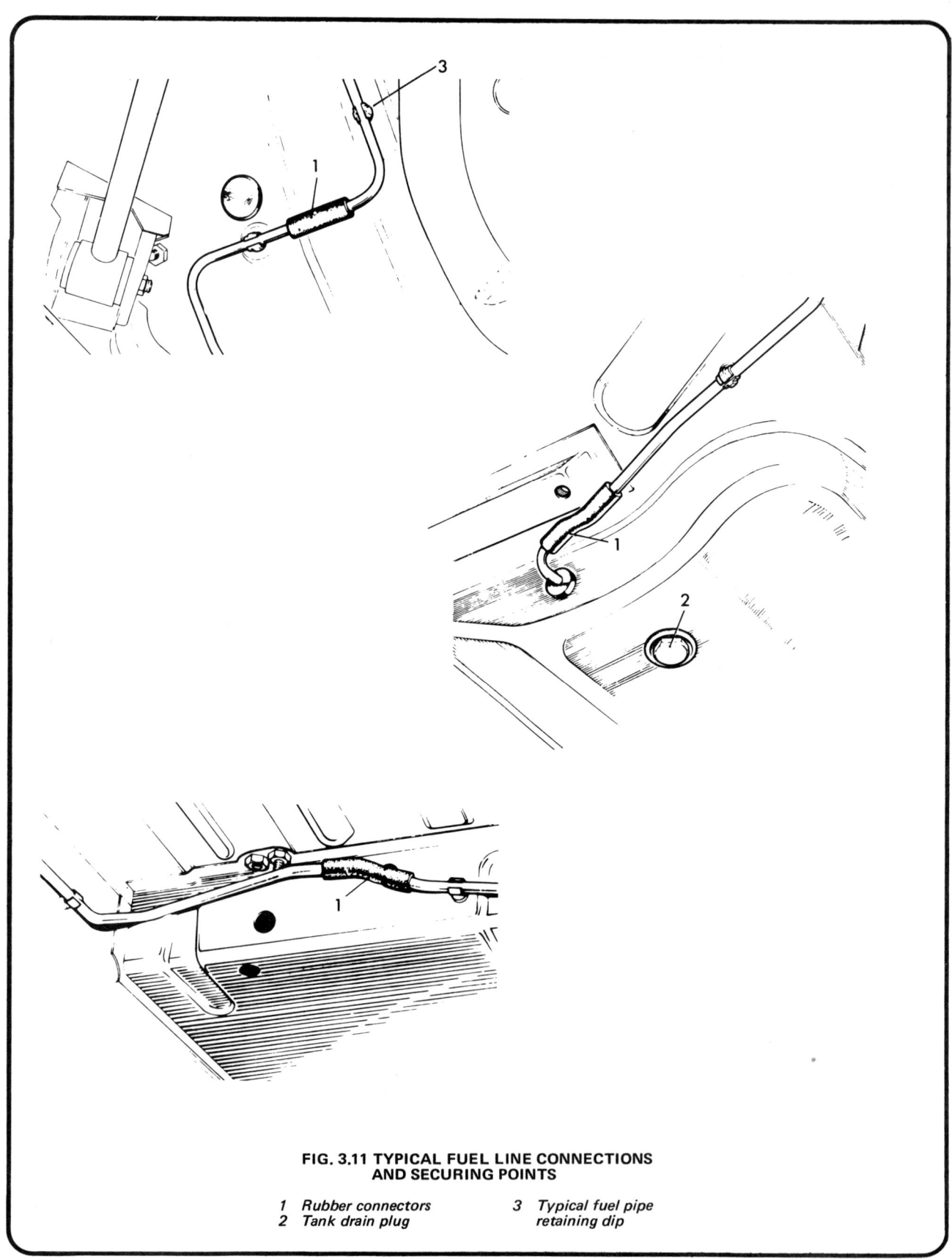

**FIG. 3.11 TYPICAL FUEL LINE CONNECTIONS
AND SECURING POINTS**

1   Rubber connectors
2   Tank drain plug
3   Typical fuel pipe
    retaining dip

25 Fault diagnosis

Unsatisfactory engine performance and excessive fuel consumption are not necessarily the fault of the fuel system or carburettor. In fact they more commonly occur as a result of ignition faults. Before acting on the fuel system it is necessary to check the ignition system first. Even though a fault may lie in the fuel system it will be difficult to trace unless the ignition is correct.

The table below therefore, assumes that the ignition system is in order.

Symptom	Reason/s	Remedy
Smell of petrol when engine is stopped	Leaking fuel lines or unions Leaking fuel tank	Repair or renew as necessary. Fill fuel tank to capacity and examine carefully at seams, unions and filler pipe connections. Repair as necessary.
Smell of petrol when engine is idling	Leaking fuel line unions between pump and carburettor Overflow of fuel from float chamber due to wrong level setting or ineffective needle valve or punctured float	Check line and unions and tighten or repair. Check fuel level setting and condition of float and needle valve and renew if necessary.
Excessive fuel consumption for reasons not covered by leaks or float chamber faults	Worn needle Sticking needle	Renew needles. Check correct movement of needle body.
Difficult starting, uneven running, lack of power, cutting out	One or more blockages Float chamber fuel level too low or needle sticking Fuel pump not delivering sufficient fuel Intake manifold gaskets leaking, or manifold fractured	Dismantle and clean out float chamber and body. Dismantle and check fuel level and needle. Check pump delivery and clean or repair as required. Check tightness of mounting nuts and inspect manifold.

Chapter 4 Ignition system

Contents

General description 1	Distributor - reassembly... 9
Contact breaker - adjustment 2	Ignition coil and ballast resistor - description, removal and
Contact breaker points - removal and replacement 3	replacement 10
Condenser - removal, testing and replacement 4	Ignition - timing 11
Distributor - lubrication 5	Spark plugs and leads 12
Distributor - removal and replacement 6	Ignition system - fault symptoms 13
Distributor - dismantling 7	Fault diagnosis - engine fails to start 14
Distributor - inspection and repair 8	Fault diagnosis - engine misfires 15

Specifications

Spark plugs

Size	14 mm
Type	Champion N9Y
Plug gap	0.025 inch (0.635 mm)
Firing order	1 - 3 - 4 - 2

Coil

Type	Lucas 16C6
Resistance at 20°C (68°F) in primary winding	1.43 to 1.58 ohms
Ballast resistor - type	Lucas 3BR
Resistance	1.3 to 1.4 ohms

Distributor

Type	Lucas 25D4
Part number	Lucas 41127
Contact points gap setting	0.014 to 0.016 in (0.356 to 0.406 mm)
Open period	$30° \pm 3°$
Closed period	$60° \pm 3°$
Direction of rotation	Ant.clockwise
Capacitor	0.20 mfd
Moving contact spring tension	18 to 24 oz (500 to 700 gms)

Ignition timing

Static setting:

Up to engine number DG 25000 H or L	9° BTDC
From engine number DG 25001 H or L	10° BTDC
Advance at 1500 rpm (distributor speed)	6° to 8°
850 rpm (distributor speed)	3½° to 5½°
550 rpm (distributor speed)	½° to 2½°
400 rpm (distributor speed)	0° to 1°

Torque wrench settings

	lb ft	kg m
Distributor to pedestal	18 - 20	2.489 - 2.765
Distributor to pedestal attachment	12 - 14	1.659 - 1.936
Spark plug	14 - 16	1.936 - 2.212

1 General description

In order that the engine may run correctly, it is necessary for an electrical spark to ignite the fuel/air charge in the combustion chamber at exactly the right moment in relation to engine speed and load. The ignition system is based on supplying low tension voltage from the battery to the ignition coil where it is converted to high tension voltage by virtue of distributor operation. The high tension voltage is powerful enough to jump the spark plug gap in the cylinders many times a second under high compression pressure, providing that the ignition system is in good working order and that all adjustments are correct.

The ignition system comprises two individual circuits known as the low tension circuit and the high tension circuit.

The low tension circuit (sometimes known as the primary circuit) comprises the battery lead to control box, lead to the ignition switch and subsequently to the low tension or primary coil windings (terminal SW). The lead from the low tension coil windings (coil terminal CB) to the contact breaker points and

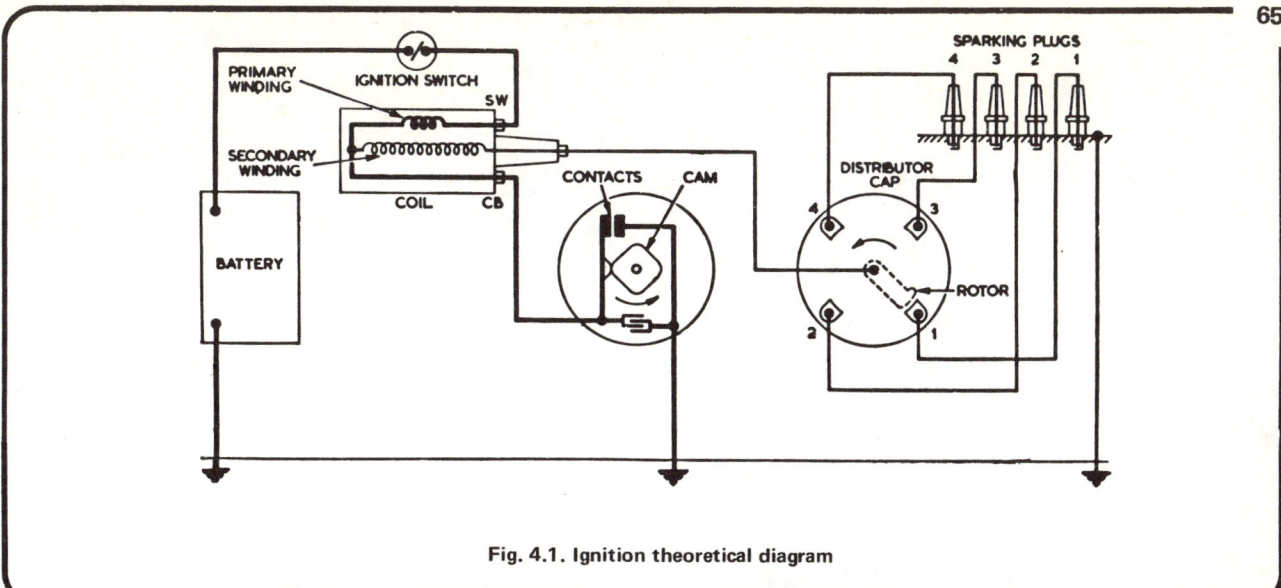

Fig. 4.1. Ignition theoretical diagram

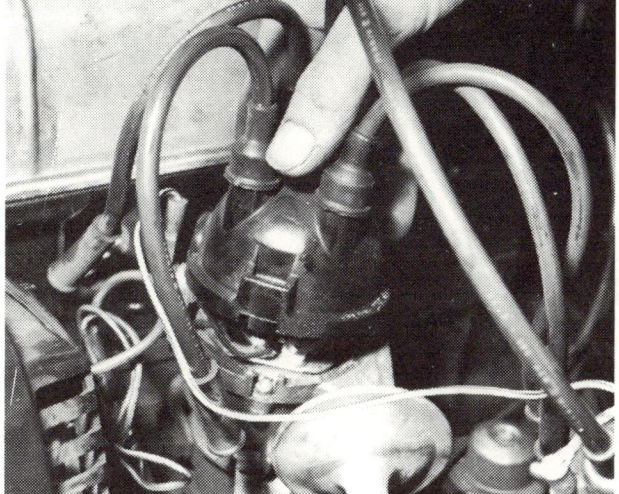

2.1a Removing the distributor cap

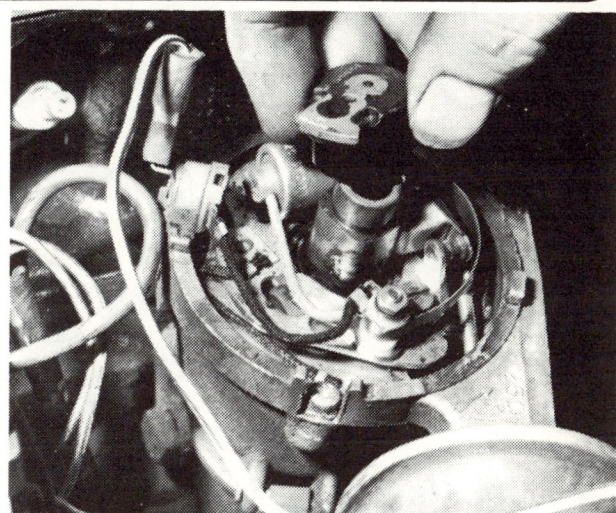

2.1b Lifting out the rotor arm

2.5a Loosening the contact plate securing screws

2.5b Adjusting the gap with a screwdriver and checking with a feeler gauge

condenser in the distributor is also in the LT circuit.

The high tension circuit (sometimes known as the secondary circuit) comprises the high tension or secondary coil winding, the heavily insulated ignition lead from the centre of the coil to the centre of the distributor cap, the rotor arm, the spark plug leads and the spark plugs.

The complete ignition system operation is as follows: low tension voltage from the car battery is changed within the ignition coil to high tension voltage by the opening and closing of the contact breaker points in the low tension circuit. High tension voltage is then fed via the carbon brush in the centre of the distributor cap to the rotor arm of the distributor. The rotor arm revolves inside the distributor cap. Each time it comes in line with one of the four metal segments in the cap, these being connected to the spark plug leads, the opening and closing of the contact breaker points causes the high tension voltage to build up, jump the gap from the rotor arm to the appropriate metal segment and via the spark plug lead, to the spark plug where it finally jumps the gap between the two spark plug electrodes, one being connected to the earth system.

The ignition time is advanced and retarded automatically to ensure the spark occurs at just the right instant for the particular load at the prevailing engine speed.

The ignition advance is controlled both mechanically and by a vacuum operated system. The mechanical governor mechanism comprises two lead weights, which move out under centrifugal force from the central distributor shaft, and so advance the spark. The weights are held in position by two light springs and it is the tension of the springs which is largely responsible for correct spark advancement.

The vacuum control comprises a diaphragm, one side of which is connected via a small bore tube to the carburettor, and the other side to the contact breaker plate. Depression in the induction manifold and carburettor, which varies with engine speed and throttle opening, causes the diaphragm to move, so moving the contact breaker plate and advancing or retarding the spark. A fine degree of control is achieved by a spring in the vacuum assembly.

2 Contact breaker - adjustment

1 To adjust the contact breaker points so that the correct gap is obtained, first release the two clips securing the distributor cap to the distributor body, and lift away the cap. Clean the inside and outside of the cap with a dry cloth. It is unlikely that the four segments will be badly burnt or scored, but if they are, the cap must be renewed. If only a small deposit is on the segments, it may be scraped away using a small screwdriver. Lift out rotor arm (photos).

2 Push in the carbon brush located in the top of the cap several times to ensure that it moves freely. The brush should protrude by at least ¼ in. (6.35 mm).

3 Gently prise the contact breaker points open to examine the condition of their faces. If they are rough, pitted or dirty, it will be necessary to remove them for resurfacing, or for replacement points to be fitted.

4 Assuming the points are satisfactory, or that they have been cleaned or replaced, measure the gap between the points by turning the engine over until the contact breaker arm is on the peak of one of the four cam lobes. A 0.015 in (0.381 mm) feeler gauge should now just fit between the points.

5 If the gap varies from this amount, slacken the contact plate securing screw and adjust the contact gap by inserting a screwdriver in the notched hole at the end of the plate, turning clockwise to decrease and anticlockwise to increase the gap. Tighten the securing screw and check the gap again (photo). (Fig.4.2).

6 Replace the rotor arm and distributor cap and clip the spring blade retainers into position.

3 Contact breaker points - removal and replacement

1 If the contact breaker points are burnt, pitted or badly worn, they must be removed and either replaced, or their faces must be filed smooth.

2 To remove the points, unscrew the terminal nut and remove it together with the washer under its head. Remove the flanged nylon bush and then the condenser lead and the low tension lead from the terminal pin. Lift off the contact breaker arm and then remove the large fibre washer from the terminal pin.

3 The adjustable contact breaker plate is removed by unscrewing one holding down screw and removing it, complete with spring and flat washer.

4 To reface the points, rub the faces on a fine carborundum stone, or on fine emery paper. It is important that the faces are rubbed flat and parallel to each other so that there will be complete face to face contact when the points are closed. One of the points will be pitted and the other will have deposits on it.

5 It is necessary to remove completely the built up deposits, but not necessary to rub the pitted point right to the stage where all the pitting has disappeared, though obviously if this is done it will prolong the time before the operation of refacing the points has to be repeated.

6 To replace the points, first position the adjustable contact breaker plate, and secure it with its screw, spring and flat washer. Fit the fibre washer to the terminal pin and fit the contact breaker arm over it. Insert the flanged nylon bush with the condenser lead immediately under its head, and the low tension lead under that, over the terminal pin. Fit the steel washer and screw on the securing nut.

7 The points are now reassembled and the gap should be set as detailed in the previous section.

4 Condenser - removal, testing and replacement

1 The purpose of the condenser (sometimes known as a capacitor) is to ensure that when the contact breaker points open there is no sparking across them which would waste voltage and cause wear. It also boosts the voltage.

2 The condenser is fitted in parallel with the contact breaker points. If it develops a short circuit, it will cause ignition failure as the points will be prevented from interrupting the low tension circuit.

3 If the engine becomes very difficult to start or begins to miss after several miles running and the breaker points show signs of excessive burning, then the condition of the condenser must be suspect. A further test can be made by separating the points by hand with the ignition switched on. If this in accompanied by a flash it is indicative that the condenser has failed.

4 Without special test equipment, the only sure way to diagnose condenser trouble is to replace a suspected unit with a new one and note if there is any improvement.

5 To remove the condenser from the distributor, take off the distributor cap and the rotor arm. Unscrew the contact breaker arm terminal nut, and remove the nut, washer and flanged nylon bush and release the condenser. Replacement of the condenser is simply a reversal of the removal proceedure. Take particular care that the condenser lead does not short circuit against any portion of the breaker plate.

5 Distributor - lubrication

1 It is important that the distributor cam is lubricated with petroleum jelly at the specified mileages, and that the breaker arm, governor weights and cam spindle, are lubricated with engine oil once every 6000 miles (10000km). In practice it will be found that lubrication every 3000 miles (5000km) is preferable although this is not recommended by the manufacturers.

2 Great care should be taken not to use too much lubricant, as any excess that might find its way onto the contact breaker

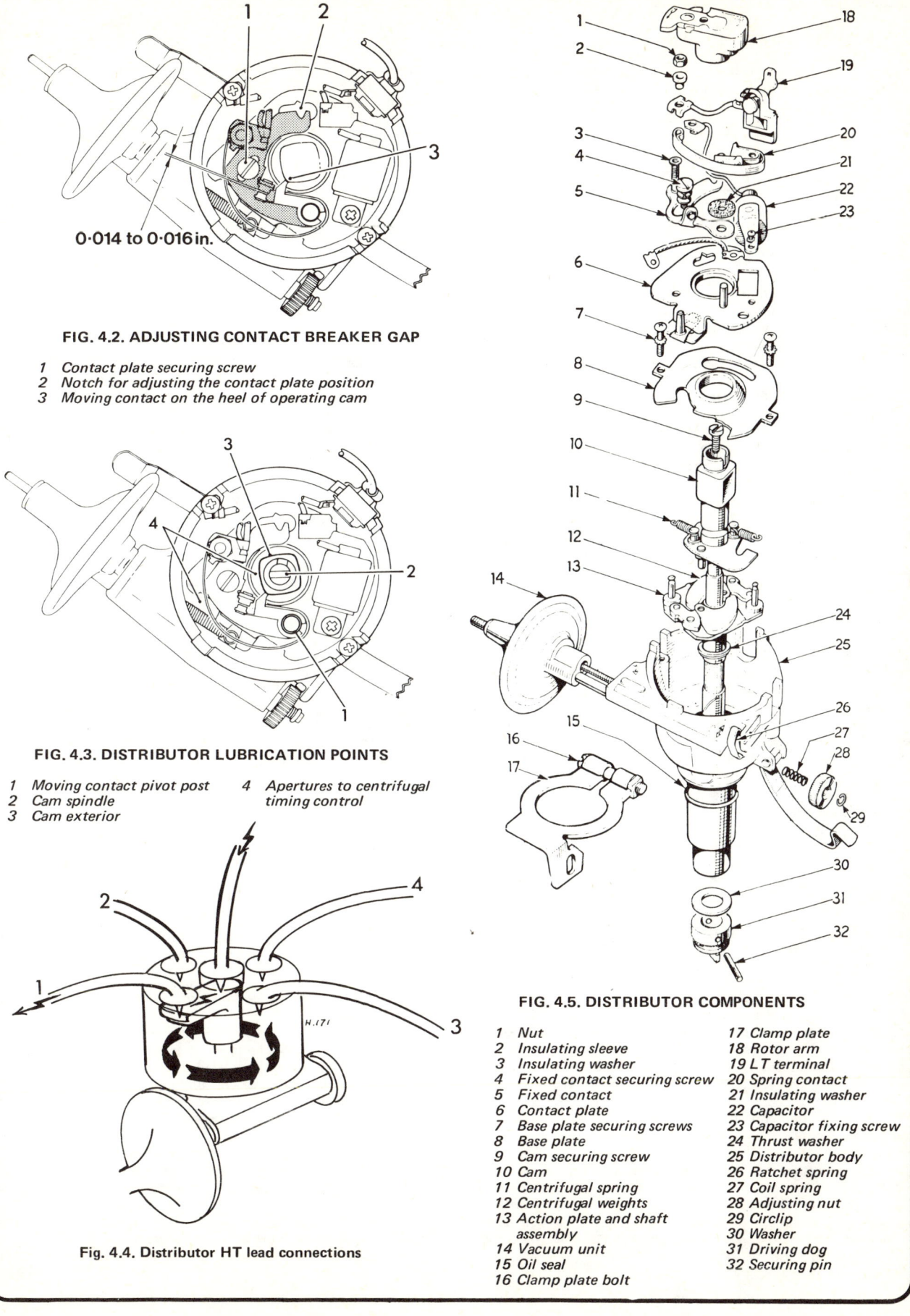

FIG. 4.2. ADJUSTING CONTACT BREAKER GAP

1 Contact plate securing screw
2 Notch for adjusting the contact plate position
3 Moving contact on the heel of operating cam

0·014 to 0·016 in.

FIG. 4.3. DISTRIBUTOR LUBRICATION POINTS

1 Moving contact pivot post
2 Cam spindle
3 Cam exterior
4 Apertures to centrifugal timing control

Fig. 4.4. Distributor HT lead connections

FIG. 4.5. DISTRIBUTOR COMPONENTS

1 Nut
2 Insulating sleeve
3 Insulating washer
4 Fixed contact securing screw
5 Fixed contact
6 Contact plate
7 Base plate securing screws
8 Base plate
9 Cam securing screw
10 Cam
11 Centrifugal spring
12 Centrifugal weights
13 Action plate and shaft assembly
14 Vacuum unit
15 Oil seal
16 Clamp plate bolt
17 Clamp plate
18 Rotor arm
19 LT terminal
20 Spring contact
21 Insulating washer
22 Capacitor
23 Capacitor fixing screw
24 Thrust washer
25 Distributor body
26 Ratchet spring
27 Coil spring
28 Adjusting nut
29 Circlip
30 Washer
31 Driving dog
32 Securing pin

points could cause burning and misfiring.

3 To gain access to the cam spindle, lift away the rotor arm. Drop no more than two drops of engine oil onto the screw head. This will run down the spindle when the engine is hot and lubricate the bearings. No more than ONE drop of oil should be applied to the pivot post (Fig. 4.3).

6 Distributor - removal and replacement

1 To remove the distributor from the engine, start by pulling the terminals off each of the spark plugs. Release the low tension cable connector from the side of the distributor. Unscrew the high tension lead retaining cap from the coil and remove the lead.

2 Unscrew the union holding the vacuum tube to the distributor vacuum housing.

3 Remove the distributor body clamp plate bolt and washers securing the clamp plate to the cylinder block distributor adaptor pedestal and lift up the distributor with the clamp plate still in position.

4 If it is not wished to disturb the ignition timing, then under no circumstances should the clamp plate bolt (16) (fig.4.5) which secures the distributor in its relative position in the clamp (17) be loosened. Providing the distributor is removed without the clamp being loosened from the distributor and the engine is not turned, the ignition timing will not be lost.

5 Replacement is a reversal of the above sequence. If the engine has been turned, it will be best to re-time the ignition. This will also be necessary if the clamp plate bolt has been loosened.

7 Distributor - dismantling

1 With the distributor removed from the car and on the bench, remove the distributor cap and lift off the rotor arm. If very tight , lever it off gently with a screwdriver.

2 Remove the contact breaker points as described in Section 3.

3 Remove the condenser (22) from the contact plate (6) by releasing its securing screw and washer (23).

4 Unlock the vacuum unit spring from its mounting pin on the moving contact plate (6).

5 Lift out the contact plate.

6 Unscrew and remove the two screws and washer (7) which hold the contact breaker base plate (8) in position, and remove the earth lead from the relevant screw. Remember to replace this lead on reassembly.

7 Lift out the contact breaker base plate.

8 Note the position of the slot in the rotor arm drive in relation to the offset drive dog at the opposite end of the distributor. It is essential that this is reassembled correctly otherwise the timing may be 180° out.

9 Unscrew the cam spindle retaining screw (9) which is located in the centre of the rotor arm drive shaft cam (10) and remove the cam spindle.

10 Lift out the centrifugal weights (12) together with their springs (11).

11 To remove the vacuum unit (14) spring off the small circlip (29) securing the advance adjustment knurled nut (28) which should then be unscrewed. With the micrometer adjusting nut removed, release the spring (27) and the micrometer adjusting nut lock spring clip (26). This is the clip that is responsible for the 'clicks' when the micrometer adjusting nut (28) is turned and it is small and easily lost, as is the circlip, so put them in a safe place. Do not forget to replace the lock spring clip on reassembly.

12 It is neccessary to remove the distributor drive shaft or spindle only if it is thought to be excessively worn, With a thin parallel pin punch, drive out the retaining pin (32) from the driving tongue collar (31) on the bottom end of the distributor drive shaft. The shaft can then be removed. Recover the thrust washers (30) and (24).

13 The distributor is now ready for inspection.

8 Distributor - inspection and repair

1 Thoroughly wash all mechanical parts in petrol and wipe dry using a clean non-fluffy rag.

2 Check the points that have been described previously. Check distributor cap for signs of tracking indicated by a thin black line between the segments. Replace the cap if any signs of tracking are found.

3 If the metal portion of the rotor arm is badly burnt or loose, renew the arm. If slightly burnt, clean the arm with a fine file. Check that the carbon brush moves freely in the centre of the distributor cover.

4 Examine the fit of the breaker plate on the bearing plate and check the breaker arm pivot for looseness or wear and renew as necessary.

5 Examine the balance weights and pivot pins for wear, and renew the weight or cam assembly if a degree of wear is found.

6 Examine the shaft and the fit of the cam assembly on the shaft. If the clearance is excessive, compare the items with new units and renew either, or both, if they show excessive wear.

7 If the shaft is a loose fit in the distributor bushes and can be seen to be worn, it will be neccesary to fit a new shaft and bushes. The old bushes in the early distributor, or the single bush in the later ones, are simply pressed out. NOTE: before inserting new bushes they should be stood in engine oil for 24 hours.

8 Examine the length of the balance weight springs and compare them with new springs. If they have stretched they should be renewed.

9 Distributor - reassembly

1 Reassembly is a straightforward reversal of the dismantling process, but there are several points which should be noted in addition to those already given in the Section on dismantling.

2 Lubricate the balance weights and other parts of the mechanical advance mechanism, the distributor shaft, and the portion of the shaft on which the cam bears, with SAE 20 engine oil, during reassembly. Do not oil excessively but ensure these parts are adequately lubricated.

3 On reassembling the cam driving pins with the centrifugal weights, check that they are in correct position so that when viewed from above, the rotor arm should be at the six o'clock position, and the small offset on the driving dog must be on the right.

4 Check the action of the weights in the fully advanced, and fully retarded positions, and ensure they are not binding.

5 Tighten the micrometer adjusting nut to the middle position on the timing scale.

6 If the oil seal (15) has stretched or is damaged, obtain and fit a new one.

7 Finally, set the contact breaker gap to the correct clearance of 0.015 in. (0.381 mm).

10 Ignition coil and ballast resistor - description, removal and replacement

This system is designed to assist engine starting under adverse conditions. A ballast resistor is positioned in series in the normal supply to the ignition coil. This unit causes a voltage drop in the circuit so that the 12-volt supply from the ignition switch may be employed to power the nominally rated 6-volt ignition coil.

During engine start the resistor is by-passed and the battery voltage (reduced from 12-volt by the starter motor load) is applied to the coil direct from the starter solenoid. This slight voltage overload provides an increased high tension voltage at the spark plugs.

1 To remove the ignition coil, pull off the two LT leads, (Lucar connectors) and the HT central lead.

2 Remove the two screws and washers that secure the coil and lift it away.

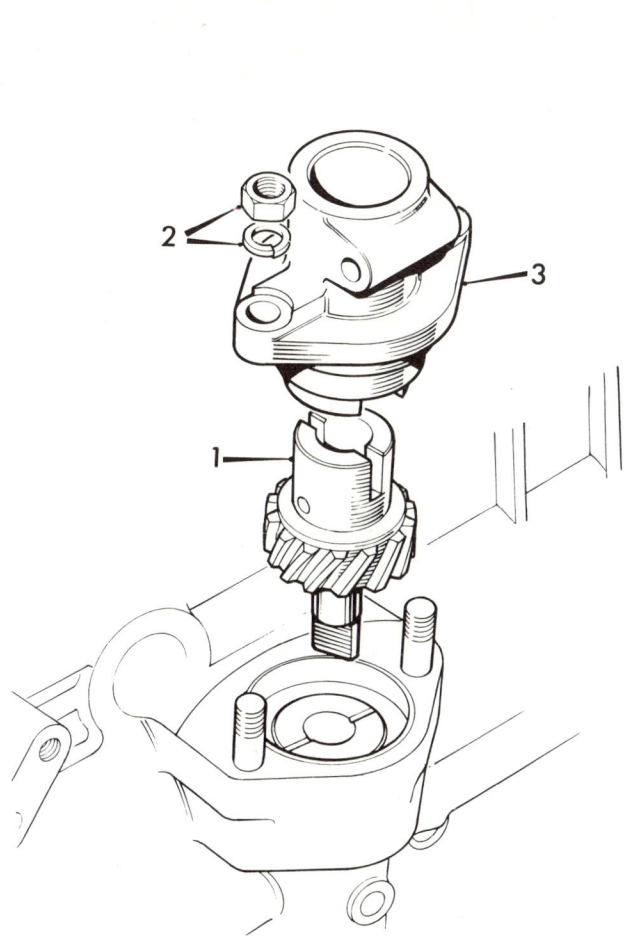

FIG. 4.6. DISTRIBUTOR DRIVE AND MOUNTING PEDESTAL

1 Drive dog   3 Pedestal
2 Nut and spring washer

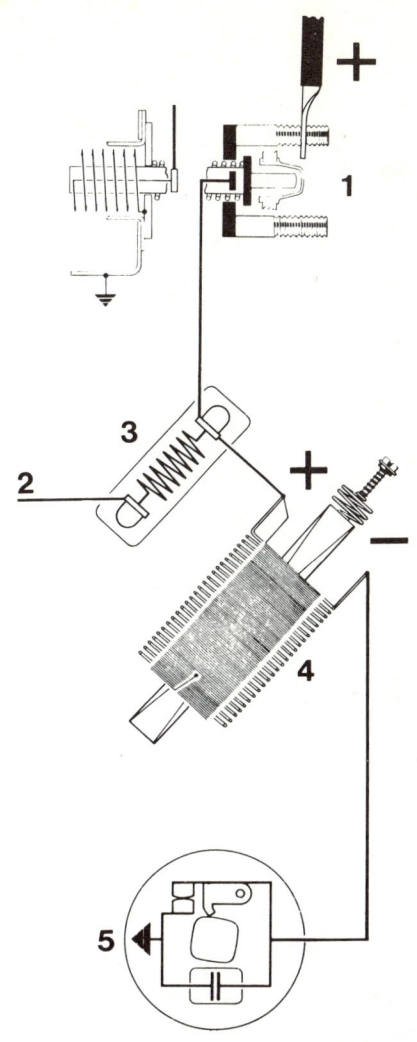

FIG. 4.7. METHOD OF CONNECTING BALLAST RESISTOR TO IGNITION COIL

1 Starter solenoid   4 Ignition coil (6 volt)
2 Normal ignition coil supply 5 Distributor
3 Ballast resistor

3 Replacement is the reversal of removal. Remember to include, in the rear screw assembly, the lug from the ballast resistor. The white/yellow wire goes to the positive terminal and the white/black wire to the negative terminal.
4 The ballast resistor is located on the left hand engine bay valance, adjacent to the ignition coil, and removal and replacement is straightforward. The white wire goes to the lower terminal and the white/yellow wire to the upper terminal (Fig.4.7).

11 Ignition - timing

1 If the clamp plate pinch bolt has been loosened on the distributor and the static timing lost, or if for any reason it is wished to set the ignition timing, proceed as follows;
2 Refer to Section 2 and check the contact breaker points. Reset as necessary.
3 Assemble the clamp plate and distributor to the pedestal, at the same time engaging the driving dog with the slot in the gear.
4 Rotate the crankshaft in the normal direction of rotation so the No 1 piston is coming up to TDC on the compression

stroke. This can be checked by removing No 1 spark plug and feeling the pressure being developed in the cylinder, or by removing the rocker cover and noting when the valves in No.4 cylinder are rocking ie the inlet valve is just opening and the exhaust valve just closing. If this check is not made it is all too easy to set the timing 180° out, as both No 1 and 4 pistons come up to TDC at the same time, but only one will be on the firing stroke.
5 The rotor arm should be pointing to No.1 segment in the distributor cap (Fig.4.9).
6 The notch on the engine pulley should now be in line with the '9° BEFORE' mark on the timing cover scale, (Fig.4.8).
7 Do not turn the crankshaft back if the marks are missed but turn in the normal direction of rotation until the marks are once again in line.
8 With the distributor cap removed, turn the milled adjusting screw (1) until approximately half the scale (3) is exposed, (Fig.4.9).
9 Slacken the clamp plate bolt (2) and, after turning the distributor body slightly anticlockwise to make sure that the contact breaker points are closed, turn the distributor body in a clockwise direction slowly until the contacts just open. Tighten

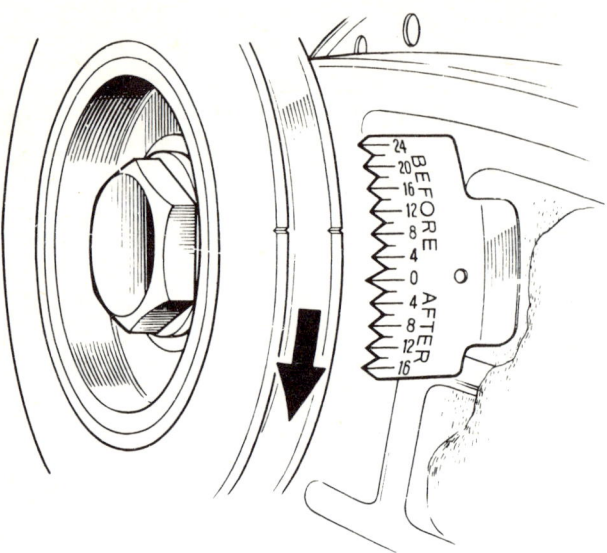

Fig. 4.8. Crankshaft pulley notch and timing scale on timing case cover. "O" is TDC

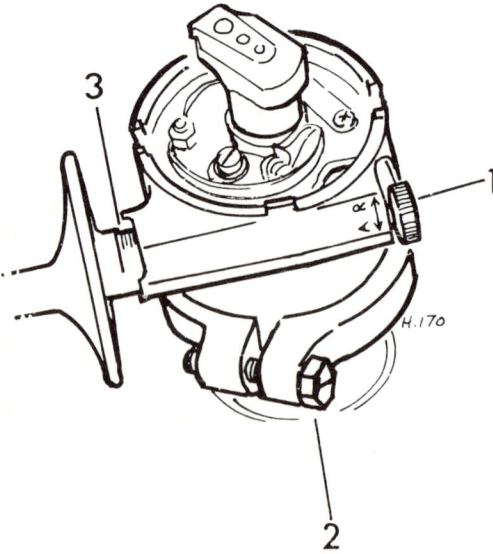

FIG. 4.9. POSITION OF ROTOR ARM FOR REFITTING DISTRIBUTOR, i.e. with rotor arm pointing to No. 1 segment in the distributor cap

1   *Adjusting screw*   3   *Scale*
2   *Clamp plate bolt*

the clamp bolt and refit the cover.

10 It should be noted that this adjustment is nominal and the final adjustment should be made under running conditions.

11 First start the engine and allow to warm up to normal temperature, and then accelerate in top gear from 30 to 50 mph (48 to 80 Km ph) listening for heavy pinking of the engine. If this occurs, the ignition needs to be retarded slightly until just the faintest trace of pinking can be heard under these operating conditions.

12 Since the ignition advance adjustment enables the firing point to be related correctly in relation to the grade of fuel used, the fullest advantage of any change of fuel will only be obtained by re-adjustment of the ignition settings.

13 This is done by varying the setting of the index scale on the vacuum advance mechanism one or two divisions, checking to make sure that the best all round result is attained.

14 Difficulty is sometimes experienced in determining exactly when the contact breaker points open. This can be ascertained most accurately by connecting a 12 volt bulb in parallel with the contact breaker points (one lead to earth and the other from the distributor low tension terminal). Switch on the ignition, and turn the advance and retard adjuster until the bulb lights up, indicating that the points have just opened.

12 Spark plugs and leads

1   The correct functioning of the spark plugs is vital for the proper running and efficiency of the engine.

2   At intervals of 6000 miles the plugs should be removed, examined and cleaned, and if worn excessively, replaced. The condition of the spark plug will also tell much about the overall condition of the engine (photo). (Fig.4.10).

3   If the insulator nose of the spark plug is clean and white with no deposits, this is indicative of a weak mixture, or too hot a plug (a hot plug transfers heat away from the electrode slowly — a cold plug transfers heat away quickly).

4   The plugs fitted as standard are Champion N9Y 14 mm. If the top and insulator nose is covered with hard black-looking deposits, then this is indicative that the mixture is too rich. Should the plug be black and oily, then it is likely that the engine is fairly worn, as well as the mixture being too rich.

5   If the insulator nose is covered with light tan to greyish brown deposits, then the mixture is correct and it is likely that the engine is in good condition.

6   If there are any traces of long brown tapering stains on the outside of the white portion of the plug, then the plug will have to be renewed as this shows that there is a faulty joint between the plug body and the insulator, and compression is being allowed to leak away.

7   Plugs should be cleaned by a sand blasting machine which will free them from carbon better than cleaning by hand. The machine will also test the condition of the plugs under compression. Any plug that fails to spark at the recommended pressure should be renewed.

8   The spark plug gap is of considerable importance. If it is too large or too small the size of the spark and its efficiency will be seriously impaired. The spark plug gap should be set to 0.025 in. (0.635 mm).

9   To set it, measure the gap with a feeler gauge, and then bend open, or close the outer plug electrode until the correct gap is achieved. The centre electrode should never be bent as this may crack the insulation and cause plug failure if nothing worse, (photo).

10 When replacing the plugs, remember to use new washers and replace the leads from the distributor in the correct firing order, which is 1 3 4 2, No.1 cylinder being the nearest one to the radiator.

11 The plug leads require no routine attention other than being kept clean and wiped over regularly. At intervals of 6000 miles (10000 km) however, pull each lead off the plugs in turn and remove them from the distributor by slackening the retaining screws. Water can seep down into these joints giving rise to a white corrosive deposit which must be carefully removed from the end of each cable.

12.2 Removing spark plug

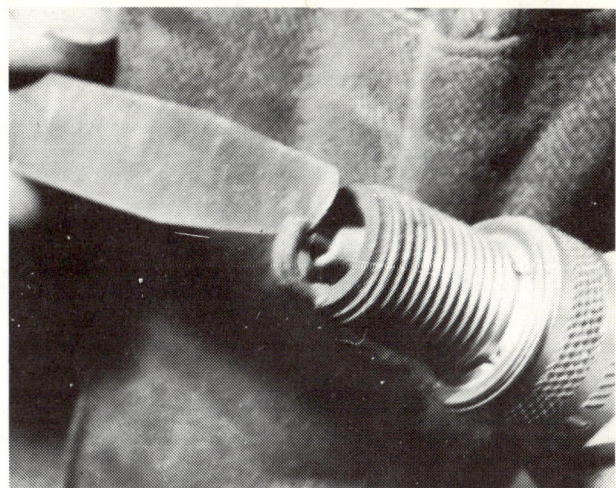

12.9 Checking spark plug gap with feeler gauge

13 Ignition system - fault symptons

There are two main symptoms indicating ignition faults. Either the engine will not start or fire, or the engine is difficult to start and misfires. If it is a regular misfire, i.e. the engine is only running on two or three cylinders, the fault is almost sure to be in the secondary, or high tension circuit. If the misfiring is intermittent, the fault could be in either the high or low tension circuits. If the engine stops suddenly, or will not start at all, it is likely that the fault is in the low tension circuit. Loss of power and overheating, apart from faulty carburation settings, are normally due to faults in the distributor or incorrect ignition timing.

14 Fault diagnosis - engine fails to start

1 If the engine fails to start and it was running normally when it was last used, first check there is fuel in the petrol tank. If the engine turns over normally on the starter motor and the battery is evidently well charged, then the fault may be in either the high or low tension circuits. First check the HT circuit. NOTE: If the battery is known to be fully charged, the ignition comes on, and the starter motor fails to turn the engine. CHECK THE TIGHTNESS OF THE LEADS ON THE BATTERY TERMINALS and also the secureness of the earth lead to its CONNECTION TO THE BODY. It is quite common for the leads to have worked loose, even if they look and feel secure. If one of the battery terminal posts gets very hot when trying to work the starter motor this is a sure sign of a faulty connection to that terminal.

2 One of the commonest reasons for bad starting is wet or damp spark plug leads and distributor. Remove the distributor cap. If condensation is visible internally, dry the cap with a rag and also wipe over the leads. Replace the cap.

3 If the engine still fails to start, check that current is reaching the plugs, by disconnecting each plug lead in turn at the spark plug end, and holding the end of the cable about 3/16 in. (5 mm) away from the cylinder block. Spin the engine on the starter motor by pressing the rubber button on the starter motor solenoid switch (under the bonnet).

4 Sparking between the end of the cable and the block should be fairly strong with a regular blue spark (hold the lead with rubber to avoid shocks). If healthy sparking is observed, then it is most probable that the plugs are faulty: remove them, re-gap them to 0.025 in. (0.635 mm) and replace. The engine should

now start. If it does not then the indications are that the fault lies in the fuel system (Chapter 3).

5 If good sparking is not evident, remove the centre HT lead from the distributor and hold it adjacent to the block.

6 Spin the engine as before, when a rapid succession of blue sparks between the end of the lead and the block indicate that the coil is in order, and that either the distributor cap is cracked; the carbon brush is stuck or worn; the rotor arm faulty; or the segments are burnt, pitted or dirty.

7 If there are no sparks from the end of the lead from the coil, then check the connections of the lead to the coil and distributor head, and if they are in order, check out the low tension circuit starting with the battery.

8 The first item to check in the LT circuit is the points; ensure that they are clean and set to the correct gap. If this is in order then move on to the coil and disconnect the terminal marked 'CB' and the low tension terminal on the side of the distributor body and connect a test lamp between these points. Turn the engine over slowly with the ignition switched on and, if the light comes on as the contact points close, and goes out as the points open, the circuit is as it should be. If the light does not function like this then there is trouble in the circuit, probably inside the coil windings or with the capacitor. Check the capacitor by applying a test lamp in series with a battery, or an Avometer or similar test meter, across the points when they are open. A reading on the meter, or the test lamp illuminating, indicates a short circuited capacitor which should be replaced. If this test is in order then disconnect all leads to the coil and check each winding with a testmeter or testlamp. If either winding is faulty the coil must be replaced.

9 If all the previous checks are satisfactory then the basic LT supply to the coil is probably at fault and must be checked through, cable by cable, in accordance with the wiring diagram in Chapter 10, using a testlamp or testmeter.

15 Fault diagnosis - engine misfires

1 If the engine misfires regularly, run it at a fast idling speed, and short out each of the plugs in turn by placing a short screwdriver across from the plug terminal to the cylinder. Ensure that the screwdriver has a wooden or plastic insulated handle.

2 No difference in engine running will be noticed when the plug in the defective cylinder is short circuited. Short circuiting the working plugs will accentuate the misfire.

3 Remove the plug lead from the end of the defective plug and hold it about 3/16 in. (5 mm) away from the block. Restart the

engine. If the spark is fairly strong and regular the fault must lie in the spark plug.

4 The plug may be loose, the insulation may be cracked or the points may have been burnt away giving too wide a gap for the spark to jump. Worse still, one of the points may have broken off. Either renew the plug, or clean it, reset the gap, and then test it.

5 If there is no spark at the end of the plug lead, or if it is weak and intermittent, check the ignition lead from the distributor to the plug. If the insulation is cracked or perished, renew the lead. Check the connections at the distributor cap.

6 If there is still no spark, examine the distributor cap for tracking. This can be recognised by a very thin black line running between two or more electrodes, or between an electrode and some other part of the distributor. Thes lines are paths which now conduct electricity across the cap thus letting it run to earth. The only answer is a new distributor cap.

7 Apart from the ignition timing being incorrect, other causes of misfiring have already been dealt with under the section dealing with the failure of the engine to start.

8 If the ignition timing is too far retarded, it should be noted that the engine will tend to overheat, and there will be a quite noticeable drop in power. If the engine is overheating and the power is down, and the ignition timing is correct, then the carburettor should be checked, as it is likely that this is where the fault lies. See Chapter 3 for details.

Measuring plug gap. A feeler gauge of the correct size (see ignition system specifications) should have a slight 'drag' when slid between the electrodes. Adjust gap if necessary

Adjusting plug gap. The plug gap is adjusted by bending the earth electrode inwards, or outwards, as necessary until the correct clearance is obtained. Note the use of the correct tool

Normal. Grey-brown deposits lightly coated core nose. Gap increasing by around 0.001 in (0.025 mm) per 1000 miles (1600 km). Plugs ideally suited to engine and engine in good condition

Carbon fouling. Dry, black, sooty deposits. Will cause weak spark and eventually misfire. Fault: over-rich fuel mixture. Check: carburettor mixture settings, float level and jet sizes; choke operation and cleanliness of air filter. Plugs can be re-used after cleaning

Oil fouling. Wet, oily deposits. Will cause weak spark and eventually misfire. Fault: worn bores/piston rings or valve guides; sometimes occurs (temporarily) during running-in period. Plugs can be re-used after thorough cleaning

Overheating. Electrodes have glazed appearance, core nose very white - few deposits. Fault: plug overheating. Check: plug value, ignition timing, fuel octane rating (too low) and fuel mixture (too weak). Discard plugs and cure fault immediately

Electrode damage. Electrodes burned away; core nose has burned, glazed appearance. Fault: initial pre-ignition. Check: as for 'Overheating' but may be more severe. Discard plugs and remedy fault before piston or valve damage occurs

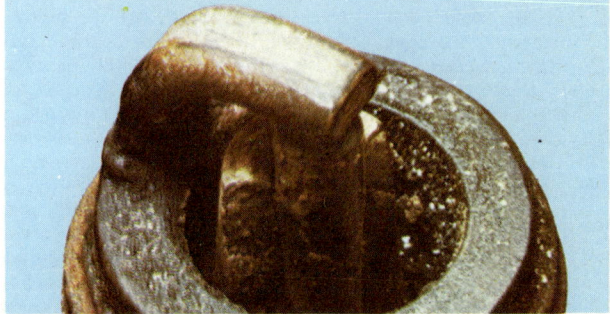

Split core nose (may appear initially as a crack). Damage is self-evident, but cracks will only show after cleaning. Fault: pre-ignition or wrong gap-setting technique. Check: ignition timing, cooling system, fuel octane rating (too low) and fuel mixture (too weak). Discard plugs, rectify fault immediately

Chapter 5 Clutch and actuating mechanism

Contents

General description 1	Clutch release mechanism - removal, inspection and replacement 8
Clutch system - bleeding 2	Clutch pedal and support bracket - removal and refitting 9
Clutch slave cylinder - removal and refitting 3	Clutch faults 10
Clutch slave cylinder - dismantling, examination and re-assembly 4	Clutch squeal - diagnosis and cure 11
Clutch master cylinder - removal and refitting 5	Clutch slip - diagnosis and cure 12
Clutch master cylinder - dismantling, examination and re-assembly 6	Clutch spin - diagnosis and cure 13
Clutch - removal, inspection and replacement 7	Clutch judder - diagnosis and cure 14

Specifications

Make	Borg and Beck
Type	Diaphragm spring. Single dry plate
Diameter	6½ in (165 mm)
Operation	Hydraulic master and slave cylinders
Drive plate	
Type	Cushion springs (4)
Facings	
Type	Mintex M19

Torque wrench settings	lb ft	kgf m
Gearbox case to clutch housing	26 - 32	3.6 - 4.4
Clutch bellhousing to engine plate	11 - 14	1.5 - 2.0
Clutch assembly to flywheel	8 - 11	1.0 - 1.5

1 General description

The clutch is fitted in order that the engine may run without being mechanically connected to the transmission. It enables the engine torque to be progressively applied to the gearbox so that the car can move off gradually from rest, and then for the gear to be changed easily as the speed increases or decreases.

The main parts of the clutch assembly are the driven plate assembly, the cover assembly and the release bearing assembly. When the clutch is in use, the driven plate assembly being splined to the input shaft, is sandwiched between the flywheel and the pressure plate by the diaphragm spring. Engine torque is, therefore, transferred from the flywheel to the clutch driven plate assembly and then to the input shaft.

By depressing the clutch pedal, the piston in the master cylinder pressurises hydraulic fluid through the clutch hydraulic pipe to the slave cylinder, the piston of which moves forward on the entry of the fluid and actuates the clutch throw out lever by means of a slot pushrod. The release bearing assembly is pushed against the diaphragm centre, releasing its pressure on the driven plate assembly, thus breaking the drive between the engine and gearbox.

When the clutch pedal is released, the pressure plate diaphragm spring forces the pressure plate into contact with the friction linings on the clutch driven plate, at the same time forcing the clutch driven plate assembly against the flywheel and so taking up the drive.

As the friction linings on the clutch driven plate wear, the pressure plate automatically moves closer to the driven plate to compensate. This makes the centre of the diaphragm spring move nearer to the release bearing, so decreasing the release bearing clearance. As the diaphragm clutch automatically compensates for wear no clutch adjustment is required nor is any facility to allow this provided.

2 Clutch system - bleeding

Whenever the clutch hydraulic system has been overhauled, a part renewed, or the level in the reservoir is too low, air will have entered the system neccessitating its bleeding. During this operation the level of hydraulic fluid in the reservoir should not be allowed to fall below half full, otherwise air will be drawn in again.

There are two methods of approaching this operation. Either the car can be jacked up and supported on axle stands, or the gearbox tunnel can be removed from inside the car (Chapter 6). Both methods are equally easy to perform, but slightly better access is gained by removing the gearbox tunnel.

1 Obtain a clean and dry glass jam jar, plastic tubing at least 12ins (305mm) long and able to fit tightly over the bleed nipple

of the slave cylinder, a supply of Castrol Girling Brake Fluid and someone to help (Fig.5.1).

2 Check that the master cylinder reservoir is full, and if not, fill it, and cover the bottom inch (25mm) of the jar with hydraulic fluid.

3 Remove the rubber dust cap from the bleed nipple on the slave cylinder and, with a suitable spanner, open the bleed nipple one turn.

4 Place one end of the tube securely over the nipple and insert the other end in the jam jar so that the tube orifice is below the level of the fluid.

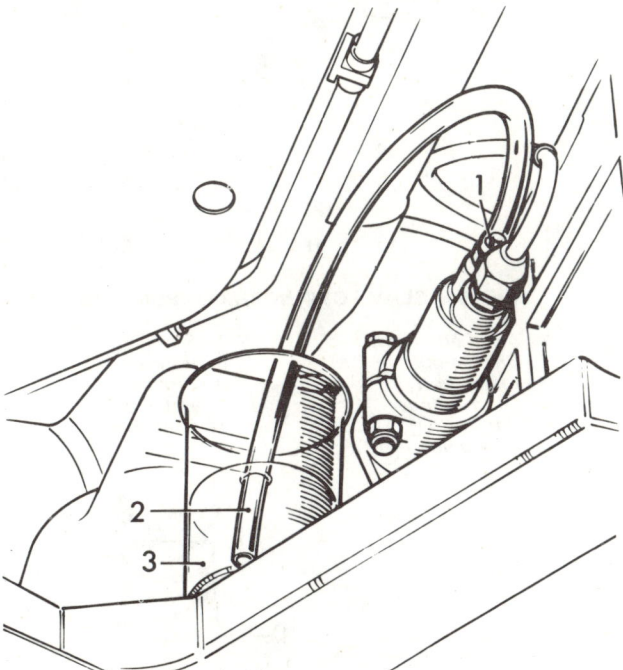

FIG. 5.1. BLEEDING THE CLUTCH HYDRAULIC SYSTEM

1 Slave cylinder bleed nipple   3 Clean glass container
2 Plastic or rubber tubing

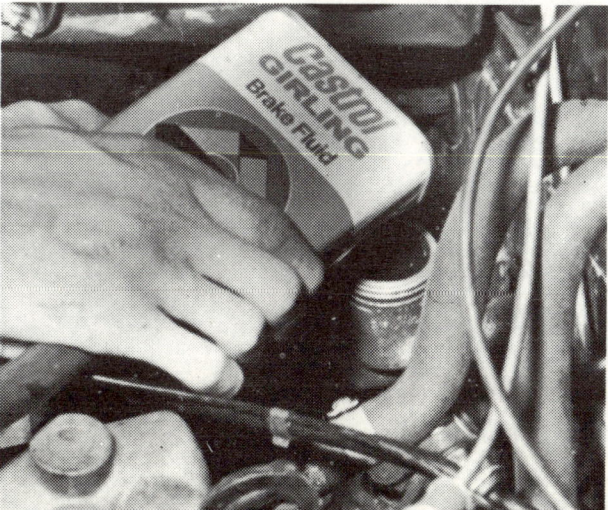

2.7 Topping up the clutch reservoir

5 The assistant should now pump the clutch pedal up and down quickly until the air bubbles cease to emerge from the end of the tubing. He should also check the reservoir frequently to ensure that the hydraulic fluid does not drop too far, so letting air into the system.

6 When no more air bubbles appear, tighten the bleed nipple on the downstroke.

7 Replace the rubber dust cap over the bleed nipple. NOTE: Never use the fluid bled from the hydraulic system immediately, for topping up the master cylinder, but allow to stand for at least twenty-four hours in a sealed air tight container to allow the minute air bubbles held in suspension to escape (photo).

3 Clutch slave cylinder - removal and refitting

The removal of the slave cylinder can be facilitated by driving the car up on a ramp, or jacking up the front end and supporting it on axle stands.

1 Before removing the slave cylinder, take off the master cylinder cap and place a piece of thin polythene over the top of the master cylinder. Screw down the cap tightly. This should prevent the fluid having to be drained off prior to slave cylinder removal.

2 Disconnect the hydraulic pipe from the slave cylinder inlet and ease it out of the way.

3 Unscrew the clamp nut sufficiently to pull the slave cylinder out of its housing, (Fig.5.2).

4 Replacement is the reversal of the removal instructions. Remember to centralise the push rod in the housing before fitting the slave cylinder in position. Line up the groove in the slave cylinder body with the clamp bolt hole and tighten the clamp bolt. Reconnect the hydraulic pipe line.

4 Clutch slave cylinder - dismantling, examination and re-assembly

1 Clean the exterior of the slave cylinder using a dry non-fluffy rag.

2 Carefully ease back the dust cover (11), (Fig.5.3), and lift away, together with the retainer (10).

3 Using pair of pointed pliers, extract the circlip (9) and, if possible, shake out the piston and seal assembly (8,7). If a low pressure air jet is available, the piston and seal may be ejected using this method. Place a rag over the open end so that when the piston is ejected it does not fly out.

4 Remove the piston seal using a non-metal pointed rod or fingers. Do not use a metal screwdriver as this could scratch the piston. Note which way round the seal is fitted. Remove the spring (5).

5 Inspect the inside of the cylinder for score marks caused by impurities in the hydraulic fluid. If there are any found, the cylinder and piston will require renewal.

6 If the cylinder is sound, thoroughly clean it out with fresh hydraulic fluid.

7 The old rubber seal will probably be swollen and visibly worn. Smear the new rubber seal with fresh hydraulic fluid and refit to the stem of the piston ensuring that the smaller periphery, or back of the seal, is against the piston. Insert the spring ensuring the small end is towards the piston.

8 Wet the piston and seal in fresh hydraulic fluid and insert the piston and seal into the bore of the cylinder. Gently ease the **edge** of the seal into the bore so that it does not roll over.

9 Refit the circlip (10) and then the dust cover (11). The slave cylinder is now ready for refitting.

5 Clutch master cylinder - removal and refitting

1 Wipe the top of the clutch master cylinder and remove the filler cap. Place some polythene sheet over the reservoir to stop

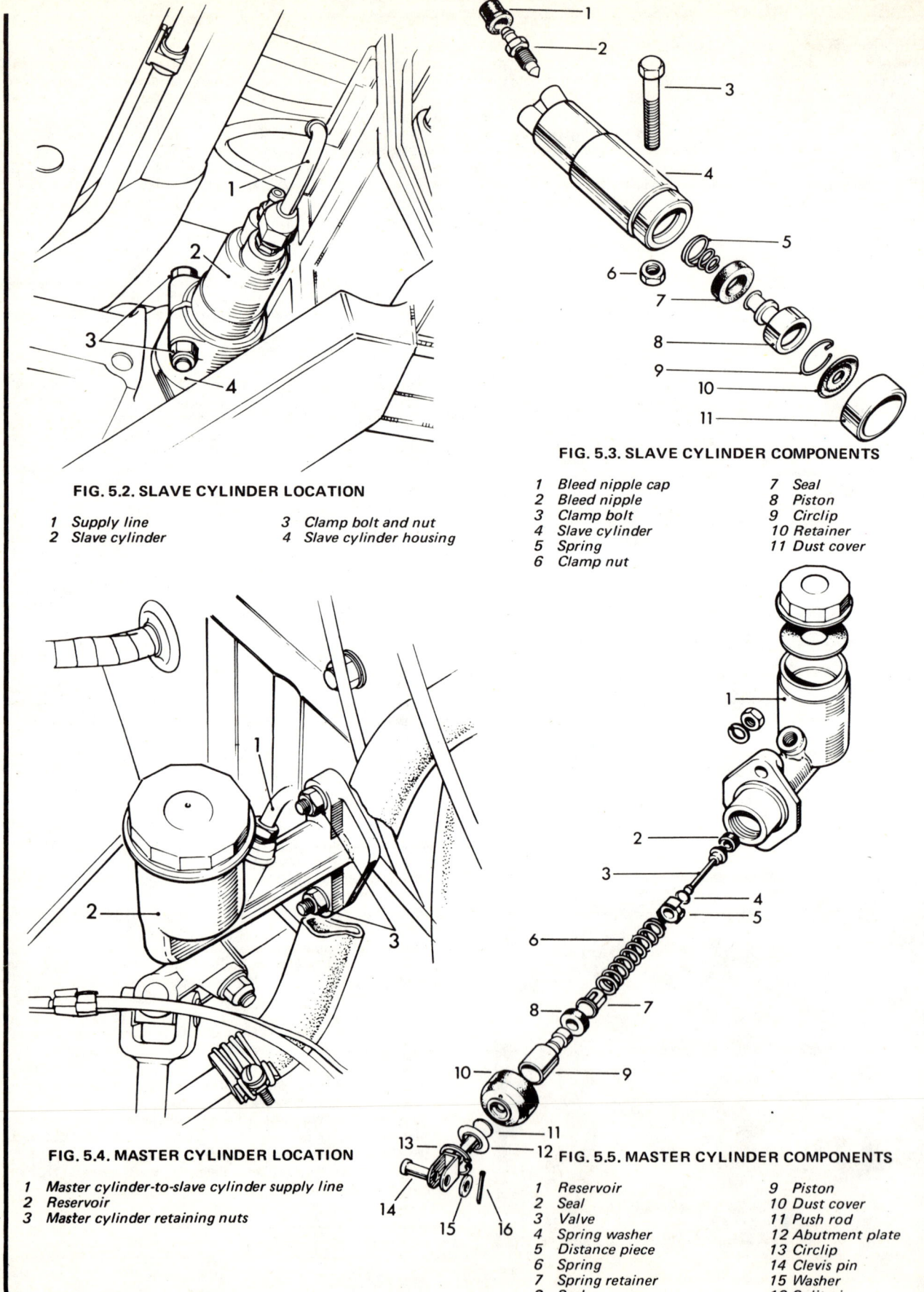

FIG. 5.2. SLAVE CYLINDER LOCATION

1 Supply line   3 Clamp bolt and nut
2 Slave cylinder   4 Slave cylinder housing

FIG. 5.3. SLAVE CYLINDER COMPONENTS

1 Bleed nipple cap   7 Seal
2 Bleed nipple   8 Piston
3 Clamp bolt   9 Circlip
4 Slave cylinder   10 Retainer
5 Spring   11 Dust cover
6 Clamp nut

FIG. 5.4. MASTER CYLINDER LOCATION

1 Master cylinder-to-slave cylinder supply line
2 Reservoir
3 Master cylinder retaining nuts

FIG. 5.5. MASTER CYLINDER COMPONENTS

1 Reservoir   9 Piston
2 Seal   10 Dust cover
3 Valve   11 Push rod
4 Spring washer   12 Abutment plate
5 Distance piece   13 Circlip
6 Spring   14 Clevis pin
7 Spring retainer   15 Washer
8 Seal   16 Split pin

loss of fluid once the hydraulic pipe is disconnected. Refit the cap (Fig.5.4).

2 Working inside the car, extract the split pin (16), (Fig.5.5.) lift away the plain washer and clevis pin (14) connecting the push rod to the clutch pedal.

3 Wipe the area around the union on the master cylinder and unscrew the union. Withdraw the pipe from the master cylinder.

4 Undo and remove the two nuts and spring washers securing the master cylinder to the two studs on the pedal support bracket.

5 Very carefully manoeuvre the master cylinder from the bulkhead, making sure that no hydraulic fluid is spilled on the paintwork as hydraulic fluid acts as a solvent.

6 Refitting is the reverse sequence to removal. It will be necessary to bleed the hydraulic system as described in Section 2.

6 Clutch master cylinder - dismantling, examination and re-assembly

If a replacement master cylinder is to be fitted , it will be necessary to lubricate the seals before fitting to the car as they have a protective coating when originally assembled. Remove the blanking plug from the hydraulic pipe union seating. Ease back and remove the pushrod dust cover so that clean hydraulic fluid can be injected at these points. Operate the piston several times so that the fluid will spread over all the internal working surfaces.

If the master cylinder is to be dismantled after removal, proceed as follows:

1 Ease back the pushrod cover (10), (Fig.5.5.) and remove the circlip (13) so that the pushrod (11) and dished washer can be withdrawn. This exposes the plunger (9) with a seal (8) attached, and thus must be removed as a unit. The assembly is separated by lifting the retainer leaf (7) over the shouldered end of the plunger. The seal (8) should then be eased off using the fingers only.

2 Depress the plunger retaining spring (6) allowing the valve stem (3) to slide through the keyhole in the retainer thus releasing the tension in the spring.

3 Detach the valve spacer distance piece (5) taking care of the spring dished washer (4) which will be found under the valve head.

4 Remove the valve seal (2) from the valve shank (3).

5 Examine the bore of the cylinder carefully for any signs of scores or ridges and, if this is found to be smooth all over, new seals can be fitted. If there is any doubt of the condition of the bore then a new cylinder must be fitted.

6 If examination of the seals shows them to be apparently oversize or swollen, or very loose in the plunger, suspect oil contamination in the system. Ordinary lubricating oil will swell these rubber seals, and if one is found to be swollen it is reasonable to assume that all seals in the clutch hydraulic system will need attention.

7 Thoroughly clean all parts in either Castrol Girling Cleaning Fluid or Industrial methylated spirits. Ensure that the by-pass ports are clean.

8 All components should be assembled wet by dipping in clean brake fluid. Fit a new valve seal (2) the correct way round so that the flat side is seating on the valve head. Place the spring dished washers (4) with the dome against the underside of the valve head. Hold it in position with the valve spacer distance piece (5) ensuring that the legs face towards the valve seal (2).

9 Replace the plunger return spring (6) centrally on the spacer, insert the retainer (7) into the spring and depress until the valve stem engages in the keyhole of the retainer.

10 Ensure that the spring is central on the spacer before fitting a new plunger seal (8) onto the plunger with the flat face against the face of the plunger.

11 Insert the reduced end of the plunger (9) into the retainer (7) until the leaf engages under the shoulder of the plunger , and press home the leaf.

12 Check that the master cylinder bore is clean and smear with clean hydraulic fluid. With the plunger suitably wetted with hydraulic fluid, carefully insert the assembly into the bore with the valve end first. Ease the lips of the plunger seal carefully into the bore.

13 Replace the pushrod (11) and refit the circlip (13) into the groove in the cylinder body. Smear the sealing areas of the dust cover with Girling Rubber Grease and pack the cover (10) with the rubber grease so as to act as a dust trap. Fit the cover to the master cylinder body. The master cylinder is now ready for refitting to the car.

7 Clutch - removal, inspection and replacement

1 Remove the gearbox as described in Chapter 6.

2 Mark the clutch cover and flywheel so that the clutch may be refitted in its original position, unless it is to be renewed. The clutch cover, pressure plate and diaphragm spring assembly must be replaced as a unit if it is found to be faulty. Only the driven plate is able to be replaced as a separate entity.

3 Progressively slacken the six pressure plate to flywheel mating bolts, a turn at a time so releasing them evenly. As they are being released, check that the pressure plate flange is not binding on the dowels, otherwise it could fly off causing an accident.

4 Lift away the six bolts and spring washers, followed by the cover assembly and driven plate. Note which way round the driven plate is fitted. The longer boss is facing towards the gearbox.

5 Using stiff brush or clean rags, clean the face of the flywheel, the pressure plate assembly and the driven plate. Note that the dust is harmful to the lungs as it contains asbestos, so do not inhale it.

6 It is important that neither oil nor grease comes into contact with the clutch facings and that absolute cleaniness is observed at all times.

7 Inspect the friction surfaces of the driven plate and, if worn, a complete new assembly must be fitted. The linings are completely worn out when the faces of the rivets are flush with the lining face. There should be at least 1/32 in. (0.8 mm) of lining material left clear of the rivet faces, or the driven plate is not worth replacing. Check that the friction linings show no signs of heavy glazing or oil impregnation. If evident a new assembly must be fitted. If a small quantity of lubricant has found its way onto the facing, due to heat generated by the resultant slipping, it will be burnt off. This will be indicated by darkening of the facings. This is not too serious provided that the grain of the facing material can be clearly indentified. Fit a new assembly if there is any doubt at all. It is important that if oil impregnation is present, the cause of the oil leak is found and rectified to prevent recurrence.

8 Carefully inspect the driven plate and flywheel contact faces for signs of overheating, distortion, cracking and scoring: if any serious evidence of scoring exists, then it will probably be necessary to replace the flywheel; if you simply replace the driven plate, you could very soon be faced with the same fault condition.

9 Mount the driven plate onto the input shaft and check for looseness or wear on the hub splines. Also check the driven plate cushion springs for damage or looseness.

10 Inspect the clutch throw-out lever assembly for wear, and obtain a new lever assembly if evident (Section 8).

11 Inspect the release bearing for wear as indicated by roughness or sloppiness between the inner and outer tracks.

12 Refitting the clutch components is the reverse sequence to removal but the following points should be noted.

13 Smear a light coating of high melting point grease to the bore of the input shaft.

14 Refit the pressure and driven plate assemblies making sure that the alignment marks previously noted, or made, are correctly matched.

15 Place the clutch disc against the flywheel with the longer end

of the hub facing outwards away from the flywheel. On no account should the clutch disc be replaced with the longer end of the centre hub facing in to the flywheel as on reassembly it will be found quite impossible to operate the clutch with the friction disc in this position.

16 Replace the clutch cover assembly loosely on the dowels. Replace the six bolts and spring washers and tighten them finger tight so that the clutch disc is gripped but can still be moved.

17 The clutch disc must now be centralised so that when the engine and gearbox are mated, the gearbox input shaft splines will pass through the splines in the centre of the driven plate hub.

18 Centralisation can be carried out quite easily by inserting a round bar or long screwdriver through the hole in the centre of the clutch, so that the end of the bar rests in the small hole in the end of the crankshaft containing the input shaft bearing bush. Ideally an old Triumph input shaft should be used.

19 Using the input shaft bearing bush as a fulcrum, moving the bar sideways or up and down will move the clutch disc in whichever direction is necessary to achieve centralisation.

20 Centralisation is easily judged by removing the bar and viewing the driven plate hub in relation to the hole in the release bearing. When the hub appears exactly in the centre of the release bearing hole all is correct. Alternatively the input shaft will fit the bush and centre of the clutch hub exactly, obviating the need for visual alignment.

21 Tighten the clutch bolts firmly in a diagonal sequence to ensure that the cover plate is pulled down evenly, and without distortion of the flange. The flywheel is prevented from turning by a spanner located between the teeth of the starter ring and a bellhousing stud.

22 Mate the engine and gearbox, bleed the slave cylinder if the pipe was disconnected and check the clutch for correct operation.

8 Clutch release mechanism - removal, inspection and replacement

In order to remove the clutch release lever and bearing it is necessary to remove the gearbox (Chapter 6) and the release mechanism is then accessible inside the bellhousing.

1 Using a thin metal drift, drive the operating lever pivot pin out of the bellhousing trunnions (1), (Fig.5.7), (photo).

2 Remove the operating lever (3) complete with the release bearing and sleeve (10, 9), (photo).

3 Place the operating lever on top of a vice and with the aid of a sawn off nail drive out the pins (8) (photo).

4 The retaining plugs (7) can then be partially levered out so as to release the bearing sleeve (9) and bearing (10) (photo).

5 Place the old bearing in a vice and carefully lever off the bearing sleeve (photo).

6 NOTE that the raised edge of the bearing is away from the sleeve and with the aid of a block of wood and a vice press the new bearing onto the old sleeve (photo).

7 Refit the sleeve to the operating arm, tap back the retaining plugs, and refit the pins. Replace the arm in the bellhousing, and finally drift in the pin and lightly stake it in place (photo).

9 Clutch pedal and support bracket- removal and refitting

1 Working inside the car, remove the parcel shelf as detailed in Chapter 12.

2 Working in the engine bay unscrew and remove the two nuts and spring washers that secure the bracket to the bulkhead.

3 Working inside the car, extract the split pin, plain washer and the clevis pin that secures the master cylinder clutch rod to the pedal.

4 Unscrew the bolt (6) (Fig.5.8) and remove, together with the spring washer (4), and plain washer (3).

5 Lift away the clutch pedal and support bracket from inside the car.

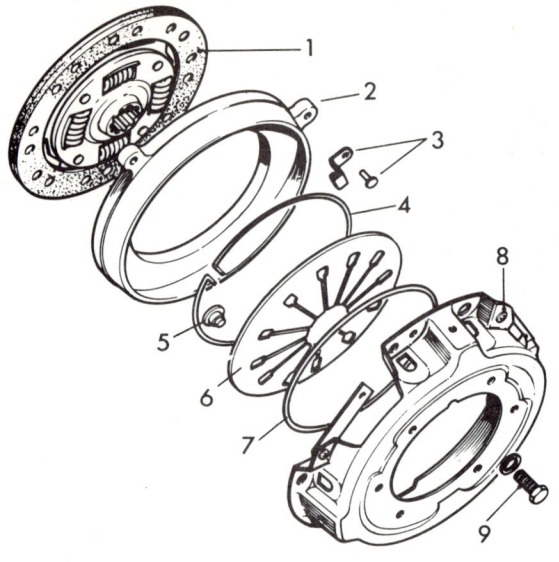

FIG. 5.6. CLUTCH COMPONENTS

1 Driven plate	6 Diaphragm spring
2 Pressure plate	7 Fulcrum ring
3 Clip and rivet	8 Clutch cover
4 Fulcrum ring	9 Cover bolt and washer
5 Rivet	

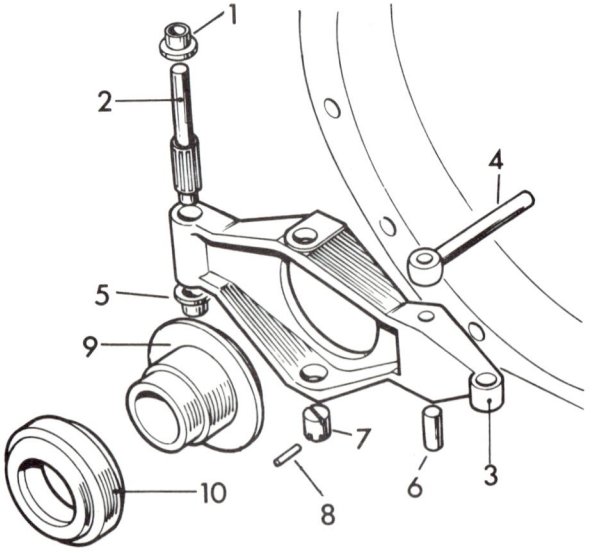

FIG. 5.7. CLUTCH RELEASE LEVER AND BEARING

1 Trunnion	6 Pushrod pivot pin
2 Pivot pin	7 Plug
3 Release lever	8 Retaining pin
4 Slave cylinder pushrod	9 Sleeve
5 Trunnion	10 Bearing

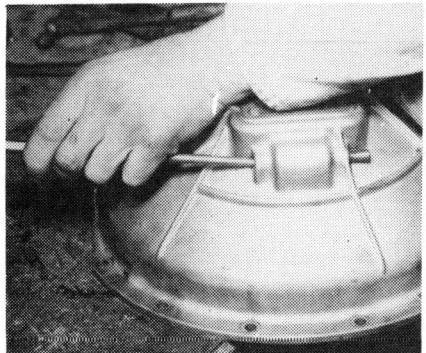

8.1 Drifting out operating lever pivot pin

8.2 Lifting out the operating lever

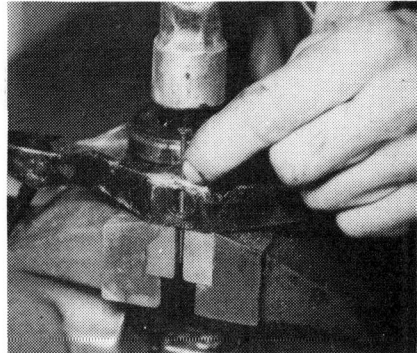

8.3 Driving out the plug retaining pins

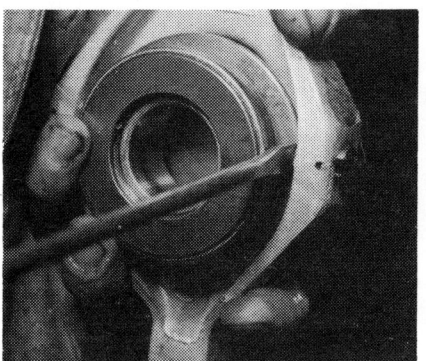

8.4 Levering out the sleeve plugs

8.5 Separating the bearing from the sleeve

8.6 Pressing a new bearing onto the old sleeve

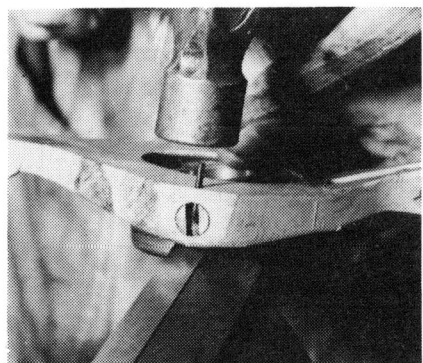

8.7 Refitting the pins that secure the sleeve plugs

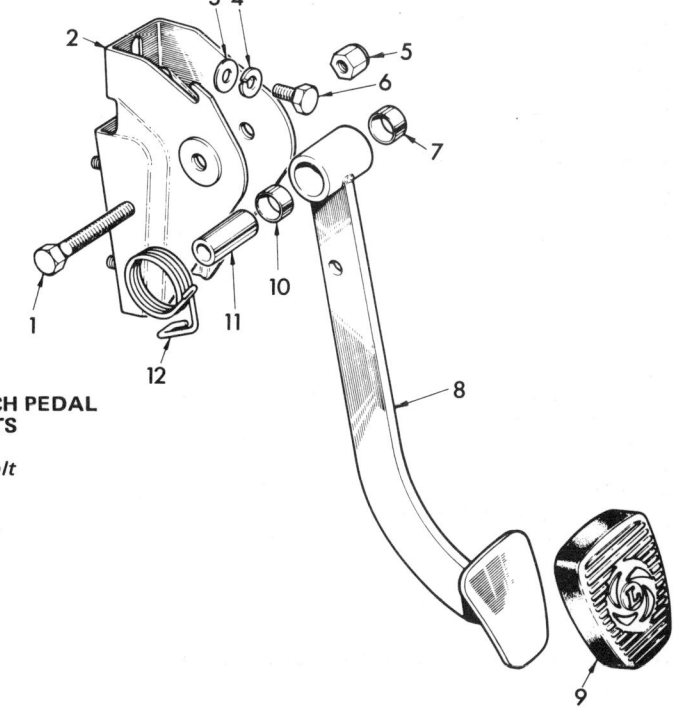

FIG. 5.8. CLUTCH PEDAL COMPONENTS

1   Pedal pivot bolt
2   Bracket
3   Plain washer
4   Spring washer
5   Nut
6   Bolt
7   Bush
8   Pedal
9   Rubber pad
10   Bush
11   Distance tube
12   Return spring

6   To dismantle the assembly, unscrew the nut (5) and remove the pivot bolt (1). The pedal assembly (8), return spring (12) and distance tube (11) may now be lifted away from the support bracket (2).

7   Check the bushes for wear by inserting the tube (11) and testing for excessive movement. If evident, the bushes may be drifted out and new bushes fitted.

8   Refitting is the reverse sequence to removal. Lubricate the bushes and pivot bolts with Castrol LM Grease.

10 Clutch faults

There are four main faults to which the clutch and release mechanism are prone:— clutch squeal, slip, spin and judder. They may occur by themselves or in conjuction with any of the other faults.

11 Clutch squeal - diagnosis and cure

1   If, on taking up the drive or when changing gear, the clutch squeals, this is sure indication of a badly worn clutch release bearing. As well as regular wear due to normal use, wear of the clutch release bearing is much accentuated if the clutch is ridden, or held down for long periods in gear, with the engine running. To minimise wear of this component, the car should always be taken out of gear at traffic lights and for similar hold ups.

2   The clutch release bearing is not an expensive item.

12 Clutch slip - diagnosis and cure

1   Clutch slip is a self evident condition which occurs when the clutch friction plate is badly worn, the release arm free travel is insufficient, oil or grease have got onto the flywheel or pressure plate faces, or the pressure plate itself is faulty.

2   The reason for clutch slip is that, due to one of the faults just listed above, there is either insufficient pressure from the pressure plate, or insufficient friction from the friction plate to ensure solid drive.

3   If small amounts of oil get onto the clutch, they will be burnt off under the heat of clutch engagement, in the process gradually darkening the linings. Excessive oil on the clutch will burn off leaving a carbon deposit which can cause quite bad slip, or fierceness, spin and judder.

4   If clutch slip is suspected, and confirmation of this condition is required, there are several tests which can be made:

a) With the engine in second or third gear and pulling lightly up a moderate incline, sudden depression of the accelerator pedal may cause the engine to increase its speed without any increase in road speed. Easing on the accelerator will then give a definite drop in engine speed without the car slowing.

b) Drive the car at a steady speed in top gear and, braking with the left leg, try and maintain the same speed by pressing down on the accelerator. Providing the same speed is maintained, a change in the speed of the engine confirms that slip is taking place.

c) In extreme cases of clutch slip, the engine will race under normal acceleration conditions.

d) If slip is due to oil or grease on the linings, a temporary cure can sometimes be effected by squirting carbon tetrochloride into the clutch. The permanent cure, of course, is to renew the clutch driven plate, and trace and rectify the oil leak.

13 Clutch spin - diagnosis and cure

1   Clutch spin is a condition which occurs when there is a leak in the clutch hydraulic actuating mechanism; the release arm free travel is excessive; there is an obstruction in the clutch either on the primary gear splines or in the operating lever itself; or oil may have partially burnt off the clutch linings and have left a resinous deposit which is causing the clutch disc to stick to the pressure plate or flywheel.

2   The reason for clutch spin is that due to any, or a combination of, the faults just listed, the clutch pressure plate is not completely freeing from the centre plate even with the clutch pedal fully depressed.

3   If clutch spin is suspected, the condition can be confirmed by extreme difficulty in engaging first gear from rest, difficulty in changing gear, and very sudden take up of the clutch drive at the fully depressed end of the clutch pedal travel as the clutch is released.

4   Check the operating lever free travel. If this is correct, examine the clutch master and slave cylinder and the connecting hydraulic pipe for leaks. Fluid in one of the rubber boots fitted over the end of either the master or slave cylinders, where fitted, is a sure sign of a leaking piston seal.

5   If these points are checked and found to be in order, then the fault lies internally in the clutch and it will be necessary to remove the clutch for examination.

14 Clutch judder - diagnosis and cure

1   Clutch judder is a self evident condition which occurs when the gearbox or engine mountings are loose or too flexible; when there is oil on the faces of the clutch friction plate or when the clutch pressure plate has been incorrectly adjusted.

2   The reason for clutch judder is that due to one of the faults just listed, the clutch pressure plate is not freeing smoothly from the friction disc, and is snatching.

3   Clutch judder normally occurs when the clutch pedal is released in first or reverse gears, and the whole car shudders as it moves backwards or forwards.

Chapter 6 Gearbox

Contents

General description 1	Gearbox - reassembly 7
Gearbox - removal and replacement 2	Gearbox cover extension - removal, overhaul and reassembly.. 8
Gearbox - dismantling 3	Gearbox top cover - removal, overhaul and reassembly ... 9
Mainshaft - dismantling and reassembly 4	Rear oil seal - removal and replacement 10
Input shaft - dismantling and reassembly 5	Rear extension - removal, overhaul and reassembly 11
Gearbox - examination and renovation 6	Gearbox - fault diagnosis 12

Specifications

Type ... ... Four forward speeds, one reverse with silent helical gears. Synchromesh on all forward gears. Remote control gear selection

Gear ratios

	Overall:	
Top, 1 : 1		4.11 : 1
Third, 1.394 : 1		5.74 : 1
Second, 2.158 : 1		8.88 : 1
First, 3.504 : 1		14.41 : 1
Reverse, 3.988 : 1		16.39 : 1

Laygear endfloat	0.007 to 0.013 in (0.18 to 0.33 mm)
Mainshaft 2nd and 3rd gear endfloat	0.000 to 0.006 in (0.00 to 0.15 mm)
First gear mainshaft endfloat	0.000 to 0.002 in (0.00 to 0.05 mm)
Oil capacity	1.42 pints (0.78 litres)
Oil type	Castrol Hypoy

Synchromesh hub springs

Axial release load: 1st/2nd	19 to 21 lb (8.6 to 9.5 kg)	
3rd/top	19 to 21 lb (8.6 to 9.5 kg)	

Torque wrench settings

	lb ft	kg m
Gearbox extension set screws	14 - 16	1.936 - 2.212
Extension to top cover studs	12 - 14	1.659 - 1.936
Flange to mainshaft	70 - 80	9.678 - 11.060
Operating shaft to gear lever	6 - 8	0.830 - 1.106
Reverse idler shaft	14 - 16	1.936 - 2.212
Speedometer sleeve attachment	14 - 16	1.936 - 2.212
Top cover attachment	6 - 8	0.830 - 1.106

1 General description

The gearbox is a constant mesh four forward and one reverse speed unit, with synchromesh fitted on all four forward speeds.

The input shaft and mainshaft are mounted in the casing on ball bearings and locate into each other on needle rollers.

The laygear cluster revolves on needle roller bearings on the fixed layshaft; endfloat is controlled by a thrust washer at each end fitted between the casing and the laygear. With the exception of reverse, all gears are helically cut.

Gear selection is by three forks running on three separate rails. The forks are held in their neutral and selection positions by spring loaded detent balls housed in each fork, which engage in grooves in the rails.

The selector lever operates the forks through a remote control which permits a short, positive action lever to be used.

The gearbox input shaft is splined and it is onto these splines that the clutch driven plate is located. The gearbox end of the input shaft is in constant mesh with the laygear cluster, and the gears formed on the laygear are in constant mesh with the gears on the mainshaft with the exception of the reverse gear. The gears on the mainshaft are able to rotate freely which means that when the neutral position is selected the mainshaft does not rotate.

When the gear change lever moves the synchromesh unit outer sleeve via the selector fork, the synchromesh cup first moves and friction caused by the conical surfaces meeting takes up initial rotational movement until the mainshaft and gear are both rotating at the same speed. This condition achieved, the sleeve is able to slide over the dog teeth of the selected gear thereby giving a firm drive. The synchromesh unit inner hub is splined to the mainshaft and because the outer sleeve is splined to the inner hub, engine torque is passed to the mainshaft and

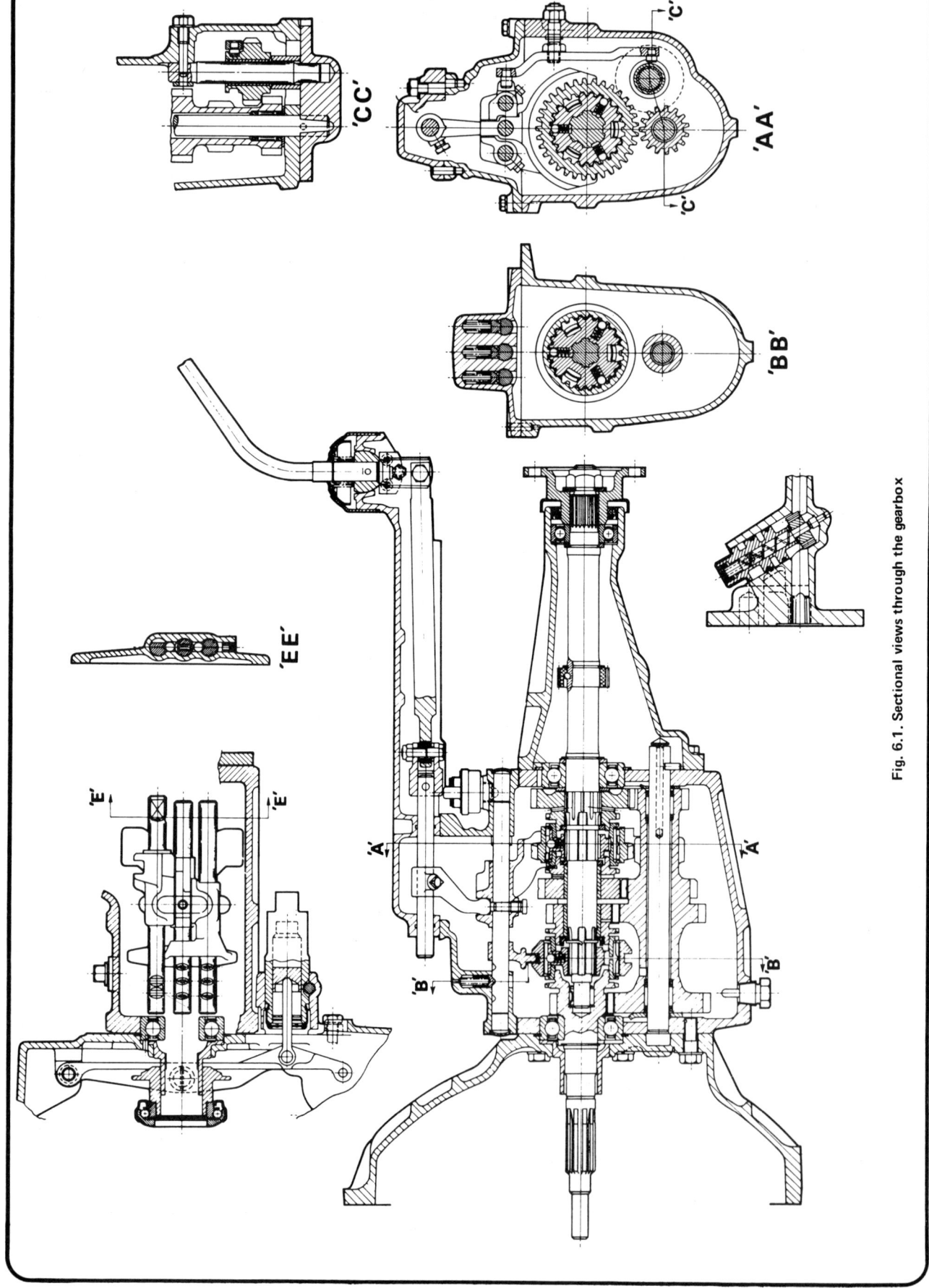

'CC'

'AA'

'C'

'C'

'BB'

'EE'

'E'

'E'

'A'

'A'

'B'

'B'

Fig. 6.1. Sectional views through the gearbox

propeller shaft. The bottom of the gearbox casing houses a drain plug, while a combined filler/level plug is on the side of the casing.

A cross sectional view of the gearbox and selector mechanism is given in Fig.6.1.

2 Gearbox - removal and replacement

The gearbox can be removed in unit with the engine, as described in Chapter 1, or, alternatively, as a separate entity. This latter method is relatively straightforward and should be used if only the gearbox requires attention.

If the gearbox rear extension, or the selector mechanism, is

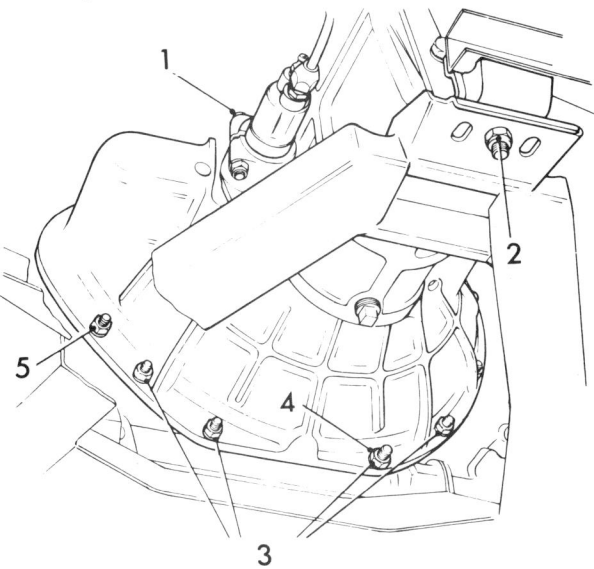

FIG. 6.2. GEARBOX AND BELLHOUSING SECURING BOLTS

1 Slave cylinder pinch bolts	4 Special locating nut
2 Mounting bracket nut	5 Starter motor lower
3 Bellhousing nuts	mounting bolt

2.13 Disconnecting the inner end of the exhaust pipe support bracket

faulty, there is no need to completely remove the gearbox since these units can be dealt with separately.

1 The vehicle should be driven onto a ramp or be jacked up and supported on axle stands or blocks. The maximum possible clearance between the car and the ground should be obtained to provide the easiest possible access.

2 Disconnect the battery, take out the carpets and drain the gearbox oil.

3 In order to remove the gearbox tunnel cover, it is necessary to remove the front seats and the parcel shelf first; details of these operations are given in Chapter 12.

4 Remove the reinforcement tube that straddles the tunnel by undoing the two set screws that secure it. Consideration should be given to carrying out operations 3 to 8 before the car is jacked up; it all hinges on what method of jacking you are using.

5 Unscrew the gear lever knob after loosening the locknut.

6 Remove the rubber grommet from the base of the gear level by releasing the four screws that secure the clamp ring and grommet to the structure.

7 Pull off the handbrake lever grip.

8 Remove the fifteen bolts and four nuts (set screws on early models) that secure the tunnel to the floor. Carefully break the seal between the tunnel and the floor and lift the tunnel cover over the gear lever.

9 Transferring your attention to beneath the car, scratch a mating mark across the propellor shaft front flange and the mainshaft drive flange and then undo the four nuts and bolts that connect them.

10 Disconnect the speedometer cable from the gearbox by undoing the knurled retaining cap.

11 Slacken the pinch bolt that secures the slave cylinder to its housing, and then withdraw the cylinder. There is no need to disconnect the hydraulic pipe to the cylinder, but ensure the complete assembly is tucked out of the way so that it will not hamper gearbox removal from the car.

12 Place a support beneath the engine sump ready to take the engine weight when the gearbox is removed. A jack with a block of wood between the jack head and the sump will suffice.

13 Disconnect the exhaust pipe from the support bracket bolted to the gearbox, then disconnect the inner end of the bracket from the gearbox mounting plate (photo).

14 Remove the nut and washer that screws the gearbox mounting bracket to the structure.

15 Remove the bellhousing - to - engine plate bolts that are accessible from beneath the car; the starter motor lower mounting bolt should also be removed as a matter of course during this operation. The remaining bellhousing retention bolts can be removed from inside the car, as can the gearbox rear mounting bracket.

16 Working in the engine bay, remove the starter motor upper mounting bolt. Remove the starter motor but note very carefully the number of spacers and distance pieces used.

17 The gearbox is now free to be manoeuvered out from inside the car. It may be necessary to raise the rear of the engine slightly to facilitate removal. Never allow the weight of the gearbox to hang on the clutch plate splines.

18 Replacement of the gearbox is the reversal of the removal procedure, but the following points should be borne in mind:
a) The clutch friction disc must be properly centred if the clutch assembly has been disturbed (Chapter 5 refers).
b) The propeller shaft should be replaced so that the mating flanges line up in the same position.
c) The same warning given in paragraph 17 also applies during reassembly: the gearbox must not be allowed to hang un-supported on the splines of the input shaft.
d) When the gearbox is in position, refit the locating bolt and nut; this will assist in replacing the remaining nuts and bolts.
e) Do not forget to replace the oil.

3 Gearbox - dismantling

1 Before any dismantling begins, thoroughly clean off the

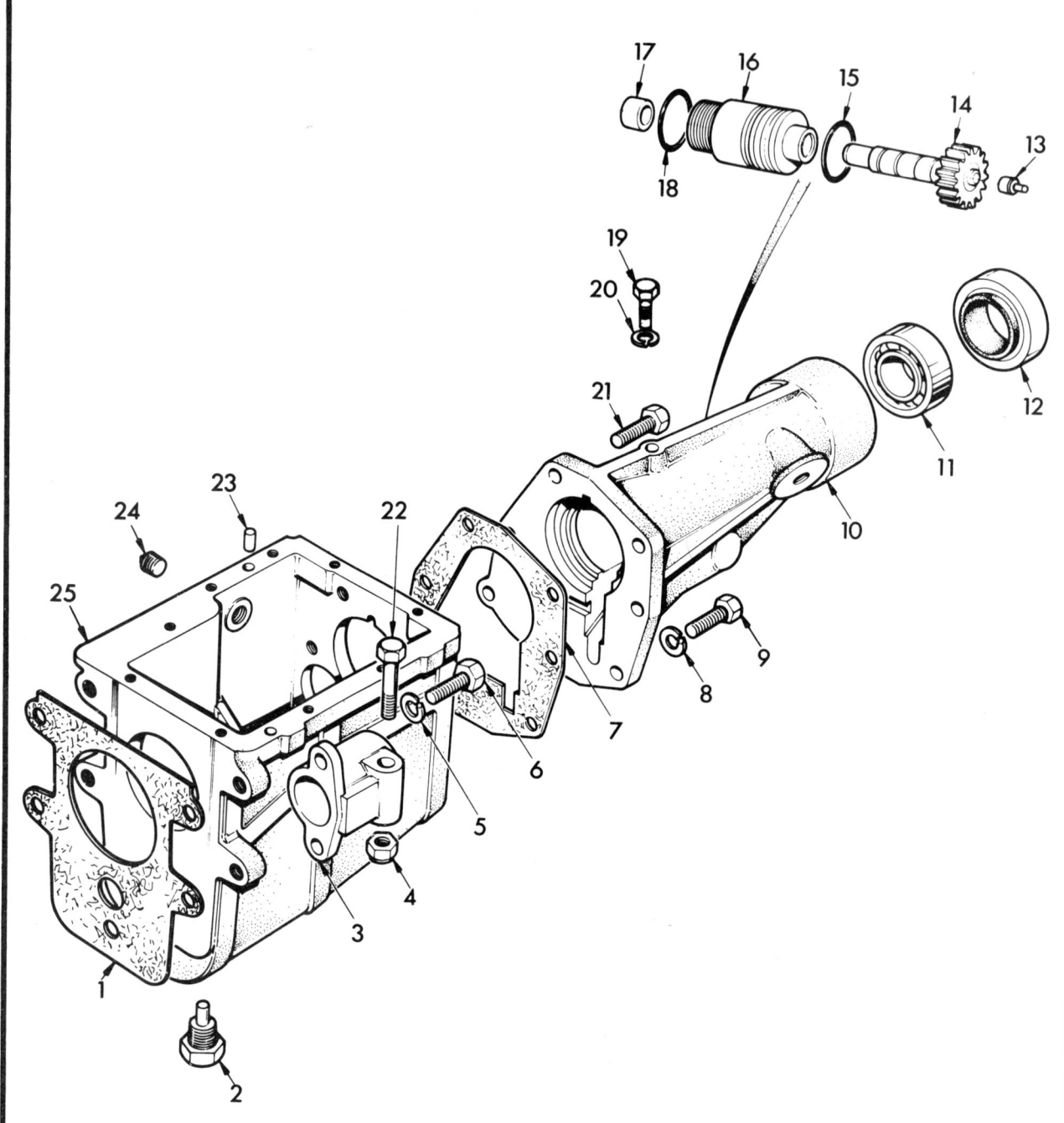

FIG. 6.3. EXPLODED VIEW OF GEARBOX EXTERNAL COMPONENTS

1 Joint washer	8 Spring washer	15 'O' ring	21 Setscrew
2 Drain plug	9 Setscrew	16 Speedometer drive	22 Pinchbolt, slave cylinder
3 Slave cylinder housing	10 Gearbox extension assembly	housing assembly	23 Dowel, top cover
4 Locknut	11 Bearing	17 Oil seal	locating
5 Spring washer	12 Oil seal	18 'O' ring	24 Screwed plug - oil
6 Setscrew	13 Thrust bearing	19 Bolt	filler level
7 Joint washer	14 Speedo driven gear assembly	20 Spring washer	25 Gearbox case

gearbox exterior with paraffin or a proprietary solvent. This will keep the working area clean and minimise the possibility of dirt and grit being transferred from the exterior to the interior. Undo the four nuts and spring washers which hold the remote control extension in place and lift off the extension and joint washer.

2 Undo the eight bolts which hold the gearbox cover to the top of the gearbox and lift off the cover.

3 The peg bolt which retains the speedometer drive housing is then unscrewed.

4 Pull the housing complete with the speedometer drive pinion out of the gearbox extension.

5 Place the mainshaft drive flange in a vice and undo the nut and spring washer which retains it in place.

6 Pull the mainshaft flange from the mainshaft.

7 Undo the bolts which retain the aluminium alloy extension to the rear of the gearbox. Note position of the longer bolt.

8 Remove the extension by tapping the underside of the mounting lug with a rawhide hammer. Lift the extension off the gearbox, together with the joint gasket.

9 Then lift the rear idler gear from the reverse gear shaft.

10 From inside the bellhousing undo the bolts which hold the bellhousing to the front of the gearbox.

11 Separate the bellhousing from the gearbox and place the former on one side. Note the single bolt with the copper washer.

12 Gently drive the layshaft out of the gearbox - preferably with a length of rod, 0.655 inch (16.6mm) in diameter and 6.5inch (165mm) long. This rod will then retain the needle roller bearings in the bore of the laycluster. The layshaft will have to be driven out from the front of the box since there is a restraining pin at the rear of the box. Now allow the laycluster to drop out of mesh with the mainshaft gear, into the bottom of the gearbox.

13 With a soft metal drift carefully tap out the input shaft, complete with bearings, forwards from inside the gearbox.

14 As soon as the bearing is clear of the gearbox casing lift the input shaft out.

15 Turning to the mainshaft, remove the centre bearing circlip and washer, and drive the mainshaft forwards into the gearbox, approximately 1¼ in. (32 mm).

16 Next, drive the bearing out of the casing from the inside. The mainshaft can then be lifted out from the inside of the casing. Place it on one side for dismantling later.

17 Raise the laygear so it is in its normal position and measure the end float with a feeler gauge. The laygear is then free to be lifted out.

18 Remove the reverse gear shaft by undoing the peg bolt and

spring washer which holds it in place.

19 Finally undo the nut and bolt and remove them together with the operating lever.

20 The gearbox is now stripped right out and must be thoroughly cleaned. The component parts of the gearbox should be examined for wear, and the laygear, input shaft and mainshaft assemblies broken down further as described in the following section.

4 Mainshaft - dismantling and reassembly

1 The component parts of the mainshaft are shown in Fig.6.6.

2 Lift the 3rd and 4th gear sychromesh hub and operating sleeve assembly from the end of the mainshaft.

3 Remove the 3rd gear synchromesh cup.

4 Using a small screwdriver ease the 3rd gear retaining circlip from its groove in the mainshaft. Lift away the circlip .

5 Lift away the 3rd gear thrust washer.

6 Slide the 3rd gear and bush from the mainshaft followed by the thrust washer. Note this is a selective thrust washer.

7 Slide the 2nd gear and bush from the mainshaft followed by the grooved washer. Note which way round it is fitted.

8 Detach the 2nd gear synchromesh cup from inside the 2nd and 1st gear synchromesh hub and lift away.

9 Slide the 2nd and 1st gear synchromesh sleeve assembly from the mainshaft. Recover the 1st gear synchromesh cup (photo).

10 Using a small electricians screwdriver lift out the two split collars from their groove in the mainshaft.

11 Slide the 1st gear and thrust washer from the mainshaft.

12 The mainshaft is now completely dismantled . Before reassembly the inspection and checking of tolerances detailed in Section 6 should be carried out. If it is considered necessary to remove the speedometer drive gear, remove the circlip and tap off the drive gear; recover the locking ball.

13 Before reassembly, ensure that all component parts are thoroughly cleaned.

14 Place the thrust washer against the back face of 1st gear.

15 Slide the 1st gear and the thrust washer onto the mainshaft.

16 Fit the two halves of the split collar into the groove in the mainshaft and push the 1st gear hard up against the collar (photo).

17 Fit the synchromesh cup onto the cone of the 1st gear (photos).

18 Slide the 1st and 2nd gear synchromesh hub and reverse gear

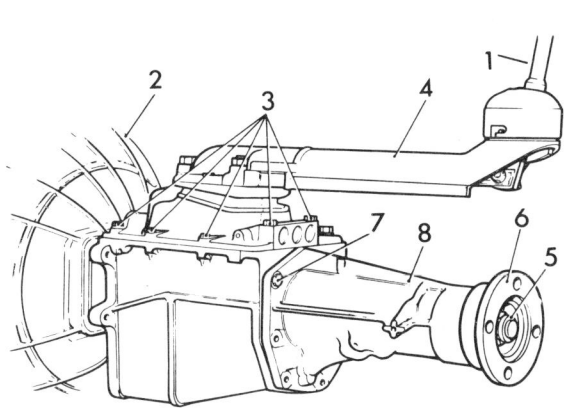

FIG. 6.4. GEARBOX COMPONENTS

1	Gear lever	5	Drive flange retaining nut
2	Bellhousing	6	Drive flange
3	Top cover bolts	7	Extension securing bolt
4	Top cover extension	8	Rear extension

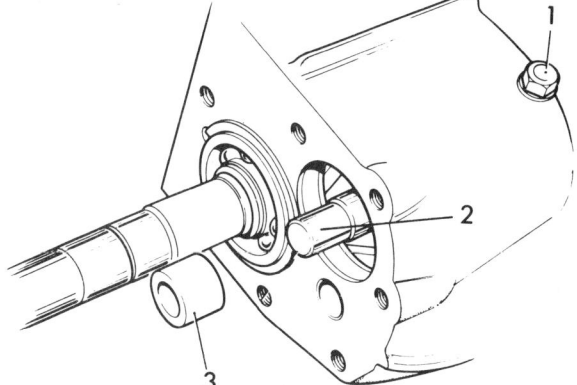

FIG. 6.5. REVERSE IDLER SHAFT REMOVAL

1	Idler shaft retaining bolt	3	Distance piece
2	Idler shaft		

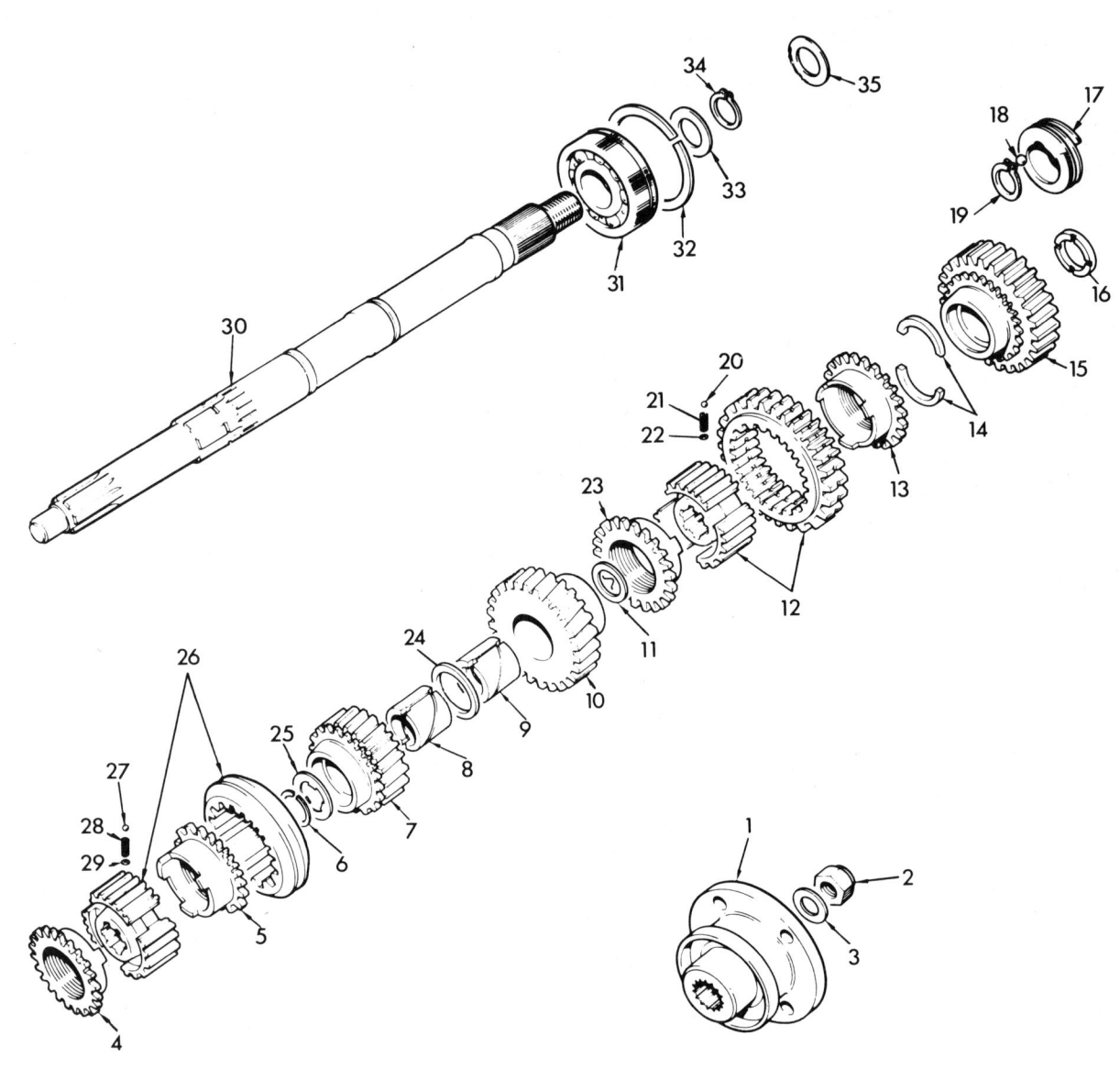

FIG. 6.6. EXPLODED VIEW OF MAINSHAFT COMPONENTS

1 Flange and stone guard	10 Gear 2nd speed	19 Circlip	28 Spring
2 Locknut	11 Washer	20 Ball bearing	29 Shim
3 Washer	12 Synchro sleeve assembly	21 Spring	30 Mainshaft
4 Synchro cup (baulking)	13 Synchro cup (baulking)	22 Shim	31 Bearing, mainshaft
5 Synchro cup (baulking)	14 Split collar	23 Synchro cup (baulking)	32 Snap ring
6 Circlip	15 1st speed gear	24 Thrust washer	33 Washer
7 3rd speed gear	16 Washer	25 Washer	34 Circlip
8 Bush 3rd speed gear	17 Speedometer driven gear (nylon)	26 Synchro sleeve assembly	35 Washer
9 Bush 2nd speed gear	18 Ball	27 Ball	

4.9 Removing the first/second synchro sleeve assembly

4.11 Remove the first gear and thrust washer

4.16 Locate the split collars

4.17A The synchromesh cup must be in an unworn condition (1st)

4.17B The first gear, split collars and synchro cup on the mainshaft

4.18 Align the 'large' splines

4.19 Now the next synchro cup (2nd)

4.20 Oil groove to the front of the mainshaft

4.21 2nd gear bush

4.22 Now 2nd gear wheel

4.23 A selective washer - 2nd and 3rd gear

4.24 The 3rd gear bush

sleeve on the mainshaft and engage it with the synchromesh cup (photo).

19 Fit the 2nd gear synchromesh cup to the synchromesh hub (photo).

20 Fit the 2nd gear washer onto the end of the mainshaft splines so that the oil groove face is towards the front of the mainshaft (photo).

21 Slide the 2nd gear bush onto the mainshaft (photo).

22 Fit the 2nd gear onto the bush on the mainshaft and engage the taper with the internal taper of the synchromesh cup (photo).

23 Fit the 2nd and 3rd gear selector washer (photo).

24 Slide the 3rd gear bush onto the mainshaft (photo).

25 Fit the 3rd gear onto the bush on the mainshaft, the cone facing the front of the mainshaft (photo).

26 Slide the 3rd gear thrust washer onto the mainshaft splines (photo).

27 Ease the 3rd gear retaining circlip into its groove in the mainshaft. Make quite sure it is fully seated (photo).

28 Fit the 3rd gear synchromesh cup onto the cone of the 3rd gear (photo).

29 Slide the 3rd and 4th gear synchromesh hub and operating sleeve assembly and engage it with the synchromesh cup (photo).

30 To replace the speedometer drivegear, turn the mainshaft until the ball detent is uppermost, replace the ball and fit the drive gear over the ball. Replace the circlip.

5 Input shaft - dismantling and reassembly

1 Place the input shaft in a vice, splined end upwards and, with a pair of circlip pliers, remove the circlip which retains the ball bearing in place. Lift away the spacer.

2 With the bearing resting on the top of open jaws of the vice and splined end upwards, tap the shaft through the bearing with a soft faced hammer. Note that the offset circlip groove in the outer track of the bearing is towards the front of the input shaft.

3 Lift away the oil flinger.

4 Remove the old caged needle roller bearing from the centre of the rear of the input shaft if it is still in place.

5 Remove the circlip from the old bearing outer track and transfer to the new bearing.

6 Replace the oil flinger and with the aid of a block of wood and vice tap the bearing into place. Make sure it is the right way round.

7 Finally refit the spacer and bearing retaining circlip.

6 Gearbox - examination and renovation

1 Carefully clean and then examine all the component parts for general wear, distortion, slackness and fit, and damage to machined faces and threads.

2 Examine the gearwheels for excessive wear and chipping of teeth. Renew them as necessary. If the laygear endfloat is above the permitted tolerance of 0.007 to 0.013 inch. (0.18 to 0.33mm) the thrust washers must be renewed. New thrust washers will almost certainly be required on any car that has completed more than 50,000 miles (80,000km). It is permissible to rub down the backs of the thrust washers to achieve the correct tolerance. The copper face must never be rubbed down (Fig.6.9).

3 Examine the layshaft for signs of wear where the laygear roller bearings bear on it, and check the laygear on a new shaft for worn bearings.

4 The three synchroniser rings are bound to be worn and it is false economy not to renew them. New rings will improve the smoothness and speed of the gearchange considerably.

5 The needle roller bearing and cage located between the nose of the mainshaft and the annulus in the rear of the input shaft is also liable to wear, and should be renewed as a matter of course.

6 Examine the condition of the three ball bearing assemblies,

4.25 Note the direction of the cone

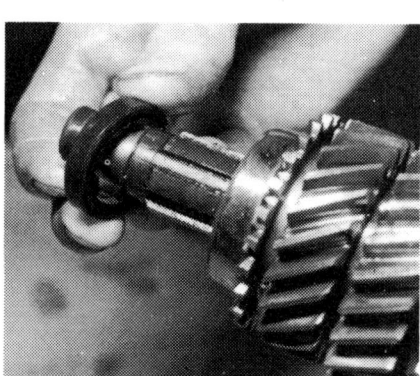
4.26 3rd gear thrust washer

4.27 Make sure it seats fully

4.28 Another synchro cup (3rd)

4.29 Meet the splines and mesh with the synchro cup

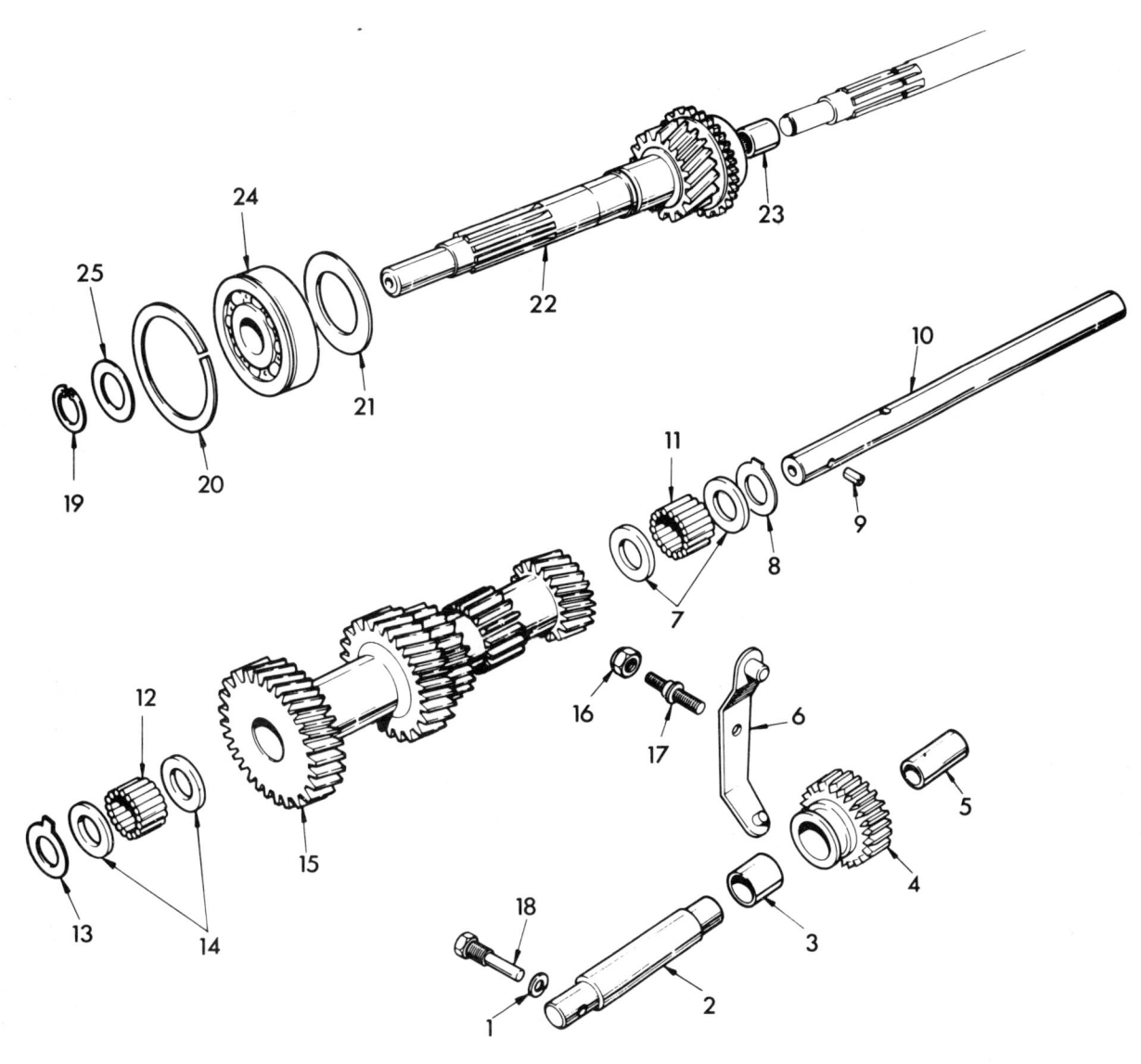

FIG. 6.7. EXPLODED VIEW OF INPUT SHAFT, LAYSHAFT AND REVERSE IDLER SHAFT COMPONENTS

1 Spring washer	7 Retaining ring	14 Retaining ring	20 Snap ring
2 Spindle	8 Thrust washer	15 Countershaft cluster gear	21 Oil thrower
3 Distance piece	9 Layshaft dowel	16 Locknut	22 Constant pinion shaft (input)
4 Reverse idler gear assembly	10 Layshaft	17 Fulcrum, reverse operating lever	23 Needle roller bearing
5 Bush	11 Needle roller	18 Bolt, reverse idler	24 Bearing
6 Reverse operating lever assembly	12 Needle roller	19 Circlip	25 Washer
	13 Thrust washer		

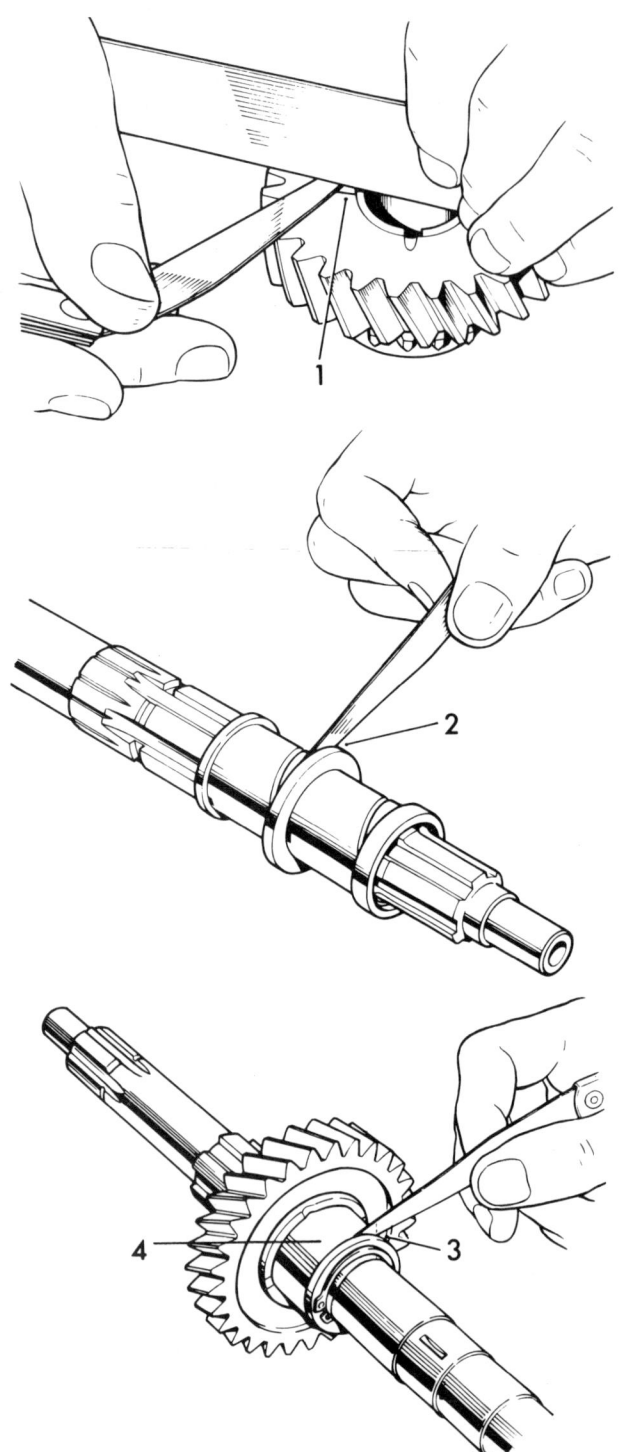

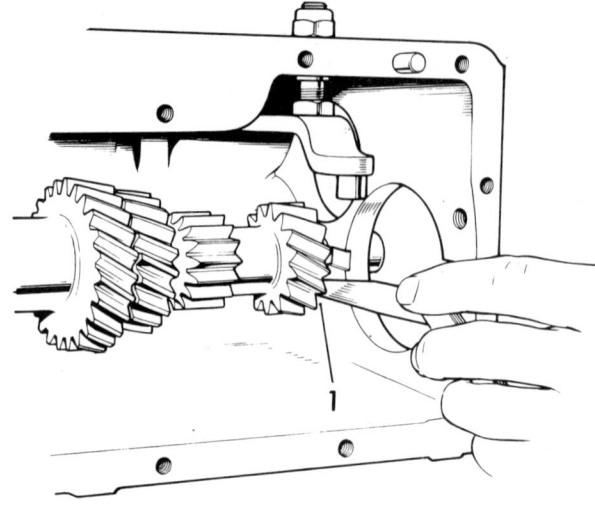

FIG. 6.9. CHECKING LAYSHAFT END FLOAT

1   *Inserting feeler gauge between layshaft gears and thrust washer*

one on the input shaft, one on the mainshaft and the other in the tail of the gearbox extension. Check them for noisy operation, looseness between the inner and outer races, and for general wear. Normally they should be renewed on a gearbox being rebuilt.

7   Examine the mainshaft bushes and fit them on the mainshaft to check for overall endfloat.

8   Fit the inner thrust washer onto the mainshaft, then one of the bushes, the washer, the remaining bush, the thrust washer, and finally the circlip. With a feeler gauge measure the endfloat between the inner thrust washer and the adjacent bush. This should be between 0.000 and 0.006 in. (0.00 and 0.15mm). If outside these figures experiment with alternative thrust washers until the endfloat is correct.

9   Measure the endfloat of the 2nd and 3rd gears on their bushes. The correct end float should be 0.002 to 0.006 in. (0.05 to 0.15mm). Either fit new bushes or lap the old ones to achieve this figure.

10 Fit the split collars, the first speed gear, the thrust washer, the bearing (or a distance tube of the same size to simulate the bearing) the distance washer and a circlip to the mainshaft. Measure the end float and adjust it to the correct limits of .000 to .002 in (.00 to .05 mm) by selectively fitting the right width washer.

11 To dismantle the synchromesh units, first wrap a length of clean rag completely round a unit and then pull off the outer synchro sleeve. The cloth will catch the spring loaded balls and springs which are bound to fly out. Compare the length of the old springs with new ones and replace any that are of incorrect length or worn. Note that an interlock plunger and ball is fitted to the second speed synchromesh hub.

12 The remote control gearchange is bound to be worn but this is dealt with in Section 8.

FIG. 6.8. CHECKING GEARBOX TOLERANCES

1   *Measuring the end float of the 2nd and 3rd gears to their bushes*
2   *Checking bush to thrust washer end float*
3   *Checking 1st gear bearing end float*
4   *Discarded bearing inner race*

7   Gearbox - reassembly

1   Screw the pivot pin into the reverse actuator until one full thread protrudes through the lever boss. Fit the actuator and pivot pin into the gear casing. Fit the plain washer and tighten the nut.

2   If the needle rollers were removed from the layshaft, replace them, holding them in with thick grease and finally retaining them in position using a tube of the dimensions given earlier. Fit

the front thrust washer into place in the casing so that its tag locates in the recess provided. Hold it in place with thick grease and centralize it by partially entering the layshaft. Lower the layshaft gear cluster assembly into position and press in the layshaft so that it ejects the tube and supports the gear cluster (photos).

3 Fit the rear thrust washer correctly into place and pass the layshaft through it. Recheck the layshaft endfloat in accordance with Section 6.2. Once the endfloat is satisfactory, press back the bearing retaining tube and allow the cluster to slide to the bottom of the casing.

4 Insert the mainshaft into the gearbox from the top. Hold it parallel in its approximate position and then press the centre bearing over the mainshaft until it can be drifted in position in the casing bearing housing (photos).

5 It will probably be necessary to place a lever in the position shown in this photo to support the mainshaft spigot when the bearing is drifted in position.

6 Fit the fourth gear synchromesh baulking onto the end of the input shaft.

7 Lubricate the needle roller bearing and fit it into the end of the input shaft (photo).

8 Fit the input shaft to the front of the gearbox casing, taking care to engage the baulk ring with the synchromesh hub (photo).

9 Tap the input bearing until the circlip is hard up against the front gearbox casing. Check that the mainshaft bearing outer track snap ring is hard up against the rear casing. Refit the washer and circlip.

10 Invert the gearbox. Fit the pin into the drilled hole in the layshaft and insert the layshaft from the rear of the casing through the layshaft gear assembly. This will push out the previously inserted tube. Line up the layshaft pin with the groove in the rear face of the casing and push the layshaft fully home (photos).

11 Fit the reverse gear shaft into the casing, align locating hole with the hole in the casing and insert the dowel bolt and washer.

Insert the idler and its bush over the shaft with the operating groove on the inside (photos).

12 Carefully engage the pin on the lower arm of the operating lever, with the groove cut on one side of the reverse gear.

13 Finally push the reverse gear fully home TAKE GREAT CARE that the reverse gear does not move forwards and disengage with the operating lever when the rear extension is being fitted.

14 If the gearbox is being rebuilt it is false economy not to renew the rear oil seal and ball race. Mount the rear extension in a vice and with the aid of a drift, drive out the oil seal and ball race from inside the extension.

15 Carefully tap a new bearing into place ensuring it is square in the bore (photos).

16 Then tap the oil seal into place with the sealing lip facing forward (photo).

17 Fit a new gasket to the rear face of the gearbox casing, and a new distance washer over the neck of the mainshaft so that it will be located behind the bearing in the rear extension (photo).

18 Carefully lower the rear extension into position tapping it home with a soft headed hammer if need be.

19 Replace the bolts and washers securing the extension in place.

20 Then refit the mainshaft drive flange: fit and tighten the locknut and washer that holds it in place (photo).

21 Refit the speedometer drive gear assembly making sure the two 'O' rings are in position in their grooves and that the hole for the lock bolt and washer is in line with the hole in the casing.

22 Fit a new gasket to the bellhousing/gearbox flange. If a new gasket is not to hand cut a new gasket from stiff brown paper. Lay the paper over the bellhousing endface, and holding the paper taut make a series of rapid gentle taps with a ball headed hammer. This will soon cut the paper to the desired shape. Proper gasket paper is even better than brown paper.

23 Offer up the bellhousing to the gearbox and fit and tighten the bottom bolt and copper washer (photo).

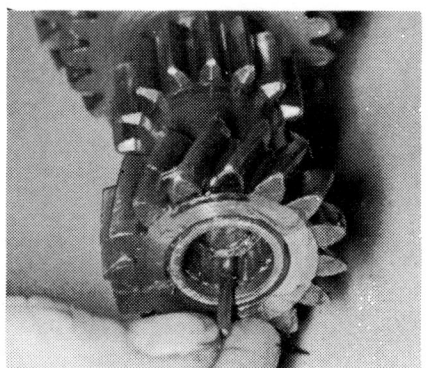
7.2a Use grease to hold the rollers

7.2b The tag must face outwards

7.4a Support the casing on a block of wood

7.4b Note the position of the large circlip

7.4c Drift in the bearing as shown

7.5 How to support the mainshaft spigot

7.7 Hold the rollers in the cage with grease

7.8 Engage the synchro hub properly

7.10a Note the pin next to his thumb

7.10b The pin in its groove

7.11a Drilled end first

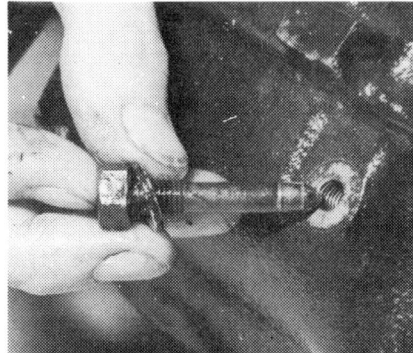

7.11b This is the dowel bolt. Note the shaped end

7.15a Face upwards for the bearing coding

7.15b Drift it in like this

7.16 Lip face inwards - tap gently

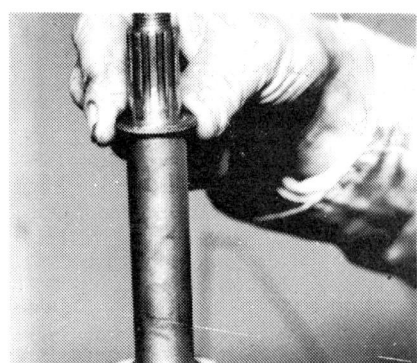

7.17 Fitting distance washer over the mainshaft

7.20 Offer up the flange

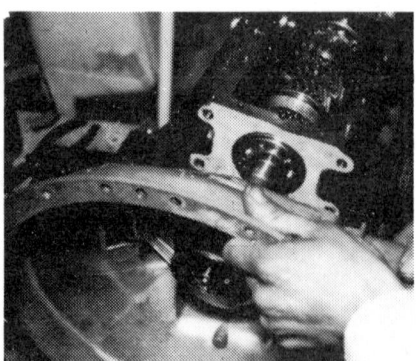

7.23 Mating bellhousing to gearbox

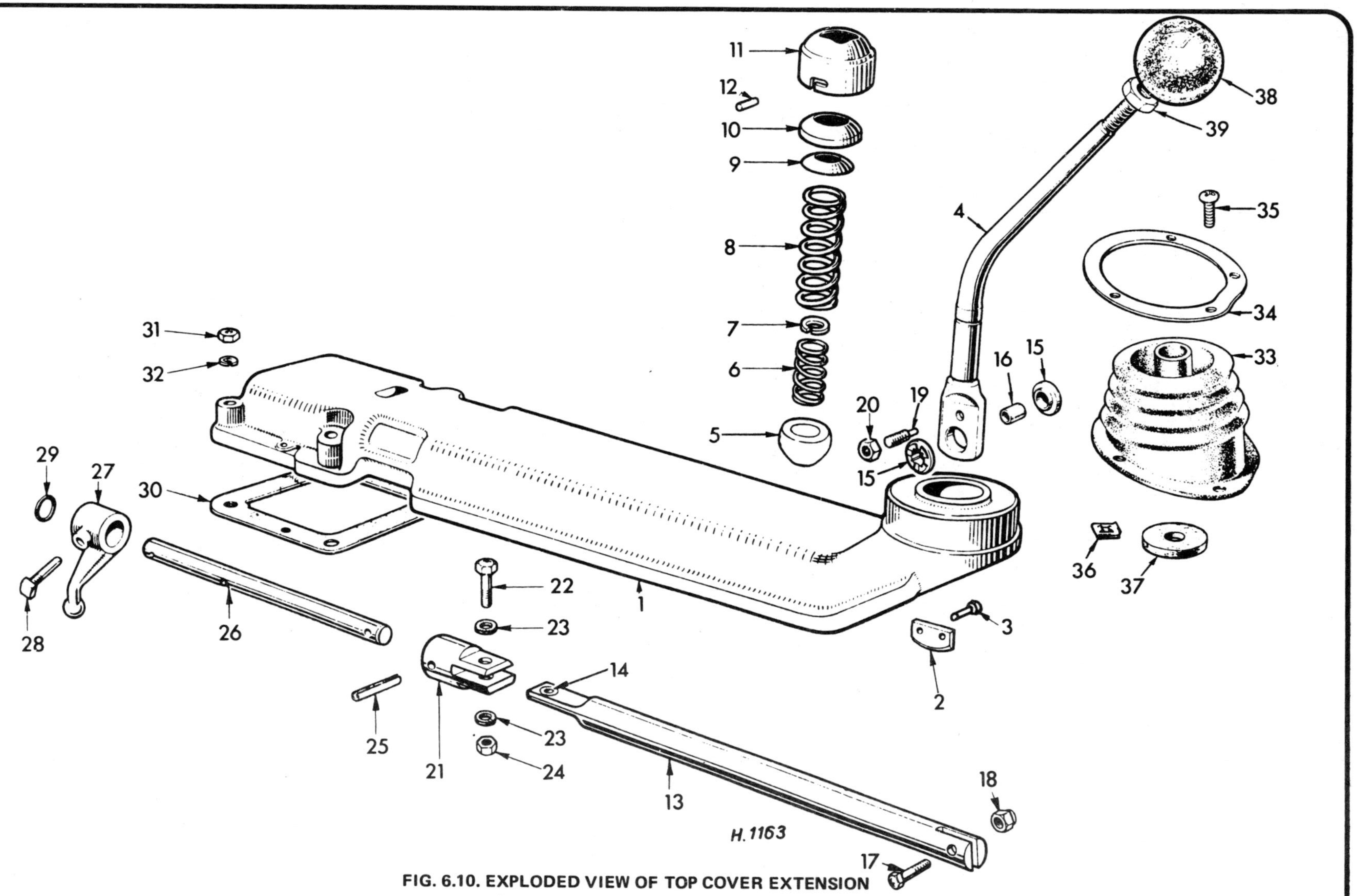

FIG. 6.10. EXPLODED VIEW OF TOP COVER EXTENSION

H.1163

1 Remote control extension	15 Gearlever bush	29 Oil seal
2 Reverse baulk plate	16 Pinch sleeve	30 Gasket
3 Rivet	17 Bolt	31 Nut
4 Gearlever	18 Nyloc nut	32 Lock washer
5 Spherical bush	19 Reverse stop screw	33 Boot (fitted to floor)
6 Reverse baulk spring	20 Lock nut	34 Boot retaining ring
7 Circlip	21 Coupling	35 Phillips screw
8 Cap retainer spring	22 Bolt	36 Nut
9 Dished inner washer	23 Aluminium washer	37 Rubber washer
10 Dished outer washer	24 Nyloc nut	38 Gearlever knob
11 Cap	25 Dowel	39 Knob lock nut
12 Dowel	26 Gearlever shaft	
13 Operating shaft	27 Internal gear lever	
14 Bush	28 Wedglok taper set bolt	

24 Select first gear on the top cover and the gearbox.
25 Fit the top cover with a new gasket; assemble the remaining bolts and washers and fully tighten according to the specifications.

8 Gearbox cover extension - removal, overhaul and reassembly

The gearbox cover extension is normally removed when evidence suggests that there is something wrong with gear selection rather than the gears themselves.
1 Remove the gear change lever as described in Section 2.
2 Working in the engine compartment, unscrew the nuts and washers securing the extension to the top cover.
3 Lift off the extension and remove the joint washer.
4 Certain items in the remote control gearchange are prone to wear and these should always be renewed when the gearbox is being overhauled. The items concerned are small and relatively inexpensive and comprise the plate, reverse gear spring, a smaller spring, the nylon ball, the bonded rubber bush and washers, and the bush and washers.
5 To renew the items on the gearlever press down and twist off the cover and remove the shield plate and larger spring (photo).
6 Undo and remove the nut and bolt which holds the gearlever to the rear remote control shaft (photo).
7 Lift out the gear lever and place it in a vice so the circlip which retains the small spring in place can be removed, and the spring and nylon ball removed (photo).
8 Fit a new nylon ball and spring and with the aid of a spanner which just fits over the gearlever tap the circlip home until it rests in its groove (photo).
9 Then fit a new bush and washer to the end of the gear lever (photo).
10 Undo the nut and bolt which holds the rear remote control rod to the fork (photo).
11 As can be seen in the photograph the old bush (bottom) had completely broken up. Press out the remains of the old bush.
12 This is most easily done in a vice using two sockets, one considerably larger, and one fractionally smaller than the bush. Place the sockets either side of the shaft and use the small socket to push the bush into the larger socket (photo).
13 Carefully press the new bush into place and reconnect the rod to the shaft using new washers. Fit the gearlever to the extension and refit the nut and bolt which secures the gear change lever to the remote control shaft (photo).
14 Then refit the larger spring and the remaining components to complete the assembly (photo).
15 If trouble had been experienced in selecting reverse gear, or it had been possible to select reverse gear without depressing the gear lever, the reverse gear stop bolt should be adjusted. If problems are still experienced after adjustment, the reverse stop bolt and plate should be replaced.
16 If the gearchange mechanism is still faulty after overhauling the extension, then the next step, detailed in Section 9, is to remove and service the gearbox top cover.

9 Gearbox top cover - removal, overhaul and installation

1 Select top gear and remove the top cover extension as detailed in Section 8.
2 Working in the engine bay, unscrew and remove the nine bolts that secure the top cover. Note that the two longer bolts fit at the rear of the cover, through the raised flange.
3 Remove the top cover and the joint gasket.
4 Position the selector shafts so that they are as far forward as possible and then drive out the welch plugs with a 1/8in (3mm) punch positioned in turn through the small holes just inside the end of the cover (photo).
5 Undo the threaded tapered locking bolts.
6 Push the reverse gear selector shaft out, followed by the other two. The two interlock balls, plunger, three selector plungers, and springs can then be removed. One spring and one

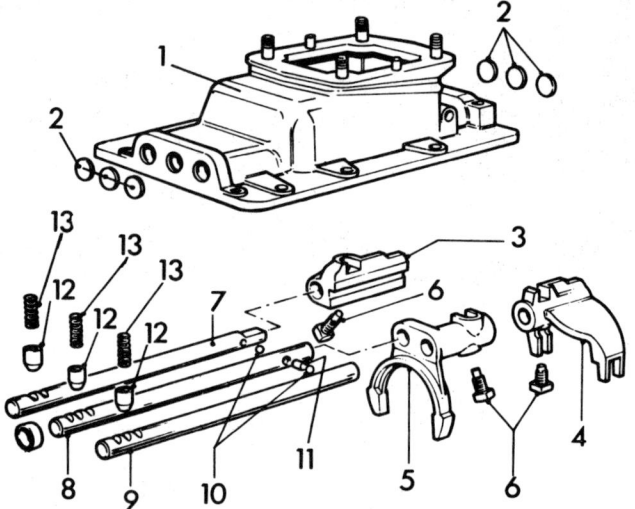

FIG. 6.11. EXPLODED VIEW OF TOP COVER

1 Cover	8 1st/2nd selector shaft
2 Welch plugs	9 3rd/4th selector shaft
3 Reverse selector	10 Interlock balls
4 1st/2nd selector	11 Interlock plunger
5 3rd/4th selector	12 Plungers
6 Taper locking pins	13 Springs
7 Reverse selector shaft	

plunger will emerge from each of the three holes indicated in the photo.
7 Reassembly commences by fitting the springs and plunger in place and then sliding the third and top selector shaft through the third and top selector fork in the top cover. Press down the selector plunger to allow the shaft to pass over it, and continue pushing the shaft home until it is in the neutral position, i.e., the plunger is resting in the centre one of the three cut outs on the shaft.
8 Replace the reverse gear selector shaft and selector fork in the same way ensuring it too is in neutral.
9 Then fit the interlock plunger to the first and second gear selector shaft, and slide the shaft into place in the selector fork, noting that the shaft also passes through the third and top selector fork. Before the shaft is fully home, drop the two interlock balls in through the centre selector shaft hole so that one ball seats each side of the transverse bore which connects the selector shaft bores. The centre selector shaft can then be pushed further in until the plunger is resting in the centre of the three cut outs, and the interlock balls and plunger are held by the shafts, (Fig. 6.12).
10 Refit the threaded tapered lock bolts and refit the welch plugs using sealing compound to give a leakproof joint.

10 Rear oil seal - removal and replacement

In order to fit a new oil seal behind the drive flange, it is necessary to disconnect the propellor shaft from the drive flange as described in Section 2.
1 Select first gear, then remove the drive flange locknut and washer.
2 Using either a puller, or gently tapping the inside of the flange right round the circumference, ease the flange out of the extension.
3 The rear oil seal will now be visible in the neck of the extension and can be prised out with some blunt-faced tool to avoid scratching the inside face of the extension.
4 Replacement is the reversal of the removal instructions. Dip the replacement seal in some light oil before reassembly and note that the protruding lip on the seal faces the bearing. Ensure that the seal enters the extension squarely and preferably use a tubular drift of the correct diameter to achieve the best results.

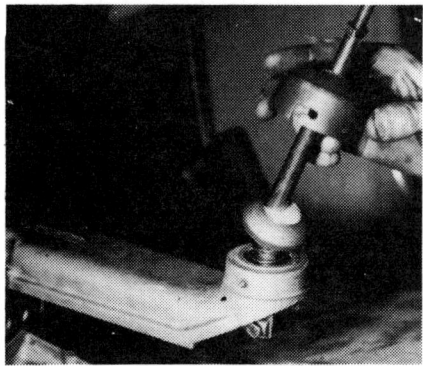
8.5 Removing gearbox extension cover

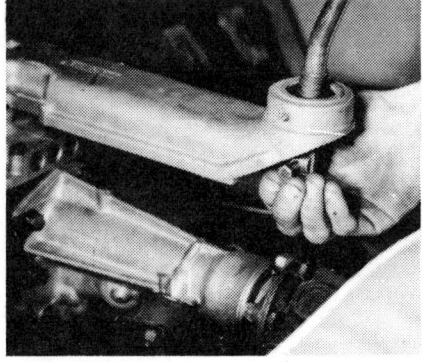
8.6 Removing gear lever securing nut

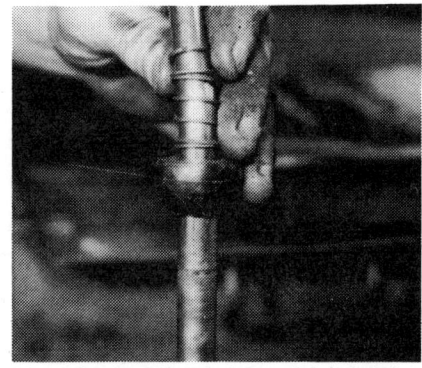
8.7 Lifting out the gear lever with integral components

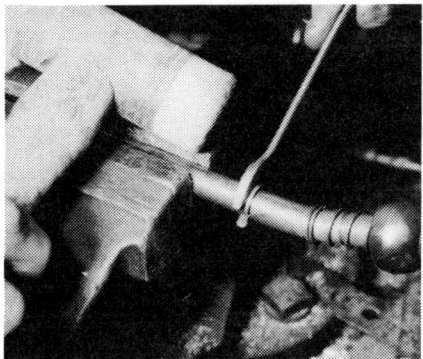
8.8 Refitting circlip

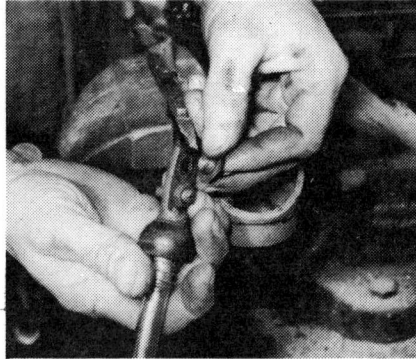
8.9 Fitting new bush and washer

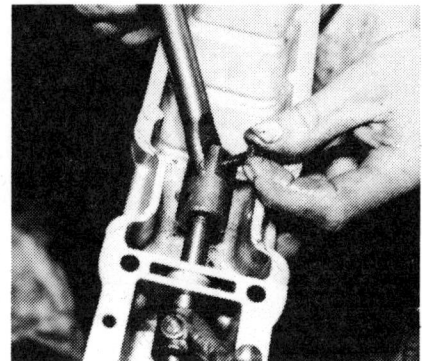
8.10 Disconnecting the remote control rod from the fork

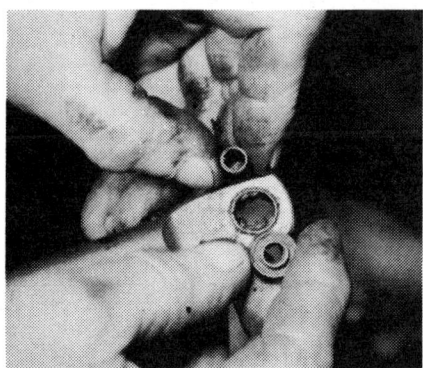
8.11 Showing a typical bush

8.12 Pressing out old bush

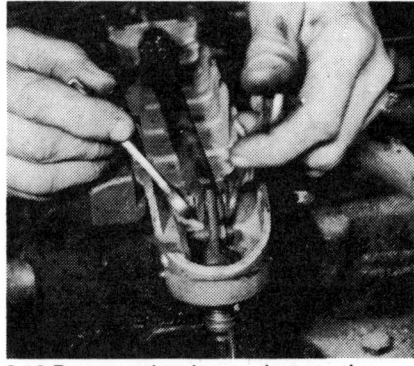
8.13 Reconnecting the gear lever to the extension rod

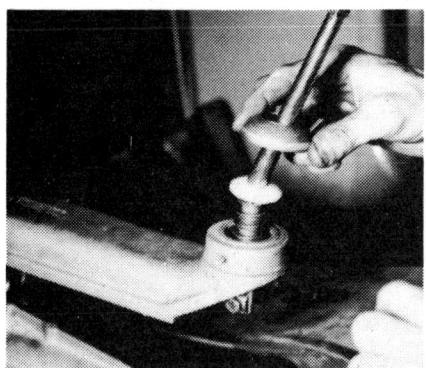
8.14 Replacing the larger spring and washers

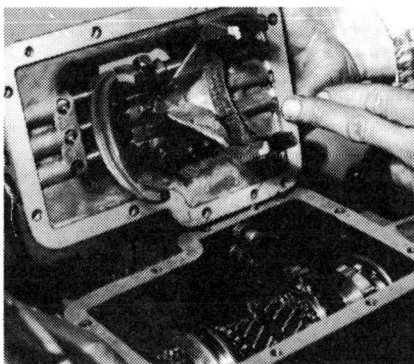
9.4 Positioning the selector shafts forward

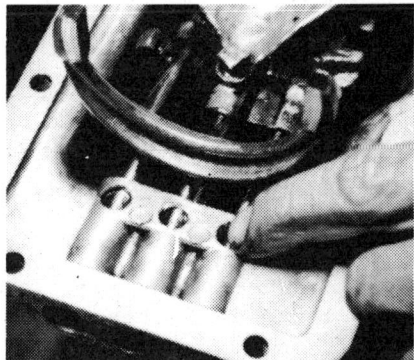
9.6 Showing the holes from which the springs and plungers will emerge

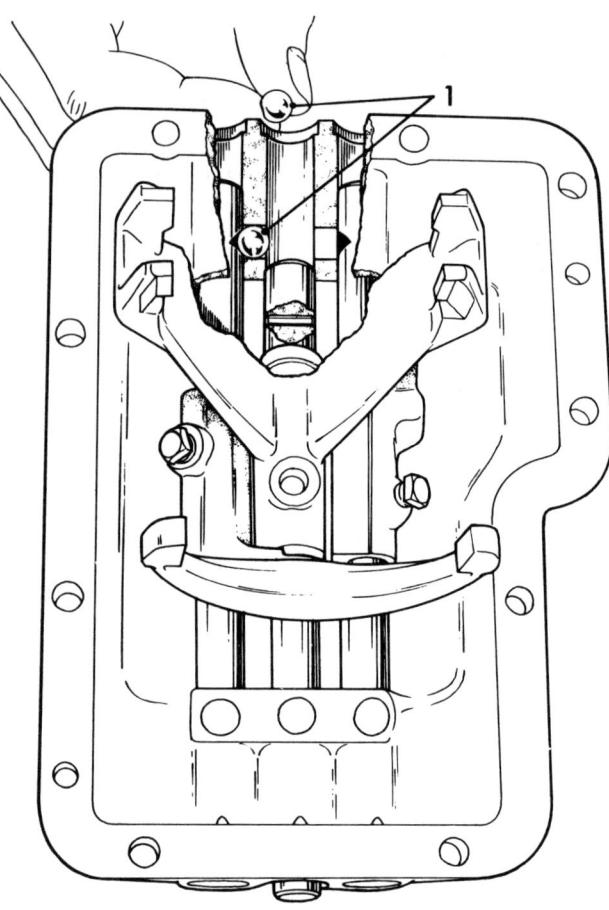

FIG. 6.12. INSERTING THE INTERLOCK BALLS

1   Interlock balls

11 Rear extension - removal, overhaul and reassembly

The rear extension houses the speedometer drive gear and the rear roller bearing; should either of these items malfunction, it is possible to remove the extension without removing the gearbox.

1 Jack up the front of the car and support it on axle stands or blocks. Drain the gearbox oil and disconnect the propellor shaft from the gearbox drive flange as described in Section 2.

2 Remove the drive flange (Section 3).

3 Support the engine under the sump, using either blocks or a jack with a piece of wood interposed between the jack head and the sump to spread the load.

4 Disconnect the exhaust support bracket from the front exhaust pipe.

5 Remove the gearbox mounting bracket by releasing the nut and washer that secures the rubber-mounted part of the bracket to the body sub-frame.

6 Disconnect the speedometer cable from the rear extension.

7 Remove the bolts and spring washers that secure the extension to the gearbox rear face. Retain the gasket thus released. This operation will also release the gearbox upper mounting bracket from its rubber- mounted main bracket.

8 Withdraw the extension over the mainshaft and place in a safe position.

9 The speedometer drive pinion can be removed from the mainshaft by releasing the circlip with a pair of circlip pliers, then sliding the gear off the mainshaft; take care not to lose the detent ball.

10 To remove the rear roller bearing it is first necessary to prise out the old seal and then drive out the bearing with a suitable drift.

11 Thoroughly clean all the components, especially the mainshaft and the inside of the casing. Inspect the casing for cracks, or oval bolt holes. Check that the area where the bearing and oil seal seats is free from scoring; if necessary rub down the area with a fine grade glass paper.

12 Replacement is the reverse of the above procedures: ensure absolute cleaniness when replacing the seal and bearing. Drift the bearing in position, ensuring that it is absolutely square with the face of the extension, then press in the oil seal with the lip facing the bearing. Fit the extension carefully over the mainshaft to avoid damaging the bearing or oil seal inner surfaces.

12 Gearbox - fault diagnosis

Faults in the gearbox can range from small buzzing noises and minor snags in engaging gears to serious faults such as loud whines, vibrations or difficulty in remaining in, or getting into gears in general. For serious faults the only thing to do is remove the gearbox and have a look, or just renew it unseen with a reconditioned or secondhand unit. For minor faults, other than those which can be positively identified as coming from the base of the gear lever, which can be easily got at, it is more a matter of how long the fault or irritating noise can be tolerated before doing something about it. Once something starts to wear to a noticeable degree other components may also deteriorate rapidly.

Unfortunately, the amount of trouble to rectify a minor fault will be the same as for a major one - removal and dismantling of the gearbox. One may save something on the cost of spares required but even this is open to doubt as accurate diagnosis can only be made when the gearbox is stripped. Some faults can go on for thousands of miles without getting noticeably worse or affecting anything else - a worn baulk ring for example. Failure of a bearing on the other hand could wreck the whole assembly in a few hundred miles. The list of faults and causes is intended to give the owner some help and guidance in deciding when to take action in the light of the degree of seriousness. All the faults require removal and dismantling of the gearbox except where stated.

Symptom	Reason/s	Remedy
Sloppy gear lever and rattles	Worn ball joint and pins or loose reverse stop plunger Loose selector lever in top cover over gearbox	Minor - can be repaired with gearbox in position. Serious - loose locking screw could drop in gearbox.
Ineffective synchromesh on one or more gears	Worn baulk rings. Worn blocker bars	Minor - can go on for many miles.
Jumps out of one or more gears	Weak detent springs Worn selector forks Worn engagement dogs Worn synchro hubs	Depends on how many gears involved and whether driving safety is affected.
Whining, roughness, vibration, allied to other faults	Bearing failure and/or overall wear	Major - could break up and lock transmission which is dangerous.
Noisy and difficult gear engagement	Clutch not operating correctly	See Chapter 5.

Chapter 7 Propeller shaft and universal joints

Contents

General description 1
Propeller shaft - removal and replacement 2
Universal joints and splines - inspection and repair 3
Universal joints - dismantling and fitting new bearings ... 4
Centre bearing - removal and replacement 5

Specifications

Note: *For details of the propeller shaft with the rear mounted splined yoke see Chapter 13.*

Type ... ...   Two piece tubular, supported by centre bearing
Universal joints sealed, needle roller bearings

1 General description

1 Engine power is transferred from the engine to the rear axle
and wheels through the gearbox and a two piece tubular propeller shaft supported in the centre by a totally enclosed bearing
which is bolted to the underframe. Fitted at each end of the rear
portion, and at the front end of the front portion, are universal
joints which allow for vertical movement of the rear axle. Each
universal joint comprises a four legged centre spider, four needle
roller bearings and two yokes (photos).
2 Fore and aft movement of the rear axle is absorbed by a
splined yoke in the front half of the propeller shaft. This sliding
joint must not be dismantled and excessive wear in the splines
will mean renewing the front half of the propeller shaft.

2 Propeller shaft - removal and replacement

1 As the two piece shaft with its centre bearing is rather an
unwieldy object it is better to remove the rear portion of the
shaft first.
2 Jack up the rear of the car, or position the rear of the car
over a pit or ramp.
3 If the rear wheels are off the ground, place the car in gear and
put the handbrake on, to ensure that the propeller shaft does not
turn when an attempt is made to loosen the four nuts securing
the propeller shaft to the rear axle.
4 The propeller shaft is carefully balanced to fine limits and it
is important for it to be replaced in exactly the same position
that it was prior to removal. Scratch a mark on the propeller
shaft and rear axle flanges, also on the flanges at the front end of
the rear portion, and the gearbox-to- propeller shaft flange, to
ensure accurate mating when the time comes for reassembly.
5 Remove the retaining nut and washer and disconnect the
right-hand side of the rear guard strap.
6 Release the four self-locking nuts and bolts that secure the
flanges at either end of the propeller shaft rear section. Remove
the rear section from the vehicle.
7 Release the nut, washer and bolt that secures the right-hand
side of the front guard strap to the floor panel.
8 Remove the four self-locking nuts and bolts that join the
gearbox flange to the propeller shaft front section flange. Some
form of support should now carry the front of the shaft while
the next operation is being carried out.
9 Moving to the centre bearing housing, remove the nuts, bolts

1.1a The front section of the propellor shaft bolted to the gearbox flange

1.1b A typical rear axle flange to propeller shaft joint (illustration
shown is of a rear type splined yoke)

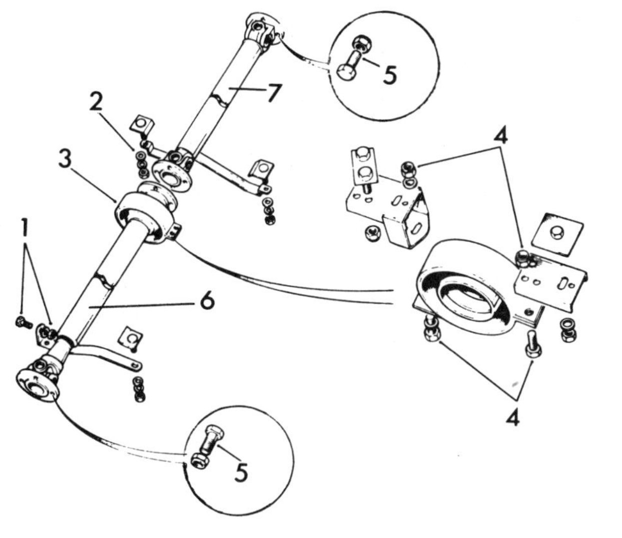

FIG. 7.1. PROPELLOR SHAFT COMPONENTS

1 Front strap righthand
   connection
2 Rear strap righthand
   connection
3 Centre bearing

4 Centre bearing mounting
   brackets
5 Drive flange bolts
6 Front section
7 Rear section

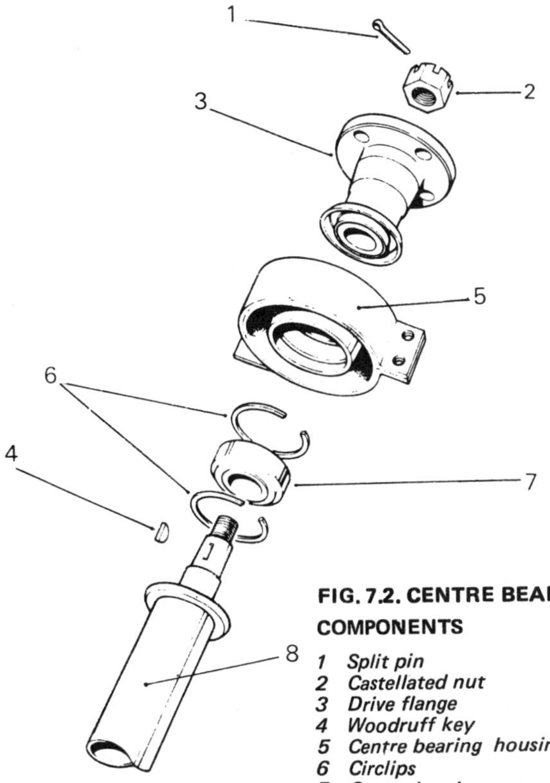

FIG. 7.2. CENTRE BEARING COMPONENTS

1 Split pin
2 Castellated nut
3 Drive flange
4 Woodruff key
5 Centre bearing housing
6 Circlips
7 Centre bearing
8 Front section of
   propellor shaft

4.1 Removing the circlips

4.2a Showing the two sockets needed to
press the cups out of the yoke

4.2b Using the sockets and a vice to
press out the cups

4.2c Lifting out the cups with a
pair of pliers

4.2d Using a hammer and socket as an
alternative method of removing the cups

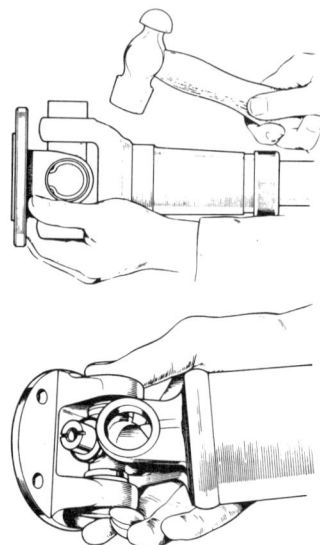

Fig. 7.3. Removing the bearing cup by lightly tapping the yoke with a hammer

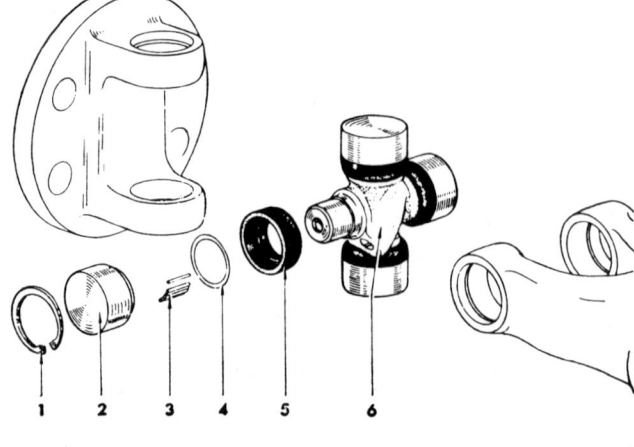

FIG. 7.4. EXPLODED VIEW OF A UNIVERSAL JOINT

1 *Circlip*   4 *Washer*
2 *Cup*   5 *Seal*
3 *Needle rollers*   6 *Spider*

and washers that secure the housing to the support brackets.
10 The front section of the propeller shaft, complete with centre bearing, can now be removed from the car.
11 Replacement of the propeller shaft is a reversal of the above procedure. Make sure that the mating marks made on the rear portion line up correctly.

3 Universal joints and splines - inspection and repair

1 Wear in the needle roller bearing is indicated by vibration or 'clunks' in the transmission, particularly when the drive is being taken up' or when going to over-run. (Backlash in the rear axle has the same effect, so check that also, if symptoms occur).
2 It is easy to check the needle roller bearings whilst the propeller shaft is still in position. Try to turn the shaft with one hand and grip the flange or sleeve on the other side of the joint with the other hand. There should be no movement between the two. If there is any, the bearings will need renewal.
3 The splines of the sliding yoke should be a smooth sliding fit, and no trace of rotational backlash or damaged splines should be apparent.
4 If worn, the old bearing and spiders will have to be discarded and a repair kit, comprising new universal joint spiders, bearings, oil seals, and retainers purchased. Check also by trying to lift the shaft and noticing any movement in the joints.

4 Universal joints - dismantling and fitting new bearings

1 Clean away all traces of dirt from the whole assembly and then remove the circlips which hold each set of needle roller bearings in position. If the circlip is tight, tap the face of the bearing cup inside it which may be jamming it in its groove (photo).
2 The bearing should come out if the edges of the yoke ears are tapped with a mallet. If, however, they are very tight, it should be possible to shift them by pressing them between the jaws of a vice, using two distance pieces. Two different size socket spanners are ideal, and it will be possible to force one out sufficiently far to enable it to be gripped by another suitable tool (pliers or vice again)and drawn out. Take care not to damage the yokes. An alternative method of removing the bearings is to use a socket and hammer as illustrated in the photo.If the bearings

have seized up or worn so badly that the holes in the yokes are oval, then a new yoke will be needed - and if this is on the propeller shaft then that will have to be acquired too, as the whole assembly is balanced and parts are not supplied separately (Fig.7.3), (photos).
3 New bearings will be supplied with new seals and circlips. Make sure the needles are correctly in position and the cup 1/3 full of grease.
4 Fit the spider to the propeller shaft yoke.
5 Engage the spider trunnion in the bearing cup and insert the cup into the yoke.
6 Fit the opposite bearing cup to the yoke and carefully press both cups into position, ensuring that the spider trunnion engages the cups and that the needle bearings are not displaced.
7 Using two flat-faced adaptors of slightly smaller diameter than the bearing cups, press the cups into the yokes until they reach the lower land of the circlip grooves. Do not press the bearing cups below this point or damage may be caused to the cups and seals.
8 Fit the circlips.

5 Centre bearing - removal and replacement

1 Remove the front half of the propeller shaft as described in Section 2.7 to 2.11.
2 Withdraw the split pin securing the castellated nut to the threaded end of the propeller shaft.
3 Unscrew the castellated nut and withdraw the drive flange from the end of the propeller shaft.
4 Remove the woodruff key from the shaft and withdraw the bearing and housing assembly from the shaft.
5 Using a screwdriver, gently ease the wire circlips from either side of the bearing and, with suitable drift and soft-faced hammer, gently tap the bearing out of the housing.
6 Inspect the bearing for evidence of wear or corrosion; there should be no excess play between the inner and outer races and the bearing should run smoothly and without undue noise.
7 To replace the bearing, fit one of the circlips in its groove, press the bearing up to it, then fit the other circlip to lock it in position. Both sides of the bearing should now be packed with a waterproof sealing compound.
8 Reassembly from now on is a direct reversal of the removal procedure.

Chapter 8 Rear axle

Contents

General description 1	Pinion oil seal - removal and replacement 4
Half shafts, bearings and oil seals - removal and replacement 2	Rear axle - removal and replacement 5
Differential assembly - removal and replacement 3	

Specifications

Type	Live axle with hypoid bevel gears and two-pinion differential.	
Oil capacity	1½ pints (0.85 litres) Castrol Hypoy	

Ratios:

Final drive	4.11 to 1	
Pinion bearing pre-load	15 to 18 lb in	(0.17 to 0.21 kg m)
Crown wheel run-out - Max	0.003 in to 0.006 in	(0.0762 to 0.1524 mm)
Optimum	0.005 in (0.127 mm)	
Differential case - maximum stretch	0.008 in	(0.2032 mm)

Torque wrench settings:

	lb ft	kg m
Hypoid housing bearing cap retainer	30 to 37	4.0 to 5.1
Brake backplate attachment	16 to 20	2.2 to 2.8
Brake adjuster to backplate	5 to 7	.7 to 1.0
Crown wheel retainer	38 to 5	5.2 to 6.2
Centre bracket to mounting bracket	16 to 20	2.2 to 2.8
Drain plug	20 to 24	2.8 to 3.3
Hypoid housing attachment	16 to 20	2.2 to 2.8
Hypoid flange to pinion	90 to 110	12.4 to 15.2
Hub to axle shaft	90 to 110	12.4 to 15.2
Propeller shaft attachment front and rear	16 to 20	2.2 to 2.8
Propeller shaft centre bearing	16 to 20	2.2 to 2.8
Rear shaft to pinion flange	26 to 32	2.6 to 4.4
Rear brake drum to hub	5 to 7	.7 to 1.0

1 General description

The main rear axle component is the hypoid differential unit which has an integral crownwheel and two-pinion differential. The crown wheel, pinion and differential are mounted as an assembly in the differential carrier and is bolted to the front of the banjo-type axle housing. This arrangement facilitates removal of the differential assembly without having to remove the rear axle as a complete unit.

The crown wheel and pinion run on opposed taper roller bearings, the bearings pre-load and meshing of the crown wheel and pinion being controlled by shims. Spring-loaded oil seals prevent oil loss at the pinion and drive shaft extremities.

Splined half-shafts transmit the drive to the rear wheels (Chapter 7) and the rear axle tube casing is insulated from the rear suspension by rubber mountings.

2 Half-shafts, bearings and oil seals - removal and replacement

1 The half shafts may be withdrawn without disturbing the differential gear. They are removed in order to renew the bearings or oil seals, or if the differential is to be removed. Read

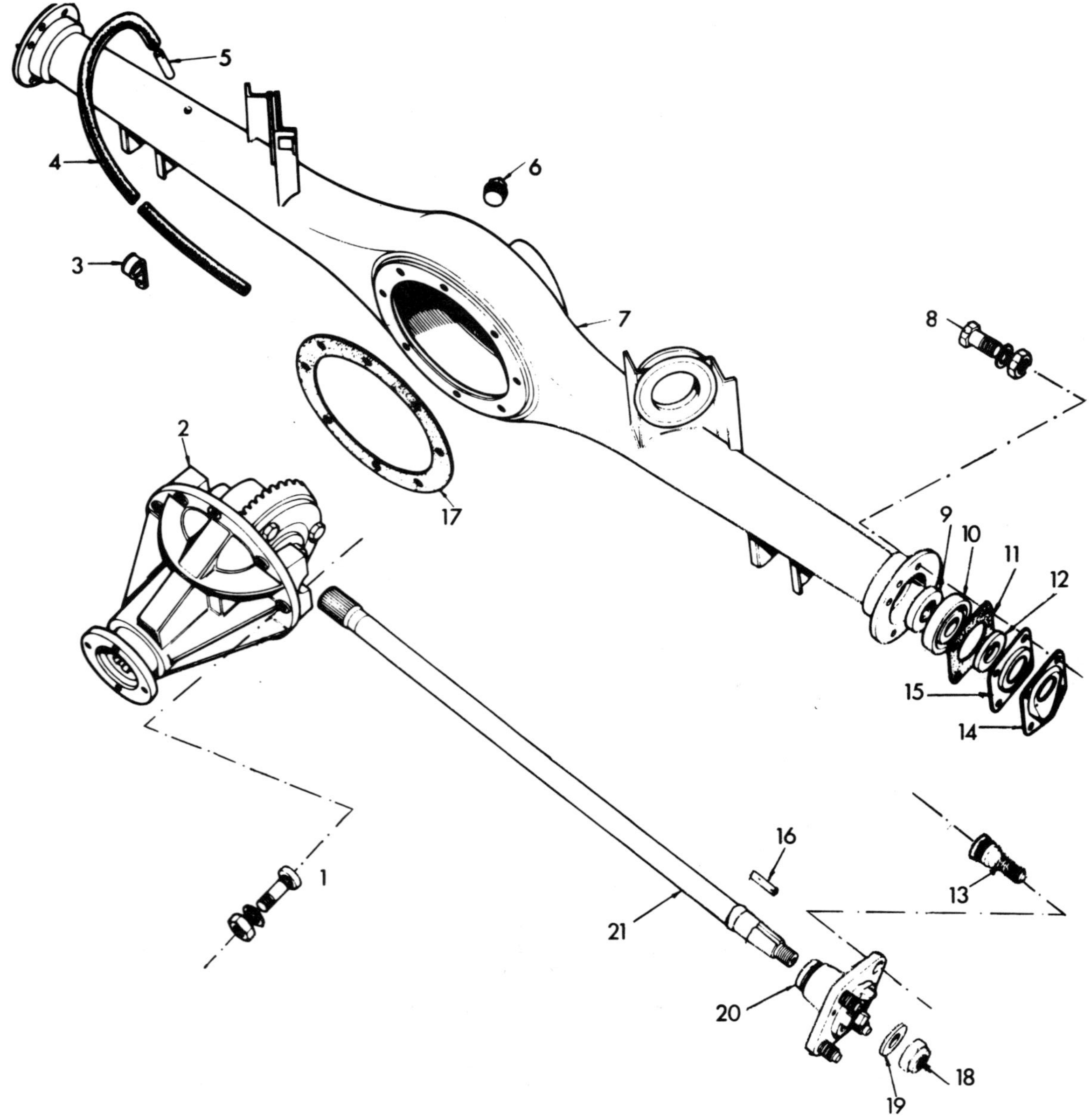

FIG. 8.1. REAR AXLE COMPONENTS

1 Nuts, washers and studs. Differential to-axle casing
2 Hypoid housing assembly, complete with gears
3 Clip
4 Breather pipe
5 Breather pipe-to-axle connector
6 Screwed plug
7 Axle casing assembly
8 Axle casing-to-back plate bolts, washer and nuts
9 Rear oil seal
10 Bearing, rear hub
11 Gasket
12 Oil seal, rear hub
13 Stud
14 Oil catcher
15 Oil seal housing
16 Key
17 Gasket
18 Nut
19 Washer
20 Rear hub and stud assembly
21 Rear axle shaft

103

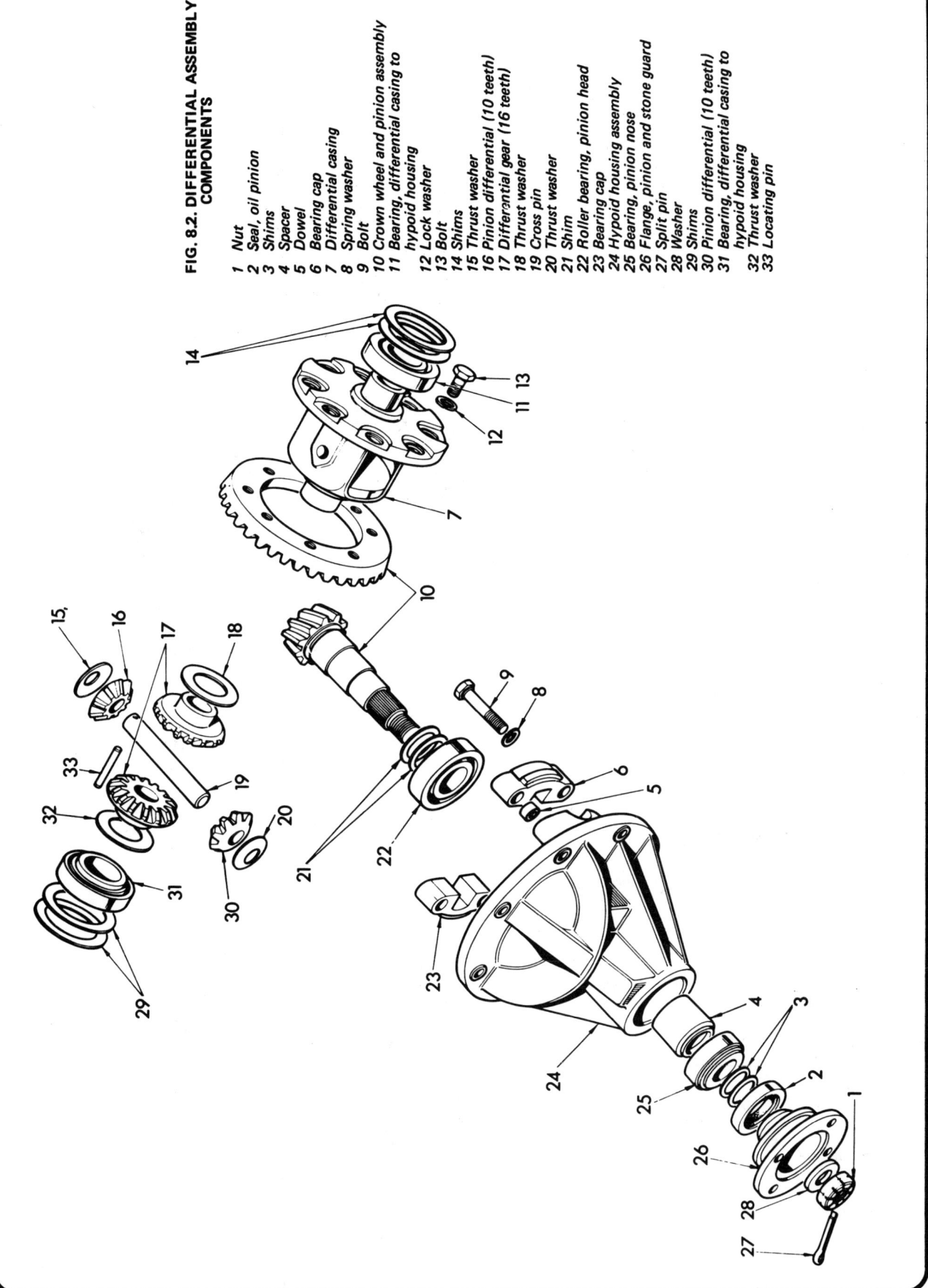

FIG. 8.2. DIFFERENTIAL ASSEMBLY
COMPONENTS

1 Nut
2 Seal, oil pinion
3 Shims
4 Spacer
5 Dowel
6 Bearing cap
7 Differential casing
8 Spring washer
9 Bolt
10 Crown wheel and pinion assembly
11 Bearing, differential casing to
   hypoid housing
12 Lock washer
13 Bolt
14 Shims
15 Thrust washer
16 Pinion differential (10 teeth)
17 Differential gear (16 teeth)
18 Thrust washer
19 Cross pin
20 Thrust washer
21 Shim
22 Roller bearing, pinion head
23 Bearing cap
24 Hypoid housing assembly
25 Bearing, pinion nose
26 Flange, pinion and stone guard
27 Split pin
28 Washer
29 Shims
30 Pinion differential (10 teeth)
31 Bearing, differential casing to
   hypoid housing
32 Thrust washer
33 Locating pin

the whole of this Section before starting work, and remember to place a container beneath the axle casing to collect the oil spillage when the axle shaft is removed. Refer to Figs. 8.1 and 8.2.

2 Jack up the car at the rear and support it firmly on proper stands. Remove the rear wheels, free the handbrake and remove the brake drums, as described in Chapter 9.

3 Remove the clevis pin from the handbrake linkage and disconnect the hydraulic brake pipe from the wheel cylinder (Chapter 9).

4 Remove the nuts and bolts securing the oil catcher plate and brake backplate to the axle casing flange and the front oil seal housing. The half shaft hub, bearing and backplate are now held in position as an assembly by the fit of the outer race of the bearing into the axle casing. Ideally the use of a proper impact hammer removal tool is needed to draw the assembly out. This consists of a flange which bolts to the wheel studs and to which is fitted a long shaft extension with a sliding weight on it. The sliding weight is hit against a flange at the extremity of the shaft and this draws the axle out. Whatever you do, this principle - of attaching a suitable bracket and striking point to the wheel studs - must be followed. No part of the axle assembly itself must be struck. A sustained pull is also quite ineffective and will probably only result in heaving the car off the stands. So get something suitable organised in advance or you will be wasting your time. One possibility is to use an old wheel rim bolted to the studs and then strike it from the inside with something suitably heavy. The success or otherwise of this method depends on access and the ability to get a good swing at it. Whatever method is used the car should be firmly supported.

5 It is essential that proper facilities are also available if the outer oil seal housing, bearing, and inner oil seal are to be renewed. The bearing has to be drawn off the outer end of the shaft. First, therefore, the hub has to be removed. It is held by a nut on to a keyed taper at the end of the shaft. A proper puller to get this off is essential, otherwise the end of the shaft may be damaged.

6 Remove the locknut and washer. After pulling off the hub, the brake back plate and oil thrower can be removed. Then the outer oil seal housing with integral seal can be pulled off the shaft.

7 Remove the Woodruff key from the axle shaft and store in a secure place.

8 Using a suitable puller, remove the bearing from the end of the axle shaft and then ease off the inner oil seal.

9 Thoroughly clean all the parts and renew the bearings if they are worn, rough or chipped. Examine the hub for cracks, a worn taper and keyway, and worn outer oil seal contacting faces. Check the shaft for straightness and wear. If necessary get expert advice from your local Triumph distributor, as wear that appears to be very small can have a considerable effect on efficiency.

10 When fitting a new bearing it should be packed with lithium-based grease, while the new oil seal should be dipped in light oil before reassembling.

11 Fit the new seal to the axle casing with the lip of the seal facing inwards.

12 Press the bearing onto the axle shaft until the measurement from the bearing face to the threaded end of the axle shaft is 2.84 inch. (69.94 mm).

13 Press a new oil seal into the outer housing after dipping it in light oil.

14 The rest of the components can be fitted in the reverse order to dismantling, remembering to fit a new gasket between the bearing and the outer oil seal housing.

15 Tighten the backplate securing nuts to 18 lb ft (2.5 Kg m) and the axle shaft nut to 85 lb ft (11.7 Kg m).

3 Differential assembly - removal and replacement

1 Jack up the car and support it on stands as for half shaft removal.

2 Mark the differential pinion and the propellor shaft drive

flange to ensure correct alignment when the assembly is replaced.

3 The half shafts should be either completely removed, as described in Section 2, or withdrawn sufficiently for the inner ends to disengage from the differential side pinions.

4 Remove the four lock nuts and bolts from the drive flange.

5 Place a container beneath the differential unit to collect the oil when the unit is removed.

6 Remove the eight locknuts and washers securing the differential assembly to the axle casing. Carefully withdraw the differential assembly from the studs and place in an extremely clean, secure position.

7 At this point, we feel it is important to stress the fact that it is not recommended that the average owner, without access to the special tools necessary, attempts to dismantle the differential assembly any further. A new or exchange differential assembly should be purchased and refitted.

8 Clean the faces of the differential and the axle casing and fit a new joint gasket lightly smeared with jointing compound.

9 Replace the parts in the reverse order, tightening the differential-to-axle casing nuts to torque of 20 lb ft (2.7 kg m).

10 Refill the axle with 1.25 pints (0.71 litres) of the recommended lubricant.

4 Pinion oil seal - removal and replacement

If oil is leaking from the front of the differential nose piece it will be necessary to renew the pinion oil seal. If a pit is not available, jack and chock up the rear of the car. It is much easier to do this job over a pit, or with the car on a ramp.

1 Mark the propeller shaft and pinion drive flanges to ensure their replacement in the same relative positions. Refer to Fig.8.7.

2 Unscrew the nuts from the four bolts holding the flanges together, remove the bolts and separate the flanges. CAUTION: place a container beneath the driving flange to collect the oil spillage when the flange and oil seal are removed.

3 Pull out the split pin and unscrew the nut in the centre of the pinion drive flange. The flange may tend to turn as pressure is applied to the nut. Although a special tool exists to prevent this, it is easier to get someone to hold it. Although it is tightened down to a torque of 90 lb ft (12.4 kg m) it can be removed fairly easily with a long extension arm fitted to the appropriate socket spanner. Remove the nut and spring washer.

4 Pull off the splined drive flange, which may be a little stubborn, in which case it should be tapped with a hide mallet from the rear; if a puller is available, so much the better. Prise out the oil seal with a screwdriver taking care not to damage the lip of its seating.

5 Replacement is a reversal of the above procedure. NOTE that the new seal must be pushed into the differential nose piece with the edge of the sealing ring facing inwards, and take great care not to damage the edge of the oil seal when replacing the end cover and drive flange. The new seal should be immersed in light oil for one hour before fitting. Smear the face of the flange which bears against the oil seal lightly with oil before driving the flange onto its splines. Tighten the nut to 90 lb ft (12.4 kg m) and insert the split pin.

6 Check the rear axle oil level and top up as necessary.

5 Rear axle - removal and replacement

1 Removal of the rear axle should be a rare occurrence; the most likely reason is if the differential unit has gone and a replacement assembly obtained from a breaker is being fitted complete, rather than just the differential carrier. Refer to Fig.8.8.

2 Jack up the rear of the car and support the body on axle or some other form of stands.

3 Remove the road wheels and release the handbrake.

4 Mark the mating faces of the propeller shaft and the differ-

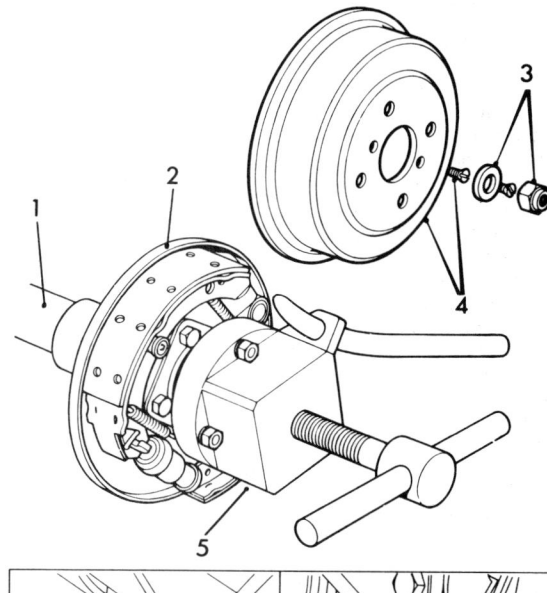

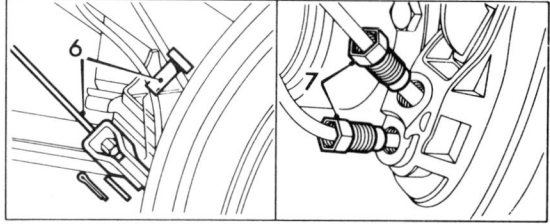

FIG. 8.3. REMOVING THE VARIOUS ITEMS PRIOR TO HALF—SHAFT REMOVAL

1 Axle shaft casing	screws
2 Brake back plate	5 Puller for removing hub
3 Wheel hub securing nut and washer	6 Clevis pins securing the handbrake cable
4 Brake drum securing	7 Brake pipe unions

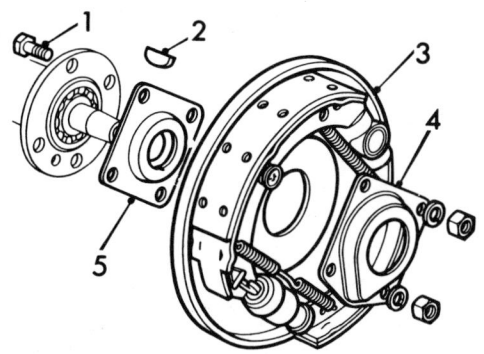

FIG. 8.4. EXPLODED VIEW OF BACK PLATE—TO—AXLE CASING SECURING METHOD

1 Bolt	4 Oil catcher
2 Woodruff key	5 Front (outer) oil seal housing
3 Brake back plate	

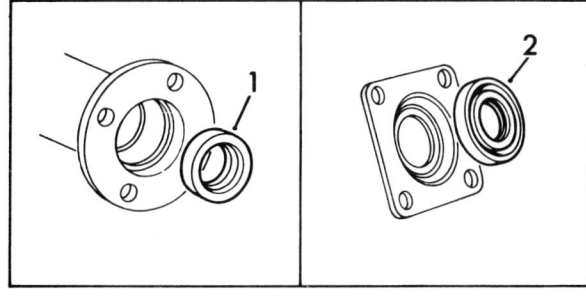

FIG. 8.5. OIL SEAL POSITIONS

1 Inner oil seal - locates in the axle casing (lip inwards)
2 Outer (front) oil seal - locates in the oil seal housing

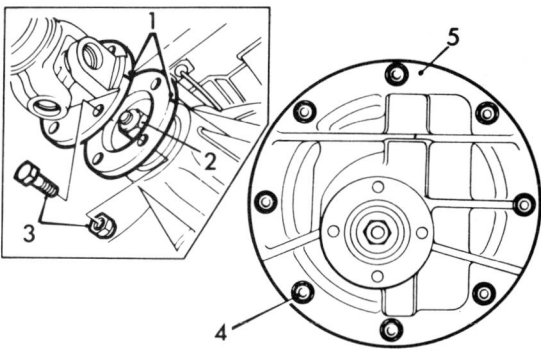

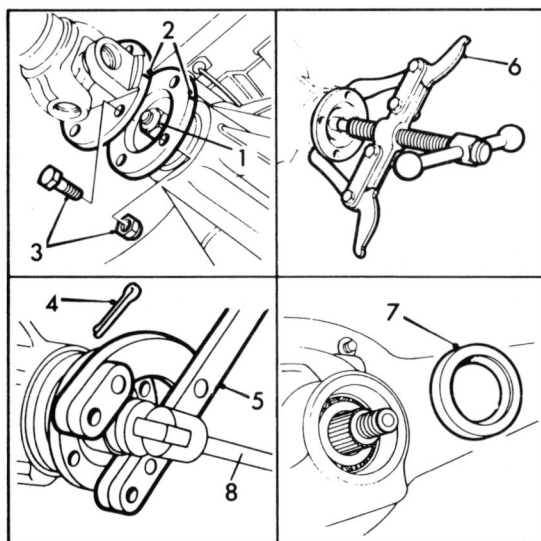

FIG. 8.6. REMOVING THE DIFFERENTIAL ASSEMBLY

1 Aligning marks
2 Drive flange retaining nut
3 Propellor shaft-to-differential flange nuts and bolts
4 Differential carrier assembly nuts
5 Differential assembly

FIG. 8.7. REMOVING THE PINION OIL SEAL

1 Drive flange retaining nut (split pin not shown)
2 Aligning marks
3 Propellor shaft-to-drive flange nuts and bolts
4 Split pin
5 Special tool that prevents drive flange turning while the nut is being removed
6 Drive flange puller
7 Oil seal
8 Socket spanner removing the nut while the drive flange is locked

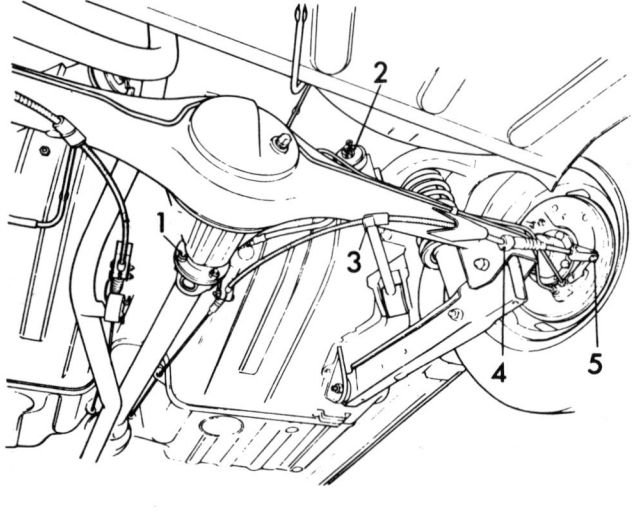

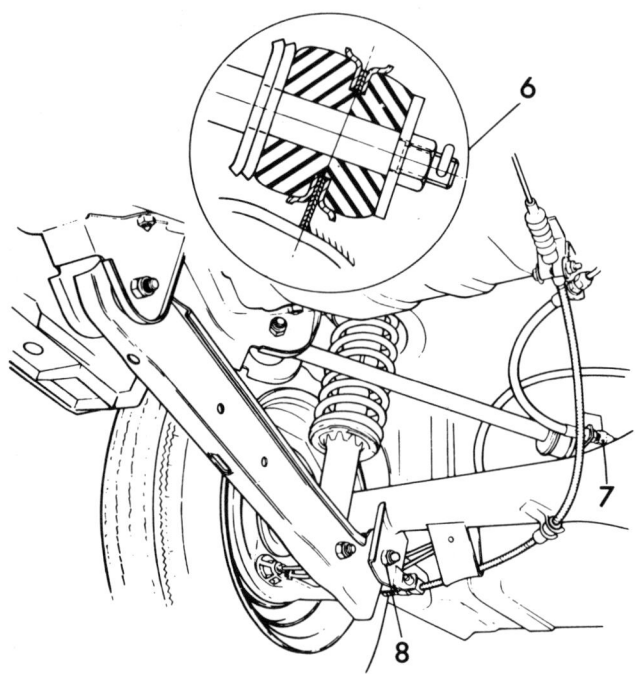

FIG. 8.8. DISCONNECTION POINTS FOR REAR AXLE REMOVAL

1 *Propellor shaft-to-differential bolts*
2 *Radius rod securing nut*
3 *Handbrake cable connection to the rear axle casing*
4 *Handbrake cable connection to the suspension bracket*
5 *Handbrake cable connection to the brake backplate*
6 *Section through radius rod locating point*
7 *Brake hose locating point*
8 *Axle housing-to-suspension arm securing nut*

ential flange, then remove the four nuts and bolts that secure these components. Allow the propeller shaft to hang down, but not to carry its weight on the centre universal joint. Support the propeller shaft if necessary.

5 Place a jack under the differential and adjust it so that it just carries the weight of the assembly.

6 Disconnect both handbrake cables at the brake backplate lever, the rear suspension bracket and the rear axle tube clip.

7 Disconnect the brake pipe union at the flexible hose and disconnect the hose from the axle bracket. Seal the pipe and hose to prevent the entry of grit.

8 Remove the nuts, washers and bushes securing the radius rods to the axle casing.

9 Remove the nuts and bolts securing the rear suspension arms to the axle.

10 Raise the axle and remove rearwards to clear the suspension arm.

11 Withdraw, carefully, the axle from beneath the car.

12 To refit the axle, position the axle below the car and support on a jack.

13 Slowly raise the jack, and engage the rear ends of the radius rods through the axle brackets: fit the bushes, washers, nuts and pins. Note that the two plain washers with bevelled edges are fitted first up against the step on the end of the radius rod. Next the inner rubber bush; the rod is then inserted through the axle bracket. Fit the outer bush over the radius rod and then a plain washer. Secure with a nut and split pin through the drilling in the end of the radius rod.

14 Engage the rear ends of the suspension arms in the axle casing brackets and fit the securing nuts and bolts.

15 Re-connect the handbrake cables to the axle clips, suspension brackets and backplate levers.

16 Re-connect the rear propeller shaft to the pinion flange, lining up with the marks made when dismantling.

Chapter 9 Braking system

Contents

General description 1	Handbrake - adjustment 15
Brake system - bleeding 2	Handbrake cable - removal and replacement 16
Flexible hose - inspection, removal and replacement.. ... 3	Brake pedal and stop light switch - removal and refitting ... 17
Brake adjustment, front and rear - general 4	
Front brake adjustment 5	SUPPLEMENT
Rear brake - adjustment 6	Disc brakes and servo unit - general description 18
Front brake shoes - inspection, removal and replacement ... 7	Front disc brakes caliper pad - removal and refitting.. ... 19
Rear brake shoes - inspection, removal and replacement ... 8	Front brake disc - removal and refitting 20
Brake master cylinder - removal and refitting 9	Front disc brake caliper - removal and refitting 21
Brake master cylinder - dismantling and reassembly 10	Front disc brake caliper - overhaul 22
Front brake wheel cylinder - removal, overhaul & reassembly.. 11	Brake master cylinder - removal and replacement 23
Rear brake wheel cylinder - removal, inspection, overhaul	Brake servo unit - description 24
and reassembly 12	Brake servo unit - removal and refitting 25
Rear brake shoe adjuster - removal and replacement 13	Brake servo unit - air filter renewal 26
Handbrake lever assembly - removal, overhaul and refitting... 14	Fault diagnosis 27

Specifications

System type	Hydraulic
Front brakes - drum	
Type	Drum - two leading shoes
Size	9 in. diameter x 1¾ in. wide (228 x 38 mm)
Number of adjusters	2
Lining area	60.5 in^2 (390 cm^2)
Swept area	99.0 in^2 (639 cm^2)
Front brakes - disc	
Disc diameter...	8¾ in (222 mm)
Disc run-out	0.006 in (0.152 cm)
Total pad area	17.4 in^2 (112.2 cm^2)
Total swept area	165 in^2 (1065 cm^2)
Minimum pad thickness	1/16 in (1.6 mm)
Rear brakes	
Type	Drum, leading and trailing shoe
Size	8 in. diameter x 1½ in. wide (204 x 38 mm)
Number of adjusters...	1
Rear lining area	37.8 in^2 (244 cm^2)
Rear swept area	75.5 in^2 (487 cm^2)
Adjustment	Manually operated adjuster
Handbrake	
Type	Centrally mounted hand lever operating rear brakes mechanically
Braking	Maximum retardation 0.92g equivalent to stopping from 30 mph in 32.5 ft (16 metres)
Hydraulic fluid	Castrol Girling Brake Fluid

Torque wrench settings	lb ft	kg m
Brake pedal mounting bolt	16 - 20	2.2 - 2.8
Brake cable to abutment bracket (717009)	5 - 7	.7 - 1.0
Brake pedal support bracket to bulkhead	26 - 32	3.6 - 4.4
Brake pedal support bracket to	7 - 9	1.0 - 1.2
Handbrake fulcrum pin	20 - 24	2.8 - 3.3
Handbrake and bracket clamp plate to floor	7 - 9	1.0 - 1.2
Master cylinder support bracket to bulkhead	16 - 20	2.2 - 2.8
Plate to body	16 - 20	2.2 - 2.8
Union four-way to chassis	7 - 9	1.0 - 1.2

1 General description

Early Toledo models were fitted with expanding brake shoes and friction drums on all four wheels. Later models, however are fitted with disc brakes on the front wheels, and a brake servo unit, as standard equipment. The disc brakes and servo unit are covered in detail at the end of the Chapter (Section 18).

The front wheels fitted with conventional drums are of the 'two-leading shoe' type of brake with individual wheel cylinders to operate each shoe.

The rear brakes are of the single leading and trailing shoe type with one wheel cylinder per wheel operating the two shoes. Attached to each of the rear wheel operating cylinders is a mechanical expander operated by the handbrake lever through a cable and lever system. This provides an independent means of rear brake application.

It is unusual to have to adjust the handbrake system, as the efficiency of this system is largely dependant on the condition of the brake linings and the adjustment of the brake shoes. The handbrake, can, however, be adjusted separately to the footbrake-operated hydraulic system.

The hydraulic brake functions in the following manner: on application of the brake pedal, hydraulic fluid under pressure is pushed from the master cylinder to the brake operating cylinders at each wheel, by means of the four-way union, steel pipes and flexible hoses shown in Fig 9.1.

The hydraulic fluid moves the pistons out, so pushing the front brake and rear brake shoes into contact with the front and rear drums. This provides an equal degree of retardation on all four wheels in direct proportion to the pressure applied to the brake pedal. Return springs between each pair of brake shoes draw the shoes together when the brake pedal is released.

It is important that the complete braking system is in the peak of condition at all times. To safeguard against any premature wear or deterioration, make sure all the 'Routine Maintenance' tasks are carried out at the time suggested.

Only Castrol Girling Brake Fluid should be used in the hydraulic system. Never leave brake hydraulic fluid in open unsealed containers as it absorbs moisture from the atmosphere which lowers the safe operating temperature of the fluid. Any fluid drained or used for bleeding the system should not be re-used.

Work performed on the hydraulic system must be done under conditions of extreme care and cleaniness.

2 Brake system - bleeding

1 Removal of all the air from the hydraulic system is essential to the correct working of the braking system, but before undertaking this, examine the fluid reservoir cap to ensure that both vent holes, one on top and the second underneath but not in line, are clear; check the level of fluid and top up if required.
2 Check all brake line unions and connections for possible seepage, and at the same time check the condition of the rubber hoses which may be perished.
3 If the condition of the wheel cylinders is in doubt check for possible signs of fluid leakage.
4 If there is any possibility of incorrect fluid having been put into the system drain all the fluid out and flush through with methylated spirits. Renew all piston seals and cups since they will be affected and could possibly fail under pressure.
5 Gather together a clean jam jar, a 9 in. (230 mm) length of tubing which fits tightly over the bleed nipple and a tin of Castrol Girling Brake Fluid.
6 To bleed the system, clean the areas around the bleed valve and start on the rear brakes by removing the rubber cup over the bleed valve and fitting a rubber tube in position.
7 Place the end of the tube in a clean glass jar containing sufficient fluid to keep the end of the tube underneath during the operation.
8 Open the bleed valve with a spanner and quickly press down

the brake pedal. After slowly releasing the pedal, pause for a moment to allow the fluid to recoup in the master cylinder and then depress again. This will force air from the system. Continue until no more air bubbles can be seen coming from the tube. At intervals make certain that the reservoir is kept topped up, otherwise air will enter at this point again (photo).
9 Repeat this operation on all four brakes, and when completed, check the level of the fluid in the reservoir and then check the feel of the brake pedal. This should be firm and free from any 'spongy' action which is normally associated with air in the system.

3 Flexible hose - inspection, removal and replacement

Inspect the condition of the flexible hydraulic hoses leading from the body mounted metal pipe to the brake backplates at the front of the car, and the single central hose at the rear of the car. If any are swollen , damaged, cut or chaffed, they must be renewed. (Fig.9.1 refers).
1 Unscrew the metal pipe union nut from its connection to the hose, and then holding the hexagon on the hose with a spanner, unscrew the attachment nut and washer.
2 The body end of the flexible hose can now be withdrawn from the chassis mounting bracket and will be quite free.
3 Disconnect the flexible hydraulic hose at the backplate by unscrewing it from the brake cylinder. NOTE: When releasing the hose from the backplate, the chassis end must always be freed first.
4 Replacement is a straight reversal of the removal procedure.

4 Brake adjustment, front and rear - general

1 Basically, the technique for adjusting the front or rear brakes is identical. The primary difference is that there are two adjusters on the front wheels, one for each cylinder, while there is only one adjuster on each rear wheel.

Whichever wheels are being adjusted, front or rear, it will be necessary to jack up that portion of the car and support it on axle stands If the rear wheels are being adjusted, ensure the handbrake is off. Always securely chock the wheels not being adjusted. (The rear drum brakes, for later models fitted with front disc brakes, are self adjusting. Special care should be taken with the automatic adjusters when re-shoeing the rear drums).

5 Front brake-adjustment

A square-ended snail cam adjuster is provided for each front brake-shoe. Rotate each adjuster clockwise (viewed from the rear of the backplate) to expand the shoe; anti-clockwise to retract the shoe.(Fig.9.2 refers).
1 Jack up the front of the car.
2 Apply a spanner to the lower adjusters on the backplate and rotate in a clockwise direction until the wheel is locked (photo).
3 Rotate the adjuster anti-clockwise until the wheel can be turned freely.
4 Repeat operations in paragraphs 2 and 3 on the upper adjuster on the backplate.
5 Repeat operations in paragraphs 2 and 4 on the opposite front wheel. If rotation of a snail cam fails to expand a brake-shoe sufficiently to lock a road wheel it is indicative of extensively worn brake linings.

6 Rear brake - adjustment

A single wedge-type adjuster with a square-ended shank is provided on the rear backplates (Fig.9.3 refers).
1 Jack up the rear of the car and release the handbrake.
2 Rotate the adjuster clockwise (viewed from the rear of the backplate) until the wheel is locked (photo).

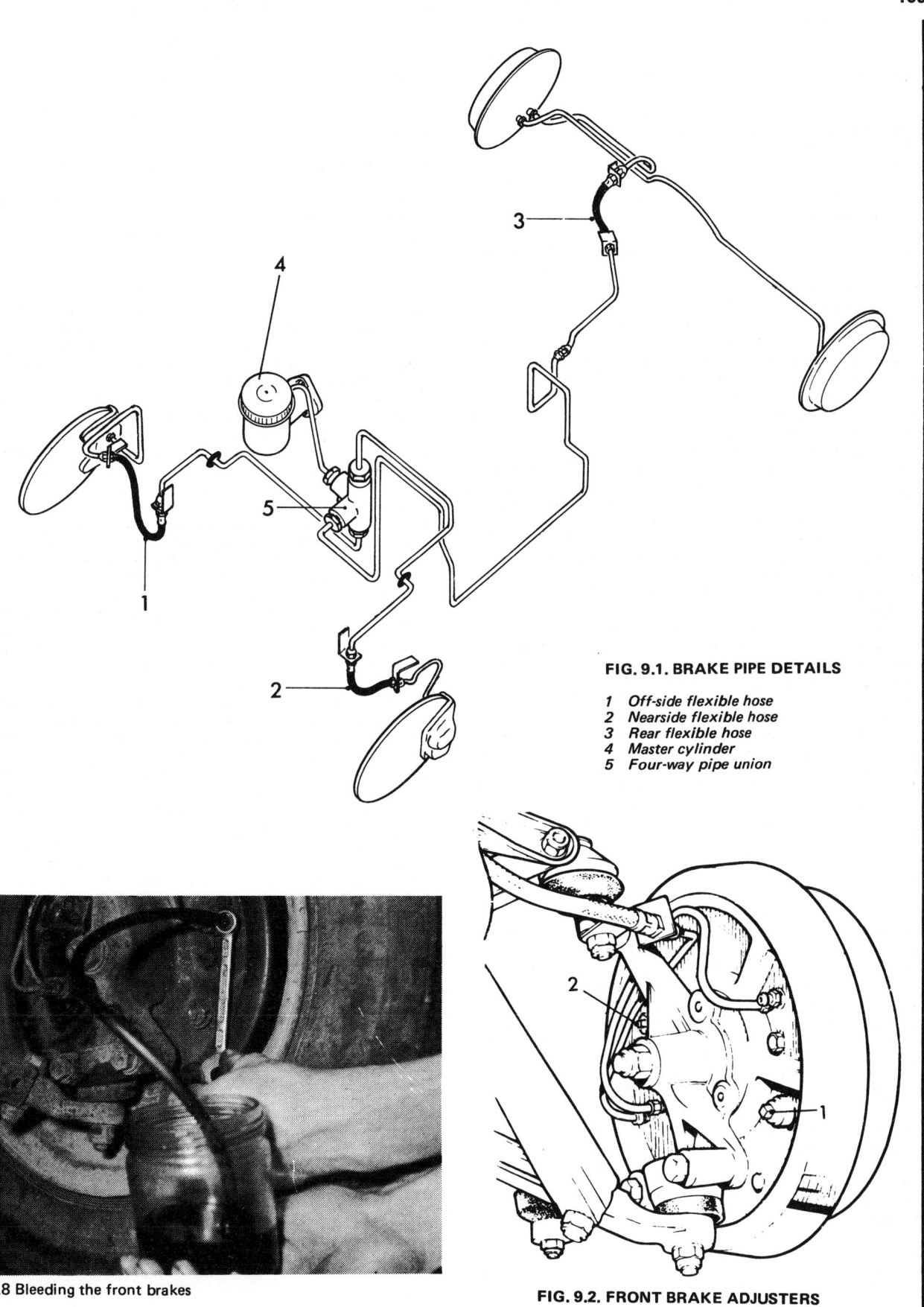

FIG. 9.1. BRAKE PIPE DETAILS

1 Off-side flexible hose
2 Nearside flexible hose
3 Rear flexible hose
4 Master cylinder
5 Four-way pipe union

2.8 Bleeding the front brakes

FIG. 9.2. FRONT BRAKE ADJUSTERS

1 Lower adjuster   2 Upper adjuster

3 Rotate the adjuster anti-clockwise until the wheel can be turned freely.

4 Repeat operations in paragraphs 2 and 3 on opposite rear wheel. Failure of an adjuster to lock a road wheel is indicative of excessively worn brake linings.

5 Spin the wheel and apply the brake hard to centralise the shoes. Recheck that it is not possible to turn the adjusting screw further without locking the shoe. NOTE: A rubbing noise when the wheel is spun is usually due to dust in the brake drum. If there is no obvious slowing of the wheel due to brake binding there is no need to slacken off the adjusters until the noise disappears. Better to remove drum and blow out the dust.

7 Front brake shoes - inspection, removal and replacement

1 Jack up the front wheel of the car until it is almost clear of the ground and slacken the wheel nuts. Raise the car until the wheel is clear and support the vehicle further by positioning on axle stands under the body. Unscrew the wheel nuts and remove the road wheel (photos).

2 Using a wide-bladed screwdriver remove the two countersunk screws which secure the drum to the hub. Withdraw the friction drum (photos).

3 If the friction area inside the drum is ridged or worn, difficulty may be experienced in pulling the drum away from the shoes. In this instance slacken off the brake shoe adjusters or tap on the perimeter of the drum with a soft-faced hammer.

4 Prise the spring plate retainers off the shoe steady pins and lift out the steady pins. Store in a secure place (photo).

5 Pull the leading edge of the lower shoe away from its location in the piston and against the pressure of the upper spring lift it clear of the cylinder. Pull the trailing edge of the shoe away from its slotted location at the back of the other cylinder. Release the tension on the spring and unhook it from the shoe and backplate. If the shoe is to be refitted mark it for correct location.

6 Repeat the previous instructions on the other shoe.

7 It is advisable, if the shoes are to be left off for some time, to secure the pistons in the wheel cylinder by binding string or wire around the cylinder; strong elastic bands may also suffice. Do not press the footbrake pedal whilst the shoes and drums are removed.

8 Avoid contaminating the linings with grease or oil as it will seriously affect the braking efficiency. Wash off any such contamination immediately with petrol.

9 When renewing the brake shoe or drums on a particular wheel, renew the corresponding parts on the opposite wheel also.

10 Use a high pressure air-line or foot pump to blow away all loose dust from the mechanism, use a dry clean cloth to wipe dust from the inside of the drums. Hard stubborn mud or dirt can be removed with a stiff brush.

11 If the linings are worn down to the rivet heads, renew them. Don't attempt to reline the shoes, obtain a complete set on an exchange basis. Heavily scored or worn friction drums should be renewed on an exchange basis and in this instance it is advisable to renew the shoes also. Renew weak or distorted springs.

8 Rear brake shoes - inspection, removal and replacement

Ensure the correct linings are fitted to the shoes, either as exchange shoes or relined by your local Triumph garage. Do not reline shoes yourself.

1 Chock the front wheels, remove the rear wheel hub cap and loosen the wheel nuts. Jack up the rear of the car and place on firm supports to avoid any accidents. Remove the wheel nuts and put in a safe place. Lift away the road wheel.

2 Using a wide bladed screwdriver, remove the two countersunk head screws (1) (Fig.9.5), holding the brake drum to the hub. Remove the brake drum (2). If the brake drum is tight, slacken off the brake adjuster. If it will not move away from the hub, use a soft faced hammer and tap outwards on the circumference rotating the drum whilst completing this operation.

3 The brake linings should be renewed if they are so worn that the rivet heads are flush with the surface of the lining. If bonded linings are fitted they must be renewed when the lining material has worn down to 1/16 in (1.6 mm) at its thinnest point.

4 Release the brake shoe web anti-rattle steady spring assembly by first rotating the locking retainer (24) 90° and lifting off the washer spring (17) and further retainer (24). Slacken off the brake adjustment if not previously done (photo).

5 Release the spring securing the distance plate to the rear brake shoe web. Remove the spring and plate (photos).

6 Make a note that the lining on the leading brake shoe is fitted towards the trailing end. Observe the position of the brake shoe return springs (8,18) the interrupted spring (18) being at the wheel cylinder end (21). Also note into which holes the springs locate in the brake shoe web.

7 To remove the brake shoe (25) lift the trailing end of the shoe from the abutment in the adjuster tappet (4) and the leading end from the wheel cylinder. Unhook the two springs (8, 18) from the shoe web and lift away. (For late type cars take

5.2 Adjusting the front brakes

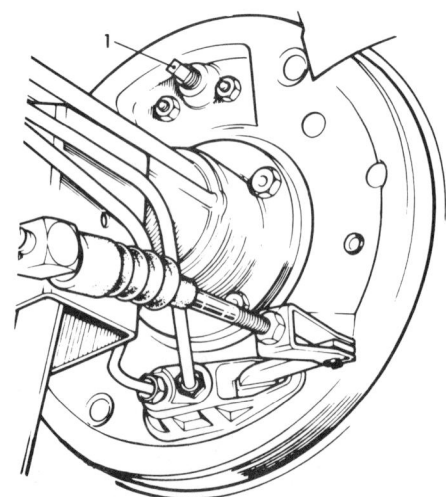

FIG. 9.3. REAR BRAKE ADJUSTER

1 Single adjuster

6.2 Adjusting the rear brakes (road wheel removed for clarity)

7.1a Removing the road wheel

7.1b Removing the road wheel

7.2a Removing the screws securing the brake drum

7.2b .... Pulling off the brake drums

7.2c .... to reveal the brake shoes

7.4 Easing the spring plates off of the steady pins

8.4 Removing the steady pin retaining cap and spring

8.5a Note the handbrake lever projecting through the shoe web; also the distance plate (washer) and its locating spring

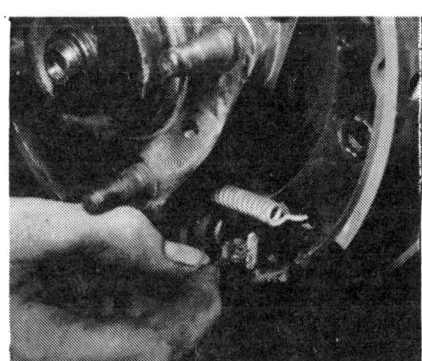

8.5b Removing the distance plate securing spring

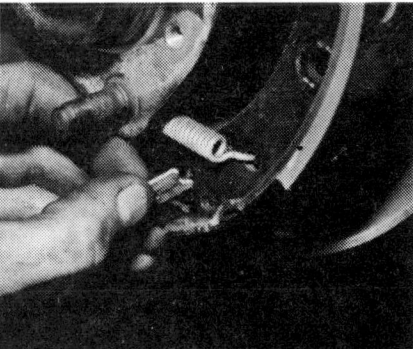

8.5c Removing the distance plate

8.7 Brake shoe with leading end removed from wheel cylinder

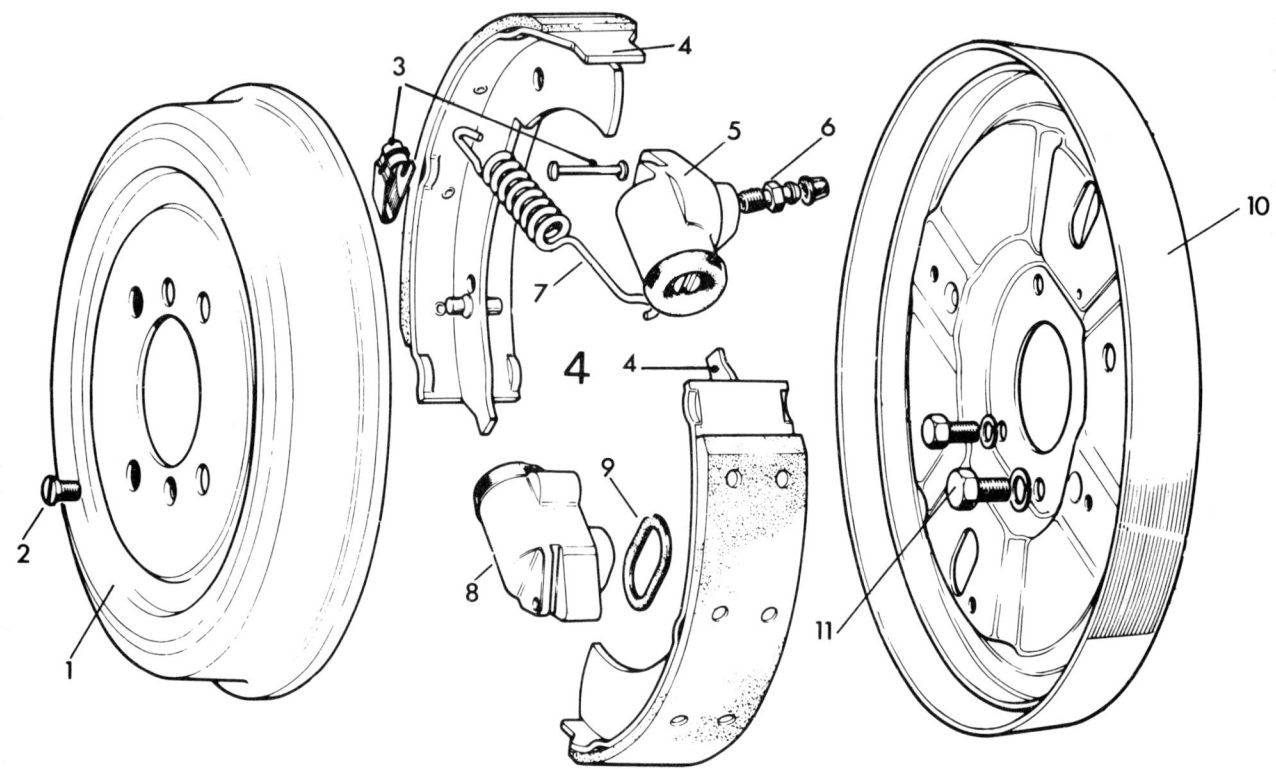

FIG. 9.4. FRONT BRAKE COMPONENTS

1	Brake drum retaining screw	4	Brake shoes	7	Spring (upper)
2	Brake drum	5	Upper wheel cylinder	8	Lower wheel cylinder
3	Steady pin and spring plate	6	Bleed screw and dust cap	9	Gasket

10	Brake backplate
11	Backplate retaining screws

off the automatic brake adjusting ratchet wheel and rotate it to its slackest position). It is recommended that strong elastic bands are used to keep the piston in the wheel cylinder. If the shoes are to be left off for a while do not at any time depress the brake pedal otherwise the piston will be ejected from the wheel cylinder causing unnecessary work (photo).

8 Thoroughly clean all traces of dust from the shoes, backplates and brake drums using a stiff brush. It is not recommended to use compressed air. Brake dust can cause judder or squeal and, therefore, it is important to clean out the brakes thoroughly.

9 Check that the piston is free in its cylinder, that the rubber dust covers are undamaged and in position, and that there are no hydraulic fluid leaks. Ensure that the handbrake lever assembly is free and also that the brake adjuster operates correctly. Lubricate the threads on the adjusting wedge with a graphite based penetrating oil.

10 Prior to reassembly, smear a trace of Castrol PH Grease to all sliding surfaces and steady posts. Do not allow any grease to come into contact with the linings or rubber parts. Refit shoes in the reverse sequence to removal taking care that the two pull off springs are located in the correct web holes, correctly positioned between web and backplate, and also that the shoes register correctly into the slotted ends of the wheel cylinder and adjuster.

11 The slotted end of the rear shoe is to the rear of the wheel cylinder, while the slotted end of the front shoe is to the front of the adjuster.

12 Do not forget to fit the distance plate between the lever and the shoe web, and to secure it with the spring.

13 Back off the adjuster and replace the brake drum, retaining

screws and road wheel. Adjust the brake. Check the correct adjustment of the handbrake and finally road test.

14 For late type cars operate the handbrake several times to activate the automatic adjusters.

9 Brake master cylinder - removal and refitting

1 Apply the handbrake, and chock the front wheels. Drain the fluid from the master cylinder reservoir by attaching a rubber tube to one of the brake bleed screws, undoing the screw one turn, and then pumping the fluid out into a suitable container by means of the brake pedal. Hold the pedal against the floor at the end of each stroke and tighten the bleed nipple. When the pedal has returned to its normal position, loosen the bleed nipple and repeat the process until the master cylinder reservoir is empty.

2 Wipe the master cylinder hydraulic pipe connection with a lean non-fluffy rag and disconnect the union. Wrap the end in a piece of clean rag to stop dirt ingress or fluid dripping onto the paintwork. Plug the master cylinder union connection to stop accidental dirt entering into the master cylinder. Details of master cylinder location and components are in Fig.9.6 and 9.7.

3 Extract the split pin from the yoke on the end of the push rod. Lift away the plain washer and withdraw the clevis pin.

4 Slacken the bolt securing the master cylinder bracket to the front spring turret. Remove the two fixing nuts and spring washers securing the master cylinder to the bulkhead and carefully ease the master cylinder away from the bulkhead. Separate the master cylinder from the bracket.

5 The master cylinder refitting procedure is the reverse to

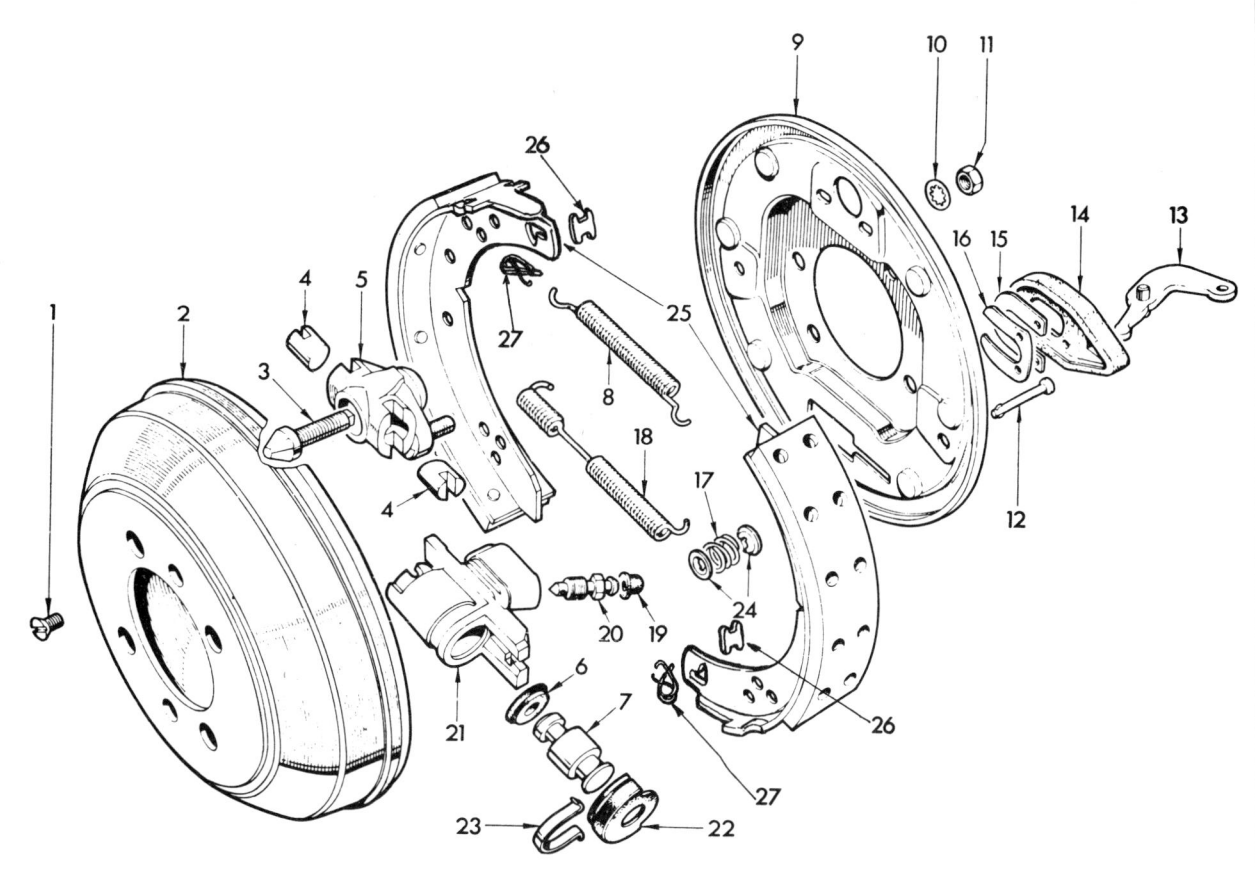

FIG. 9.5. REAR BRAKE COMPONENTS

1 Screw	8 Spring	15 Abutment plate	22 Dust excluder
2 Brake drum	9 Backplate	16 Spring plate - retaining	23 Clip
3 Expander - adjuster	10 Spring washer	17 Spring	24 Retainer - steady pin
4 Tappet	11 Nut	18 Spring	25 Brake shoes
5 Adjuster housing	12 Steady pin	19 Dust cap	26 Distance plate
6 Piston seal	13 Handbrake lever	20 Bleed nipple	27 Distance plate retaining
7 Piston	14 Dust excluder	21 Hydraulic cylinder	spring

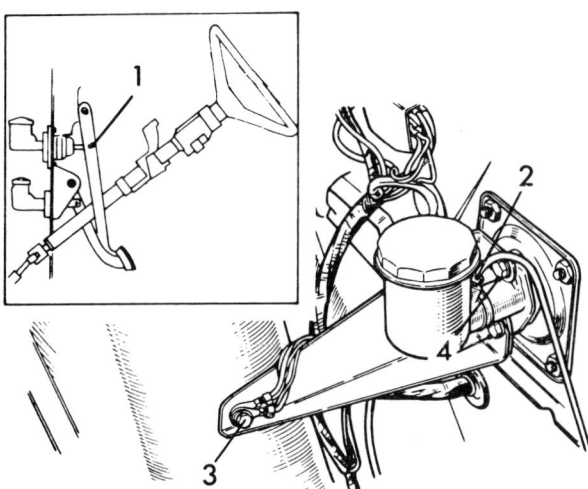

FIG. 9.6. MASTER CYLINDER LOCATION

1 Push rod connection to brake pedal
2 Brake pipe union
3 Bracket securing bolt
4 Master cylinder securing bolt

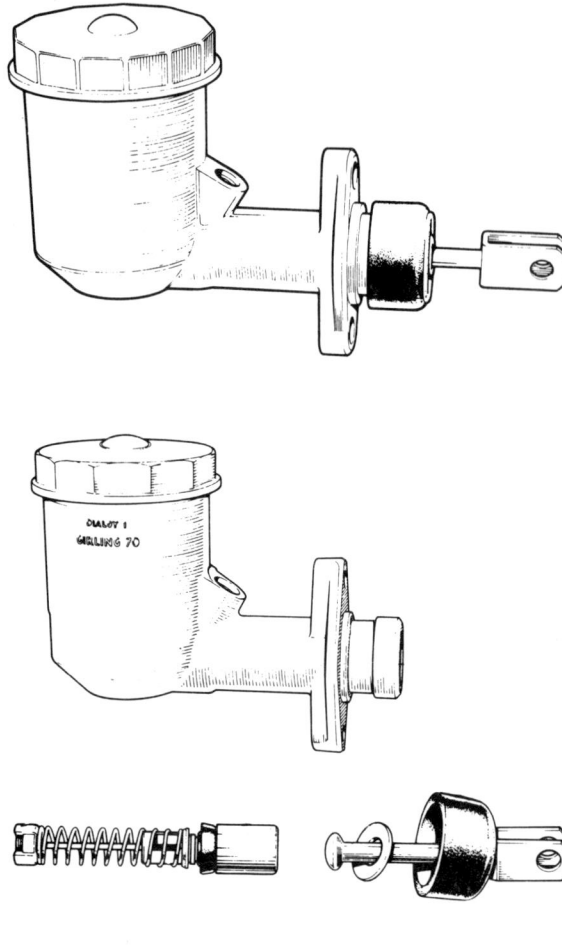

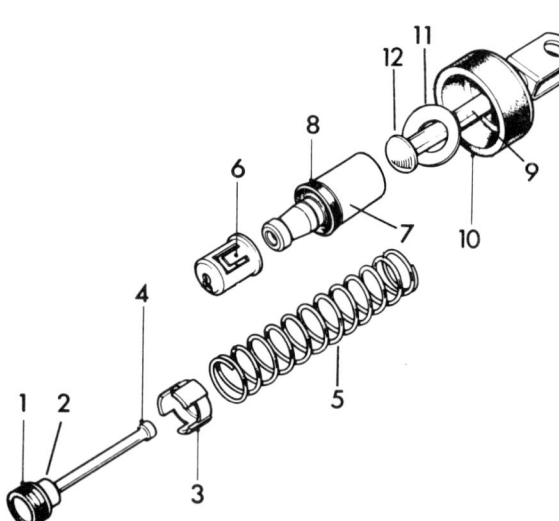

**FIG. 9.7. MASTER CYLINDER COMPONENTS –
EXPLODED AND ASSEMBLED**

1 Valve seal
2 Spring (valve seal)
3 Distance piece
4 Valve shank
5 Plunger return spring
6 Retainer

7 Plunger
8 Plunger seal
9 Push rod
10 Dust cover
11 Circlip
12 Push rod stop

removal but care must be taken when offering up to the bulkhead that the pushrod is in line with the brake pedal. Once connections have been made the complete hydraulic system must be bled and the car road tested.

10 Brake master cylinder - dismantling and reassembly

If a replacement master cylinder is to be fitted , it will be necessary to lubricate the seals before fitting to the car as they have a protective coating when originally assembled. Remove the blanking plugs from the hydraulic pipe union seating. Ease back and remove the pushrod dust cover so that clean brake fluid can be injected at these points. Operate the piston several times so that the fluid will spread over all internal working surfaces.

If the master cylinder is to be dismantled after removal proceed as follows:

1 Ease back the pushrod cover (10) (Fig 9.7.) and remove the circlip (11) so that the pushrod (9) and dished washer (12) can be withdrawn. This exposes the plunger (7) with a seal (8) attached, which must be removed as a unit. The assembly is separated by lifting the retainer leaf (6) over the shouldered end of the plunger. The seal (8) should then be eased off using the fingers only.

2 Depress the plunger return spring (5) allowing the valve shank (4) to slide through the keyhole in the retainer (6), thus releasing the tension in the spring.

3 Detach the valve spacer distance piece (3) taking care of the spring dished washer (2) which will be found under the valve head.

4 Remove the valve seal (1) from the valve shank (4).

5 Examine the bore of the cylinder carefully for any signs of scores or ridges, and if this is found to be smooth all over, new seals can be fitted. If there is any doubt of the condition of the bore then a new cylinder must be fitted.

6 If examination of the seals shows them to be apparently oversize or swollen, or very loose on the plunger, suspect oil contamination in the system. Ordinary lubricating oil will swell these rubber seals, and if one is found to be swollen it is reasonable to assume that all seals in the braking system will need attention.

7 Thoroughly clean all parts in either Girling Cleaning Fluid or Industrial Methylated spirits. Ensure that the bypass parts are clean.

8 All components should be assembled wet by dipping in clean brake fluid. Fit a new valve seal (1) the correct way round so that the flat side is seating on the valve head. Place the spring dished washer (2) with the dome against the underside of the valve head. Hold it in position with the valve spacer distance piece (3) ensuring that the legs face towards the valve seal (1).

9 Replace the plunger return spring (5) centrally on the spacer, insert the retainer (6) into the spring and depress until the valve shank (4) engages in the keyhole of the retainer (6).

10 Ensure that the spring is central on the spacer before fitting a new plunger seal (8) onto the plunger (7) with the float face against the face of the plunger.

11 Insert the reduced end of the plunger (7) into the retainer (6) until the leaf engages under the shoulder of the plunger, and press home the leaf.

12 Check that the master cylinder bore is clean, and smear with clean brake fluid. With the plunger suitably wetted with brake fluid, carefully insert the assembly into the bore with the valve end first. Ease the lips of the plunger seal carefully into the bore.

13 Replace the pushrod (9) and refit the circlip (11) into the groove in the cylinder body. Smear the sealing areas of the dust cover with Girling Rubber Grease and pack the cover (10) with the rubber grease so as to act as a dust trap. Fit the cover (10) to the master cylinder body. The master cylinder is now ready for refitting to the car.

11 Front brake wheel cylinder - removal, overhaul and re-assembly

1 If it is suspected that one or more of the wheel cylinders is malfunctioning, jack up the suspect wheel and remove the brake drum. Front wheel cylinder details all shown in Fig. 9.8.

2 Inspect for signs of fluid leakage around the wheel cylinder and if there are any, proceed as described in paragraph 5.

3 Next get someone to press the brake pedal very gently a small amount. Watch the wheel cylinder and see that the piston moves out a little. On no account let it come right out or it will need reassembly and bleeding. On releasing the pedal pressure make sure that the retraction springs on the shoes move the piston back into position without delay.

4 If there is a leak, or the piston does not move (or only moves very slowly under excessive pressure), then the rubber piston seals will need renewal at least.

5 Remove the brake shoes as described in Section 7. Clean down the rear of the backplate using a stiff brush. Place a quantity of rag or a tray under the backplate to catch any hydraulic fluid that may issue from the open pipe or wheel cylinder.

6 Seal the reservoir cap with a piece of polythene.

7 Disconnect the feed pipe union from the front wheel cylinder, or, disconnect the feed pipe and transfer pipe unions from the rear wheel cylinder.

8 Remove the two nuts and spring washers securing the cylinder to the backplate. Withdraw the cylinder.

9 Cleanliness is essential when overhauling the wheel cylinders: the working area should be free of dirt and the hands must be kept perfectly clean. If particles of dirt enter the cylinders they will scratch the highly polished bores and piston sides, which will provide an escape route for the fluid when it is under pressure. The components should be washed only in methylated spirits or clean brake fluid. Petrol or other solvents will have a detrimental effect on the seals and dust covers. It is advisable to renew the seals, whatever the condition once the cylinders have been dismantled.

10 Take off the rubber dust cover and shake out the piston, seal and spring.

11 Clean and examine the cylinder bores and the pistons for score marks and wear. Use a magnifying glass to examine in detail. Discard the cylinder if it is badly scored.

12 Lubricate the cylinder bore and the new seal with brake fluid.

13 Refit the spring with the large coils at the bottom of the cylinder.

14 Assemble the seal to the piston with the larger lip towards the bottom of the cylinder. Ease the piston and seal assembly in the cylinder, making sure that the bottom lip does not get trapped or turned back on itself.

15 Refit the rubber cap and ensure that it fits in the groove around the neck of the cylinder.

16 Refit the cylinder to the backplate in the reverse manner to removal.

17 Replace the brake shoes, drums and road wheel, and finally, adjust the brakes. Remove the polythene from under the reservoir cap.

12 Rear brake wheel cylinder - removal, inspection, overhaul and reassembly

The same general conditions relating to removal of a front wheel cylinder also apply in the case of a rear wheel cylinder. Since, however, the cylinders and their method of mounting on the brake backplate are slightly different the series of operations is given in full.

1 Remove the brake drum and brake shoes as described in Section 8. Clean down the rear of the backplate using a stiff brush. Place a quantity of rag under the backplate or a tray to catch any hydraulic fluid that may issue from the open pipe or wheel cylinder.

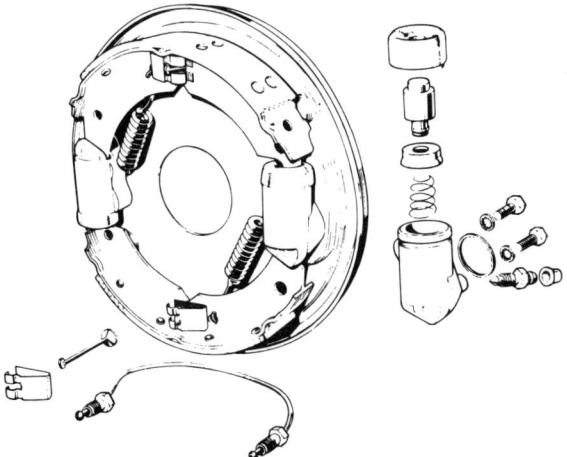

Fig. 9.8. Dismantling front wheel brake assembly and wheel cylinder

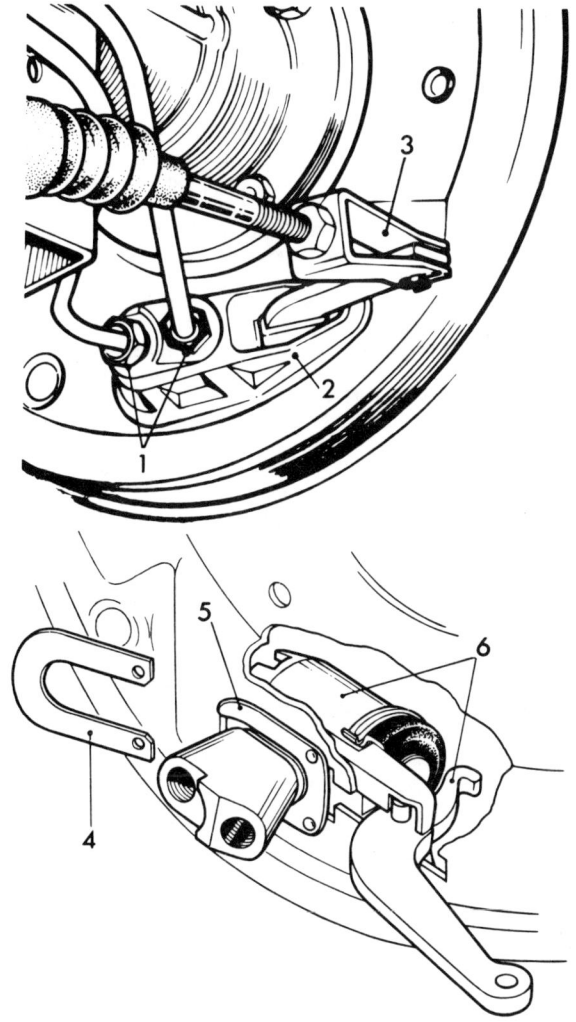

FIG. 9.9. REMOVING REAR WHEEL CYLINDER

1 Feed and transfer pipe unions
2 Rubber boot
3 Cable fork connected to brake lever
4 Horseshoe clip
5 Spring plate
6 Wheel cylinder and handbrake lever assembly

2 Place a piece of polythene under the reservoir cap and screw down the cap tightly. Carefully detach the hydraulic pipe from the rear of the wheel cylinder. The left-hand rear cylinder has only one feed pipe connected, while the right-hand cylinder has a feed pipe and a transfer pipe connected. Also disconnect the handbrake cable from the handbrake lever assembly (13) (Fig 9.5) at the rear of the backplate by removing the split pin and extracting the clevis pin noting that the head is uppermost. Remove the rubber boot (14).

3 Using a wide bladed screwdriver separate the horseshoe clip and wheel cylinder retaining spring plate (16), and carefully pull the horseshoe clip towards the front of the car.

4 Withdraw the handbrake lever assembly (13) from the wheel cylinder, followed by the spring plate and shaped distance washer which is held in position by a retaining spring. Carefully pull the wheel cylinder assembly from the hub side of the brake backplate.

5 Ease away the clip (23) followed by the piston dust cover (22) and withdraw the piston (7) from the cylinder. Remove the piston seal (6) using a non-metal pointed rod, or fingers. Do not use a metal screwdriver as this could scratch the piston.

6 Inspect the inside of the cylinder for score marks. If any are found the cylinder and piston will require renewal. NOTE: If the wheel cylinder requires renewal ensure that the replacement is the same diameter as originally fitted.

7 If the cylinder is sound, thoroughly clean it out with fresh hydraulic fluid.

8 The old rubber seal will probably be swollen and visibly worn. Smear the new rubber seal with hydraulic fluid and re-assemble in the cylinder. Fit a new dust seal (22) and retaining clip (23).

9 Using Castrol PH Grease smear the backplate where the wheel cylinder slides, and refit the brake wheel cylinder ensuring it is the correct way round.

10 Replace the handbrake lever assembly (13) not forgetting the shaped distance washer and its retaining spring. Install the spring plate with the open end towards the front of the car, and with the dimples towards the differential. Fit the horseshoe clip from the front of the cylinder, ensuring the holes in the end engage with the dimples on the spring plate. Check that the cylinder is free to float in the backplate.

11 Refit the rubber cover (14), connect the hydraulic pipe to the wheel cylinder and the handbrake cable to the handbrake lever. Replace the clevis pin with the head uppermost, and lock using a new split pin.

12 Replace the brake shoes, drum and road wheel and finally adjust the brakes. Remove the polythene from the reservoir cap.

13 Rear brake shoe adjuster - removal and replacement

1 Should it be found necessary to remove the brake adjuster, first remove the road wheel, brake drum and brake shoes. Release the adjuster retaining nut (11) (Fig.9.5) and lift away the star washer (10). The adjuster can now be lifted away from the backplate.

2 Check that the screw (3) can be screwed both in and out to its fullest extent without showing signs of tightness.

3 Lift away the two tappets and thoroughly clean the adjuster assembly. Inspect the adjuster body and tappets for signs of excessive wear and fit new parts as necessary.

4 Lightly smear the tappets with Castrol PH Grease and re-assemble. Double check correct operation by holding the two tappets between the fingers and rotating the wedge whereupon the two tappets should move out together.

5 Refitting is the reverse procedure to dismantling. The two adjuster retaining nuts should be tightened to a torque wrench set to between 4 and 5 lb ft. (0.55 and 0.69 kg m).

14 Handbrake lever assembly - removal, overhaul and refitting

1 Chock the front wheels, release the handbrake, jack up the

rear of the car and support on firmly based stands.

2 Working under the car, extract the split pin securing the compensator clevis pin. Lift away the plain washer and withdraw the clevis pin noting that the head is uppermost.

3 Now working inside the car, take out the two bolts securing each front seat slide to the floor panels and lift away the two front seats.

4 Remove the front seat safety belt, inboard eyebolts and lift out the carpeting.

5 Remove the handbrake lever rubber gaiter and, using a socket, undo and remove the four handbrake assembly floor mounting bolts. Refer to Fig. 9.10.

6 Pull the handbrake lever assembly upwards and forwards so as to expose the cable attachment clevis pin. Extract the split pin, lift away the plain washer and withdraw the clevis pin.

7 Lift the handbrake lever assembly away from the inside of the car.

8 To dismantle the handbrake assembly, remove the nut and fulcrum pin from the handbrake mounting bracket. Withdraw the ratchet and bushes from the handbrake lever.

9 Using an electric drill cut away the riveted head of the pawl fulcrum pin. With a suitable diameter parallel pin punch drift out the pin, and remove the pawl.

10 The handbrake button and spring will tend to fly off, unless restrained, when the pawl is removed. Withdraw the release rod (button) and spring.

11 The parts should be washed down and the teeth of the ratchet segment and pawl examined for wear. Also examine the handbrake lever for cracks, and the various holes for ovality. Obtain new parts if worn.

12 To reassemble, first fit the spring over the release rod, apply a little Castrol LM Grease to the rod and spring and insert both through the hole in the grip.

13 Holding the grip in one hand, depress the button at the end of the release rod with the thumb and fit the radiused lug of the pawl into the hooked end of the release rod.

14 Carefully line up the hole in the pawl with the holes in the lever and insert the pin once it has been lightly greased. Rivet over the end of the pin.

15 To refit the handbrake lever assembly is the reverse sequence to removal.

15 Handbrake - adjustment

1 If the handbrake is in need of adjustment, excessive travel of the lever is taken up automatically when the rear brakes are adjusted. After high mileages it is possible that the handbrake cables will have stretched and will need to be adjusted.

2 With the rear wheels free off the ground and chocks under the front wheels to prevent any forward movement, ensure the handbrake is fully off, and then lock each brake drum by screwing the brake adjusters in as far as possible.

3 Remove the split pin from the clevis pin and pull out the clevis pin to free the fork from the brake lever.

4 Loosen the locknut and screw the fork onto the threaded rod until the clevis pin can be fitted to the fork and the brake lever without pulling the lever from the off position or straining the cable.

5 Fit the fork to the brake lever with the clevis pin and secure with a split pin. Slacken off the rear brake adjusters in the normal way until adjustment is correct. Lower the car to the ground.

6 Apply the handbrake, noting the number of clicks of the rachet before the rear brakes are fully applied. The adjustment may be considered correct if there are four clicks. If incorrect, re-adjust the position of the nut and repeat the instructions in paragraph 5.

16 Handbrake cable - removal and replacement

1 Chock the front wheels, jack up the rear of the car and

FIG. 9.10. HANDBRAKE COMPONENTS

1 Pawl, handbrake
2 Bracket - handbrake mounting
3 Clamp plate, between handbrake and boot
4 Boot - handbrake lever
5 Split pin
6 Washer
7 Clevis pin
8 Compensator link cable
9 Bracket - handbrake mounting
10 Washer
11 Pin, fulcrum, handbrake lever
12 Bush
13 Spring washer
14 Bolt
15 Setscrew
16 Nut
17 Spring washer
18 Split pin
19 Washer
20 Fork end, handbrake cable
21 Nut, locking
22 Pin, clevis
23 Nut
24 Handbrake cable assembly
25 Grommet, handbrake cable
26 Nut
27 Washer
28 Spring compensator support
29 Plug
30 Clevis pin
31 Washers
32 Split pin
33 Grip, handbrake lever
34 Spring, pawl release
35 Rod assembly, pawl release
36 Lever, handbrake
37 Compensator, (handbrake)
38 Locknut
39 Pin, fulcrum, pawl to lever
40 Bolt
41 Washer
42 Bush

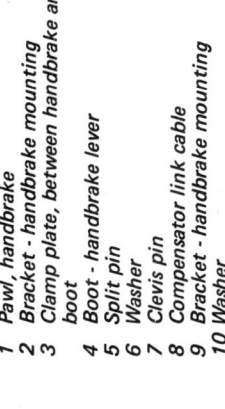

support with stands or blocks. Release the handbrake.

2 Disconnect the cable fork from the backplate lever by removing the split pin and clevis pin. Remove the nut securing the cable rear support to the suspension bracket and detach the cable support.

3 Release the cable sheath and rubber bush from the clip on the axle casing.

4 Withdraw the cable fork through the bracket on the axle casing.

5 Remove the pinch bolt, nut and plain washers from the cable sheath front bracket.

6 Withdraw the cable sheath rearwards clear of the front bracket and ease the cable wire downwards.

7 Release the nipple on the front end of the cable from the handbrake compensator, and withdraw the cable.

8 To replace the cable expand the brake shoes in the rear drum and lock the wheel.

9 Engage the nipple on the front end of the cable in the hand brake compensator.

10 Slide the cable sheath in the bracket. Fit the bolt, plain washers and nut. Do not overtighten the pinch bolt. Slide the rubber boot rearwards to engage the cable sheath.

11 Thread the cable fork through the bracket on the axle casing.

12 Insert the rubber bush and cable sheath into the axle casing clip.

13 Attach the cable sheath rear support to the suspension bracket and secure it with the nut.

14 Adjust the fork at the rear end of the cable so that the clevis pin engages the fork and backplate lever.

15 Ensure that the handbrake compensator remains central.

16 Fit the split pin to the clevis pin and slacken the brake adjuster on the backplate. Re-adjust the handbrake as described in Section 15.

17 Brake pedal and stop light switch - removal and refitting

1 Refer to Chapter 12 and remove the parcel shelf.

2 Working inside the car, extract the split pin and remove the plain washer from the end of the clevis pin securing the master cylinder push rod yoke to the pedal.

3 Disconnect the pedal return spring.

4 To remove the pedal from the bracket, unscrew the nylon nut and withdraw the bolt retaining the pedal assembly in the bracket. Lift away the pedal assembly return spring and distance tube from the support bracket.

5 Wash down the component parts and check the pedal bushes for wear by refitting the distance tube. If excessive rocking movement is evident, carefully drift out the old bushes and insert new ones.

6 Reassembly and refitting the pedal is the reverse sequence to removal.

7 If, for some reason, it is also required to remove the brake pedal mounting bracket, it will also be necessary to remove the facia (Chapter 12) and the windscreen wiper linkage (Chapter 10).

8 The brake stop light switch is adjacent to the brake pedal arm above the steering column. Having located it, disconnect the two Lucar connectors.

9 Slacken the large hexagon nut and unscrew the switch from the nut, which, together with the washer can remain in situ.

10 When a new switch is fitted, take care not to overtighten the nut or the plastic threads of the switch may be damaged. A little time is necessary to set the adjustment for a new switch. Remember that the ignition must be switched on to get the battery feed to the switch.

18 Disc brakes and servo unit - general description

While all early models of the Toledo destined for the United Kingdom market had conventional drum brakes both front and rear, later models are now being fitted with front wheel disc

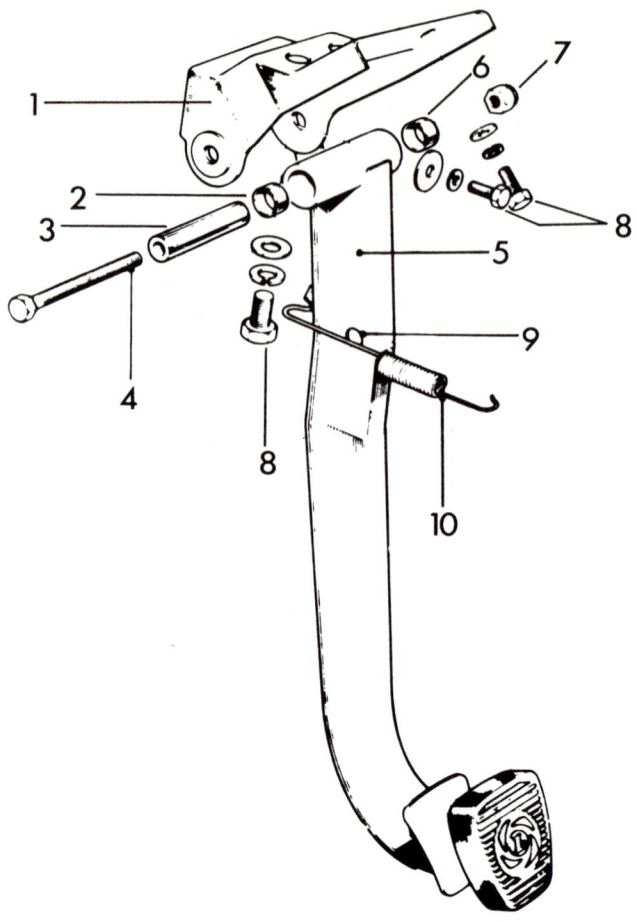

FIG. 9.11. BRAKE PEDAL COMPONENTS

1	Pedal bracket	7	Locknut
2	Bush	8	Bracket securing bolts
3	Distance tube	9	Connection hole for master
4	Pivot bolt		cylinder yoke
5	Pedal	10	Return spring
6	Bush		

brakes and a vacuum servo unit as standard equipment.

The front disc brakes are of the conventional caliper design. Each half of the caliper contains a piston which operates in a bore both being interconnected so that under hydraulic pressure these pistons move towards each other. By this action they clamp the rotating disc between two friction pads so slowing rotational movement of the disc. Special seals are fitted between the piston and bore and these seals are able to distort slightly when the piston moves to apply the brake. When the hydraulic pressure is released the seals return to their natural shape and draw the pistons back slightly so giving a running clearance between the pads and disc. As the pads wear, the piston is able to slide through the seal so allowing wear to be taken up.

The front disc brakes are self adjusting. A brake vacuum servo unit is fitted between the brake pedal and master cylinder to add to the pressure on the master cylinder pushrod when the brake pedal is being depressed.

19 Front disc brake caliper pad - removal and refitting

1 Chock the rear wheels, apply the handbrake, jack up the front of the car and support on firmly based axle stands. Remove the road wheel.

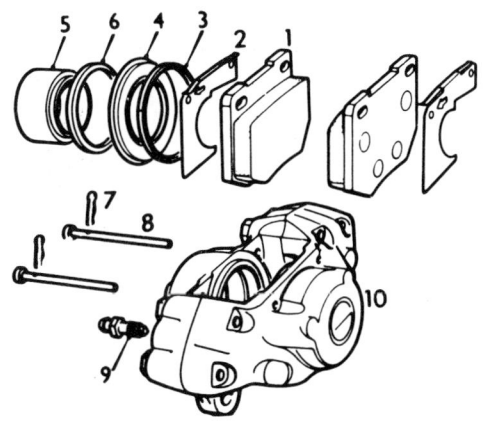
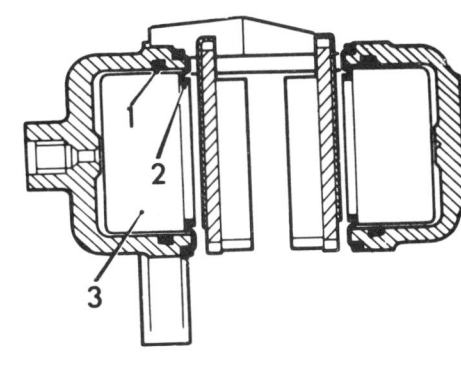

FIG. 9.12. FRONT DISC BRAKE CALIPER COMPONENT PARTS

1 Pad	4 Dust cover	7 Spring clip	10 Caliper body
2 Anti-squeak shim	5 Piston	8 Retaining pin	
3 Dust cover retaining ring	6 Sealing ring	9 Bleed screw	

Inset: Correct fitted position of piston seal and dust cover
1 Piston seal   2 Dust cover   3 Piston

2 Extract the two pad retaining pin spring clips and withdraw the two retaining pins (Fig.9.12).

3 Lift away the brake pads and anti-rattle shims noting which way round the shims are fitted.

4 Inspect the thickness of the lining material and, if it is less than 1/16 inch. (1.6 mm) the pads must be renewed. If one of the pads is slightly more worn than the other, it is permissible to change these round.

5 If new pads are being fitted always replace with high quality branded pads of similar specification to those given at the start of this chapter.

6 To refit the pads, it is first necessary to extract a little brake fluid from the system. To do this, fit a plastic bleed tube to the bleed screw and immerse the free end in 1 in. (25 mm) of hydraulic fluid in a jar. Slacken off the bleed screw one complete turn and press back the pistons into their bores. Tighten the bleed screw and remove the bleed tube.

7 Wipe the exposed end of the pistons, and in the recesses of the caliper free of dust or road dirt.

8 Re-fitting the pads is now the reverse sequence to removal. In addition:
a) The anti-squeal shims are fitted with the arrows pointing upwards.
b) If it is suspected that air has entered the system during the operation described in paragraph 6, the system must be bled as described in Section 2.

9 Wipe the top of the hydraulic fluid reservoir and remove the cap. Top up and depress the brake pedal several times to settle the pads. Recheck the hydraulic fluid level.

20 Front brake disc - removal and refitting

1 Chock the rear wheels, apply the handbrake, jack up the front of the car and support on firmly based axle stands. Remove the road wheel.

2 Refer to Section 21 and remove the caliper assembly.

3 Using a wide bladed screwdriver ease off the hub grease cap.

4 Straighten the hub nut retainer locking split pin ears and extract the split pin. Remove the nut retainer and then undo and remove the nut and splined washer.

5 Withdraw the complete front hub assembly from the spindle (Chapter 2).

6 To separate the disc from the hub, first mark the relative position of the hub and disc. Undo and remove the four bolts securing the hub to the disc and separate the two parts.

7 Should the disc surfaces be grooved and a new disc not obtainable, it is permissible to have the two faces ground by an engineering works (but only so far). Score marks are not serious provided that they are concentric but not excessively deep. It is however far better to fit a new disc rather than to re-grind the original one.

8 To refit the disc to the hub make sure that the mating faces are very clean and then line up the previously made alignment marks if the original parts are to be used. Secure with the four bolts which should be tighened in a progressive and diagonal manner to a final torque wrench setting of 38 to 45 lb ft (5.25 to 6.22 kg m).

9 Refitting is now the reverse sequence to removal but the following additional points should be noted:
a) Before refitting the caliper check the disc run-out at a 4.75 in. (120.7 mm) radius of the disc. The run-out must not exceed 0.006 in. (0.152 mm). If necessary remove the disc and check for dirt on the mating faces. Should these be clean reposition the disc on the hub.
b) The hub bearing endfloat must be adjusted as described in Chapter 11.

21 Front disc brake caliper - removal and refitting

1 Apply the handbrake, chock the rear wheels, jack up the front of the car and support on firmly based stands. Remove the road wheel.

2 Wipe the top of the master cylinder reservoir, unscrew the cap and place a piece of polythene sheet over the top. Refit the cap . This is to stop hydraulic fluid syphoning out during subsequent operations.

3 Wipe the area around the caliper flexible hose to metal pipe union and also metal pipe to caliper connection. Unscrew the union nuts, and lift away the metal pipe (Fig 9.13).

4 Undo and remove the two bolts and spring washers securing the caliper to the vertical link. Lift the caliper from the disc.

5 Refitting the caliper is the reverse sequence to removal. In addition:
a) The two caliper securing bolts should be tightened to a torque wrench setting of 50 lb ft (6.9 kg m).
b) Bleed the brake hydraulic system as described in Section 2.
c) Depress the brake pedal several times to reset the pads in their correct operating position.

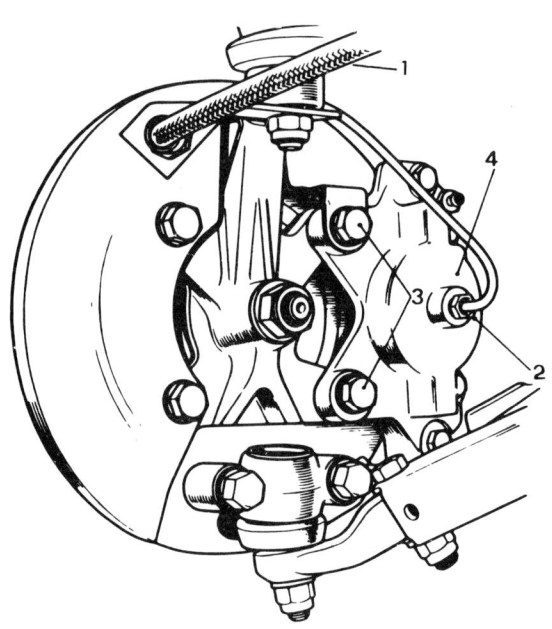

FIG. 9.13. DISC BRAKE CALIPER MOUNTING DETAILS

1 Flexible hose
2 Brake pipe union connection to caliper
3 Caliper retaining bolts
4 Caliper body

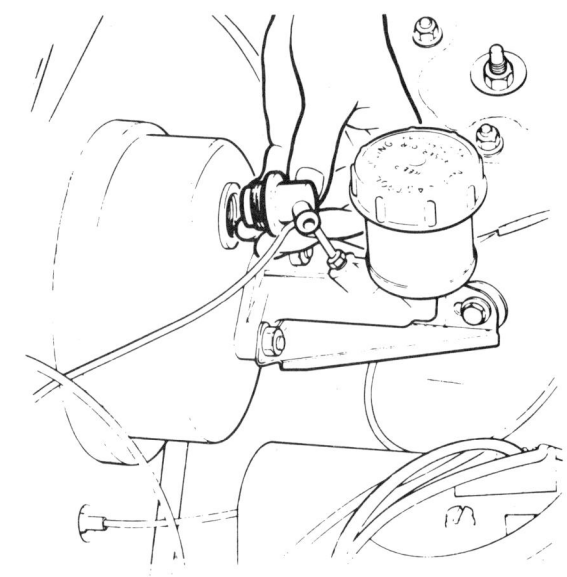

Fig. 9.15. Disconnecting the non-return valve

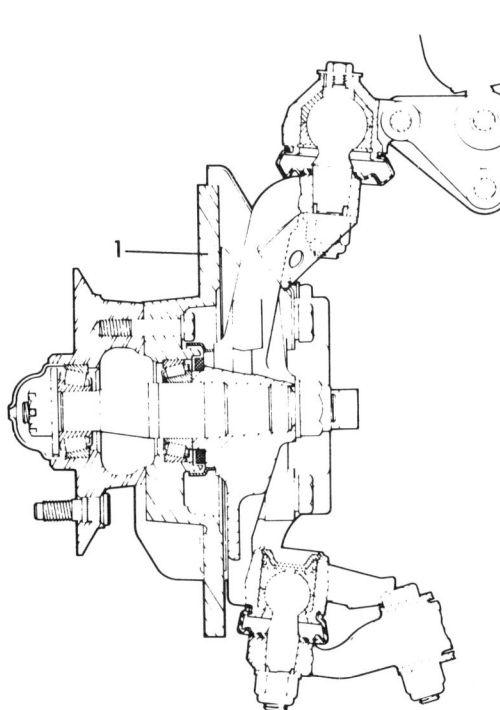

FIG. 9.14. SECTION THROUGH FRONT WHEEL HUB SHOWING THE BRAKE DISC

1 Disc

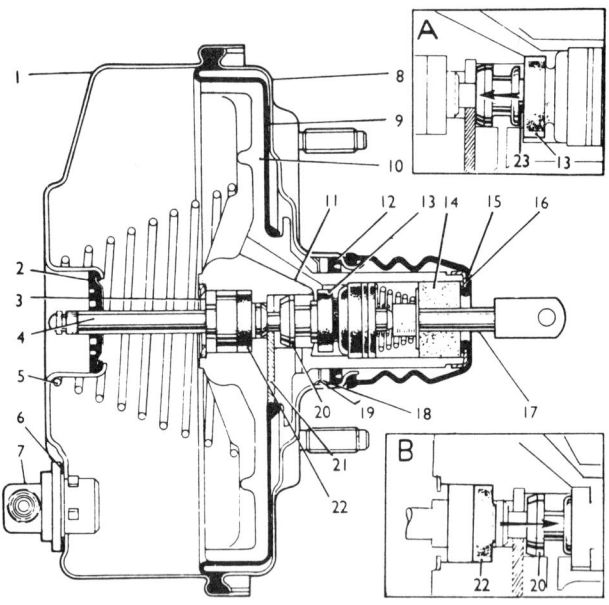

FIG. 9.16. SECTIONAL VIEW OF SERVO UNIT

1 Front shell
2 Seal and plate assembly
3 Retainer (sprag washer)
4 Pushrod - hydraulic
5 Diaphragm return spring
6 'O' ring
7 Non-return valve
8 Rear shell
9 Diaphragm
10 Diaphragm plate
11 Vacuum port
12 Seal
13 Control valve
14 Filter
15 Dust cover
16 End cap
17 Valve operating rod assembly
18 Bearing
19 Retainer
20 Control piston
21 Valve retaining plate
22 Reaction disc
23 Atmospheric port

Insets: A Control valve closed, control piston moved forward - atmospheric port open.
B Pressure from diaphragm plate causes reaction disc to extrude, presses back control piston and closes atmospheric port.

22 Front disc brake caliper - overhaul

1 Extract the two pad retaining pin spring clips and withdraw the two retaining pins (Fig 9.12).
2 Lift away the brake pads and anti-squeak shims noting which way round the shims are fitted.
3 Temporarily reconnect the caliper to the hydraulic system. Do not allow the caliper to hang on the flexible hose, but support its weight. Using a small G clamp hold the piston in the mounting half of the caliper. Carefully depress the foot- brake pedal with the bleed nipple open so as to bleed the system, and then close the nipple. Depress the footbrake again and this will push the piston in the rim half of the caliper outwards. Release the dust cover retaining ring and the cover. Depress the foot-brake again until the piston has been ejected sufficiently to continue removal by hand. It is advisable to have a container or tray available to catch any hydraulic fluid once the piston is removed.
4 Using a tapered wooden rod or an old plastic knitting needle, carefully extract the fluid seal from its bore in the caliper half.
5 Remove the G clamp from the mounting half piston. Temporarily refit the rim half piston and repeat the operations in paragraph 3 and 4.
6 Thoroughly clean the internal parts of the caliper using methylated spirits. Any other fluid cleaner will damage the internal seals between the two halves of the caliper. DO NOT SEPARATE THE TWO HALVES OF THE CALIPER.
7 Inspect the caliper bores and pistons for signs of scoring and, if evident, a new assembly should be fitted.
8 To reassemble the caliper, first wet a new fluid seal with Castrol Girling Brake Fluid and carefully insert it into its groove in the rim half of the caliper seating, ensuring that it is correctly fitted. Refit the dust cover into its special groove in the cylinder.
9 Release the bleed screw in the caliper one complete turn. Coat the side of the piston with hydraulic fluid and with it positioned squarely in the top of the cylinder bore, ease the piston in until approximately 5/16 in. (7.94 mm) is left protruding. Engage the outer lip of the dust cover in the piston groove and push the piston into the cylinder as far as it will go. Fit the dust cover retaining ring.
10 Repeat the operations in paragraph 8 and 9 for the mounting half of the caliper.
11 Fit the pads and anti-squeak shims into the caliper and retain in position with the two pins and spring clips.
12 The caliper is now ready for refitting.

23 Brake master cylinder - removal and replacement

When a vacuum servo unit is fitted, the removal technique for the master cylinder is very slightly different form that detailed in Section 9.
1 Drain the hydraulic fluid from the reservoir and master cylinder as described in Section 9.
2 Wipe the area around the hydraulic pipe union on the master cylinder. Undo the union nut and lift out the hydraulic pipe.
3 Undo and remove the two nuts and spring washers that secure the master cylinder to the servo unit and remove the bolt that secures the earth wires and the front end of the master cylinder bracket to the valance.
4 Lift away the master cylinder taking care not to allow any hydraulic fluid to drip onto the paintwork.
5 Refitting is the reverse sequence to removal.

24 Brake servo unit - description

A vacuum servo unit can be fitted into the brake hydraulic circuit in series with the master cylinder, to provide power assistance to the driver when the brake is depressed.

The unit operates by vacuum obtained from the induction manifold and comprises basically a booster diaphragm and a non-return valve.

The servo unit and hydraulic master cylinder are connected together so that the servo unit piston rod acts as the master cylinder pushrod. The driver's braking effort is transmitted through another pushrod to the servo unit piston and built-in control system. The servo unit piston does not fit tightly into the cylinder, but has a strong diaphragm to keep its edges in constant contact with the cylinder wall so assuring an air tight seal between the two parts. The forward chamber is held under vacuum conditions created in the inlet manifold of the engine and, during periods when the brake pedal is not in use, the controls open a passage to the rear chamber so placing it under vacuum. When the brake pedal is depressed, the vacuum passage to the rear chamber is cut off and the chamber opened to atmospheric pressure. The consequent rush of air pushes the servo piston forward in the vacuum chamber and operates the main pushrod to the master cylinder. The controls are designed so that assistance is given under all conditions and, when the brakes are not required, vacuum in the rear chamber is estab-lished when the brake pedal is released. Air from the atmosphere entering the rear chamber is passed through a small air filter.

25 Brake servo unit - removal and refitting

1 Refer to Section 23 and remove the brake master cylinder.
2 Slacken the hose clip and detach the vacuum hose from the servo connector.
3 Refer to Chapter 12 and remove the front parcel tray.
4 Straighten the ears of the split pin retaining the servo to brake pedal push rod clevis pin. Extract the split pin, lift away the plain washer and withdraw the clevis pin.
5 Undo and remove the four nuts and spring washers that secure the servo unit to the mounting bracket. Lift away the servo unit.
6 Refitting the servo unit is the reverse sequence to removal. It is important that the servo operating rod is attached to the BOTTOM hole of the two holes in the brake pedal lever. Bleed the brake hydraulic system as described in Section 2.

26 Brake servo unit - air filter renewal

Under normal operating conditions the vacuum servo unit is very reliable and does not require overhaul except possibly at very high mileages. In this case it is far better to obtain a service exchange unit, rather than repair the original.

However, the air filter may be renewed and fitting details are given. This will not however, repair any fault.
1 Pull back the dust cover and slide up the push rod.
2 Using a screwdriver ease out the end cap and then with a pair of scissors cut off the old air filter.
3 Make a diagonal cut through the new air filter element and fit over the pushrod. Hold in position and refit the end cap.
4 Reposition the dust cover on the servo unit body.

For 'Fault diagnosis ' see next page

27 Fault diagnosis

Symptom	Reason/s	Remedy
PEDAL TRAVELS ALMOST TO FLOORBOARDS BEFORE BRAKES OPERATE		
Leaks and air bubbles in hydraulic system	Brake fluid level too low	Top up master cylinder reservoir. Check for leaks.
	Wheel cylinder or caliper leaking	Dismantle wheel cylinder or caliper clean fit new rubbers and bleed brakes.
	Master cylinder leaking (bubbles in master cylinder fluid)	Dismantle master cylinder, clean, and fit new rubbers. Bleed brakes.
	Brake flexible hose leaking	Examine and fit new hose if old hose leaking Bleed brakes.
	Brake line fractured	Replace with new brake pipe. Bleed brakes.
	Brake system unions loose	Check all unions in brake system and tighten as necessary. Bleed brakes.
Normal wear	Linings over 75% worn	Fit replacement shoes and brake linings.
BRAKE PEDAL FEELS SPRINGY		
Brake lining renewal	New linings not yet bedded-in	Use brakes gently until springy pedal feeling leaves.
	Brake drums or discs badly worn and weak or cracked	Fit new brake drums or discs.
	Master cylinder securing nuts loose	Tighten master cylinder securing nuts. Ensure spring washers are fitted.
BRAKE PEDAL FEELS SPONGY AND SOGGY		
Leaks or bubbles in hydraulic system	Wheel cylinder or caliper leaking	Dismantle wheel cylinder or caliper, clean, fit new rubbers, and bleed brakes.
	Master cylinder leaking (bubbles in master cylinder reservoir)	Dismantle master cylinder, clean, and fit new rubbers and bleed brakes. Replace cylinder if internal walls scored.
	Brake pipe line or flexible hose leaking	Fit new pipe line or hose.
	Unions in brake system loose	Examine for leaks, tighten as necessary.
BRAKES UNEVEN AND PULLING TO ONE SIDE		
Oil or grease leaks	Linings and brake drums or discs contaminated with oil, grease, or hydraulic fluid	Ascertain and rectify source of leak, clean brake drums fit new linings.
	Tyre pressures unequal	Check and inflate as necessary.
	Brake backplate caliper or disc loose	Tighten backplate caliper or disc securing nuts and bolts.
	Brake shoes or pads fitted incorrectly	Remove and fit shoes or pads correct way round.
	Different type of linings fitted at each wheel	Fit the linings specified all round.
	Anchorages for front or rear suspension loose	Tighten front and rear suspension pick-up points including spring locations.
	Brake drums or discs badly worn, cracked or distorted	Fit new brake drums or discs.
BRAKES TEND TO BIND DRAG OR LOCK-ON		
Incorrect adjustment	Brake shoes adjusted too tightly	Slacken off rear brake shoe adjusters two clicks.
	Handbrake cable over-tightened	Slacken off handbrake cable adjustment.
	Master cylinder pushrod out of adjustment giving too little brake pedal free movement	Reset to specifications.
Wear or dirt in hydraulic system or incorrect fluid	Reservoir vent hole in cap blocked with dirt	Clean and blow through hole.
	Master cylinder by-pass port restricted - brakes seize in 'on' position	Dismantle, clean, and overhaul master cylinder. Bleed brakes.
	Wheel cylinder seizes in 'on' position	Dismantle, clean and overhaul wheel cylinder. Bleed brakes.
Mechanical wear	Drum brake shoe pull-off springs broken, stretched or loose	Examine springs and replace if worn or loose.
Incorrect brake assembly	Drum brake shoe pull-off springs fitted wrong way round, omitted, or wrong type used	Examine, and rectify as appropriate.

Chapter 10 Electrical system

Contents

General description 1	Windscreen wiper motor - removal, overhaul and replacement 19
Battery - removal and replacement 2	Flasher circuit - fault tracing and rectification 20
Battery - maintenance and inspection 3	Horns - fault tracing and rectification 21
Battery - electrolyte replenishment 4	Headlight units - removal and replacement 22
Battery - charging 5	Headlamp beam adjustment 23
Alternator - general description 6	Front parking and flasher lamp bulbs - removal & replacement 24
Alternator - functional check 7	Stop, tail and rear flasher bulbs - removal and replacement ... 25
Alternator - removal and refitting 8	Interior roof lamp - removal and refitting 26
Alternator - adjusting the drive belt 9	Rear number plate light bulb - removal and replacement ... 27
Alternator - dismantling, overhaul and reassembly 10	Ignition/starter switch - removal and replacement 28
Starter motor - general description 11	Windscreen wiper switch - removal and replacement... ... 29
Starter motor - testing on engine 12	Steering column combination switch - removal and replacement 30
Starter motor - removal and replacement 13	
Starter motor inertia drive - removal and replacement ... 14	Fuse box and fuses - removal and replacement 31
Starter motor - dismantling and reassembly 15	Voltage stabiliser - removal and replacement 32
Windscreen wiper mechanism - maintenance 16	Temperature and fuel gauge - removal and replacement ... 33
Windscreen wiper arms - removal and replacement 17	Speedometer and cable - removal and replacement 34
Windscreen wiper mechanism - fault diagnosis and rectification 18	Fault diagnosis 35

Specifications

Battery ... ... 12-volt (negative earth) lead-acid
    Capacity ... ... 40 AH

Alternator
    Type ... ... Lucas 15 ACR
    Output ... ... 318 watts (28 amperes)
    Control unit ... ... Integral with alternator
    Stator phases 3

Starter motor
    Type ... ... Lucas M35J
    Brush spring tension ... ... 28 oz (0.8 kg)
    Minimum brush length ... ... 3/8 in (9.5 mm)
    Lock torque ... ... 7 lb ft (0.96 kg m) with 350 to 375 amp load
    Torque at 1000 rpm ... ... 4.4 lb ft (0.61 kg m) with 260 to 270 amp
    Light running current ... ... 65 amp at 8000 to 10,000 rpm

Windscreen wiper motor
    Type ... ... AC Delco 7975284

Running speed - with linkage arm disconnected from crank pin and
terminal voltage of 14 volts
    Normal speed ... ... 54 to 64 rev/min

Running current - with linkage arm disconnected from crank pin and
terminal voltage of 14 volts
    Normal speed ... ... 1.5 amp
    Armature endfloat ... ... None

Light bulbs   **Watts**
Headlamps - two rectangular
    LH Dip 75/60
    RH Dip - normal 45/40
    Front parking lamps 5

Front flasher lamps ...	...	...	...	...	...	...	21
Rear flasher lamps ...	...	...	...	...	...	...	21
Tail/stop lamps ...	...	...	...	...	...	...	5/21
Plate illumination lamps ...	...	...	...	...	...		5
Luggage boot illumination ...	...	...	...	...	...		2.2
Roof lamp ...	...	...	...	...	...	...	6
Instrument illumination ...	...	...	...	...	...		2.2
Warning lights ...	...	...	...	...	...		2.2

1 General description

The electrical system is of the 12-volt type and the major components comprise a 12-volt battery of which the negative terminal is earthed, a Lucas alternator which is fitted to the front left hand side of the engine and is driven from the pulley on the front of the crankshaft, and a starter motor which is mounted on the rear left hand side of the engine.

The battery supplies current for the ignition, lighting and other electrical circuits, and provides a reserve of electricity when the current consumed by the electrical equipment exceeds that being produced by the alternator. Normally an alternator is able to meet any demand placed upon it.

The battery is charged by a Lucas 15 ACR alternator and a description of the latter will be found in Section 6.

When fitting electrical accessories to cars with a negative earth system it is important, if they contain silicone diodes or transistors, that they are connected correctly, otherwise serious damage may result to the component concerned. Items such as radios, tape recorders, electronic tachometers, automatic dipping, parking lamps and anti-dazzle mirrors should all be checked for correct polarity.

It is important that the battery positive lead is always disconnected if the battery is to be boost charged or if any body or mechanical repairs are to be carried out, using electric arc welding equipment, otherwise serious damage can be caused to the more delicate instruments, specially those containing semi-conductors.

2 Battery - removal and replacement

1 The battery is in a special carrier fitted on the righthand wing valance of the engine compartment. It should be removed once every three months for cleaning and testing. Disconnect the positive and then the negative leads from the battery terminals by slackening the clamp retaining nuts and bolts or by unscrewing the retaining screws if terminal caps are fitted instead of clamps.

2 Unscrew the clamp bar retaining wing nuts and lower to the side of the battery. Carefully lift the battery out of its compartment. Hold the battery vertical to ensure that none of the electrolyte is spilled.

3 Replacement is a direct reversal of this procedure. NOTE: Replace the negative lead before the positive lead and smear the terminals with petroleum jelly (vaseline) to prevent corrosion. NEVER use an ordinary grease as applied to other parts of the car.

3 Battery - maintenance and inspection

1 Normal weekly battery maintenance consist of checking the electrolyte level of each cell to ensure that the separators are covered by ¼ in. (6 mm) of electrolyte. If the level has fallen, top up the battery using water only. Do not overfill. If a battery is overfilled or any electrolyte spilled, immediately wipe away the excess as electrolyte attacks and corrodes any metal it comes into contact with very rapidly.

2 If the battery has the Auto-fil device as fitted on original production of the car, a special topping up sequence is required. The white balls in the Auto-fil battery are part of the automatic topping up device which ensures correct electrolyte level. The vent chamber should remain in position at all times except when topping up or taking specific gravity readings. If the electrolyte level in any of the cells is below the bottom of the filling tube top up as follows:

a) Lift off the vent chamber cover.

b) With the battery level, pour distilled water into the trough until all the filling tubes and trough are full.

c) Immediately replace the cover to allow the water in the trough and tubes to flow into the cells. Each cell will automatically receive the correct amount of water (photo), (Fig.10.1)

3 As well as keeping the terminals clean and covered with petroleum jelly, the top of the battery, and especially the top of the cells, should be kept clean and dry. This helps prevent corrosion and ensures that the battery does not become partially discharged by leakage through dampness and dirt.

4 Once every three months remove the battery and inspect the battery securing bolts, the battery clamp plate, tray and battery leads for corrosion (white fluffy deposits on the metal which are brittle to touch). If any corrosion is found, clean off the deposit with ammonia and paint over the clean metal with anti-rust anti-acid paint.

5 At the same time inspect the battery case for cracks. If a crack is found, clean and plug it with one of the proprietary compounds marketed by such firms as Holts for this purpose. If leakage through the crack has been excessive then it will be necessary to refill the appropriate cell with fresh electrolyte as detailed later. Cracks are frequently caused to the top of the battery case by pouring in distilled water in the middle of winter AFTER instead of BEFORE a run. This gives the water no chance to mix with the electrolyte and so the former freezes and splits the battery case.

6 If topping up the battery becomes excessive and the case has been inspected for cracks that could cause leakage, but none are found, the battery is being overcharged and the voltage regulator will have to be checked and reset.

7 With the battery on the bench at the three monthly interval check, measure the specific gravity with a hydrometer to determine the state of charge and condition of the electrolyte. There should be very little variation between the different cells and, if a variation in excess of 0.025 is present, it will be due to either:

a) Loss of electrolyte from the battery at some time caused by spillage or a leak, resulting in a drop in the specific gravity of the electrolyte when the deficiency was replaced with distilled water instead of fresh electrolyte.

b) An internal short circuit caused by buckling of the plates or similar malady pointing to the likelihood of total battery failure in the near future.

8 The specific gravity of the electrolyte for fully charged conditions at the electrolyte temperature indicated, is listed in Table A. The specific gravity of a fully discharged battery at different temperatures of the electrolyte is given in Table B.

TABLE A
Specific gravity - battery fully charged

1.268 at 100°F or 38°C electrolyte temperature
1.272 at 90°F or 32°C electrolyte temperature
1.276 at 80°F or 27°C electrolyte temperature
1.280 at 70°F or 21°C electrolyte temperature
1.284 at 60°F or 16°C electrolyte temperature
1.288 at 50°F or 10°C electrolyte temperature
1.292 at 40°F or 4°C electrolyte temperature
1.296 at 30°F or -1.5°C electrolyte temperature

3.2a Removing the battery filler cover

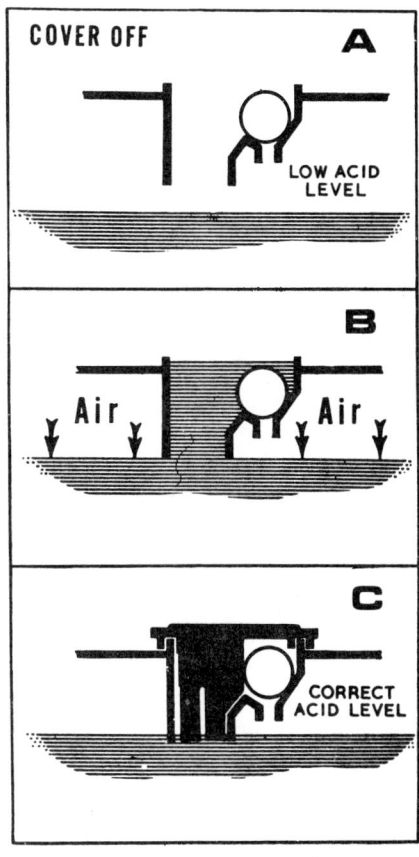

FIG. 10.1. PRINCIPLE OF AUTO-FIL DEVICE

A *The cell vent hole is sealed by the ball which seats firmly on it.*
B *During topping-up, this forms an air-lock when the acid level rises to the bottom of the filling tube. The level in the cell can then rise no further. As the topping-up continues, this fills each tube and then the trough.*
C *The air-lock is broken by the ball being lifted. Water in the trough and tubes flows into each cell which is automatically filled to the correct level.*

TABLE B
Specific gravity - battery fully discharged

1.098 at 100°F or 38°C electrolyte temperature
1.102 at 90°F or 32°C electrolyte temperature
1.106 at 80°F or 27°C electrolyte temperature
1.110 at 70°F or 21°C electrolyte temperature
1.114 at 60°F or 16°C electrolyte temperature
1.118 at 50°F or 10°C electrolyte temperature
1.122 at 40°F or   4°C electrolyte temperature
1.126 at 30°F or -1.5°C electrolyte temperature

4 Battery - electrolyte replenishment

1 If the battery is in a fully charged state and one of the cells maintains a specific gravity reading which is 0.025 or more lower than the others and a check of each cell has been made with a voltage meter to check for short circuits (a four to seven second test should give a steady reading of between 1.2 and 1.8 volts), then it is likely that electrolyte has been lost from the cell with the low reading at some time.
2 Top the cell up with a solution of 1 part sulphuric acid to 2.5 parts of water. If the cell is already fully topped up draw some electrolyte out of it with a pipette. The toal capacity of each cell is ¾ pint (0.43 litres).
3 When mixing the sulphuric acid and water NEVER ADD WATER TO SULPHURIC ACID - always pour the acid slowly onto the water in a glass container. IF WATER IS ADDED TO SULPHURIC ACID IT WILL EXPLODE.
4 Continue to top up the cell with the freshly made electrolyte and then recharge the battery and check the hydrometer readings.

5 Battery - charging

1 In winter time when heavy demand is placed upon the battery, such as when starting from cold, and much electrical equipment is continually in use, it is a good idea to occasionally have the battery fully charged from an external source at the rate of 3.5 to 4 amps.
2 Continue to charge the battery at this rate until no further rise in specific gravity is noted over a four hour period.
3 Alternatively, a trickle charger, charging at the rate of 1.5 amps can be safely used overnight.
4 Specially rapid 'boost' charges which are claimed to restore the power of the battery in 1 to 2 hours are most dangerous as they can cause serious damage to the battery plates through overheating.
5 While charging the battery note that the temperature of the electrolyte should never exceed 100°F.

6 Alternator - general description

The main advantage of the alternator lies in its ability to provide a high charge at low revolutions. Driving slowly in heavy traffic with a dynamo invariably means little if any charge is reaching the battery. In similar conditions even with the wiper, heater, lights and perhaps radio switched on, the 15 ACR alternator will ensure a charge reaches the battery.

An important feature of the alternator is a built in output control regulator, based on 'thick film' hybrid integrated micro-circuit technique, which results in Model 15 ACR being a self-contained generating and control unit.

The system provides for direct connection of a charge indicator light, and eliminates the need for a field switching relay or warning light control unit, necessary with former systems.

The alternator is of a rotating field, ventilated design. It comprises principally, a laminated stator on which is wound a star connected 3-phase output winding; a twelve pole rotor carrying the field windings - each end of the rotor shaft runs in ball

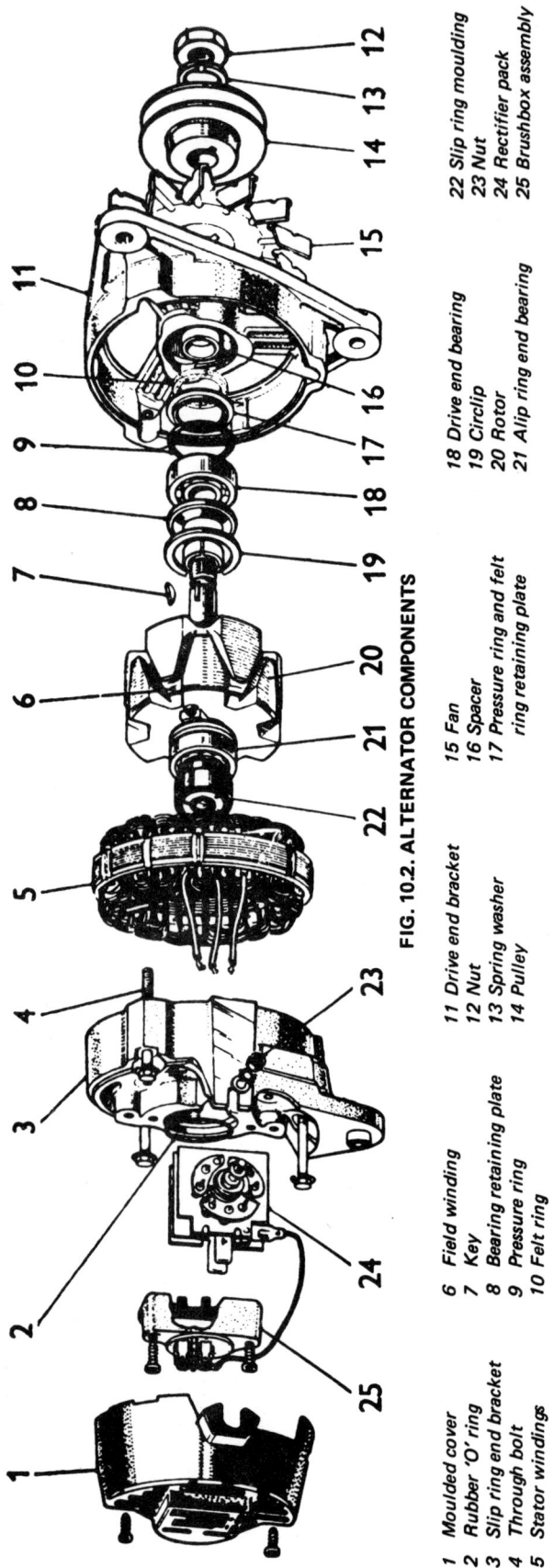

FIG. 10.2. ALTERNATOR COMPONENTS

1 Moulded cover
2 Rubber 'O' ring
3 Slip ring end bracket
4 Through bolt
5 Stator windings
6 Field winding
7 Key
8 Bearing retaining plate
9 Pressure ring
10 Felt ring
11 Drive end bracket
12 Nut
13 Spring washer
14 Pulley
15 Fan
16 Spacer
17 Pressure ring and felt
   ring retaining plate
18 Drive end bearing
19 Circlip
20 Rotor
21 Slip ring end bearing
22 Slip ring moulding
23 Nut
24 Rectifier pack
25 Brushbox assembly

race bearings which are lubricated for life; natural finish alum-inium die cast end brackets, incorporating the mounting lugs; a rectifier pack for converting the AC output of the machine to DC for battery charging; and an output control regulator.

The rotor is belt driven from the engine through a pulley keyed to the rotor shaft. A pressed steel fan adjacent to the pulley draws cooling air through the machine. This fan forms an integral part of the alternator specification. It has been designed to provide adequate air flow with a minimum of noise, and to withstand the high stresses associated with maximum speed. Rotation is clockwise viewed on the drive end. Maximum con-tinuous rotor speed is 12500 rpm.

Rectification of alternator output is achieved by six silicon diodes housed in a rectifier pack and connected as a 3-phase full-wave bridge. The rectifier pack is attached to the outer face of the slip ring end bracket and contains also three 'field' diodes; at normal operating speeds, rectified current from the stator output windings flows through these diodes to provide self-excitation of the rotor field, via brushes bearing on face-type slip rings.

The slip rings are carried on a small diameter moulded drum attached to the rotor shaft outboard of the slip ring end bearing. The inner ring is centred on the rotor shaft axle, while the outer ring has a mean diameter of ¾ in. (20 mm) approximately. By keeping the mean diameter of the slip rings to a minimum, relative speeds between brushes and rings, and hence wear, are also minimal. The slip rings are connected to the rotor field winding by wires carried in grooves in the rotor shaft.

The brush gear is housed in a moulding screwed to the outside of the slip ring and bracket. This moulding thus encloses the slip ring and brush gear assembly, and, together with the shielded bearing, protects the assembly against the entry of dust and moisture.

The regulator is set during manufacture and requires no further attention. Briefly the 'thick film' regulator comprises resistors and conductors screen printed onto a 1 in. (25.4mm) square alumina substrate. Mounted on the substrate are Lucas semi-conductor dice consisting of three transistors, a voltage reference diode and a field recirculation diode, and also two capacitors. The internal connections between these components and the substrate are made by special Lucas patented con-nectors. The whole assembly is 1/16 in. (1.59mm) thick, and is housed in a recess in an aluminium heat sink, which is attached to the slip ring bracket. Complete hermetic sealing is achieved by a silicone rubber encapsulant to provide enviromental pro-tection.

Electrical connections to external circuits are brought out to Lucar connector blades, these being grouped to accept a moulded connector socket which ensures correct connections.

7 Alternator - functional check

The alternator functional check is normally performed when it is suspected that the malfunction lies within the alternator, and is not simply a case of adjusting the fan belt tension. Normally, the first indication of failure is the ignition warning light illumin-ating: if this cannot be remedied by adjusting fan belt tension, or by observing and rectifying disconnected or broken leads to the alternator or control box, then the following checks should be carried out.

WARNING:

It is not recommended that an owner without the basic electrical knowledge or necessary equipment should attempt to delve into the alternator's internals, since it is a complex and expensive item, and one may easily cause more expense than is saved.

1 The first check is to ensure that the alternator can produce the correct current, and should be performed as near as possible to the alternator's normal operating temperature.

2 Disconnect the multi-socket connector from the end of the alternator, then remove the moulded cover.

3 Connect up a test circuit as shown in Fig.10.3. The polarity

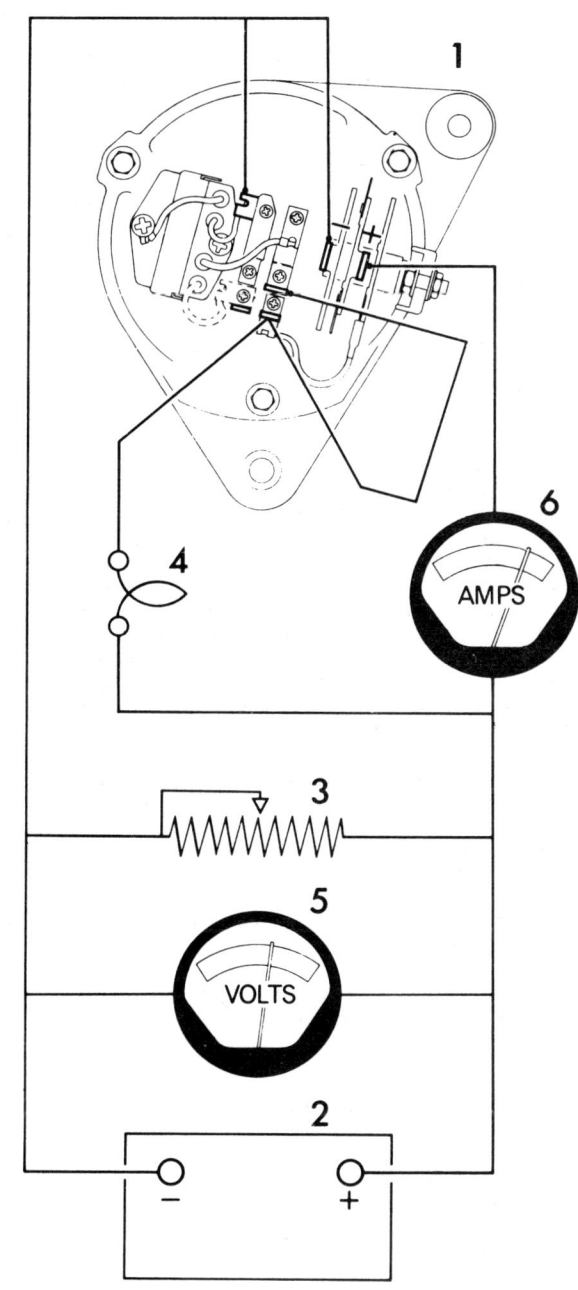

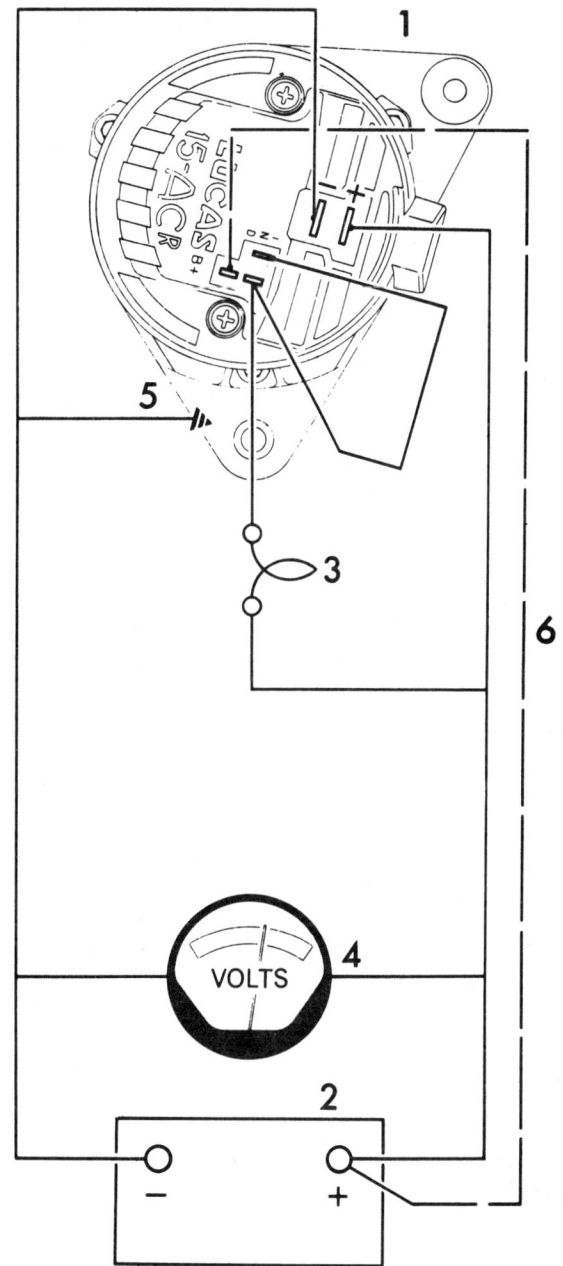

FIG. 10.3. ALTERNATOR OUTPUT TEST CIRCUIT

1   Alternator
2   Battery ... ...   12 volt
3   Variable resistor ...   0–15 ohm–35 amp
4   Light ... ...   12 volt–2.2 watt
5   Voltmeter ... ...   0–20 volt
6   Ammeter ... ...   0–40 amp

FIG. 10.4. ALTERNATOR CONTROL UNIT TEST CIRCUIT

1   Alternator
2   Battery ... ...   12 volt
3   Bulb ... ...   12 volt–2.2 watt
4   Voltmeter ... ...   0–20 volt
5   Earth connection to alternator body

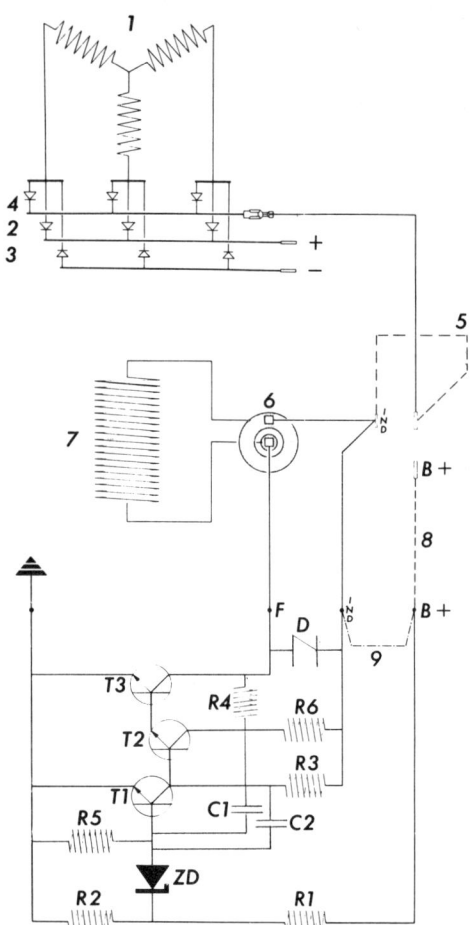

FIG. 10.5. ALTERNATOR THEORETICAL CIRCUIT

1   Stator windings
2   Live side output diodes
3   Earth side output diodes
4   Field winding supply diodes
5   Harness loop - Circuit is made when multi-socket connector
    is fitted and broken when connector is removed.
6   Brushes and slip rings
7   Field winding
8   Internal B+ connection
R3 Resistor -   Restricts T2 base current supplied from field
    winding supply' diodes.
T2 Intermediate transistor - Controls T3 base current direct.
R6 Resistor - Restricts T3 base current supplied from 'field wind-
    ing supply' diodes.
T3 Output transistor - Controls field winding earth return circuit.
R1 and R2 Potential divider - Senses battery reference voltage.
ZD Zener diode - Voltage sensitive component. Opposes passage
    of current until breakdown voltage — approximately 8 volts
    — is reached. Controls T1 base current direct.
T1 Input transistor -   Controls T2 base current by diverting-
    current passing through R3 to earth when ZD is conducting.
C1 and R4 Capacitor and Resistor - Prevents transistor overheat-
    ing by providing a positive feed back circuit to ensure quick
    switching of transistors from 'fully on' to 'fully off'.
D   Surge quench diode - Connected across field winding. Protects
    T3 from field winding high induced voltage surge and
    smoothes field winding current.
C2 Condenser - Radio interference suppression.

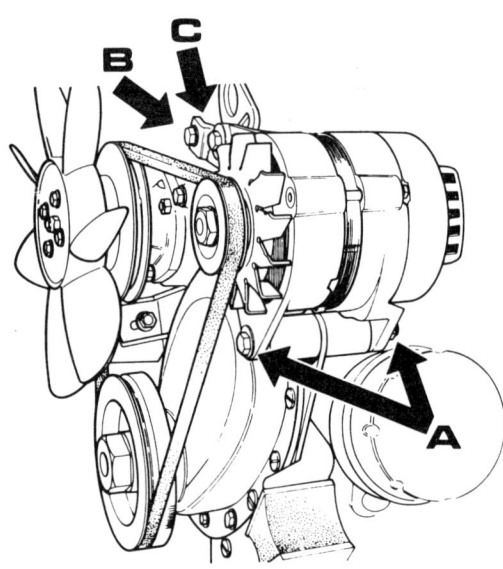

FIG. 10.6. ALTERNATOR SECURING BOLTS

A   Main pivot bolt   B   Mounting bracket bolt
          C   Adjustment bolt

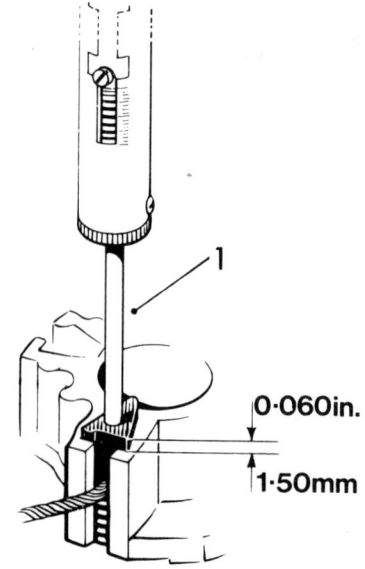

FIG. 10.7. MEASURING SPRING BRUSH PRESSURE

1   Spring balance

of the connections MUST be correct, or irreparable damage can be caused.

4 Do not connect the variable resistor across the battery for longer than is necessary to perform the check.

5 Run the engine and gradually increase the speed. At 620 engine rpm (1500 alternator rpm.) the test light should be extinguished.

6 Hold the speed at approx. 2480 engine rpm. (6000 alternator rpm). Adjust the variable resistor so that the voltmeter reads 14 volts. The ammeter reading should now be approximately 28 amps. If this figure is not achieved, it indicates that the alternator is faulty and needs replacement.

7 In order to check the control unit, proceed as for alternator checking, except that the test circuit should be as that given in Fig.10.4. There is no need to remove the moulded alternator cover for this test; make the connections from the access gained when the multi-socket connector is removed.

8 Start the engine and gradually increase the speed. The light should go out at an engine speed of 620 rpm. (1500 alternator rpm.) Increase the speed and then hold it steady at 2480 engine rpm. (6000 alternator rpm.) The voltmeter should be steady at 14.0 to 14.4 volts. If the reading is not steady within the limits but the alternator is satisfactory then the control unit is defective and must be renewed.

8 Alternator - remove and refit

1 Disconnect the multi-socket connectors from the end face of the alternator.

2 Slacken the main mounting bolt assembly and the two adjustment bracket bolts.

3 Push the alternator towards the engine and remove the drive belt from the pulley.

4 Remove the outer adjustment bracket bolt.

5 Support the weight of the alternator and withdraw the main mounting bolt. Lift the alternator away from the vehicle.

6 Refitting is the reverse of removal, ensure that fan belt tension is adjusted when the alternator is finally in position.

9 Alternator - adjusting the drive belt

1 Slacken the main mounting bolt assembly and the two adjustment bracket bolts (Fig. 10.6).

2 Carefully lever the alternator away from the engine to tension the belt. CAUTION: To prevent bearing damage when tensioning the belt use a lever of soft material preferably wood - applied to the alternator drive end bracket. Do not lever on any other part of the alternator.

3 Tighten the three bolts.

4 Check the belt tension; movement should be 0.75 to 1.00 in. (20 to 25mm) at the mid-point of the longest run.

10 Alternator - dismantling, overhaul and reassembly

Since the alternator is a very complex component we do not recommend that the average home mechanic dismantle the unit any further than brush box level. Any further work should be carried out by a qualified auto electrician, preferably with access to Triumph tools and test equipment.

If a functional check has revealed no output from the alternator, the brushes can be checked as follows:

1 To clean the brushes first remove the alternator from the car, and clean the outside. Then remove the moulded end cover (two screws). Remove the brush box and control unit by disconnecting the "Lucar" connectors, and taking out three screws.

2 Check that the brushes protrude at least 0.060 in. (1.50 mm) from the brush box when free. Use a modified spring balance to check that the spring pressure is 7 to 10 oz when the faces of the brushes are flush with the brush box. Renew the brush box assembly if either of these limits is not reached (Fig.10.7

refers).

3 Clean the brushes with a petrol-moistened cloth and check that they move freely in the brush box. If necessary polish the sides of the brush lightly, using a smooth file.

4 Check that the slip rings are smooth and clean, cleaning them with a petrol-moistened cloth. If the slip rings show any burn marks, polish these off using very fine glasspaper. Never use emery cloth, as this will leave particles embedded in the slip ring, and do not machine the slip rings as this may affect the high speed performance of the alternator.

5 The resistance of the field coil winding can be measured between the slip rings using an Avometer or similar testmeter; this should be 4.33 ohms approx. A 110-volt AC test lamp or an insulation resistance meter (megger) may be used between each slip ring and the rotor to ensure that the insulation has not broken down. Renew the rotor if it is defective.

6 Replacement is the reverse to the removal instructions.

11 Starter motor - general description

The Lucas M35 J starter motor is of the inertia type, and has a series-wound, four-pole, four-brush motor with an extended shaft which carries a conventional inertia drive.

The armature shaft rotates in two porous bronze bushes. A squared extension of the shaft protrudes to enable the shaft to be rotated to clear any jamming between the inertia drive and engine flywheel ring gear, The armature features a face-type moulded commutator.

A plastic brush box is riveted to the commutator end bracket. It holds four wedge-shaped brushes and captive coil springs. The brushes are keyed to ensure correct fitting.

The field winding is a continously wound strip with no joints. One end is attached to two brush flexibles, while the other is attached to a single flexible which is earthed to the yoke.

The yoke is windowless and has no through-bolts . The commutator end bracket is secured by four screws which align with tappings in the yoke. The drive end bracket is attached by two slot-headed bolts which screw into tappings provided in the end faces of two of the pole-shoes.

The principle of operation of the inertia type starter motor is as follows: When the ignition switch is turned, current flows from the battery to the starter motor solenoid switch which causes it to become energized. Its internal plunger moves inwards and closes an internal switch so allowing full starting current to flow from the battery to the starter motor. This creates a powerful magnetic field to be induced into the field coils which causes the armature to rotate.

Mounted on helical splines is the drive pinion which, because of the sudden rotation of the armature, is thrown forwards along the armature shaft and so into engagement with the flywheel ring gear. The engine crankshaft will then be rotated until the engine starts to operate on its own and, at this point, the drive pinion is thrown out of mesh with the flywheel ring gear.

12 Starter motor - testing on engine

1 If the starter motor fails to operate, then check the condition of the battery by turning on the headlamps. If they glow brightly for several seconds and then gradually dim, the battery is in an uncharged condition.

2 If the headlamps continue to glow brightly and it is obvious that the battery is in good condition then check the tightness of the battery wiring connections (and in particular the earth lead from the battery terminal to its connection on the body frame). Check the tightness of the connections at the relay switch and at the starter motor. Check the wiring with a voltmeter for breaks or shorts due to failure of insulation.

3 If the wiring is in order then check that the starter motor switch is operating. To do this press the rubber covered button in the centre of the relay switch. If it is working the starter motor will be heard to 'click' as it tries to rotate. Alternatively

check it with a voltmeter.

4 If the battery is fully charged, the wiring in order, and the switch working but the starter motor fails to operate then it will have to be removed from the car for examination. Before this is done, ensure that the starter pinion has not jammed in mesh with the flywheel, check by turning the square end of the armature shaft with a spanner. This will free the pinion if it is stuck in engagement with the flywheel teeth.

13 Starter motor - removal and replacement

1 Disconnect the positive and the negative terminals from the battery.

2 Disconnect the lead from the starter motor terminal by removing the nut and spring washer.

3 Note the relationship between the starter motor, shims if fitted, packing and clutch housing.

4 Working from below the engine, remove the lower mounting bolt.

5 Working from above the engine, remove the upper mounting bolt (photo).

6 Working from below the engine, withdraw the starter motor downwards from the vehicle complete with the packing and shims if fitted (photo).

7 Refitting is the reverse sequence to removal. Make sure that the starter motor cable, when secured in position by its terminal retaining nut, does not touch any part of the body or power unit which could damage the insulation.

14 Starter motor inertia drive - removal and replacement

1 To dismantle the starter motor drive, first use a press or large valve spring compressor to push the retainer clear of the circlip which can then be removed. Lift away the retainer and main spring.

2 Slide off the remaining parts with a rotary action of the armature shaft.

3 It is most important that the drive gear is completely free from oil, grease and dirt. With the drive gear removed, clean all parts thoroughly in paraffin. Under no circumstances oil the drive components. Lubrication of the drive components could easily cause the pinion to stick.

4 Reassembly of the starter motor drive is the reverse sequence to dismantling. Use a press or the large valve spring compressor to compress the spring and retainer sufficiently to allow a new circlip to be fitted to its groove on the shaft.

15 Starter motor - dismantling and reassembly

Should it be necessary to dismantle the starter motor completely, the following operations, used in conjunction with Fig.10.8, will facilitate overhaul. Bear in mind, though, that it may be more economical in terms of money plus time, to purchase on exchange unit.

The other factor that may mitigate against overhaul is the need for special tools and test gear.

1 To strip the starter remove the two bolts holding the drive end bracket to the yoke, and take off that bracket, withdrawing the armature. Remove the thrust washer from the brush end of the armature.

2 Undo the four small bolts holding on the commutator end bracket. Pull the bracket aside. Note the way the flexible cable from the field windings to the brushes is fitted. Then undo these brushes.

3 To separate the armature from the drive end bracket and inertia drive, remove the inertia drive, and slide the drive end bracket from the shaft.

4 Inspect the laminations for score marks. These may indicate a bent shaft, worn bearings or a loose pole shoe.

5 Clean the commutator with a petrol-moistened cloth. If the commutator is in good condition it will be smooth and free from pits or burned spots.

6 If necessary, polish the commutator with fine glass-paper. If the commutator is badly scored it will need skimming. Mount the armature in a lathe and rotate at high speed. Using a very sharp tool, take a light cut. Polish with fine glass-paper. Do not cut below the minimum skimming thickness given in the Specifications. Do not undercut insulators between segments.

7 Inspect the porous bronze bearing bushes for wear and renew as necessary. To renew the commutator end bracket bush drill out the two rivets and discard the plate and felt seal. Screw a ½ in. (12.70mm) tap squarely into the bush and withdraw. Prepare the porous bronze bush by immersing it in thin engine oil for 24 hours. Using a highly polished, shouldered mandrel suitably dimensioned and a suitable press, fit the bush. Do not ream the bush after fitting or its porosity may be impaired. Assemble the brush box, commutator end bracket felt seal and plate. Secure with two rivets.

8 To renew the drive end bracket bush, remove the inertia drive, and slide the drive end bracket from the shaft. Support the bracket and press out the bush. Prepare the porous bronze bush by immersing it in thin engine oil for 24 hours. Using a highly polished, shouldered, mandrel suitably dimensioned and a suitable press, fit the bush. Do not ream the bush after fitting or its porosity may be impaired.

9 The brushes should be renewed if worn down to a length of 0.375 in (9.53mm).

10 The commutator end bracket brushes are supplied attached to a new terminal post. Withdraw the two brushes from the brush box. Withdraw the terminal post and remove the insulation piece. Reverse to assemble. Retain the longer flexible under the clip.

11 The field winding brushes are supplied attached to a common flexible. Cut old flexibles 0.250 in. (6 mm) from the joint. Solder the new flexible to the ends of the old flexible. Do not attempt to solder direct to the field winding strip as the strip may be produced from aluminium.

12 Check the field winding insulation from the yoke as follows. Drill out the rivet at the earth connection. Apply the normal 110-volt a.c. test-lamp circuit to the field winding and yoke. Do not attempt to disconnect the flexible from the field winding strip as the strip may be produced from aluminium.

13 To renew the field winding, drill out the rivet at the earth connection. Using a wheel-operated screwdriver, slacken the four pole-shoe screws. Remove two diametrically opposite screws and pole-shoes. Slacken the remaining two screws sufficient to allow the field winding to be withdrawn from the yoke. Reverse to assemble.

14 Assembly is the reverse of dismantling.

a) Insert the two field winding brushes into the brush box with the flexibles positioned as shown.

b) Position the commutator end bracket and secure it with four 4 B.A. bolts.

c) Fit the thrust washer.

d) Insert the drive end bracket, armature and inertia drive assembly complete into the yoke.

e) Fit the two drive end bracket bolts and spring washers.

16 Windscreen wiper mechanism - maintenance

1 Renew the windscreen wiper blades at intervals of 12000 miles (20,000 km) or more frequently if necessary.

2 The linkage which operates the wiper arms from the motor should be greased, and the washer round the two pivot housings should be lubricated with several drops of glycerine, every 6000 miles (10000 km).

17 Windscreen wiper arms - removal and replacement

1 Before removing a wiper arm, turn the windscreen switch on and off to ensure the arms are in their normal parked position

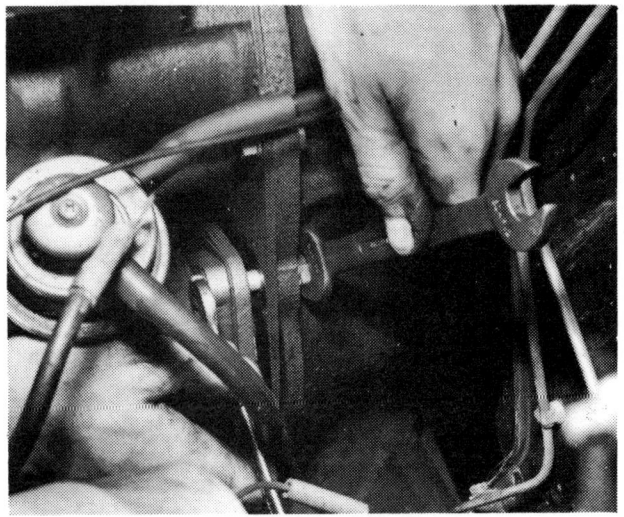

13.5 Removing the upper mounting bolt

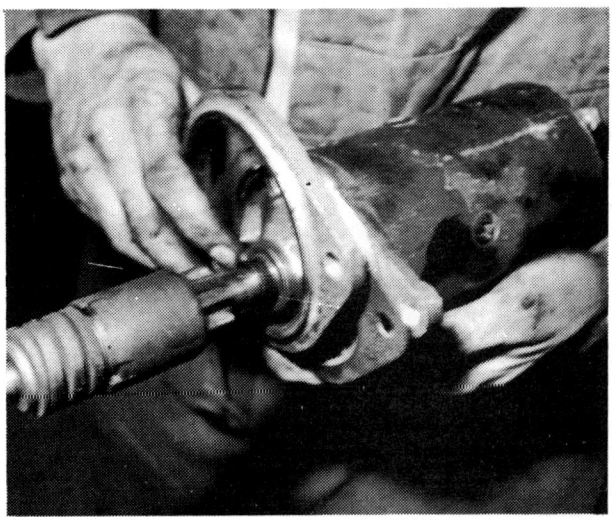

13.6 Note the packing piece and shim

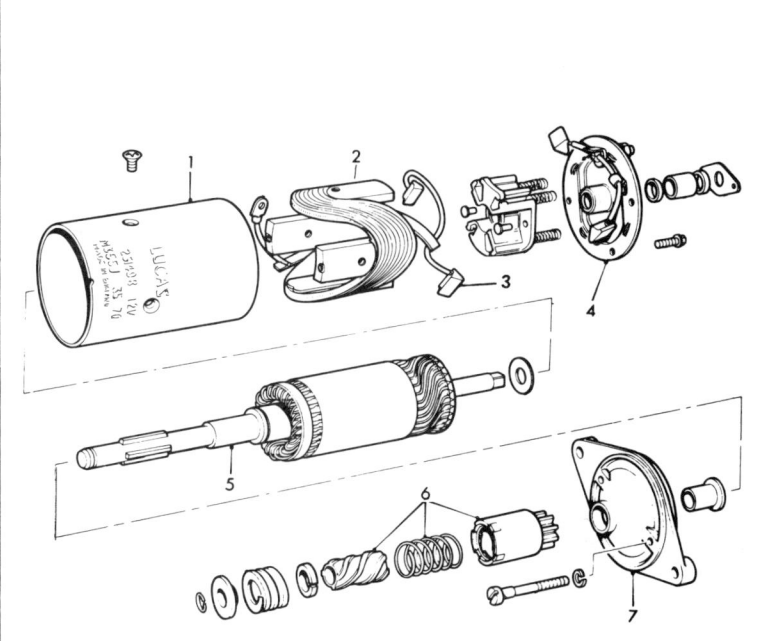

FIG. 10.8. STARTER MOTOR COMPONENTS

1	Body	5	Commutator
2	Field coils	6	Drive
3	Brushes	7	Drive end bracket
4	Commutator end bracket		

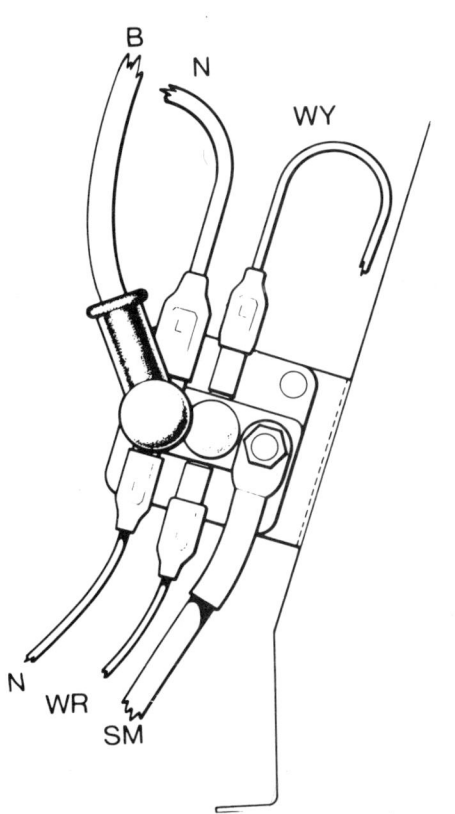

FIG. 10.9. STARTER SOLENOID CONNECTIONS

B	Battery lead
N	Brown wire
WY	White/yellow wire
N	Brown wire
WR	White/red wire
SM	Starter motor lead

parallel with the bottom of the windscreen. Lift the wiper arm and blade from the screen so that it falls back to the service position.

2   To remove an arm, place a screwdriver blade between the arm head and the locknut on the mounting post; then twist to lift the clip from the spindle groove.

3   When replacing an arm, place so it is in correct relative position and then press the arm head fully onto the splined drive. Lower the arm to the screen.

18 Windscreen wiper mechanism - fault diagnosis and rectification

Should the windscreen wipers fail, or work very slowly, then check the terminals for loose connections, and make sure the insulation of the external wiring is not broken or cracked. If this is in order, check the current the motor is taking by connecting up a 1-20 ammeter in the circuit and turning on the wiper switch. Consumption should be 1.5 amps.

If no consumption is passing through, check the A3-A4 fuse. If the fuse has blown, replace it after having checked the wiring of the motor and other electrical circuits served by this fuse. If the fuse is in good order, check the wiper switch.

If the wiper takes a very high current, check the wiper blades for freedom of movement. If this is satisfactory check the motor mountings and linkages for tightness. Should all appear to be well, the motor will have to be stopped and checked for tightness of the armature in its bearings or insufficient end float.

If the motor takes a very low current, ensure that the battery is fully charged. Check the brushes for wear and freedom of movement once the commutator end frame has been removed. Finally check the armature by substitution, if this part is suspect.

19 Windscreen wiper motor – removal, overhaul and replacement

1   The parts of the windscreen wiper motor are shown in Fig.10.12. Before removing the motor, disconnect the battery.

2   Remove the nut that secures the motor shaft to the crank.

3   Remove the three screws, washers, spacers and bushes that secure the motor to the support bracket.

4   Lift off the motor and disconnect the four Lucar connectors. Remove the motor and place it on a clean area of the workbench.

5   Release the three clips from the end frame.

6   Carefully withdraw the end frame and armature 0.25 in. (6 mm).

7   Use two small screwdrivers to hold back the two brushes and continue withdrawal. Ensure that the brushes are not contaminated with grease.

8   Remove the two brushes and springs.

9   Pull the armature from the end frame against the action of the permanent magnets.

10 Remove the single screw and Lucar blade.

11 Remove the gear cover and brush plate joined together by single wire.

12 Carefully lever retainer from the shaft.

13 Withdraw wormwheel and pinion assembly. Using pliers, carefully unscrew locknut. Screw out thrust screw.

14 Remove the motor shaft nut and withdraw the crank.

15 Remove the rubber sealing ring and washer.

16 Withdraw the final gear and thrust washer.

17 Withdraw the thrust washer.

18 Remove any dust with a brush or compressed air jet. Do not, allow any liquid cleaner into contact with the field coils.

19 Inspect the commutator for signs of burning or pitting, and if evident, clean with a little fine glass paper. Wash away any dust with petrol.

20 If any major part of the motor requires renewal, it is better to obtain a new motor rather than try to recondition a well worn one.

21 Reassembly is the reverse sequence to removal.

The following additional points should, however, be noted:

a) To renew the brushes it is necessary to unsolder the connections and re-solder on the new ones. Ensure the tags are well cleaned, and that a hot iron and coved solder are used, or you may finish up with a 'dry joint', i.e. a joint that looks good but in fact has no electrical continuity.

b) During assembly the gearbox should be generously lubricated with high temperature water resistant grease.

c) Ensure that the earth brush is not hidden under the brush plate and that the brushes are not contaminated with grease.

d) Fit the two springs and brushes and retain them deep in the brush box using slave clips locally made from paper clips or similar wire. Carefully insert armature shaft through the bearing, screwing in as required to engage wormgear. Ensure that the brushes are not contaminated with grease and that commutator clears brushes. Continue insertion until endframe is 0.25 in. (6 mm) from seat. When the brushes are over the commutator remove the slave clips (Fig.10.10).

e) Adjust the armature endfloat as follows: Slacken the locknut and screw out the screw to free position. Connect the motor in series with a 12-volt battery and ammeter. Run the motor with the crank free and note the current increases by 0.1 amp - maintain in this position and tighten locknut.

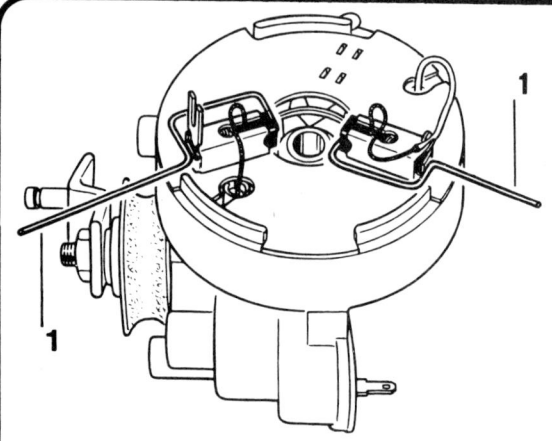

FIG. 10.10. SECURING WINDSCREEN WIPER MOTOR BRUSHES WITH SLAVE CLIPS DURING RE—ASSEMBLY

1 Slave clips

Fig. 10.11. Windscreen wiper linkage

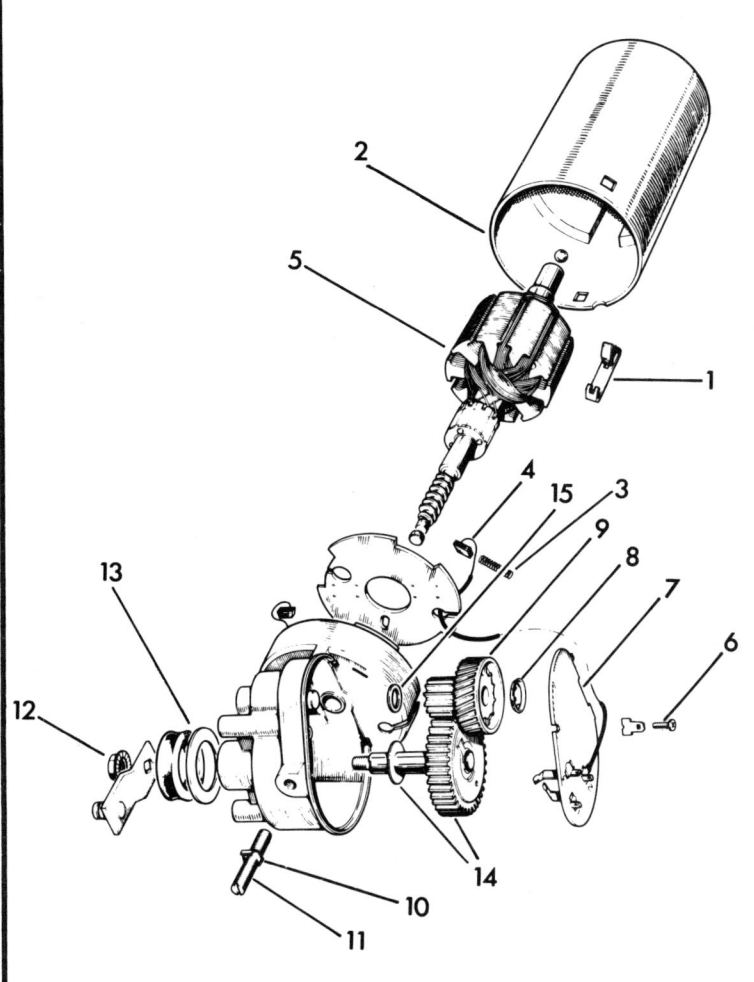

**FIG. 10.12. WINDSCREEN WIPER MOTOR
COMPONENTS**

1 Clips
2 End frame
3 Spring
4 Brush
5 Armature
6 Screw
7 Gear cover
8 Retainer
9 Helical gear and pinion
10 Locknut
11 Thrust screw
12 Crank arm nut
13 Sealing ring and washer
14 Final gear and thrust
   washer
15 Thrust washer

**FIG. 10.13. WINDSCREEN WIPER MOTOR
WIRING DIAGRAM**

+ Supply
1 Facia switch
   Used when single-speed wiper motor is fitted to vehicle.
   Terminal 4 is not used.

PARK	1 to 2
ON	2 to 3

2 Normal supply brush
3 High speed brush. (Two-speed wiper motor only)
4 Permanent magnet
5 Earth brush
6 Final gear slip ring arrangement
7 Static contacts

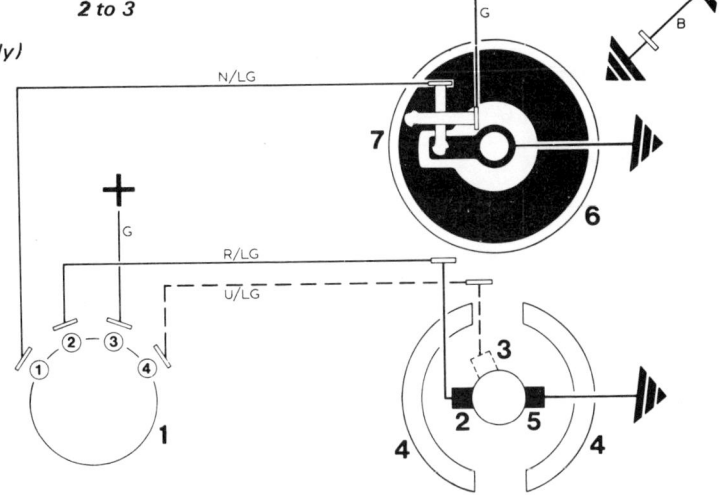

20 Flasher circuit - fault tracing and rectification

1   The flasher unit consists of a small alloy cylindrical container positioned under the facia panel.

2   If the flasher unit works twice as fast as usual when indicating either right or left, this is a sure sign of a broken filament in the front or rear indicator on the side operating too quickly.

3   If the external flashers are working but the internal flasher warning light has ceased to function, check the filament of the warning bulb and replace as necessary.

4   With the aid of the wiring diagram check all the flasher circuit connections if a flasher bulb is sound but does not work.

5   With the ignition turned on, check that current is reaching the flasher unit by connecting a voltmeter between the 'plus' or B terminal and earth. If this test is positive connect the 'plus' or B terminal and the L terminal and operate the flasher switch. If the flasher bulb lights up, the flasher unit itself is defective and must be replaced as it is not possible to dismantle and repair it.

21 Horns - fault tracing and rectification

1   If a horn works intermittently or fails completely, first check the wiring leading to it for short circuits and loose connections. Also check that the horn is firmly secured and that there is nothing lying on the horn body.

2   The horn should never be dismantled but it is possible to adjust it. This adjustment is to compensate for wear only and will not affect the tone. At the rear of the horn is a small adjustment screw on the broad rim, nearly opposite the two terminals. Do not confuse this with the large screw in the centre.

3   Turn the adjustment screw anticlockwise until the horn just fails to sound. Then turn the screw a quarter of a turn clockwise, which is the optimum setting.

4   It is recommended that if the horn is to be reset in the car the fuse should be removed and replaced with a piece of wire, otherwise the fuse will blow due to the continous high current required for the horn in continual operation.

22 Headlight units - removal and replacement

Two type of headlamps are fitted; pre-focus type or sealed beam type. If a prefocus lamp fails the bulb can be replaced. With a sealed beam unit, however, it is necessary to replace the complete unit.

1   Remove the two nuts and washers from the rim studs inside the appropriate wheelarch. It may be necessary to remove a wheel to obtain access to these nuts (photo).

2   Remove the four screws and washers that retain each grille and rim assembly at the front of the car (photo).

3   Release the three screws that secure the rim and light unit (photo).

4   **Sealed beam type.** Ease the lamp out of the recess and pull the connector block from the rear of the unit (photo).

5   **Pre-focus bulb type.** Gently lift the lamp forwards and pull the connector from the rear of the lamp. Disengage the locking clip and withdraw the bulb.

6   Reassembly is the reverse sequence to removal.

23 Headlight beam - adjustment

The headlights may be adjusted for both vertical and horizontal beam positions by the two screws, these being shown in Fig.10.16. For vertical movement screw B should be used and horizontal movement screw A.

They should be set so that on full or high beam, the beams are set slightly below parallel with a level road surface. Do not forget that the beam position is affected by how the car is normally loaded for night driving, and set the beams with the car loaded to this position.

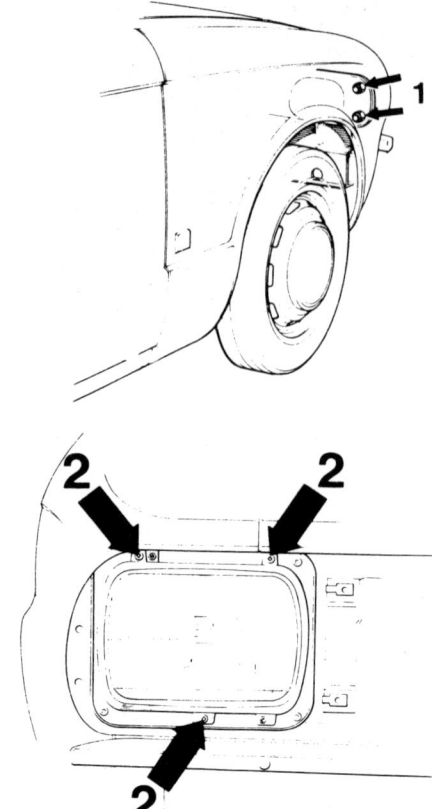

FIG. 10.14. HEADLAMP ASSEMBLY RETAINING NUTS AND SCREWS

1   Nuts inside the wheel arch. (There are four other screws that secure the grille and headlamp rim).
2   Light unit and rim securing screws.

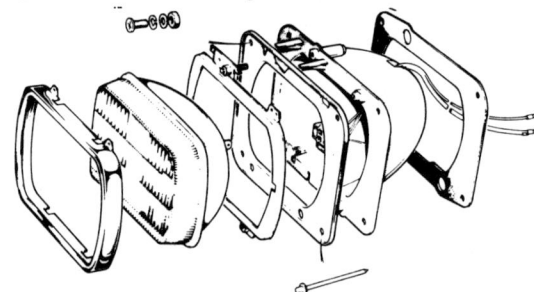

Fig. 10.15. Exploded view of headlamp unit

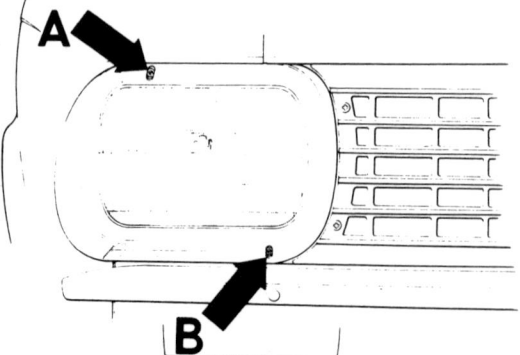

FIG. 10.16. HEADLAMP ADJUSTING SCREWS

A   Horizontal adjustment screw
B   Vertical (height) adjustment screw

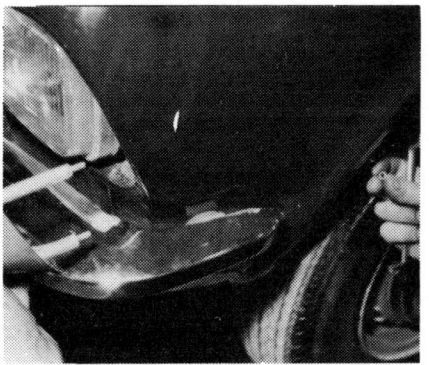
22.1 Removing the nuts in the wheel arch

22.2 ... and the screws in the grille front

22.3 ... and the rim screws

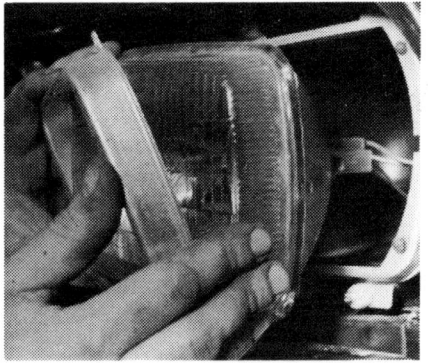
22.4a Lifting out the rim and lamp unit

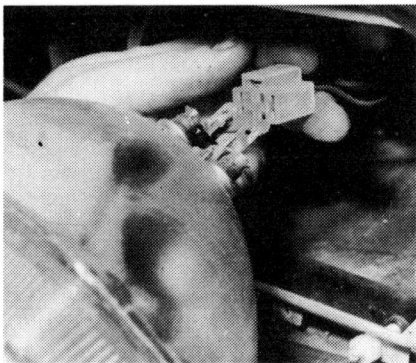
22.4b ... and releasing the connector

24.1a Removing the screws

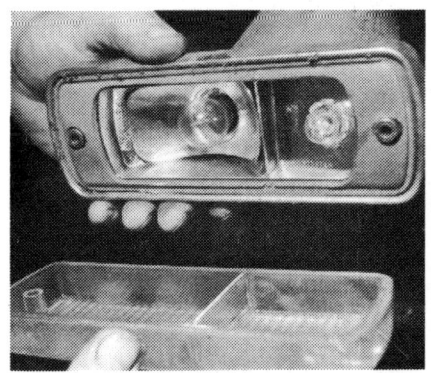
24.1b Lifting away the lens

25.4a Removing the lamp holders

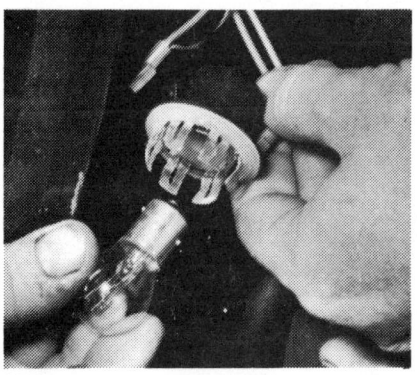
25.4b ... and the bulb

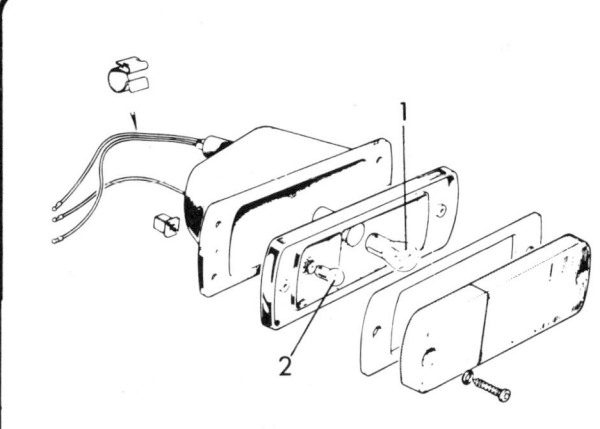

FIG. 10.17. EXPLODED VIEW OF FRONT PARKING AND FLASHER LAMP UNIT

1 Flasher bulb

2 Parking bulb

Although this adjustment can be approximately set at home, it is recommended that this be left to a local garage who will have the necessary equipment to do the job more accurately.

24 Front parking and flasher lamp bulbs - removal and replacement

1 Undo and remove the two screws securing the lamp lens to the lamp body and lift away the lenses (photos).
2 Either bulb is retained by a bayonet fixing, so to remove a bulb push in slightly and rotate in an anticlockwise direction.
3 Refitting is the reverse sequence to removal. Take care not to tighten the two lens retaining screws as the lenses can be easily cracked.

25 Stop, tail and rear flasher bulbs - removal and replacement

1 Open the luggage boot and remove the floor covering; if working on the right hand lamp, remove the floor panel also.
2 Remove the two screws and withdraw the side trim panel.
3 Disconnect the Lucar connector from the requisite bulb.
4 Pull the bulb holder from the lamp base and remove the bulb from the bayonet fitting (photos).
5 Replacement is the reverse of the removal instructions.

26 Interior roof lamp - removal and refitting

1 Isolate the battery.
2 Rotate the lens until the two screws are exposed; remove the screws and lower the lamp (photos).
3 Remove the festoon lamp.
4 Reverse the removal instructions to replace the lamp.

27 Rear number plate light bulb - removal and replacement

1 Open the luggage boot and remove the two screws securing the cowled rims.
2 Peel back the rubber lip and remove the lens.
3 Remove the bulb.
4 Refitting is the reverse of the removal instructions but ensure the cowled rim is fitted so that light is directed towards the number plate.

28 Ignition/starter switch - removal and replacement

1 Isolate the battery.
2 Remove the two screws and lift away the nacelle upper half. Remove the single screw and detach the nacelle lower half.
3 Prise off the trim board from its four retaining clips under the facia panel.
4 Disconnect the harness plug that is associated with the ignition switch cables.
5 Remove the three screws securing the parcel tray finisher; then, using a Phillips screwdriver, remove the two small screws securing the ignition switch to the steering column lock. Withdraw the switch. If it is required to remove the switch from the car it will be necessary to remove the tape securing the harness to the column.
6 Refitting is the reversal of removal instructions, but remember to ensure that the lockshaft and switch are aligned by virtue of the correct positioning of the keyway.

29 Windscreen wiper switch - removal and replacement

1 Isolate the battery.
2 Locate the hole in the underside of the switch knob, and insert a thin-bladed screwdriver to depress the spring clip. Pull

the knob from the shaft while the spring is depressed.
3 Unscrew the bezel and manoeuvre the switch out of its housing. Note the cable connections and then disconnect the three Lucar connectors.
4 Note the relative positions of the two water pipes and then pull them off the connecting nozzles. The switch can now be lifted clear.
5 Replacement is the reversal of the removal instructions. Ensure that the switch is securely attached to the spacer; if not tighten the slotted ring.

30 Steering column combination switch - removal and replacement

This switch is a combined headlamp dip/flasher, horn, direction indicator selection switch.
1 Isolate the battery.
2 Remove the two screws and lift off the nacelle upper half. Remove the single screw and detach the nacelle lower half.
3 Prise off the trim board from the four clips securing it under the facia.
4 Disconnect the harness plug associated with the switch.
5 Remove the two screws that secure the clamp and switch. Unwind any tape that binds the harness to the column. Withdraw the combined switch and harness.
6 Replacement is the reversal of the removal instructions.

31 Fuse box and fuses – removal and replacement

The fuse box is positioned on the bulkhead. The unit contains two operational fuses and has provision to house two spares. The fuses are protected by a pull-off plastic cover.

Failure of a particular fuse is indicated when all the circuits protected by it become inoperative. If a new fuse fails establish the cause and rectify the fault before fitting a second replacement.
1 To change a faulty fuse, it is first essential to indentify the fuse:

The fuse fed by a brown cable from the battery protects the following circuits:

    Horn
    Headlamp flash
    Luggage boot lamp
    Roof lamp

The fuse fed by a white cable from ignition/starter switch protects the following circuits:

    Temperature indication
    Fuel indication
    Heater
    Reverse lamp (optional extra)
    Windscreen wiper
    Stop lamp
    Turn signal

2 To remove the fuse box, first isolate the battery. Remove the fusebox cover and disconnect the cable plug-in connectors, noting their colour and with which tags they are associated. Remove the two screws that secure the box to the bulkhead and lift it away.
3 Replacement is the reversal of the removal instructions. If you are replacing the same fusebox, it is well worthwhile cleaning the connectors with some fine emery paper.

32 Voltage stabilizer - removal and replacement

The voltage stabilizer is mounted on the bulkhead above the fuse box. Its function is to provide a stabilized voltage to the temperature and fuel indicaters on the instrument panel in order to obtain an accurate, consistent reading that does not vary with battery voltage. One indication of failure of this unit would be both indicators giving inaccurate readings simultaneously.

26.2a Remove the screws

26.2b ... and lower the lamp

34.2 Easing the speedometer out of the facia

34.3 ... and disconnecting the bulb holders

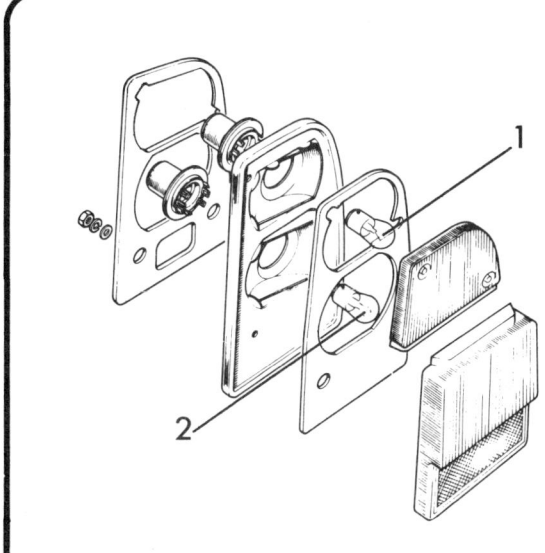

FIG. 10.18. EXPLODED VIEW OF TAIL, STOP AND FLASHER LAMP UNIT

1 *Flasher bulb*   2 *Stop/tail bulb*

1 Disconnect the Lucar connectors, noting cable connections.
2 Remove the single securing screw and lift the unit away. Replace in the reverse manner.

33 Temperature and fuel gauge - removal and replacement

1 Isolate the battery.
2 Remove the trim board from under the facia panel by prising it out of the four spring clips.
3 Unscrew the two knurled nuts that secure the instrument to the facia panel. The inboard nut must be removed, while the outboard nut need only be loosened. Withdraw the instrument.
4 Both gauges are secured to the instrument with two screws; these can be removed after the instrument is withdrawn sufficiently to obtain access to the screws. It may be found necessary to disconnect the Lucar connectors, the panel light bulb holder and the turn signal warning light bulb holders.
5 Refit in the reverse manner to removal. Ensure that the earth lead eyelet is under the spring washer and knurled nut. Check that all bulb holders and Lucar connectors are replaced in their correct positions (Fig.10.19 refers).

34 Speedometer and cable - removal and replacement

1 Disconnect the battery.

2 Unscrew the two knurled nuts, spring washers and release the clamp brackets. Pull the speedometer forward until it is possible to obtain access at the rear (photo).
3 Pull out the panel light bulb holders and unscrew the trip reset knurled nut at the attachment to the facia support rail (photo).
4 Depress the lever to release the catch from the annular groove in the boss. Pull the cable away from the instrument.
5 To remove the cable completely, jack up the car sufficiently high to allow access to the gearbox extension. Unscrew the knurled nut from the speedometer drive.
6 Note the cable run in relation to other adjacent components from the speedometer down to the body panel aperture. Manoeuvre the cable downwards through the grommet and detach it from the vehicle.
7 The inner cable can be removed on its own with a pair of long-nosed pliers, gripping the end of the inner cable and pulling it out. This can be carried out as soon as the instrument is separated from the combined inner and outer cable. Take care that the greasy inner cable does not contaminate the upholstery as it is withdrawn.
8 Replacement is the reverse of the removal instructions. The cable inner should be greased sparingly and fed into the cable outer, rotating it slightly to ease engagement of the squared end with the drive gear. Leave about one inch protruding to aid mating with the instrument.

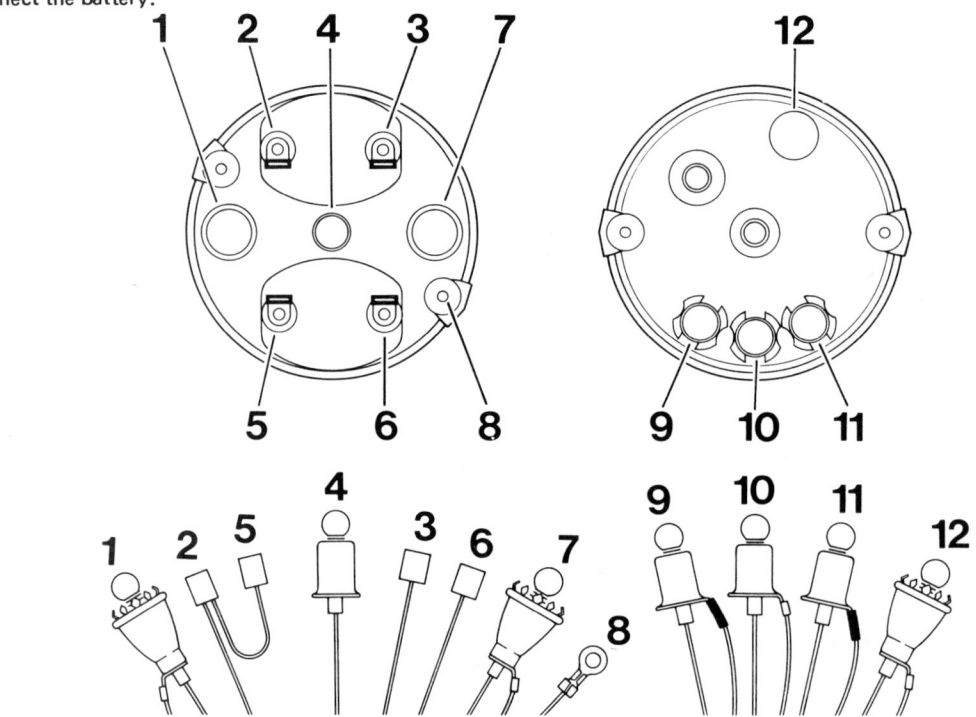

FIG. 10.19. CONNECTIONS TO GAUGES AND WARNING LIGHTS

No.	Colour Code	Connection	Component
1	GW and B	Bulb holder	R.H. turn signal warning light
2	L G	Lucar	Temperature indicator
3	GU	Lucar	Temperature indicator
4	R	Bulb holder	Instrument illumination
5	L G	Lucar	Fuel indicator
6	GB	Lucar	Fuel indicator
7	GR and B	Bulb holder	L.H. turn signal warning light
8	B	Eyelet	Earth
9	W and NY	Bulb holder	Ignition warning light
10	W and WN	Bulb holder	Oil pressure warning light
11	UW and B	Bulb holder	Main beam warning light
12	R and B	Bulb holder	Instrument illumination

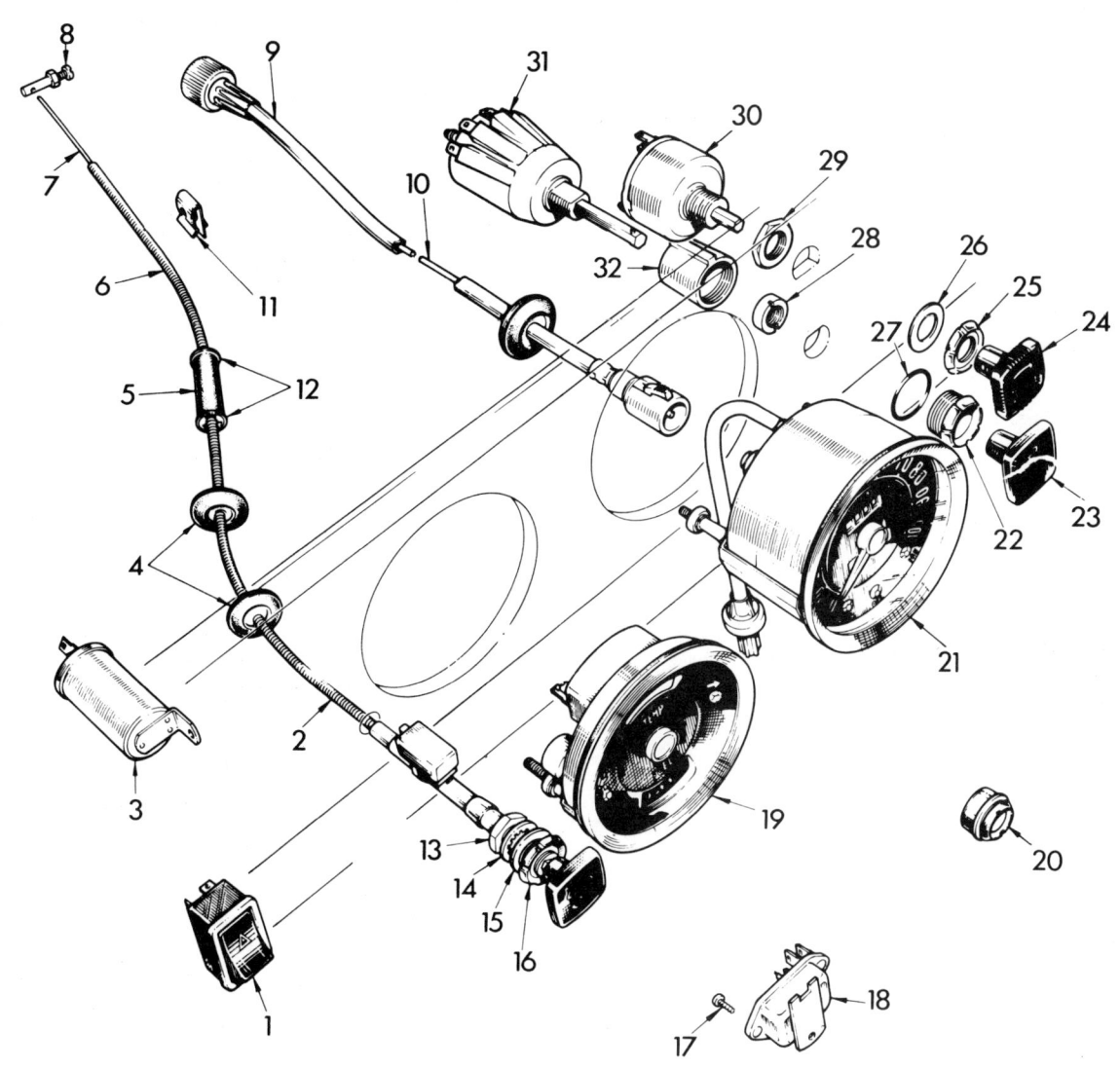

FIG. 10.20. INSTRUMENTS AND SWITCHES ON THE FACIA PANEL

1	Hazard warning switch (not fitted on U.K. models)	17	Screw
2	Choke outer cable - primary	18	Voltage stabilizer
3	Flasher unit	19	"2 in 1" instrument gauge
4	Grommets	20	Dual brake warning light (not fitted on U.K. models)
5	Connecting sleeve	21	Speedometer assembly
6	Choke outer cable - secondary	22	Bezel
7	Choke inner cable	23	Windscreen wiper switch
8	Pivot and screw assembly	24	Light selector switch
9	Speedometer outer cable	25	Bezel
10	Speedometer - inner cable	26	Rubber washer
11	Clip	27	PVC washer
12	Retaining plate	28	Spacer nut
13	Locking nut	29	Locknut
14	Spring washer	30	Light switch unit
15	Rubber washer	31	Windscreen wiper and washer switch
16	Bezel	32	Spacer

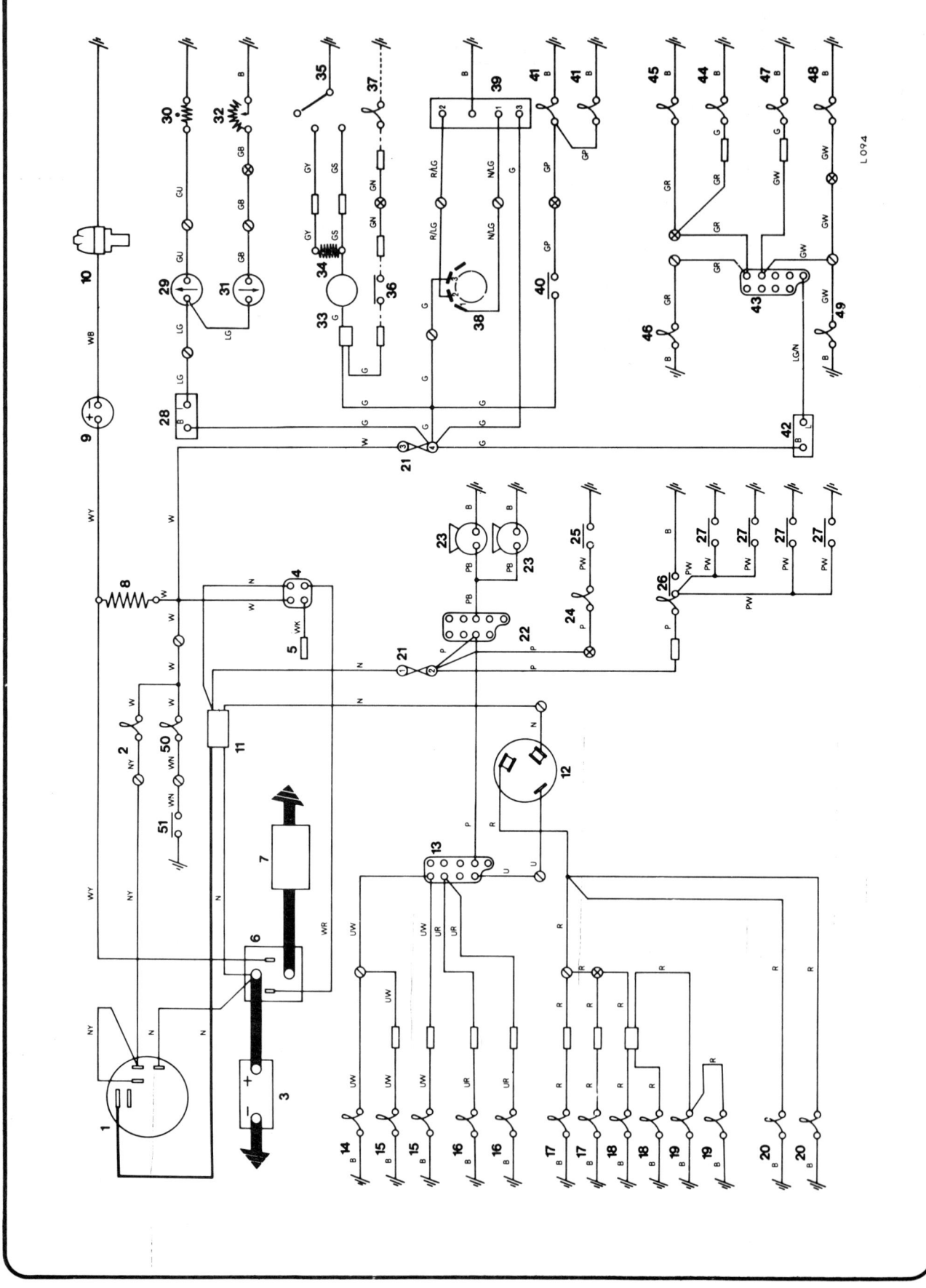

L094

FIG.10.21. WIRING DIAGRAM

1 Alternator
2 Ignition warning light
3 Battery
4 Ignition/starter switch
5 Radio supply
6 Starter solenoid
7 Starter motor
8 Ballast resistor
9 Ignition coil—6-volt
10 Ignition distributor
11 Connector block
12 Master light switch
13 Main/dip/flash switch
14 Main beam warning light
15 Main beam
16 Dip beam
17 Front parking lamp

18 Plate illumination lamp
19 Tail lamp
20 Instrument illumination
21 Fuse
22 Horn switch
23 Horn
24 Luggage boot lamp
25 Luggage boot lamp switch
26 Roof lamp
27 Door switch
28 Voltage stabilizer
29 Temperature indicator
30 Temperature transmitter
31 Fuel indicator
32 Fuel tank unit
33 Heater motor
34 Heater resistor

35 Heater switch
36 Reverse lamp switch (optional extra)
37 Reverse lamp switch (optional extra)
38 Windscreen wiper switch
39 Windscreen wiper motor
40 Stop lamp switch
41 Stop lamp
42 Turn signal flasher unit
43 Turn signal switch
44 L.H. front flasher lamp
45 L.H. rear flasher lamp
46 L.H. turn signal warning light
47 R.H. front flasher lamp
48 R.H. rear flasher lamp
49 R.H. turn signal warning light
50 Oil pressure warning light
51 Oil pressure switch

Colour Code

N Brown   U Blue   R Red   P Purple   G Green   L/G Light Green   W White   Y Yellow   S Slate   B Black   K Pink

35 Fault diagnosis

Symptom	Reason/s	Remedy
STARTER MOTOR FAILS TO TURN ENGINE		
No voltage at starter motor	Battery discharged	Charge battery.
	Battery defective internally	Fit new battery.
	Battery terminal leads loose or earth lead not securely attached to body	Check and tighten leads.
	Loose or broken connections in starter motor circuit	Check all connections and check any that are loose.
	Starter motor switch or solenoid faulty	Test and replace faulty components with new.
Voltage at starter motor: motor still does not function	Starter motor pinion jammed in mesh with ring gear	Disengage pinion by turning squared end of armature shaft.
	Starter brushes badly worn, sticking, or brush wires loose	Examine brushes, replace as necessary, tighten down brush wires.
	Commutator end face dirty, worn, or burnt	Clean end face of commutator.
	Starter motor armature faulty	Overhaul starter motor, fit new armature.
	Field coils earthed	Overhaul starter motor.
STARTER MOTOR TURNS ENGINE VERY SLOWLY		
Electrical defects	Battery in discharged condition	Charge battery.
	Starter brushes badly worn, sticking, or brush wires loose	Examine brushes, replace as necessary, tighten down brush wires.
	Loose wires in starter motor circuit	Check wiring and tighten as necessary.
STARTER MOTOR OPERATES WITHOUT TURNING ENGINE		
Dirt or oil on drive gear	Starter motor pinion sticking on the screwed sleeve	Remove starter motor, clean starter motor drive.
Mechanical damage	Pinion or ring gear teeth broken or worn	Fit new gear ring, and new pinion to starter motor drive.
STARTER MOTOR NOISY OR EXCESSIVELY ROUGH ENGAGEMENT		
Lack of attention or mechanical damage	Pinion or ring gear teeth broken or worn	Fit new ring gear, or new pinion to starter motor drive.
	Starter drive main spring broken	Dismantle and fit new main spring.
	Starter motor retaining bolts loose	Tighten starter motor securing bolts. Fit new spring washer if necessary.
BATTERY WILL NOT HOLD CHARGE FOR MORE THAN A FEW DAYS		
Wear or damage	Battery defective internally	Remove and fit new battery.
	Electrolyte level too low or electrolyte too weak due to leakage	Top up electrolyte level to just above plates.
	Plate separators no longer fully effective	Remove and fit new battery.
	Battery plates severely sulphated	Remove and fit new battery.
	Drive belt slipping	Check belt for wear, replace if necessary, and tighten.
	Battery terminal connections loose or corroded	Check terminals for tightness, and remove all corrosion.
	Alternator not charging properly	Remove and overhaul alternator.
	Short in lighting circuit causing continual battery drain	Trace and rectify.
IGNITION LIGHT FAILS TO GO OUT, BATTERY RUNS FLAT IN A FEW DAYS		
Alternator not charging	Drive belt loose and slipping, or broken	Check, replace, and tighten as necessary.
	Brushes worn, sticking, broken or dirty	Examine, clean, or replace brushes as necessary.
	Brush springs weak or broken	Examine and test. Replace as necessary.
	Slip rings dirty, greasy, worn or burnt	Clean slip rings.
	Diodes faulty in rectifier pack	Change faulty diodes.
	Stator open - circuit	Renew stator.

WIPERS

Wiper motor fails to work	Blown fuse	Check and replace fuse if necessary.
	Wire connections loose, disconnected, or broken	Check wiper wiring. Tighten loose connections.
	Brushes badly worn	Remove and fit new brushes.
	Armature worn or faulty	If electricity at wiper motor remove and overhaul and fit replacement armature.
	Field coils faulty	Purchase reconditioned wiper motor.
Wiper motor works slowly and takes excessive current	Commutator dirty, greasy, or burnt	Clean commutator thoroughly.
	Link rods bent or unlubricated	Examine link rod and straighten out if necessary. Lubricate generally.
	Armature bearings dry or unaligned	Replace with new bearings correctly aligned.
	Armature badly worn or faulty	Remove, overhaul, or fit replacement armature.
Wiper motor works slowly and takes little current	Brushes badly worn	Remove and fit new brushes.
	Commutator dirty, greasy or burnt	Clean commutator thoroughly.
	Armature badly worn or faulty	Remove and overhaul armature or fit replacement.
Wiper motor works but wiper blades remain static	Drive shaft or link rods faulty	Replace as necessary.
	Wiper motor gearbox parts badly worn	Overhaul or fit new gearbox.

Chapter 11 Suspension, dampers and steering

Contents

General description 1	Steering wheel - removal and replacement 13
Front hub bearings - removal and refitting 2	Rack and pinion steering gear - removal and refitting ... 14
Front hub bearings - adjustment 3	Rack and pinion steering gear - dismantling, overhaul and
Front spring and damper - removal and refitting ... 4	reassembly 15
Front suspension upper wishbone arms - removal, rebushing	Steering column (early models) - removal and refitting ... 16
and refitting 5	Steering column (later models) - removal and refitting ... 17
Front lower wishbone arm - removal, rebushing and replace-	Steering column - dismantling, overhaul and reassembly 18
ment 6	Steering wheel intermediate shaft - removal, inspection
Front suspension vertical link upper ball joint - removal, over-	and refitting 19
haul and refitting 7	Outer ball joint assembly - removal and replacement ... 20
Steering arm - removal, joint overhaul and reassembly ... 8	Front wheel alignment 21
Rear hub assembly - removal and refitting 9	Rear wheel alignment 22
Rear damper - removal, inspection and refitting 10	Front wheel camber 23
Radius rod - removal and refitting 11	Fault diagnosis 24
Rear suspension arm - removal and refitting 12	

Specifications

Suspension

Front	Independent, double wishbones, coil springs and dampers
Rear	Trailing suspension arm, with coil springs and dampers

Steering

Type	Alford and Adler, rack and pinion
Steering wheel diameter	16 in (405 mm)
Number of turns - lock to lock	3 turns
Wheel alignment	0 to 1/16 in toe-in (0 to 1.588 mm)
Camber (unladen)	
Front	$\frac{1}{2}^o$ negative to $1\frac{1}{2}^o$ positive
Rear	$1\frac{1}{4}^o$ positive $\pm 1^o$
	$1\frac{1}{2}^o$ negative $\pm \frac{1}{2}^o$
Castor	$2\frac{1}{4}^o \pm 1^o$
King pin inclination	$6\frac{1}{2}^o \pm 1^o$
Turning circle	29 ft 9 in between kerb

Chassis

Wheelbase	8 ft 0 5/8 in (2454 mm)
Track	
Front	4 ft 5 in (1348 mm)
Rear	4 ft 2 in (1270 mm)
Ground clearance (static unladen)	4½ in (114 mm)
Weight:	
Dry (excluding extra equipment)	16 cwt (815 Kg)
Kerb (including fuel, oil, tools and water)	17 cwt (865 Kg)
Max gross vehicle weight	24 cwt (1230 Kg)

Wheels and tyres

Wheels	Steel disc type, 4 stud fitting
Rim size	13 in diameter. 4J section
Tyres	5.20 - 13 tubeless
Type	Dunlop D75 cross-ply

Pressures

Front	22 lb/sq in (1.55 Kg/sq cm)
Rear	26 lb/sq in (1.82 Kg/sq cm)

TORQUE WRENCH SETTINGS

	lb ft	Kg m
Front suspension		
Hub to stub axle	5 to 6	0.70 to 1.00
Damper to damper plate on upper wishbone	26 to 32	3.6 to 4.4
Lower ballpin attachment	38 to 45	5.2 to 6.2
Lower wishbone attachments	26 to 32	3.6 to 4.4
Rear mounting sub frame to body	26 to 32	3.6 to 4.4
Rear damper assembly to lower link	30 to 37	4.1 to 5.1
Stub axle to vertical link	50 to 65	7 to 9
Stub to front sub frame	30 to 37	4.1 to 5.1
Strut to lower wishbone	50 to 65	7 to 9
Tie rod to vertical link	50 to 65	7 to 9
Upper wishbone to fulcrum shaft	38 to 45	5.2 to 6.2
Upper ball housing and damper plate to wishbone ...	20 to 24	2.8 to 3.3
Wheel to hub	38 to 45	5.2 to 6.2
Rear suspension		
Lower link to body	30 to 37	4.1 to 5.1
Upper link to body bracket	30 to 37	4.1 to 5.1
Rear suspension mounting bracket forward fixing ...	16 to 20	2.2 to 2.8
Wheel to hub	38 to 45	5.2 to 6.2
Rear damper detail	7 to 9	1.0 to 1.2
Damper assembly to lower link	30 to 37	4.1 to 5.1
Damper assembly to body	7 to 9	1.0 to 1.2
Steering		
Clamp to steering column	7 to 9	1.0 to 1.2
Flexible joint to steering unit and universal joint ...	7 to 9	1.0 to 1.2
Lower support tube to body	7 to 9	1.0 to 1.2
Rack to subframe	11 to 14	1.5 to 2.8
Steering column support to lower rail	7 to 9	1.0 to 1.2
Support bracket to dash front	7 to 9	1.0 to 1.2
Steering wheel retaining nut	26 to 32	3.6 to 4.4
Universal joint to steering column	16 to 20	2.2 to 2.8
Chassis - engine mountings		
Engine and rear engine plate to transmission unit ...	16 to 20	2.2 to 2.8
Engine and rear engine plate to transmission unit ...	26 to 32	3.6 to 4.4
Rubber to crossmember front engine mounting	16 to 20	2.2 to 2.8
Rear engine rubber to mounting plate	20 to 24	2.8 to 3.3
Starter motor attachment	26 to 32	2.6 to 4.4

1 General description

The front suspension is of a low periodicity independent design using rubber bushed double wishbones. The combined coil spring and telescopic damper is fitted between the upper wishbones and a turret incorporated in the front wheel arch inner panel.

The front suspension units are mounted on a sub-frame and this is rubber insulated at its four mounting points to the body side members.

The inner ends of the upper wishbones are carried on rubber bushes on a long fulcrum bolt located in a shimmed mounting bracket bolted to the sub-frame. The camber angle may be altered by adjusting the thickness of the shim pack.

The upper wishbones outer ends are double bolted and attached by sandwich action to a flanged bracket. This is an integral part of the upper ball housing for the vertical link and the two damper mounting plates. The upper hole in each of the damper mounting plates positions the through bolt for the lower rubber mounting of the telescopic damper.

There is a flange on the outside of the damper body which provides a seating for the lower end of the coil spring. The upper end of the spring locates in a dished plate which is attached to the turret incorporated in the wheel arch and it is to this that the upper end of the damper is secured.

The lower wishbone comprises an arm which is rubber bushed on a trunnion at its inner end, embodied in the lower end of the mounting bracket, and a strut. The open end of the strut holds the wishbone arm and is bolted to this at its outer end.

The inner end of the strut is rubber insulated from, and secured to, the sub-frame by a nyloc nut. This strut also carries out the functions of a radius arm.

The rear suspension comprises coil springs and concentrically mounted shock absorbers carried by trailing arms. The arms are anchored to the vehicle body at the forward end, and to the axle casing at the rear. Two upper radius rods connect the body and axle tube tops; their effect is to combine the functions of torque reaction links and stiffening members.

The steering system is rack and pinion. This comprises a rack having teeth which engage with a pinion carried on a short shaft, the top of which is splined to accept a universal joint coupling. The rack and pinion gears are accommodated in an oil tight housing.

The pinion gear is mounted at an angle to the rack. It is positively located by a bush at the bottom of the housing, and a ball bearing and retainer at its upper end. The rack is fitted with a spring loaded damper to ensure constant mesh between the pinion and rack teeth. The shaped damper plunger bears on the plain portion of the rack.

For lubrication, a grease plug is fitted to the top of the damper cap nut which must be removed to fit a grease nipple when lubrication is required.

The outer ends of the rack housing tubes are fitted with rubber gaiters. These gaiters enclose the inner tie rod members and prevent dirt ingress as well as loss of lubricant.

Splined and locked to the upper end of the pinion shaft by a bolt, is a adaptor which is coupled to a second or upper adaptor using a flexible plate and four bolts and rubber bushes on either side of the plate.

The upper adaptor is splined to the shaft of a universal coupling, the upper yoke of which is fitted on the lower end of the steering column inner member. This in turn is splined and the steering wheel is attached to it. The inner column is mounted in two bush assemblies.

The steering column incorporates a steering lock, and driver protection is afforded by a padded steering wheel hub and collapsible steering column.

2 Front hub bearings - removal and refitting

1 Jack up the front of the car and support on firmly based axle stands. Remove the wheel trim and the road wheel.
2 Drum brake models: Refer to Chapter 9 and back off the brake adjusters. Undo and remove the two countersunk screws securing the brake drum to the hub. Remove the brake drum if it is tight, tap around its circumference with a soft faced hammer.
3 Disc brake models: Refer to Chapter 9 and remove the disc brake caliper. It will also be necessary to remove the nut and bracket securing the brake hose to the vertical link.
4 Using a wide bladed screwdriver carefully ease off the grease cap.
5 Straighten the split pin ears and extract the split pin. Undo and remove the hub nut and withdraw the thrust washer. The hub may now be drawn from the axle stub complete with the oil seal.
6 Remove the outer bearing cone.
7 Using a screwdriver ease out the felt seal from the inlet bearing shield, then remove the inner bearing shield and the inner bearing cone.
8 If the bearings are to be renewed carefully drift out the bearing cups working from the inside of the hub.
9 Thoroughly wash all parts in paraffin and wipe dry using a non-fluffy rag.
10 Inspect the bearing for signs of rusting, pitting or overheating. If evident, a new set of bearings must be fitted.
11 Inspect the oil seal journal face of the stub axle shaft for signs of damage. If evident, either polish with fine emery tape, or if very bad a new stub axle will have to be fitted.
12 To reassemble, if new bearings are to be fitted carefully drift in the new bearing cups using a piece of tube of suitable diameter. Make sure they are fitted the correct way round with the tapers facing outwards. Press them in until they are tight against the hub inner flanges.
13 Work some high melting point grease into the inner bearing cone and fit it into the hub.
14 Next, fit the inner bearing shield with the lip facing outwards. Lubricate a new felt seal and press it into the inner bearing shield.
15 Fit the hub to the axle stub. Work some high melting point grease into the outer bearing cone and fit it in the hub.
16 Refit the washer and nut.
17 It is now necessary to adjust the hub bearing end float and full information will be found in Section 3. Don't forget to fit the split pin when adjustment is complete.
18 Refit the grease cap, road wheel and wheel trim. Lower the front of the car to the ground.

3 Front hub bearings - adjustment

1 Jack up the front of the car and support on firmly based axle stands.
2 Remove the wheel trim, road wheel and grease cap.
3 Straighten the split pin ears and extract the split pin.
4 Tighten or slacken the castellated nut as necessary to obtain 0.002 to 0.008 in. (0.0508 to 0.2032mm) end float. This is preferably measured with a dial gauge, or if not available, feeler gauges will have to suffice; measure between the inner face of the locknut and the washer.

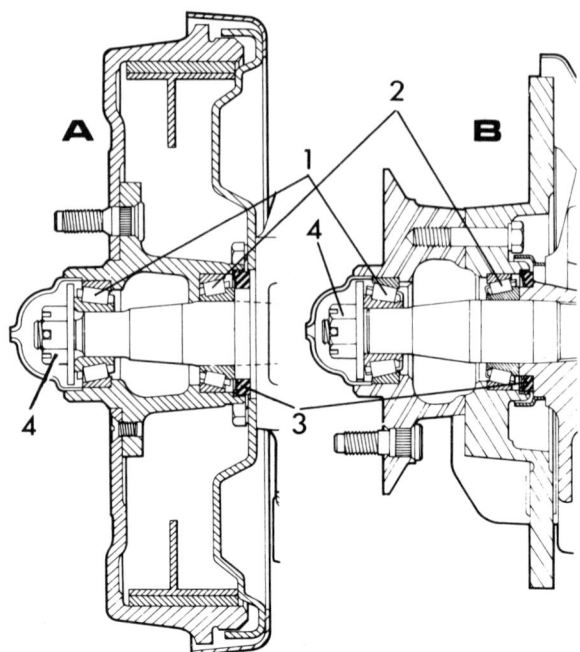

FIG. 11.1. SECTION THROUGH FRONT WHEEL HUB

A Drum brake	B Disc brake
1 Outer bearing	3 Oil seal
2 Inner bearing	4 Stub axle locknut wheel

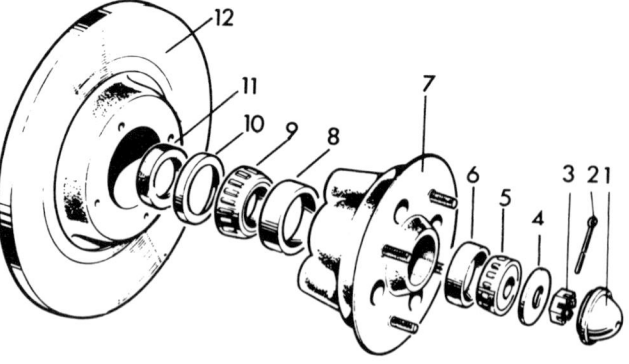

**FIG. 11.2. EXPLODED VIEW OF FRONT WHEEL HUB
— (DISC BRAKES)**

1 Hubcap	7 Hub
2 Split pin	8 Bearing track
3 Locknut	9 Inner bearing
4 Washer	10 Bearing shield
5 Outer bearing	11 Oil seal
6 Bearing track	12 Brake disc

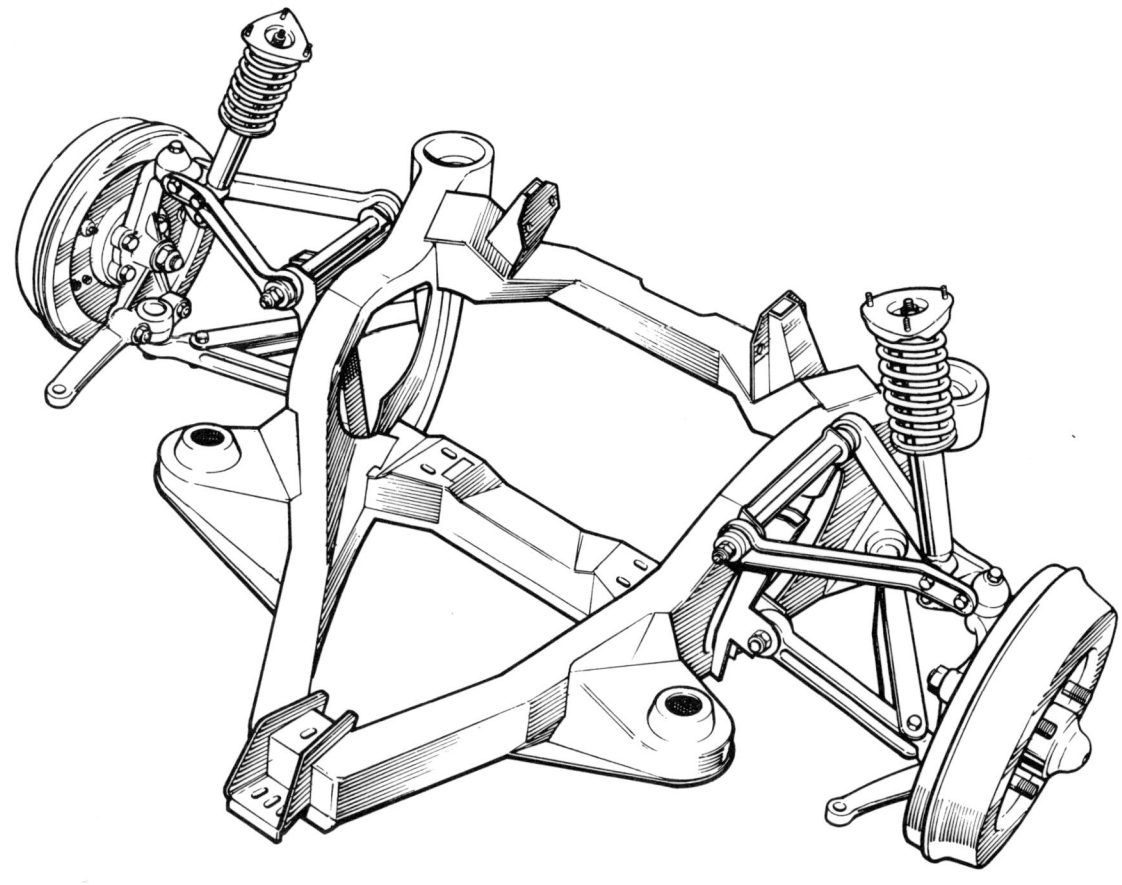

Fig. 11.3. Front sub-frame and suspension — general arrangement

5   Fit a new split pin and place in position without moving the locknut more than one section. Lock the assembly by opening the ears of the split pin.

6   Fit the grease cap and replace the road wheel and wheel trim. It will be observed that the end float setting achieved can cause a considerable amount of movement when the tyre is 'rocked'. Do not reduce the end float any further provided it has been set correctly as described. The bearings must not on any account be pre-loaded.

4   Front spring and damper - removal and refitting

1   Before commencing work, a special tool will be necessary to compress the coil spring so that the dampers can be released from the spring. Due to the strong tension of the spring do not use any other means for reasons of personal safety.

2   Apply the handbrake firmly and chock the wheel on the opposite side of the car to be worked upon. Remove the front wheel trim and slacken the wheel nuts. Jack up the car and place on axle stands. Remove the road wheel.

3   Support the weight of the front disc and hub assembly to prevent it dropping in the subsequent operations.

4   Undo and remove the nut and bolt that connects the bottom of the damper to the suspension upper wishbone fishplates. Then slacken the two bolts securing the damper mounting plates to the wishbone and ball joint.

5   Undo and remove the three nuts with plain and spring washers from the top of the turret in the side of the engine compartment.

6   Lift away the front spring and damper from the wheel arch.

7   If it is necessary to separate the spring from the damper take the assembly along to the local Triumph garage who will have the necessary equipment to do the work. Should however, the special tool be available then follow the instructions in the subsequent paragraphs. Instead of the special Triumph tool, a standard spring 'keep' can be used if one is exceptionally careful.

8   Using the press, compress as many coils as possible of the road spring, just enough to relieve the load from the damper top nuts.

9   Undo and remove the locknut, nut, washer, rubber bush and cap from the top of the damper.

10   Very carefully release the load from the road spring and then lift away the parts from the press.

11   Withdraw the damper from the upper spring plate and road spring.

12   Check the spring with the specifications and if outside the tolerances it must be replaced. In any event it is good policy to fit a new rubber insulator to the top spring coil. If one spring is replaced, then good practice dictates that its companion spring is also replaced.

13   Inspect the damper for signs of a damaged or dented body, bent piston rod, slackened mounting flange or fluid leakage. If evident, a new damper should be fitted as it is not a serviceable item.

14   If the damper appears to be mechanically sound, hold the unit vertically, and slowly extend and compress it approximately ten times through its full operating range. Resistance must be considerable and constant whilst being extended and compressed. It is well worth while fitting a new rubber bush to the eye at the bottom of the damper. This can sometimes cure quite

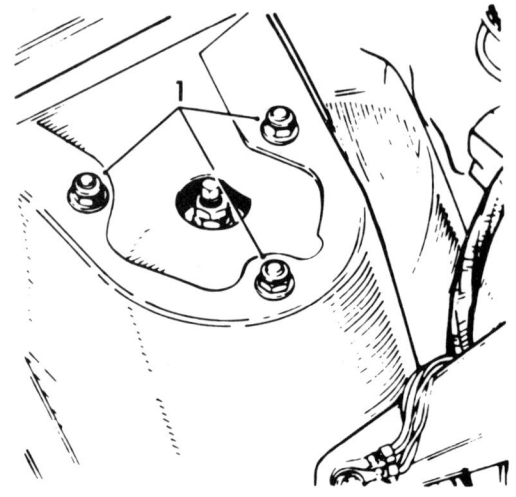

FIG.11.4. FRONT DAMPER MOUNTING

1 Mounting plate nuts

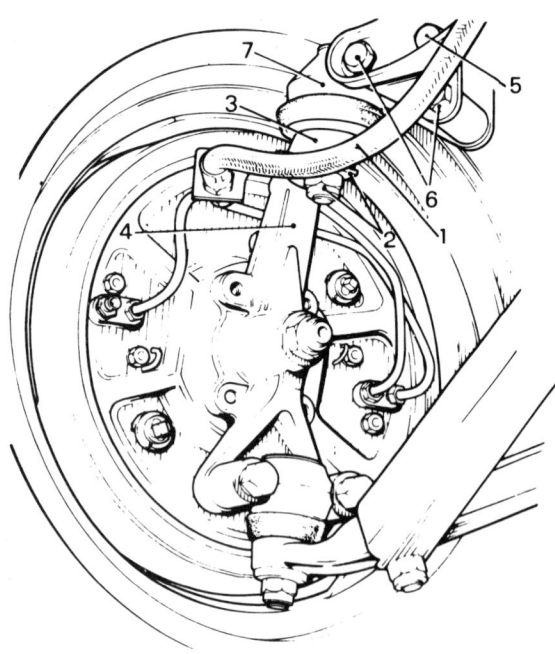

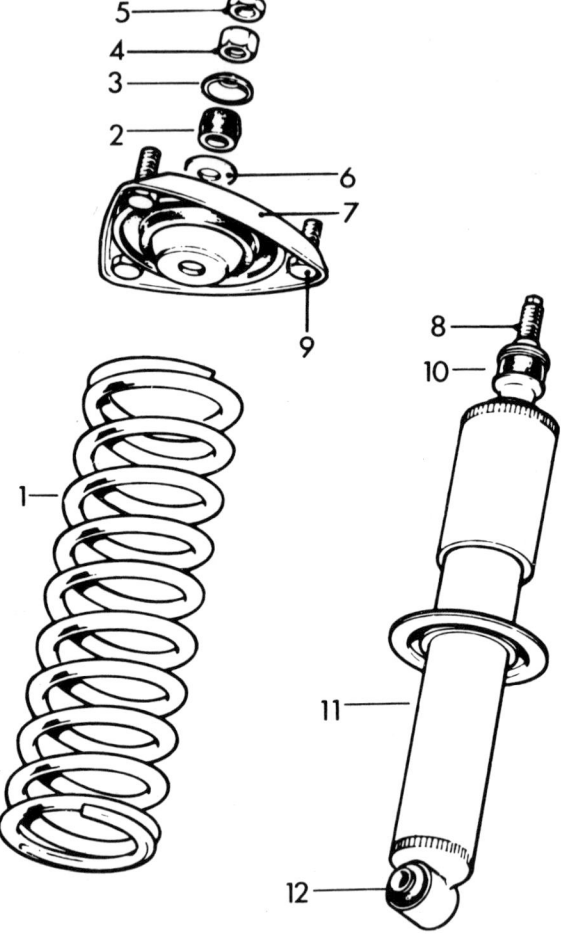

FIG. 11.5. FRONT DAMPER AND SPRING ASSEMBLY

1	Coil spring	7	Mounting plate
2	Rubber bush	8	Damper rod
3	Dished washer	9	Bolt
4	Nut	10	Damper upper bush
5	Locknut	11	Damper body
6	Washer	12	Damper lower bush

FIG.11.6 UPPER BALL JOINT REMOVAL

1	Brake hose	5	Damper lower mounting bolt
2	Ball pin securing nut and washer	6	Ball joint and upper wish-bone bolts
3	Ball joint shank	7	Ball joint housing
4	Vertical link		

a few squeals or knocks.

15 Should there be none; only slight resistance in one or both directions; excessive resistance or a pocket of no resistance when the direction is reversed, a new damper must be obtained.

16 To reassemble the spring and damper, first fit the washers and rubber to the top of the damper.

17 Extend the damper and insert it into the road spring and upper spring plate.

18 Using the special spring press, compress the road spring sufficiently to enable the completion of the damper attachment to the upper spring plate.

20 Refitting the spring and damper assembly is the reverse sequence to removal. It is however, important that before the bolt is fully tightened, the vehicle is loaded by placing 150 lbs on each seat (the rear seat must be considered as two seats). Tighten the bolt securely.

5 Front suspension upper wishbone arms - removal, rebushing and refitting

1 Apply the handbrake firmly and chock the wheels on the opposite side of the car to that to be worked upon. Remove the front wheel trim and slacken the wheel nuts. Jack up the car and support on axle stands. Remove the road wheel.

2 Support the weight of the disc and hub or drum and hub assembly, depending which is fitted.

3 Remove the two bolts which clamp the upper wishbone arms to the steering upper ball joint.

4 Release the bolt and nut securing the inner end of the lower wishbone to the wishbone bracket: ease the lower wishbone out of the bracket.

5 Detach the ball joint from the wishbone.

6 Remove the four nuts and bolts (three upper and one lower) that secure the wishbone bracket to the sub-frame. Withdraw the wishbone bracket and any packing shims that are fitted behind it. Carefully note exactly what shims are removed; this is most critical since they are used to set the wheel camber.

7 Remove the nyloc nut and washer at the forward end of the upper wishbone fulcrum shaft and withdraw the front wishbone arm and inner washer.

8 Withdraw the fulcrum shaft, rear wishbone arm and plain washers.

9 Inspect the rubber bushes for wear. If evident, new bushes will have to be fitted, and for this operation either a press or a large bench vice will be necessary.

10 Obtain a piece of tube with an internal diameter slightly larger than the external diameter of the bush. Place it behind the bush and, using a piece of rod slightly smaller in diameter than the bush outer diameter, push out the old bush.

11 Using coarse emery cloth, clean the eye of the suspension arm and lubricate with Castrol Rubber Grease.

12 Place a bolt in the tube of the new rubber bush and press into position.

13 Inspect the wishbone bracket for fractures or evidence of corrosion, and check the fulcrum shaft for fractures, corrosion or score marks. Replace if damaged.

14 Dismantling and inspection of the ball joints is covered in Section 7.

15 Refitting the bracket and wishbones is essentially the reverse of dismantling; but for anyone who is a little unsure of the various techniques we are giving the complete sequence of operations.

16 Check the position and tightness of the two nuts on the end of the fulcrum shaft. They should be located on the shaft with one full thread projecting beyond the locknut. The locknut should be tightened to 46 to 50 lbf ft (6.23 to 6.77 kgf m).

17 Fit the outer plain washer, upper rear wishbone arm (cranked end away from nuts) and inner plain washer to the fulcrum shaft.

18 Insert the fulcrum shaft into the rear of the wishbone bracket.

19 Fit the inner plain washer, upper front wishbone arm (cranked end towards rear arm), plain washer and nyloc nut. Do not tighten the Nyloc nut at this stage.

20 Fit the wishbone bracket and shim(s) to the subframe and secure with the four bolts and nuts. It is extremely important that the same shims that were removed are refitted, or the wheel camber will be lost.

21 Fit the lower wishbone to the wishbone bracket and secure with the bolt and nut. Do not tighten at this stage.

22 Engage the ball joint in the upper wishbone and insert the triangular plates. Fit the two bolts and nuts to the wishbone arms, plates, and ball joint stem.

23 Fit the lower end of the damper to the wishbone and secure with the nut and bolt.

24 Tighten the three nuts and bolts securing the ball joint and damper to the wishbone.

25 Remove the string or wire used to relieve the weight of hub assembly from the brake hose.

26 Fit the road wheel and remove the jack, then tighten the nut and bolt securing the lower wishbone to the suspension bracket.

27 Tighten the Nyloc nut on the upper fulcrum shaft to 46 to 50 lbf ft (6.23 to 6.77 kgf m).

28 If any new component has been fitted , it is recommended that the wheel camber angle is checked at a Triumph garage and reset as necessary.

6 Front lower wishbone arm - removal, rebushing and replacement

1 Apply the handbrake firmly and chock the wheels on the opposite side of the car to that worked upon. Remove the front wheel trim and slacken the wheel nuts. Jack up the car and support on axle stands. Remove the road wheel.

2 Support the weight of the disc or hub assembly. Undo and remove the nut and plain washer securing the ball joint to the lower wishbone arm.

3 Using a universal ball joint separator and suitable thrust pad, separate the lower wishbone arm from the steering arm.

4 Undo and remove the nut and bolt securing the radius arm to the lower wishbone arm.

5 Undo and remove the nut and bolt securing the lower wishbone arm to the lower wishbone bracket. Lift away the lower wishbone arm.

6 Inspect the rubber bush for wear and fit a new one as described in Section 5 paragraph 9-12 inclusive.

7 Refitting the lower wishbone arm is the reverse sequence to removal.

7 Front suspension vertical link upper ball joint - removal, overhaul and refitting

1 Apply the handbrake firmly and chock the wheel on the opposite side of the car to that to be worked upon. Remove the front wheel trim and slacken the wheel nuts. Jack up the car and support on axle stands. Remove the road wheel.

2 Support the vertical link and hub assembly with a cord or wire to avoid stressing the flexible brake hose.

3 Detach the hose support bracket from the vertical link.

4 Undo and remove the nut and plain washer securing the ball joint to the vertical link. Using a universal ball joint separator and suitable thrust pad, separate the ball joint pin from the vertical link.

5 Undo and remove the two nuts and bolts clamping the upper wishbone arms to the joint. Lift away the old joint.

6 The upper ball joint should be rebuilt if vertical play within the joint exceeds 0.010 in. (0.254 mm).

7 Remove the gaiter and circlip. Lift away all the component parts and wash in paraffin. Inspect for wear or damage.

8 To remove the socket, use a grooving chisel and partially dismantle the socket. Fit a new socket using the ball to press it in, in a vice.

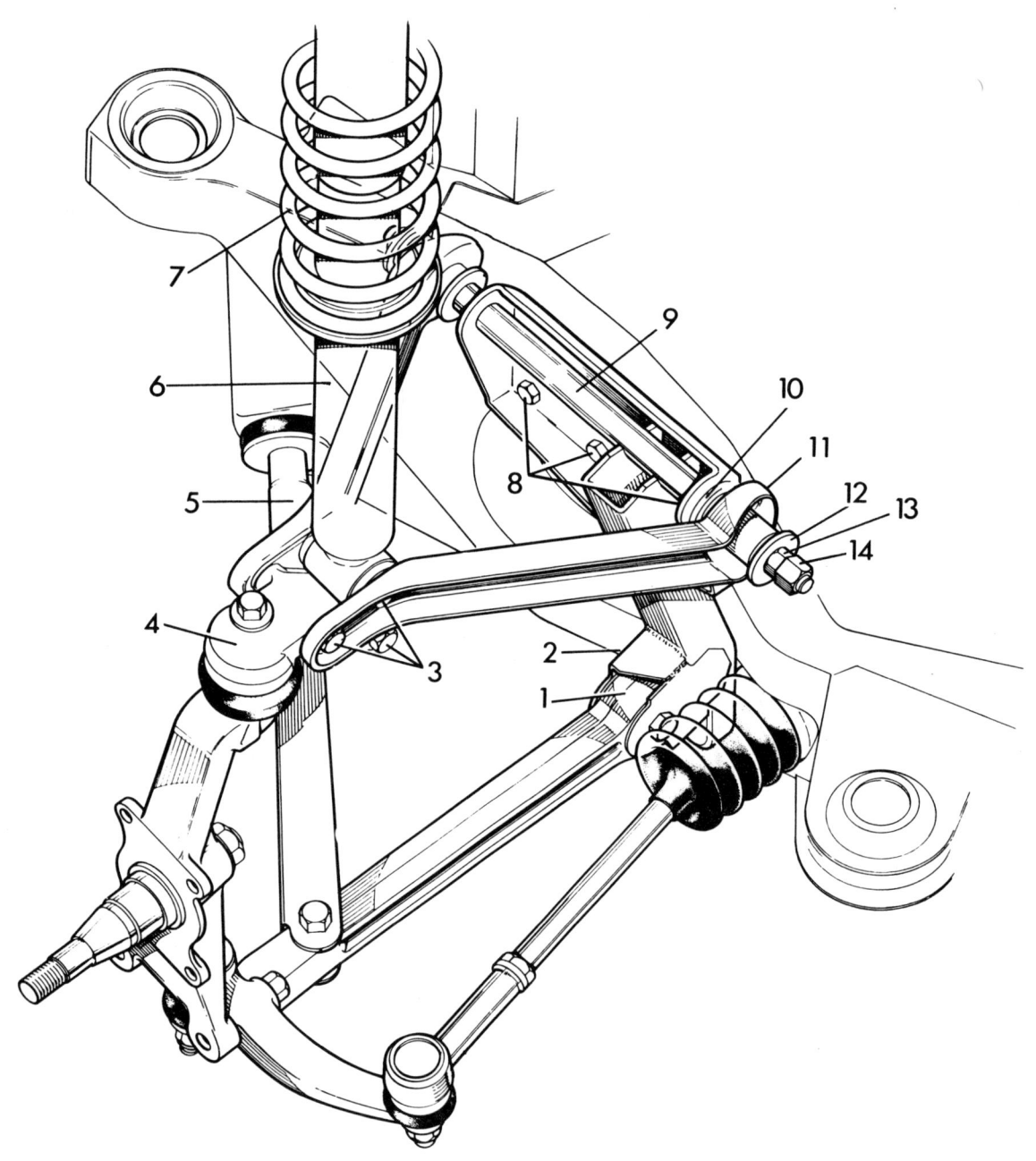

FIG.11.7 FRONT SUSPENSION COMPONENTS

1 Lower wishbone arm
2 Mounting bracket
3 Bolts securing ball joint and damper
4 Ball joint
5 Radius arm
6 Damper
7 Coil spring
8 Wishbone bracket mounting bolts
9 Fulcrum shaft
10 Inner washer
11 Wishbone arm
12 Outer washer
13 Nut
14 Locknut

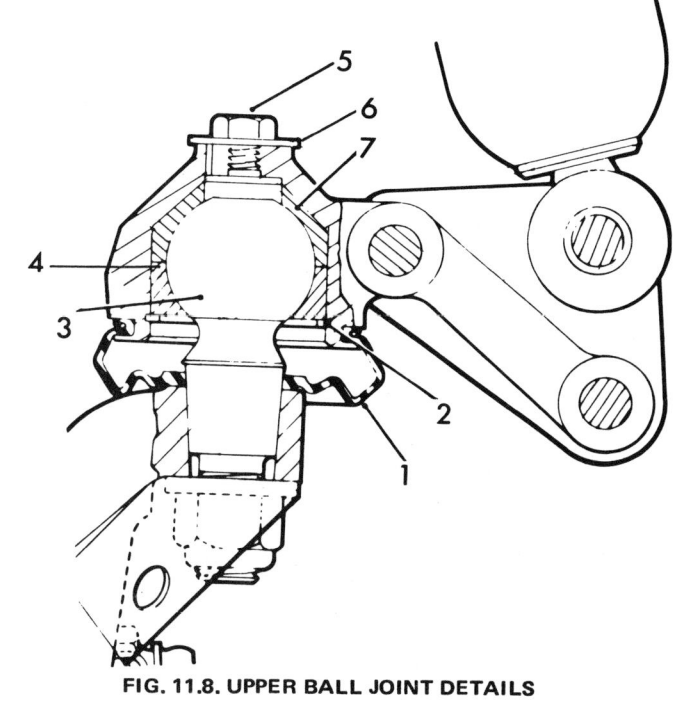

FIG. 11.8. UPPER BALL JOINT DETAILS

1 Rubber boot	5 Plug
2 Circlip	6 Washer
3 Balljoint	7 Ball upper seat
4 Ball lower seat	

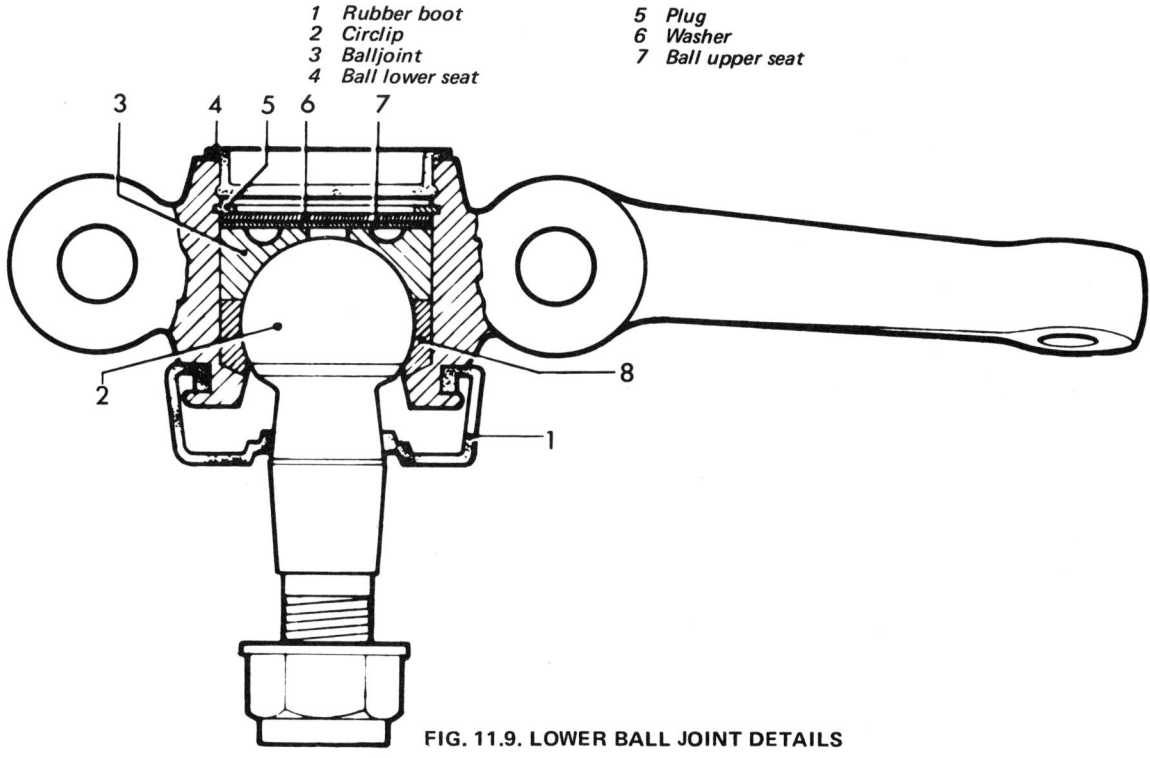

FIG. 11.9. LOWER BALL JOINT DETAILS

1 Rubber boot	3 Ball upper seat	5 Circlip	7 Spring disc
2 Ball joint	4 Sealing cap	6 Top cover	8 Lower ball seat

9 Remove the ball and fit the metal lower socket. Tap round the metal socket with a soft metal drift to make sure it has seated properly.

10 Assemble the joint dry, selecting the correct thickness of lower socket to give a maximum of 0.004 in. (0.102 mm) end play. Rotate the ball to ensure it is able to rotate freely at all positions.

11 Three alternative sizes of lower ball seat are available, also shims of 0.005 and 0.010 inch. (0.127 and 0.254 mm). Select a combination of these to achieve the correct end-float.

12 Dismantle the joint and lubricate well with grease. Reassemble the joint and insert 1/3 ounce of grease in the gaiter and apply a grease gun to the top grease point.

13 Refitting the new ball assembly is the reverse sequence to removal. The circlip retaining the lower seat must be fitted with its open end at right angles to the ball housing shank.

8 Steering arm - removal, joint overhaul and reassembly

1 Apply the handbrake fully and chock the wheels on the opposite side of the car to that to be worked upon. Remove the front wheel trim and slacken the wheel nuts. Jack up the car and support on axle stands. Remove the road wheel.
2 Undo and remove the nut and plain washer securing the steering rack outer ball joint to the steering arm.
3 Using a universal ball joint separator and suitable thrust pad separate the ball joint pin from the steering arm.
4 Undo and remove the two bolts and spring washers which secure the arm to the vertical link.
5 Separate the steering arm from the lower wishbone, first undoing and removing the nut and spring washer and then using a universal ball joint separator and suitable thrust block.
6 Remove the polythene sealing cap and circlip. Lift away all the component parts and wash in paraffin. Inspect for wear or damage.
7 To remove the lower socket, use a grooving chisel and partially dismantle the socket. Fit a new lower socket with the elongation of the ball pin hole at right angles to the steering arm mounting face. This will place the two tags on a diameter which lies parallel to the mounting face. Insertion of the socket will be easily accomplished by using the ball to press it into the steering arm in a bench vice.

8 Tap the end of the ball with the threads suitably protected to ensure the socket seats fully.
9 Reassembly and refitting is now the reverse sequence to removal. All joint components should be liberally coated with grease. The spring disc must be fitted with its concave side towards the ball upper seat.

9 Rear hub assembly - removal and refitting

1 Chock the front wheels, jack up the rear of the car and place on firmly based axle stands.
2 Remove the wheel trim and road wheel. Apply the handbrake.
3 Undo and remove the axle shaft nut and washer.
4 Release the handbrake and refer to Chpater 9. Back off the brake adjuster. Remove the two countersunk screws that retain the brake drum and pull off the brake drum.
5 Using a universal puller and suitable thrust block pull the hub from the end of the axle shaft.
6 Remove the axle shaft key.
7 Refitting the rear hub assembly is the reverse sequence to removal. The axle shaft nut must be tightened to the torque wrench setting given in the Specifications.
8 Replacing a rear hub oil seal is covered in Chapter 8 which details removal of half shafts and their associated bearings and oil seals.

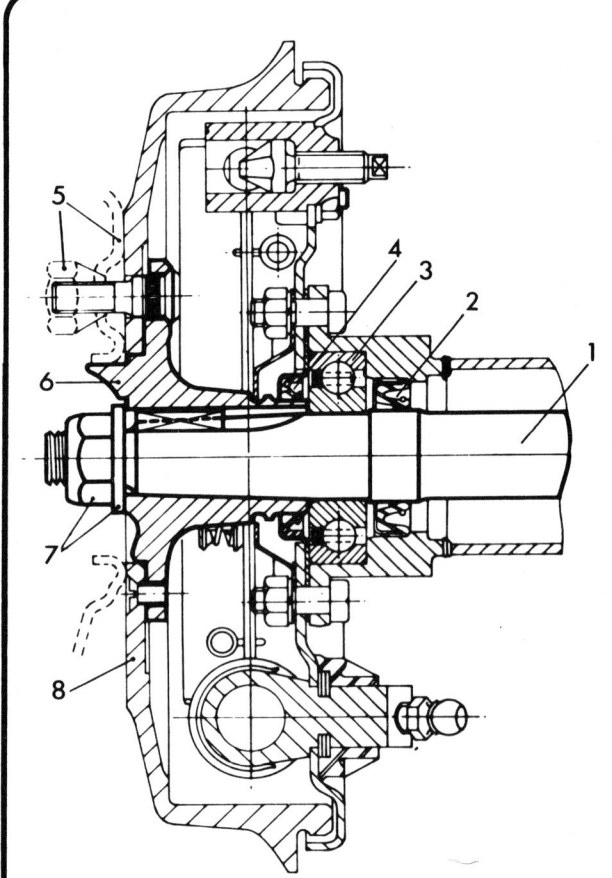

FIG. 11.10. SECTION THROUGH REAR WHEEL HUB

1	Axle shaft	6	Hub
2	Inner oil seal	7	Hub retaining nut and washer
3	Bearing		
4	Outer oil seal	8	Brake drum
5	Wheel nut		

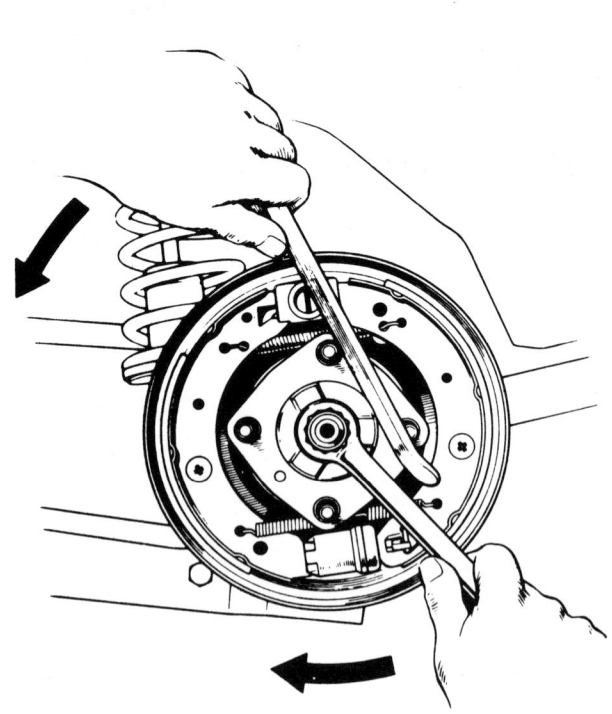

Fig. 11.11. Illustrating the correct method of tightening the rear hub retaining nut: this prevents any undue load being placed on the crown wheel and pinion

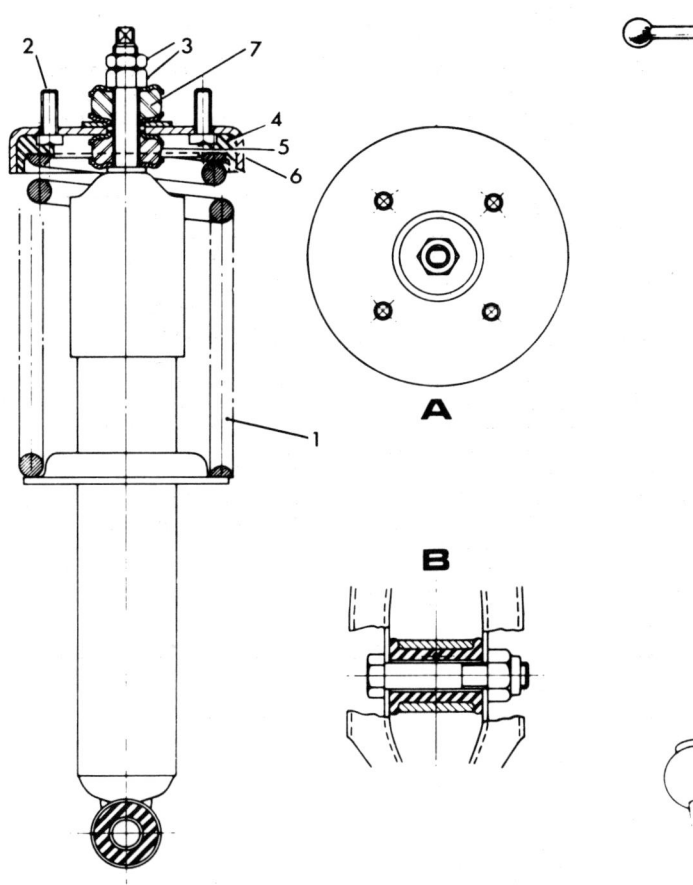

FIG. 11.12. SECTION THROUGH REAR DAMPER AND COIL SPRING ASSEMBLY

1 Coil spring
2 Mounting stud
3 Damper nut and
    locknut
4 Rubber insulating ring
5 Lower rubber bush and
    washers
6 Mounting flange
7 Upper-rubber bush
    and washers

Inset (A):   Plan of mounting flange
Inset (B):   Section through lower damper bush

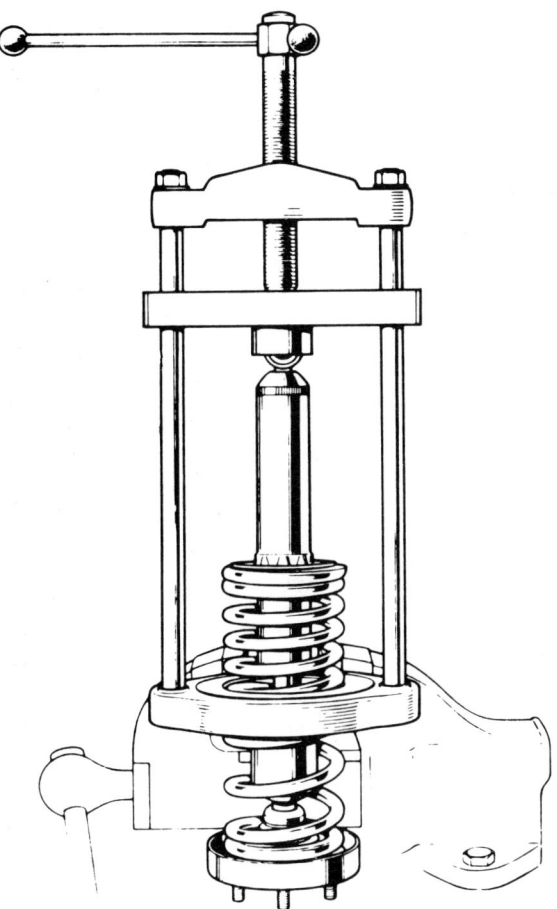

Fig. 11.13. Using special tool to compress the coil spring

10 Rear damper - removal, inspection and refitting

1 Jack up the rear of the car and support on firmly based axle stands located under the main longitudinal chassis members. Support the weight of the axle on the side from which the damper is to be removed.
2 Remove the four nuts and plain washers securing the damper upper mounting studs to the top of the rear spring turret, inside the boot.
3 Release the nut and bolt securing the lower end of the damper to the rear suspension arm.
4 Remove the nut and bolt that secures the front end of the rear suspension arm to the body. Lower the rear suspension arm from its mounting bracket; this will provide sufficient access to withdraw the damper, complete with coiled spring, from its location.

5 If it is considered necessary to separate the spring from the damper it is necessary to either obtain a special tool, S4221A with adaptors 5 and 18, from a Triumph Agent, or use a spring 'Keep'. If these precautions are not followed, injury to the person doing the dismantling could well result from the spring 'flying'.

6 Either compress the spring with the special tool or fit the spring 'Keep'. Remove the locknut and plain nut securing the damper rod to the mounting flange. Then withdraw the mounting flange complete with upper rubber bush, washers and spring insulating ring. This will leave the lower rubber bush and washers on the damper rod; withdraw these and then lift away the coiled spring (still compressed) (Fig.11.13).
7 To test the shock absorber alternatively compress and extend it throughout its full movement. If the action is jerky or weak, either it is worn or there is air in the hydraulic cylinder. Continue to compress and extend it and if the action does not become more positive a new shock absorber should be obtained. If the shock absorber is showing signs of leaking it should be discarded as it is not possible to overhaul it.
8 Check the bushes and if they show signs of deterioration a new set of rubbers should be obtained. These can be removed and refitted as described in Section 5.
9 The coil spring should be checked against the specifications and if outside the stated tolerances, should be discarded and a new spring fitted.
10 Replacement is the reverse of removal operations. Ensure that a new insulating ring is fitted to the spring top coil, and that the centre of the flange engages the collar of the lower bush washer.

11 Radius rod - removal and refitting

1   Under normal circumstances it will not be necessary to remove the radius arms except when the rubber bushes have worn. To remove the radius rod, jack up the rear of the car and support on firmly based stands. Also support the weight of the rear suspension by placing a jack under the rear axle. Remove the road wheels.

2   Undo and remove the front securing nut and bolt and withdraw from the radius rod eye. Draw the radius rod from its mounting and recover the rubber bushing.

3   Now working at the rear of the radius rod, release the split pin, remove the clamping nut and lift away the plain washer. Lift off the rear half of the rubber bushing. Draw the radius rod forwards and lift away from the underside of the car. Remove the second half of the rubber bushing.

4   Refitting is the reverse sequence to removal. Do not lubricate the rubber bushings. New bushing can be fitted to the eye of the radius rod using the technique outlined in Section 5. Ensure the position of the bushes and washers conform to the sequence shown in Fig. 11.14.

12 Rear suspension arm - removal and refitting

1   Jack up the rear of the car and support it on axle stands. Locate a jack under the rear axle.

2   Remove the nut and bolt securing the lower end of the damper to the suspension arm.

3   Release the nut and bolt securing the forward end of the suspension arm to the body bracket.

4   Remove the nut and bolt that secures the rear end of the suspension arm to the rear axle tube bracket. Then detach the suspension arm from the damper, and lift it out of the two brackets.

5   Inspect the suspension arm for fractures, corrosion or evidence of ovality in the bush housings (after the bushes have been pressed out). New bushes can be fitted to the arm providing that the housings are in good order. Press the bushes in using packing material and a vice; ensure they are centralised before refitting the suspension arm to the car in the reverse manner to removal.

13 Steering wheel - removal and replacement

1   Disconnect the battery earth terminal for safety reasons.

2   Undo and remove the two screws securing the steering wheel pad assembly to the steering wheel. Lift away the wheel pad assembly.

3   Disengage the steering lock, mark the position of the steering wheel hub relative to the inner column and, with a socket, undo the steering wheel retaining nut. Withdraw the ignition key from the switch then remove the three screws clamping the two nacelle halves together: withdraw the nacelle halves.

4   Using the palms of the hands as near to the steering wheel as possible, thump it from its splines on the inner column.

5   Refitting the steering wheel is the reverse sequence to removal. Tighten the steering wheel securing nut to a torque wrench setting of 26 to 32 ft lbs (3.6 to 4.4 kg m). If there are no scribe marks present when you come to refit the steering wheel, set the road wheels straight ahead with the steering wheel spokes horizontal.

14 Rack and pinion steering gear - removal and refitting

1   Chock the rear wheels, apply the handbrake , jack up the front of the car and support on firmly based stands.

2   Undo the nyloc nut securing the tie rod ends to the steering arms. Lift away the nut and plain washer.

3   Using a universal ball joint separator, detach the tie rod ends from the steering arms.

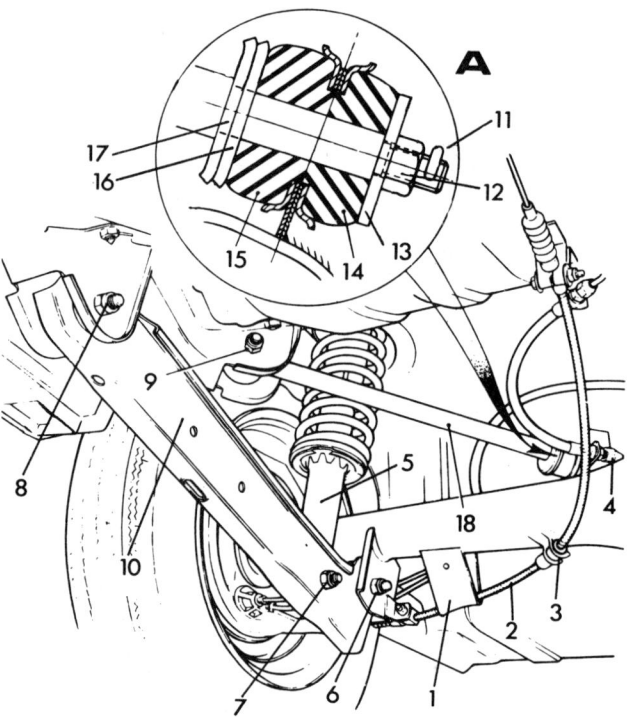

FIG. 11.14. REAR SUSPENSION COMPONENTS AND ANCILLARIES

1 Handbrake cable support bracket	9 Radius rod connection to body
2 Handbrake cable	10 Suspension arm
3 Cable location point	11 Radius rod spring pin
4 Brake hose union	12 Radius rod to axle securing nut
5 Damper	13 Washer
6 Suspension arm connection to axle	14 Outer rubber bush
7 Damper lower mounting anchorage	15 Inner rubber bush
8 Suspension arm connection to body	16 Dished washer
	17 Dished washer
	18 Radius rod

Inset: Section through radius rod bushes

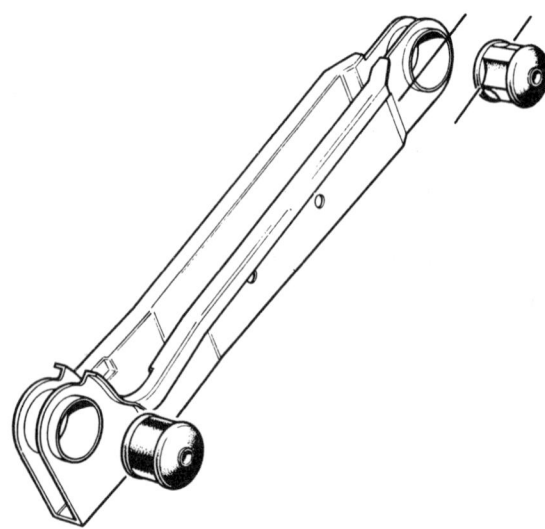

Fig. 11.15. Rear suspension arm bushes

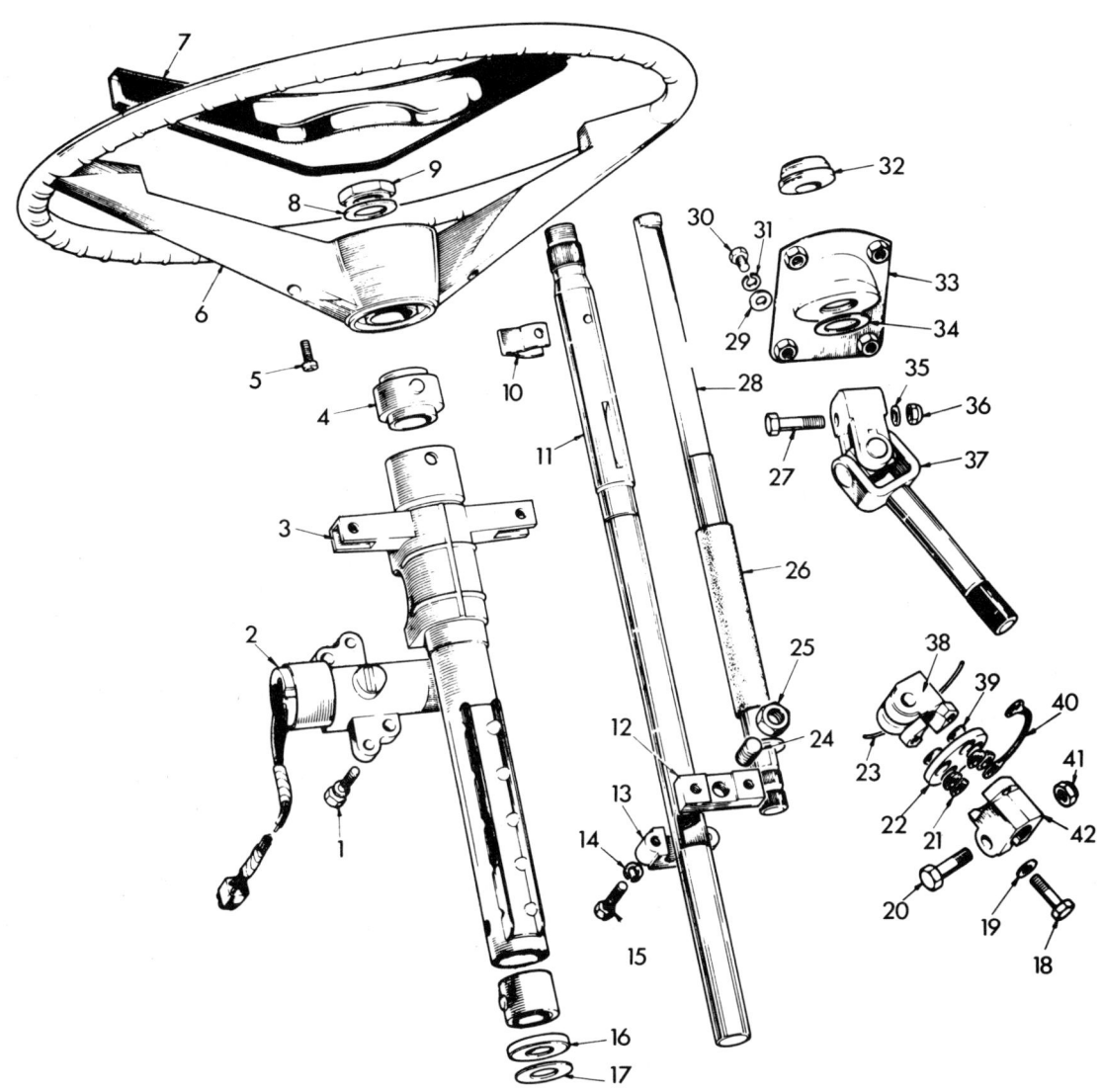

FIG. 11.16. STEERING WHEEL AND COLUMN COMPONENTS

1	Bolt, lock to outer housing	22	Flexible joint plate
2	Ignition switch and lock	23	Locking wire
3	Outer housing assembly, upper steering column	24	Locating screw
4	Bearing (upper)	25	Nut
5	Screw	26	Distance tube (cardboard)
6	Steering wheel	27	Bolt
7	Centre pad, steering wheel	28	Lower steering column assembly
8	Washer	29	Washer
9	Nut, securing steering wheel	30	Bolt
10	Clip - trafficator cancelling	31	Split washer
11	Upper steering column assembly	32	Bearing (lower)
12	Locating plate	33	Bracket, lower steering column support
13	Clamp, steering column	34	Washer
14	Split washer	35	Washer
15	Bolt	36	Locknut
16	End cap, outer tube	37	Universal joint assembly
17	Washer, end cap	38	Adaptor
18	Bolt	39	Bush (rubber) between plate and adaptor
19	Washer	40	Conductor strip
20	Bolt	41	Locknut
21	Bush (rubber) between plate and adaptor	42	Adaptor

4 Undo and remove the nuts, washers, U bolts, and locating plates securing the steering rack assembly to the front sub-frame.
5 Mark the relative positions of the intermediate shaft coupling and the rack pinion shaft.
6 Remove the pinch bolt from the intermediate shaft lower flexible coupling.
7 Ease the rack forward to disengage the pinion shaft, from the flexible coupling and withdraw the rack from the vehicle.
8 If the assembly is to be dismantled, remove all traces of road dirt or oil by washing in paraffin and wiping dry with a non—fluffy rag.
9 To refit the steering rack assembly first fit new rubber bushes and a new nylon damping plug.
10 Carefully position the rack in the sub-frame in a reverse manner to removal.
11 Engage the pinion shaft splines in the intermediate shaft flexible coupling, ensuring that the previously marked scribe lines are aligned. If no scribe marks are present it will be necessary to centralize the rack shaft, locate the rack in its fitted position and ensure that the steering-wheel spokes are horizontal before engaging the pinion shaft in the flexible coupling.
12 Fit and tighten the pinch bolt in the flexible coupling, and check that the rack mounting rubbers are correctly located.
13 Fit the bearer plate under the rack mounting rubber (not pinion side).
14 Fit the rack clamp brackets and 'U' bolts, then compress the rack rubbers and tighten the 'U' bolts.
15 Refit the tie rod ends to the steering arms and remove the axle stands. Lower the car to the ground.
16 Set the front wheels in the straight ahead position, and secure the steering couplings with the upper column and the steering wheel and direction indicator cancelling clip in the straight ahead position.
17 As the front wheel alignment will probably have been disturbed, the car should be taken to the local Triumph garage to have the wheel alignment reset as necessary.

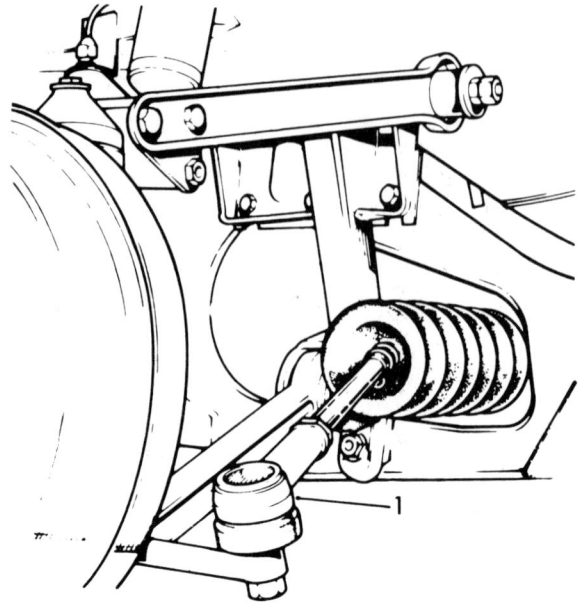

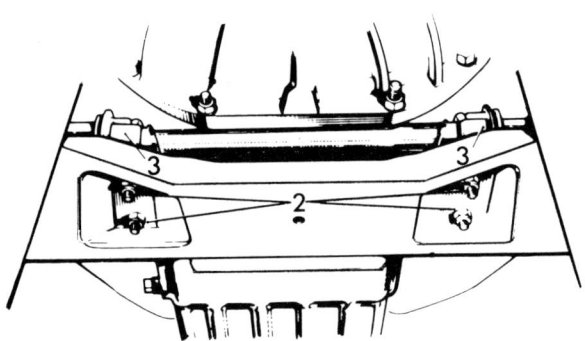

15 Rack and pinion steering gear - dismantling, overhaul and reassembly

1 With the exterior of the assembly clean and free of dirt and oil, release the gaiter clips and slide both gaiters outwards.
2 Slacken the locknuts and unscrew both tie rod assemblies from the rack.
3 Withdraw the small coil spring from each end of the rack.
4 Bend up the tab washer tab, unscrew the sleeve nut and remove the tab washer, shims and thrust cup. Slaken the locknuts and unscrew the tie rod ends from their tie rods.
5 Remove the locknut, gaiters, clips and cup nut from each tie rod.
6 Undo and remove the locknuts. Unscrew the cap nut and remove the shims, spring and pressure pad from the housing.
7 Unscrew and withdraw the plug holding the pinion assembly to the rack housing.
8 Carefully detach the rubber O ring from its groove in the retainer. Invert the plug and fit into the pinion shaft. Engage the two short bolts in the tapped holes in the plug and tighten to grip the pinion shaft. Using two screwdrivers, prise the pinion shaft clear of the housing. Next, remove the circlip securing the ball-race to the pinion shaft and withdraw the ball-race.
9 Finally, withdraw the rack from the tube.
10 Thoroughly wash all components and then inspect for wear or damage. Should the pinion bearings be worn a complete new steering rack must be obtained.
11 Check the bush in the end of the rack tube for wear. If evident, it may be removed, using a suitable diameter drift, and a new one inserted using a bench vice to press it into position.
12 With all parts ready for reassembly carefully insert the rack into the tube and refit the pinion.
13 Fit the pressure pad and cap nut to the rack tube. Tighten the plug to just remove all end float and, using feeler gauges,

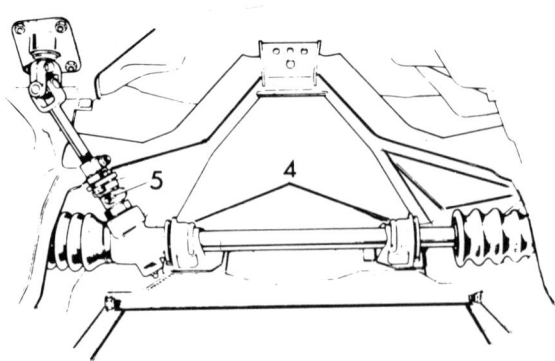

FIG. 11.17. DISCONNECTION POINTS TO REMOVE RACK AND PINION STEERING GEAR

1 *Tie rod*	4 *'U' bolts*
2 *'U' bolt nuts*	5 *Intermediate shaft pinch*
3 *Rubber mountings*	*bolt;*

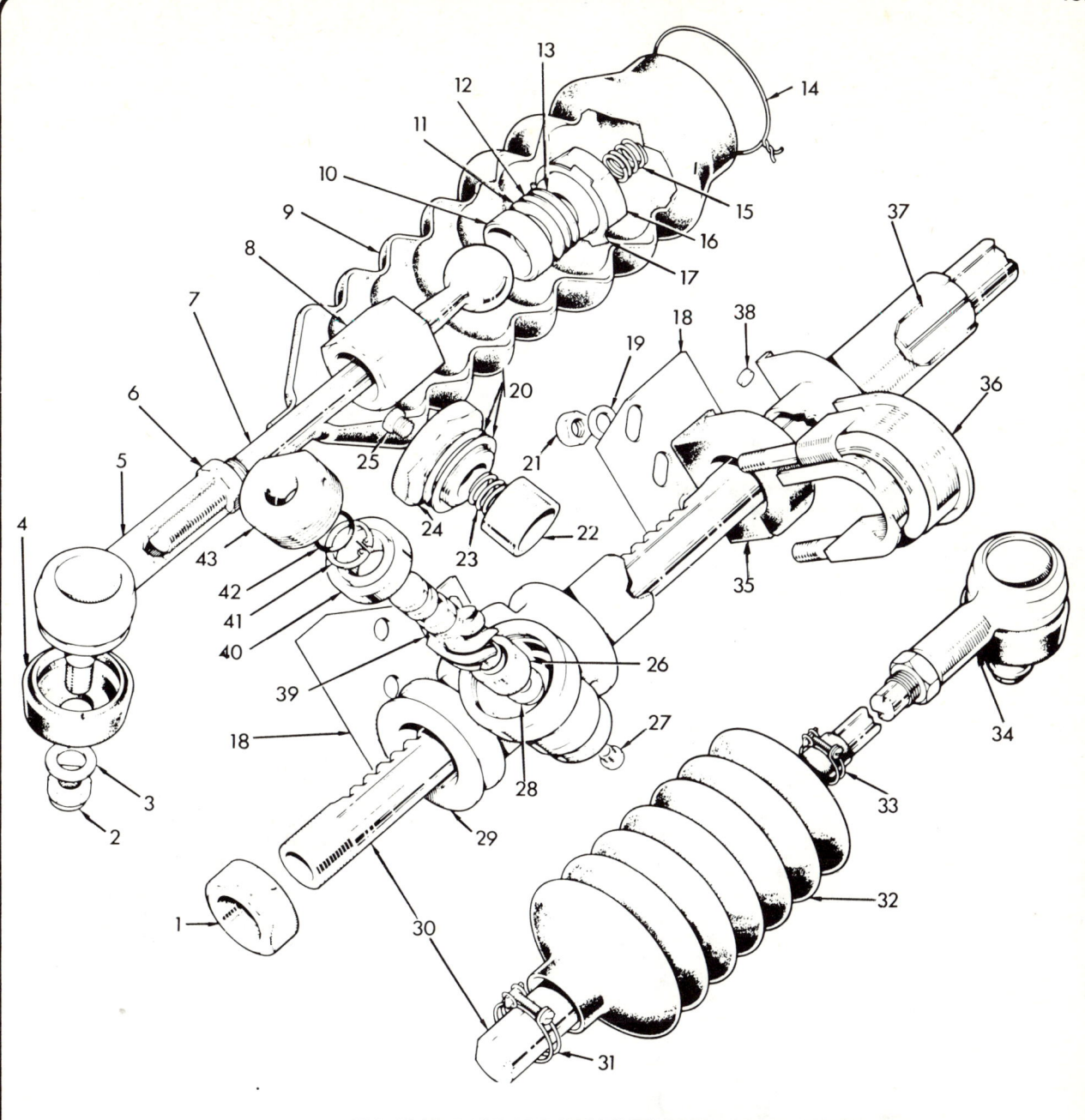

FIG. 11.18. RACK AND PINION STEERING GEAR COMPONENTS

1	Nut, locking ball pin on rack	20	Shim (.004 inch) pinion adjusting
2	Ball joint locknut	21	Nut
3	Washer	22	Plunger
4	Gaiter assembly	23	Spring plunger
5	Outer ball joint assembly	24	Cap, screwed, retaining plunger
6	Locknut, ball joint to ball pin	25	Grease plug in screwed cap
7	Ball pin	26	Bush, pinion lower
8	Ball housing	27	Grease nipple in screwed cap
9	Gaiter (rubber)	28	End cover
10	Ball socket	29	Housing, rack and pinion R.H.S.
11	Shim (.002 inch)	30	Steering rack
12	Shim (.004 inch)	31	Gaiter securing clip
13	Shim (.010 inch)	32	Gaiter (rubber)
14	Gaiter inner locking wire	33	Gaiter securing clip
15	Spring, inner ball joint	34	Outer ball joint assembly
16	Sleeve, adaptor	35	Mounting rubber
17	Washer, tab locking ball housing to sleeve	36	Clamp, rack and pinion housing
18	Locating plate	37	Bush, rack tube
19	Washer	38	Plug (fitted in housing)

Note: All shims are a selective fit on assembly

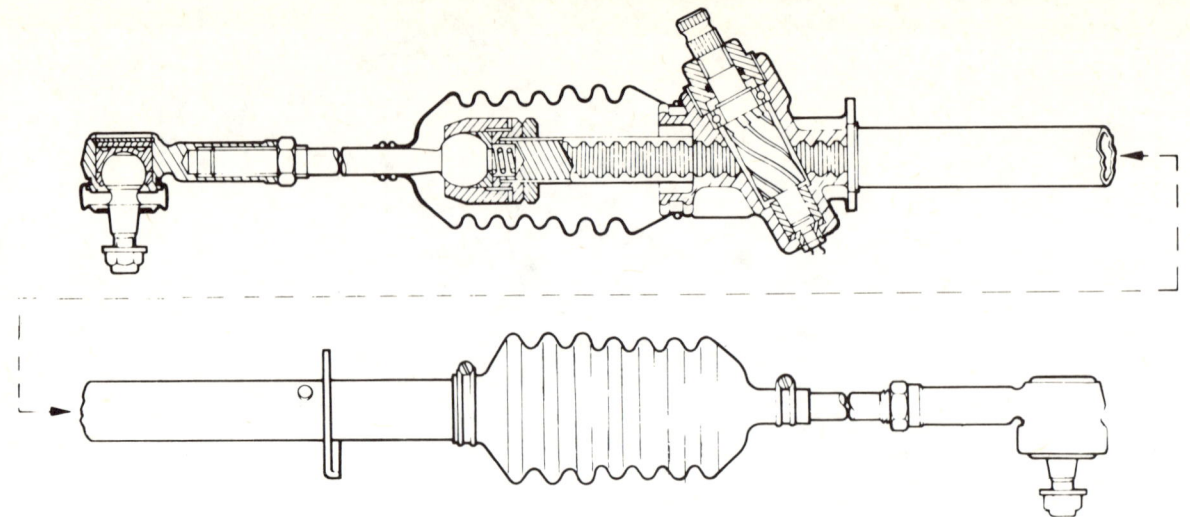

Fig. 11.19. Section through assembled rack and pinion steering gear (refer to Fig. 11.18 for component details)

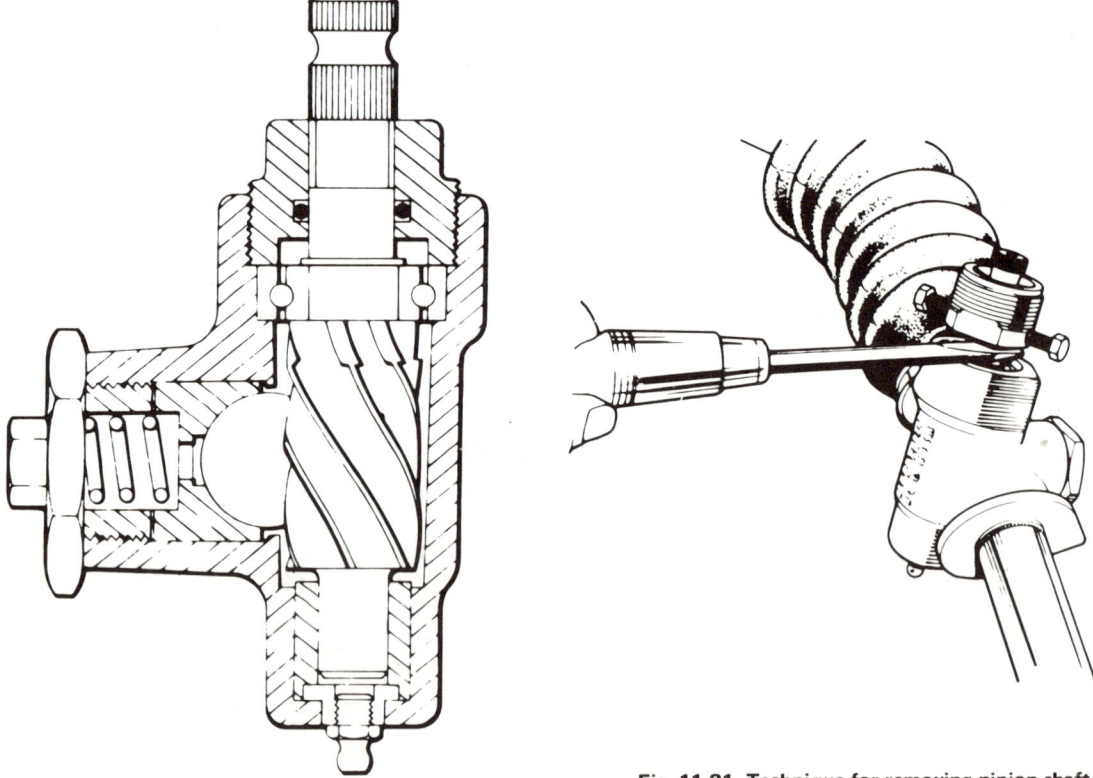

Fig. 11.21. Technique for removing pinion shaft

Fig. 11.20. Section through pinion shaft and pressure pad assembly (refer to Fig. 11.18 for component details)

measure the clearance between the cap nut and housing faces.

14 Unscrew and remove the cap nut and pad.

15 Make up a shim pack equal to the cap/ housing clearance previously determined plus 0.006 in. (0.152mm) nominal end float.

16 Pack the assembly with grease and assemble the cap nut, shim pack, spring and pad to the housing. Tighten the cap nut.

17 Obtain a small spring scale and a piece of metal bar about twelve inches (305 mm) long. Attach the metal bar to the pinion and, with the spring scale , measure the force required to rotate the pinion shaft at a radius of eight inches (203 mm) through three quarters of a turn either side of the mid position. This force must not exceed 2 lbs and for the remainder of the rack travel, 3 lbs.

18 Should these figures be exceeded, adjust by adding or substracting shims from beneath the cap nut.

19 Continue reassembly by sliding the cap nut over the tie rod and insert the thrust cap into the cap nut.

20 Position the tab washer over the sleeve nut and screw this fully into the cap nut.

21 With the cap nut held in a vice, pull and push the tie rod so as to estimate the approximate amount of ball lift.

22 Make up a shim pack slightly thicker than the estimated ball lift and insert this between the thrust cap and the sleeve nut.

23 Add or remove shims to obtain the required 0.0005 to 0.003 in. (0.0127 to 0.0762 mm) ball lift when the sleeve nut is firmly screwed into the cap nut.

24 Test the ball to make sure that it can now move freely in the joint. Should tightness occur at any point. increase the shim thickness sufficiently to overcome this. Shims are available in 0.002, 0.004 and 0.010 in. (0.051, 0.102 and 0.254mm) sizes.

25 When adjustment is correct, lock the assembly by bending the tabs of the tab washer over the sleeve nut and the cap nut.

26 Repeat the above sequence for the second inner ball joint.

27 Fit one locknut and spring to each end of the rack and screw on the tie rod assemblies. Adjust the position of the tie rod assemblies. The distance between the inner and outer tie—ball joint centres should be 9.3/16 in. (233.4mm). Tighten the two locknuts to a torque of 80 lb ft (11 kg m).

28 Pack the ends of the rack shafts and tie rod inner ball joints with clean grease and fit and secure the gaiters. The unit is now ready for refitting to the vehicle.

16 Steering column (early models) - removal and refitting

1 Disconnect the battery as a safety measure.

2 Disconnect the plug-in connectors for the ignition starter circuits and for the horn/trafficator/lights. It is well worth while marking the respective plug and sockets in order to facilitate replacement.

3 Withdraw the ignition key and remove the three screws clamping the nacelle halves together; remove the nacelle.

4 Remove the trafficator/horn stalk and brackets by releasing the two screws from the clamp bracket.

5 Next to be removed are the two nuts and spring washers securing the steering column clamp bracket to the column upper support bracket: detach the clamp bracket and spring clips.

6 Remove the pinch bolt and nut securing the lower end of the column to the intermediate shaft universal joint.

7 Carefully withdraw the steering column complete with the steering wheel. The wheel can be removed as described in Section 13, if required.

8 Reassembly is the reverse of the removal instructions. However, several important points to note when replacing the steering column are given at the end of Section 17, when an almost exactly similar operation is carried out.

17 Steering column (later models) - removal and refitting

1 Disconnect the battery for safety reasons, and then proceed as for the operation in paragraphs 2,3 and 4 of the preceding

Section.

2 Remove the parcel shelf as described in Chapter 12.

3 Release the pinch bolt and nut securing the lower end of the steering column to the universal joint.

4 Remove the two bolts securing the steering column clamp bracket to the column upper support bracket. These bolts are of the shear-headed type and removal is accomplished using a drill and an 'Easiout' extractor.

5 Remove the steering column bracket and spring clip. Withdraw the steering column complete with steering wheel.

6 Refitting is the reverse of removal instructions. The following points need careful attention to ensure that the safety aspect of reassembly is observed:

a) Locate the steering column assembly in position and engage the lower end of the column in the bottom bush fitted to the scuttle.

b) Fit the nylon washer to the lower end of the column and with the road wheels straight ahead and the steering wheel spokes horizontal, engage the column splines in the universal joint.

c) Fit and tighten the pinch bolt and nuts.

d) Fit the spring clip, clamp bracket, and two new shear bolts to the column.

e) Tighten the shear bolts evenly and shear off the heads. The remaining reassembly operations are straightforward and are not detailed.

18 Steering column - dismantling, overhaul and reassembly

1 With the steering column assembly removed from the car it can readily be dismantled into its constituent parts. The most likely components to need replacing are the lower bushes.

2 Remove the steering wheel as described in Section 13.

3 Release the two bolts and washers that secure the safety clamp in position, then pull the lower column downwards and out from inside the upper column.

4 Withdraw the upper column from the housing holding it central to avoid damaging or disturbing the bushes.

5 The bushes can be removed by inserting an electrician's screwdriver through the locating hole and depressing the rubber locating dowel; the bushes can then be drifted out. It is necessary to remove the end cap before the lower bush can be removed.

6 With the steering column dismantled, examine it thoroughly for fractures, distortion, corrosion or badly worn bushes. It is good practice to renew the bushes in any event, having stripped the assembly so far. If any other components are worn or damaged they must be replaced; never try to 'patch-up' any steering component - it just isn't worth it.

19 Steering wheel intermediate shaft - removal, inspection and refitting

1 The intermediate shaft is normally replaced when it is apparent that any play in the steering is not in the rack and pinion, or the ball joints, but is in the intermediate shaft universal joints. This can be detected by disconnecting the pinion shaft universal joint, and an assistant holding the steering wheel firmly, twisting the intermediate shaft in both directions and noting any excess play or knocks.

2 To remove the intermediate shaft, remove the upper and lower pinch bolts, and the nuts securing the intermediate shaft to the steering column and steering rack pinion.

3 Remove the "U" bolts securing the rack to the sub-frame, then ease the rack forward to release the pinion shaft from the intermediate shaft flexible coupling.

4 Pull the intermediate shaft from the steering column.

5 In order to remove the flexible coupling, it is necessary to remove the pinch bolt securing the coupling and pull it off the shaft.

6 Inspect the shaft for fractures or corrosion, and the universal

and flexible couplings for excess play or other evidence of deterioration. Fit new parts where necessary.

7 Reassembly is the reverse to removal. Remember to set the road wheels to the straight-ahead position, and with the steering-wheel spokes horizontal, connect the intermediate shaft universal joint to the column and the flexible joint to the rack pinion. The remainder of the refitting operations are straightforward.

20 Outer ball joint assembly - removal and replacement

1 If the tie-rod outer ball joints are worn it will be necessary to renew the whole ball joint assembly as they cannot be dismantled and repaired. To remove a ball joint, free the ball joint shank from the steering arm and mark the position of the locknut on the tie-rod accurately to ensure near accurate 'toe-in' on reassembly.

2 Slacken off the ball joint locknut, and holding the tie-rod by its flat with a spanner, to prevent it from turning, unscrew the complete ball assembly from the rod. Replacement is a straightforward reversal of this process. the distance between the inner and outer tie-rod ball joint centres should be 9.3/16 in. (233.4 mm). Visit your local Triumph agent to ensure that toe-in is correct.

21 Front wheel alignment

1 The front wheels are correctly aligned when they are turning in at the front 0-1/16 in. (0-1.588 mm). It is important that this measurement is taken on a centre line drawn horizontally and parallel to the ground through the centre line of the hub. The exact point should be in the centre of the sidewall of the tyre and not on the wheel rim which could be distorted and so give inaccurate readings.

2 The adjustment is effected by loosening the locknut on each tie-rod ball joint and also slackening the rubber gaiter clip holding it to the tie-rod, both tie-rods being turned equally until the adjustment is correct.

3 This is a job best left to your local Triumph garage, as accurate alignment requires the use of special equipment. If the wheels are not in alignment, tyre wear will be heavy and uneven, and the steering will be stiff and unresponsive.

22 Rear wheel alignment

It is important that the rear wheel toe out and camber angles are always checked every time the rear suspension has been dismantled. To do this accurately measuring equipment is necessary and will usually be found at Triumph garages. This check should be entrusted to them.

23 Front wheel camber - setting up

Apart from checking toe-in, the only other adjustment possible is the camber of the wheels. This is accomplished by removing or fitting shims behind the front suspension bracket. However, since this operation requires specialised measuring equipment, it is virtually impossible for the home owner to do it himself with anything like the degree of accuracy that is required. For that reason we recommend that the operation be carried out by a Triumph agent.

24 Fault diagnosis

Symptom	Reason/s	Remedy
STEERING FEELS VAGUE, CAR WANDERS AND FLOATS AT SPEED		
General wear or damage	Tyre pressures uneven	Check pressures and adjust as necessary.
	Dampers worn	Test, and replace if worn.
	Steering gear ball joints badly worn	Fit new ball joints.
	Suspension geometry incorrect	Check and rectify.
	Steering mechanism free play excessive	Adjust or overhaul steering mechanism.
	Front suspension and rear suspension pick-up points out of alignment	Normally caused by poor repair work after a serious accident. Extensive rebuilding necessary.
STIFF & HEAVY STEERING		
Lack of maintenance or accident damage	Tyre pressures too low	Check pressures and inflat tyres.
	No oil in steering gear	Top up steering gear.
	No grease in steering and suspension ball joints	Clean nipples and grease thoroughly.
	Front wheel toe-in incorrect	Check and reset toe-in.
	Suspension geometry incorrect	Check and rectify.
	Steering gear incorrectly adjusted too tightly	Check and readjust steering gear.
	Steering column badly misaligned	Determine cause and rectify (usually due to bad repair after severe accident damage and difficult to correct).
WHEEL WOBBLE & VIBRATION		
General wear or damage	Wheel nuts loose	Check and tighten as necessary.
	Front wheels and tyres out of balance	Balance wheels and tyres and add weights as necessary.
	Steering ball joints badly worn	Replace steering gear ball joints.
	Hub bearings badly worn	Remove and fit new hub bearings.
	Steering gear free play excessive	Adjust and overhaul steering gear.
	Front springs weak or broken	Inspect and renew as necessary.

Chapter 12 Bodywork and underframe

Contents

General description	1
Maintenance - body and chassis	2
Maintenance - upholstery and carpets	3
Minor body repairs	4
Major chassis and body repairs	5
Maintenance - locks and hinges	6
Door rattles - tracing and rectification	7
Front door - remove and refit	8
Rear door - remove and refit	9
Door hinges, front and rear - removal and refitting	10
Front door - dismantling and reassembly	11
Rear door - dismantling and reassembly	12
Striker plate - removal, replacement and adjustment ...	13
Windscreen glass - removal and replacement	14

Front and rear seat - removal and refitting	15
Facia panel - removal and refitting	16
Parcel shelf - removal and refitting	17
Heater unit and fan motor - removal and replacement ...	18
Heater air flow control cable - removal and refitting ...	19
Heater water valve - removal and replacement	20
Heater fan motor switch - removal and replacement ...	21
Bonnet lock - removal and refitting	22
Bonnet lock control cable - removal and refitting ...	23
Bonnet - removal and refitting	24
Boot lid - removal and refitting	25
Boot lid locks - removal and refitting	26
Bumpers and mounting brackets - removal and refitting	27

1 General description

The Toledo body is constructed from rust-proofed steel on the monocoque principle; a sub-frame at the front supports some of the major components, including suspension, gearbox and steering gear; it also braces the structure.

Two or four-door versions are available; in this Chapter it is assumed that four doors are fitted.

Toughened safety glass is fitted to all windows; the windscreen has a specially toughened 'zone' in front of the driver. In the event of the windscreen shattering this 'zone' breaks into much larger pieces than the rest of the screen thus giving the driver much better vision than would otherwise be possible.

The front seats are of the adjustable bucket type whilst the rear seat is a bench seat, without a central arm rest.

The instruments are all housed in two dials located on the facia panel in front of the driver.

A heater and demister unit provides fresh air of a selected temperature to the interior of the car. Air flow can be increased by the use of a two-speed booster fan. Through-flow ventilation is provided by the use of interior ducts at the base of the back light. Two face-level air ducts are located each side of the facia panel and the ducts can be adjusted to suit the passengers' requirements. Exterior non-return ducts at the top of the backlight assist rear window demisting.

2 Maintenance - body and chassis

1 The condition of the car's bodywork is of considerable, importance as it is on this that the second-hand value of the car will mainly depend. It is usually more difficult to repair neglected bodywork than to renew mechanical assemblies. The hidden portions of the body, such as the wheel arches, the underframe and the engine compartment, are equally important, although obviously not requiring such frequent attention as the immediately visible paintwork.

2 Once a year, or every 12000 miles (20000 Km) it is recommended that you visit your local main agent and have the underside of the body steam cleaned. This will take about 1½ hours. All traces of dirt and oil will be removed and the underside can then be inspected carefully for rust, damaged hydraulic pipes, frayed electrical wiring and similar maladies. The car should be greased on completion of this job.

3 At the same time the engine compartment should be cleaned in a similar manner. If steam cleaning facilities are not available, then brush Gunk or a similar cleaner over the whole engine and engine compartment with a stiff brush, working it well in where there is an accumulation of oil and dirt. Do not paint the ignition system; protect it with oily rags when the Gunk is washed off. As the Gunk is washed away it will take with it all traces of oil and dirt, leaving the engine looking bright and clean.

4 The wheel arches should be given particular attention, as under-sealing can easily come away here and stones and dirt thrown up from the road wheels can soon cause the paint to chip and flake, and so allow rust to set in. If rust is found, clean down the bare metal with wet and dry paper, paint on an anti-corrosive coating such as Kurust, or if preferred, red lead, and renew the paintwork and undercoating.

5 The bodywork should be washed once a week or when dirty. Thoroughly wet the car to soften the dirt and then wash the car down with a soft sponge and plenty of clean water. If the surplus dirt is not washed off very gently, in time it will wear the paint down as surely as wet and dry paper. It is best to use a hose if this is available. Give the car a final wash down and then dry with a soft chamois leather to prevent the formation of spots.

6 Spots of tar and grease thrown up from the road can be removed by a rag dampened in petrol.

7 Once every three, or six months if wished, give the bodywork and chromium trim a thoroughly good wax polish. If a chromium cleaner is used to remove rust on any of the car's plated parts, remember that the cleaner also removes part of the chromium, so use sparingly.

3 Maintenance - upholstery and carpets

1 Remove the carpets or mats and thoroughly vacuum clean the interior of the car three months , or more frequently if necessary.

2 Beat out the carpets and vacuum clean them if they are very dirty. If the upholstery is soiled, apply an upholstery cleaner with a damp sponge and wipe off with a clean dry cloth.

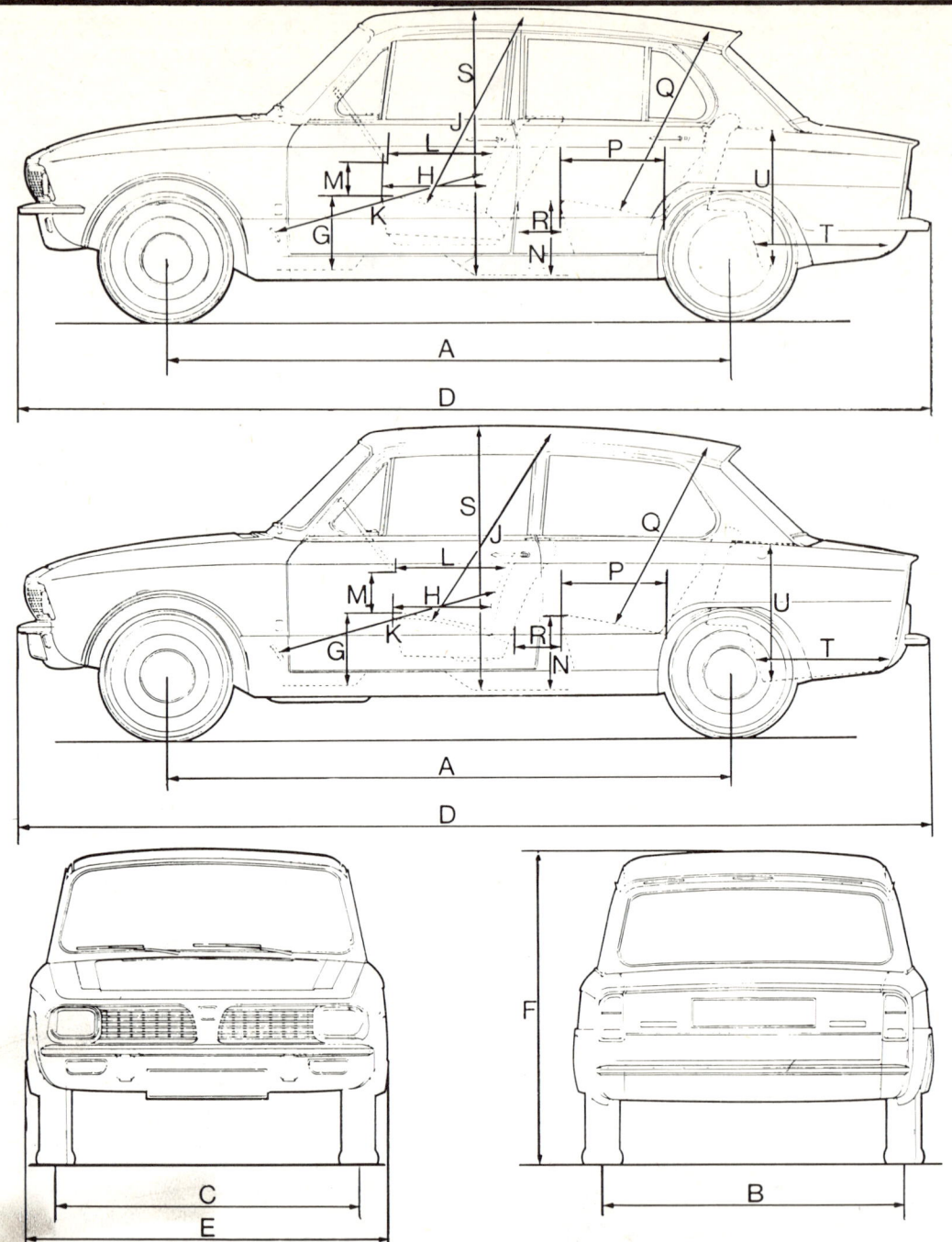

FIG.12.1. BODYSHELL DIMENSIONS (TOP: 4 DOOR, BOTTOM: 2 DOOR)

			ft/inches	mm					ft/inches	mm
A	Wheelbase		8ft. 0.5/8	2454	M	Steering wheel clearance from front seat cushion			6½	165
B	Rear track		4ft. 2	1270						
C	Front track		4ft. 5	1348						
D	Overall length		13ft.0.1/8	3965	N	Rear seat height — floor to cushion			13	330
E	Overall width		5ft. 1¼	1568	P	Rear seat depth			18	457
F	Overall height		4ft. 6	1372	Q	Headroom — from rear seat cushion			33½	852
G	Front seat height— floor to cushion		13 in.	330	R	Rear legroom	Max.		12½	318
H	Front seat depth		17½	445			Min.		6½	165
J	Headroom — front front seat cushion		36	914	T	Luggage compartment depth	Max.		33	837
K	Front squab to clutch pedal	Max.	39	991			Min.		26	660
		Min.	33	838	U	Luggage compartment height	Max.		17	432
L	Steering wheel clearance from front seat squab	Max.	19	483			Min.		13½	343
		Min.	13	330						

4 Minor body repairs

1   Usually at least once in a car's life, minor body damage takes place.

2   Major damage must be repaired by your local Triumph garage, but there is no reason why you cannot successfully beat out, repair and re-spray minor damage yourself. The essential items which the owner should gather together to ensure a really professional job are :-

a)   A plastic filler such as Holts Cataloy.

b)   Paint whose colour matches exactly that of the bodywork, either in a can for application by a spray gun or in a aerosol spray.

c)   Fine cutting paste.

d)   Medium and fine grade wet and dry paper.

3   Never use a metal hammer to knock out small dents as the blows tend to scratch and distort the metal. Knock out the dent with a mallet or rawhide hammer and press on the underside of the dented surface a metal dolly or smooth wooden block roughly contoured to the normal shape of the damaged area.

4   After the worst of the damaged area has been knocked out, rub down the dent and surrounding area with medium wet and dry paper and thoroughly clean away all traces of dirt.

5   The plastic filler comprises a paste and hardener which must be thoroughly mixed together. Mix only a small portion at a time as the paste sets hard within five to fifteen minutes depending on the amount of hardener used.

6   Smooth on the filler with a knife or stiff plastic to the shape of the damaged portion and allow to thoroughly dry, a process which takes about six hours. After the filler has dried it is likely that it will have contracted slightly, so spread on a second layer of filler if necessary.

7   Smooth down the filler with fine wet and dry paper wrapped round a small flat block of wood. Continue until the whole area is perfectly smooth and it is impossible to feel where the filler joins the rest of the paintwork.

8   Spray on from an aerosol can, or with a spray gun, an anti-rust undercoat, smooth down with wet and dry paper, and then spray on two coats of the final finish using a circular motion.

9   When thoroughly dry, polish the whole area with a fine cutting paste to smooth the re-sprayed area into the remainder of the wing or panel and to remove the small particles of spray paint which will have settled round the area.

10 This will leave the area looking perfect with not a trace of the previous unslightly dent.

5 Major chassis and body repair

1   Major chassis and body repair work cannot be successfully undertaken by the home mechanic. Work of this nature should be entrusted to a competent body repair specialist who should have the necessary jigs, welding and hydraulic equipment, as well as skilled panel beaters, to ensure a proper job is done.

2   If the damage is severe, it is vital that on completion of repair the chassis is correctly aligned. Less severe damage may also have twisted or distorted the chassis although this may not be visible immediately. It is therefore, always best on completion of a repair to check for twist and squareness to ensure that all is correct.

3   To check for twist, position the car on a clean level floor, place a jack under each jacking point, raise the car and take off the wheels. Raise or lower the jacks until the sills are parallel with the ground. Depending where the damage occurred, using an accurate scale, take measurements at the suspension mounting points and if comparable readings are not obtained it is an indication that the body is twisted.

4   After checking for twist, check for squareness by taking a series of measurements on the floor. Drop a plumb line and bob weight from various mounting points on the underside of the body and mark these points on the floor with chalk. Draw a straight line between each point and measure and mark the middle of each line. A line drawn on the floor starting at the front and finishing at the rear should be quite straight and pass through the centres of the other lines. Diagonal measurements can also be made as a check for squareness.

6 Maintenance - locks and hinges

Once every 6,000 miles (10,000 Km) or 6 months, the door bonnet and boot hinges should be oiled with a few drops of engine oil from an oil can. The door striker plates can be given a thin smear of grease to reduce wear and ensure free movement.

7 Door rattles - tracing and rectification

1   The most common cause of door rattles is a misaligned, loose or worn striker plate but other causes may be:

a)   Loose door handles, window winder handles or door hinges.

b)   Loose, worn or misaligned door lock components.

c)   Loose or worn remote control mechanism.

Or a combination of these.

2   If the striker catch is worn as a result of door rattles renew it and adjust as described later in this Chapter.

3   Should the hinges be badly worn then they must be renewed

8 Front door - remove and refit

1   Refer to Section 11 and remove the trim pad.

2   Mark the outline of the hinge plate on the door frame using a soft pencil or something similar.

3   Remove the water curtain, then having gained access to the

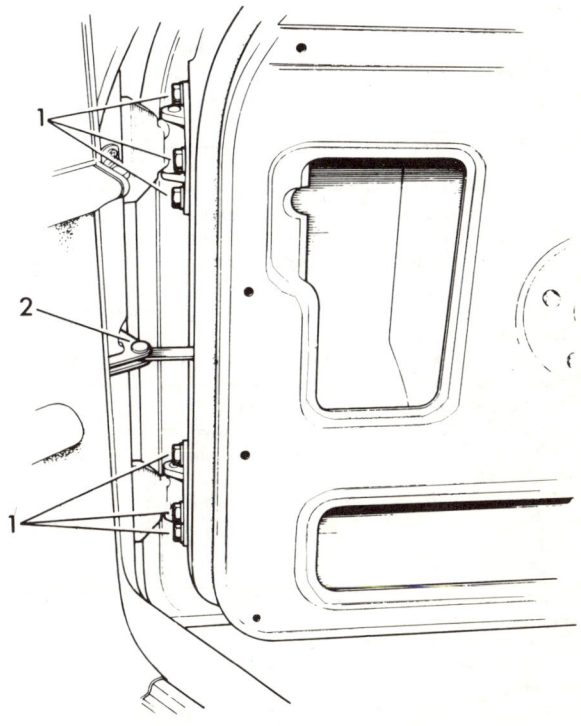

FIG.12.1A FRONT DOOR SECURING POINTS

1   Hinge plate bolts   *2   Checkstrap*

door inner section, drill out the rivet that retains the check strap. Remove the check strap.

4 With an assistant taking the weight of the door, remove the six bolts and spring washers that secure the door.

5 Refitting the door is the reverse sequence to removal. Should it be necessary to adjust the position of the door in the aperture leave the locknuts slightly loose and reposition the door by trial and error. Fully tighten the locknuts.

9 Rear door - remove and refit

1 Remove the two bolts and spring washers that secure the retaining strap.

2 Mark the position of the hinge plates on the door frame and, with the door supported, remove the six bolts and spring washers that secure them.

3 Refitting is the reverse to removing. Adjust the position of the hinges as necessary to achieve an accurate fit in the door frame.

10 Door hinges, front and rear - removal and refitting

1 Remove the door (Sections 8 or 9).

2 To remove the front door hinges, first remove the two bolts and washers that secure the driver's side of the parcel shelf and the two screws and washers that retain the side trim.

3 Ease the parcel shelf slightly upwards, and the side trim slightly away from the door frame, in order to gain access to the inner hinge fixings.

4 Mark the outline of the hinge plates and then undo the three nuts and washers that secure each hinge plate to the door frame. Withdraw the hinges.

5 To remove the rear door hinges it is only necessary to remove the rear door and then release the three bolts and washers that secure each hinge to the door.

6 Refitting is the reverse of removal. Line up the hinges with the previously made marks. Adjust the hinge position as necessary.

11 Front door - dismantling and reassembly

1 Unscrew and remove the interior lock plunger knob.

2 To remove the window winder, depress the bezel and press out the retaining pin. Very often the shank of a nail will suffice for this purpose. Remove the handle and bezel.

3 Remove the armrest by releasing the two screws and washers that secure it.

4 It is now possible to remove the trim pad: prise it off the sixteen clips that secure it. Use a wide bladed tool without any sharp edges and apply gentle but firm pressure.

5 In order to remove the door lock, the water curtain must first be removed. Then release the four linkage clips and undo the four screws that secure the lock. Pull the lock clear.

6 The remote control linkage is released by removing the three screws and washers that retain the handle, and detaching the clip from the handle.

7 The next series of operations are reasonably delicate since they concern the removal of the window glass-so take that extra special bit of care.

8 Remove the anti-drum stiffener.

9 Wind the glass fully down and detach the regulator arm from the channel.

10 Remove the single bolt and washer that secures the forward glass stop to the bottom of the regulator assembly.

11 Release the glass vertical channel by removing the single bolt and two washers that secures it at the bottom bracket.

12 Carefully remove the window channel rubbers by easing them out of the door glass apertures and the associated clips.

13 Using extreme care, turn the glass sideways and lift it out through the aperture: try and avoid scratching it on the rubber

seal clips.

14 The regulator can now be removed by releasing the four bolts and washers that secure it to the door frame. Withdraw the regulator.

15 The final part to be removed from the door is the ventilator. First remove the top glass sealing rubber.

16 Then, using an electric drill, remove the two pop rivets located in the angled frame.

17 Pull the glass clear of the vent runner and lift out the vent assembly.

18 The parts are now ready for inspection and refitting. Should the window winder or door lock mechanism prove to be faulty, the complete unit must be renewed as individual service parts are not available.

19 Refitting the door parts is the reverse sequence to removal. Lubricate well all moving parts. It is recommended if there are signs of excessive internal rusting of the door panels, that the rust be removed with a suitable solvent and the interior of the door be painted with a lead paint. Check that the drain holes are free of rust and dirt.

12 Rear door - dismantling and reassembly

The rear door is dismantled in essentially the same manner as the front door (Section 11) from the point of removing the various control handles. The next step is the removal of the trim pad and door internal mechanisms.

1 Using a wide bladed screwdriver carefully prise away the door trim pad from the door inner panel. There are fifteen spring clips securing it in position.

2 To detach the remote control linkage, remove the spring clips by prising them out of their recesses with a screwdriver.

3 Undo and remove the three screws securing the handle to the door inner panel.

4 Lift away the window regulator control linkage.

5 To remove the regulator undo the three screws securing the glass stop. Lift away the glass stop.

6 Carefully lower the door glass. Undo and remove the four screws, disengage the regulator arm from the door glass channel and lift the regulator mechanism away from the door.

7 To remove the door lock, undo and remove the four screws and lift away the lock assembly.

8 To remove the door handle, undo and remove the three screws and lift away the door handle.

9 The door glass and ventilator may next be removed. Allow the glass to rest in the bottom of the door and remove the inner and outer weather strips.

10 Undo and remove the two screws and clips which secure the anti-drum stiffener. Lift away the stiffener.

11 Carefully pull the weatherstrip from the ventilator area of the door to expose the securing pop rivet.

12 Remove the pop rivet using a drill.

13 Remove the glass sealing rubber from the top of the door.

14 Undo and remove the screw located at the bottom of the quarter light stanchion. Carefully pull the stanchion away from the glass and remove it.

15 The door quarter light glass assembly may now be lifted out of the door frame.

13 Striker plate - removal, replacement and adjustment

1 If it is wished to renew a worn striker plate, mark its position on the door pillar so a new plate can be fitted in the same position.

2 To remove the plate, simply undo and remove the two screws which hold the plate in position. Replacement is equally straightforward.

3 To adjust the striker plate, close the door and then push it hard against its sealing rubber. The door edge furthest from the hinges should move in approximately 3/32 in. (2.4 mm).

4 Slacken the door striker plate screws and adjust the plate

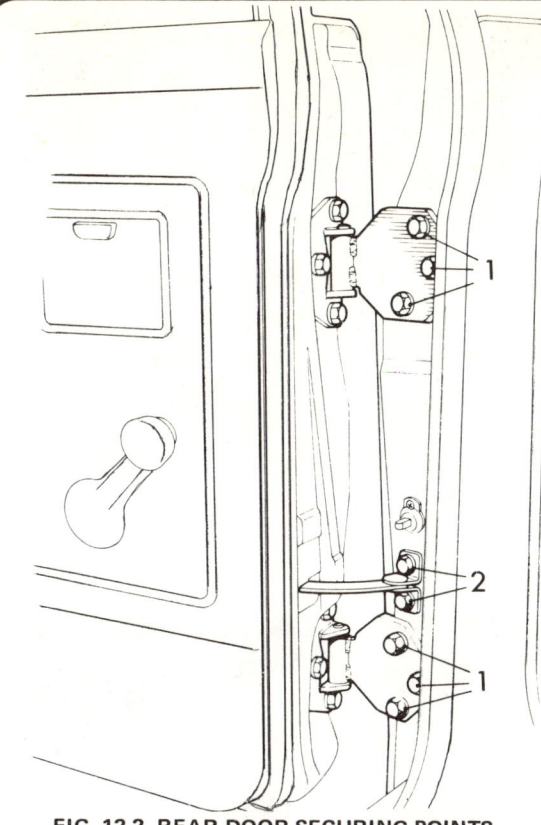

FIG. 12.2. REAR DOOR SECURING POINTS

1　Hinge plate bolts　　　2　Check strap bolts

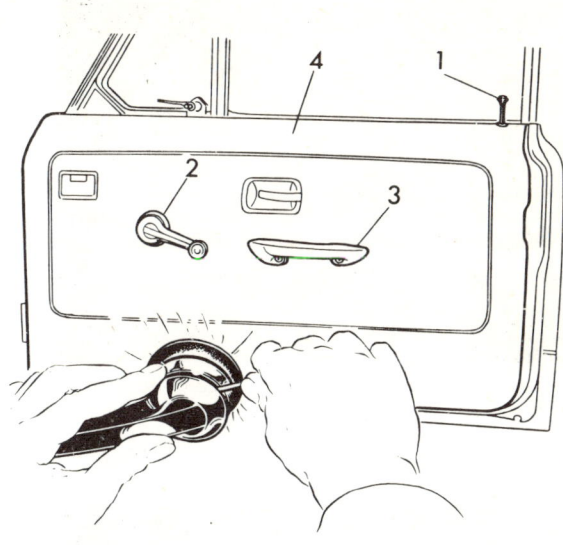

FIG. 12.4. DISMANTLING THE FRONT DOOR

1　Plunger knob　　　　　3　Arm rest
2　Window winder　　　　4　Trim pad

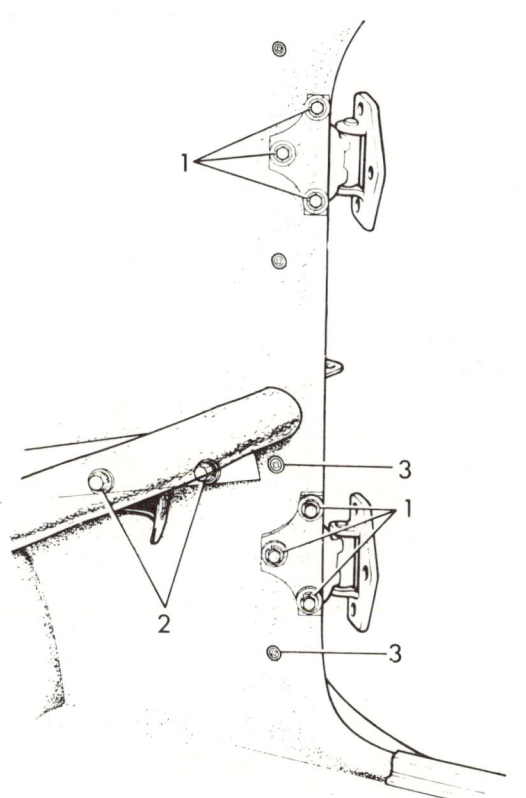

FIG. 12.3. REMOVING FRONT DOOR HINGES

1　Hinge bolts beneath　　2　Parcel shelf bolts
　the trim　　　　　　　3　Trim retaining screws

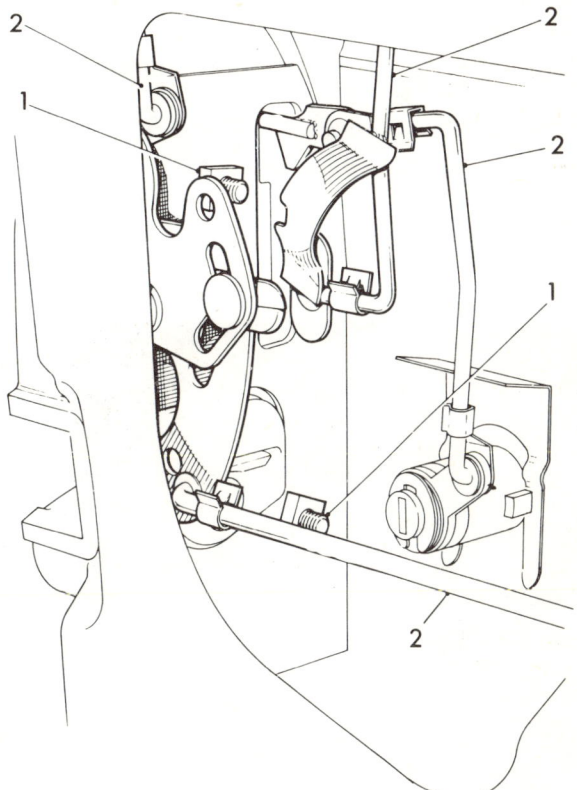

FIG. 12.5. REMOVING THE DOOR LOCK

1　Lock retaining screws　　2　Linkages

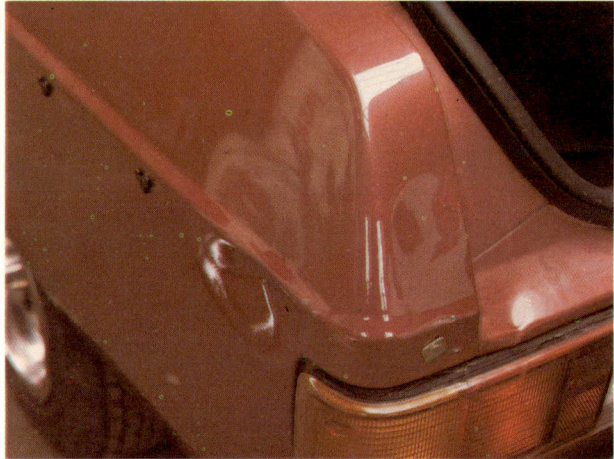

This sequence of photographs deals with the repair of the dent and scratch (above rear lamp) shown in this photo. The procedure will be similar for the repair of a hole. It should be noted that the procedures given here are simplified - more explicit instructions will be found in the text

In the case of a dent the first job - after removing surrounding trim - is to hammer out the dent where access is possible. This will minimise filling. Here, the large dent having been hammered out, the damaged area is being made slightly concave

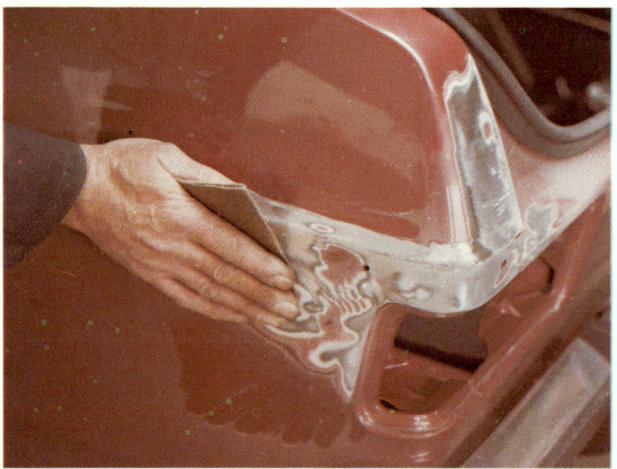

Now all paint must be removed from the damaged area, by rubbing with coarse abrasive paper. Alternatively, a wire brush or abrasive pad can be used in a power drill. Where the repair area meets good paintwork, the edge of the paintwork should be 'feathered', using a finer grade of abrasive paper

In the case of a hole caused by rusting, all damaged sheet-metal should be cut away before proceeding to this stage. Here, the damaged area is being treated with rust remover and inhibitor before being filled

Mix the body filler according to its manufacturer's instructions. In the case of corrosion damage, it will be necessary to block off any large holes before filling - this can be done with zinc gauze or aluminium tape. Make sure the area is absolutely clean before ...

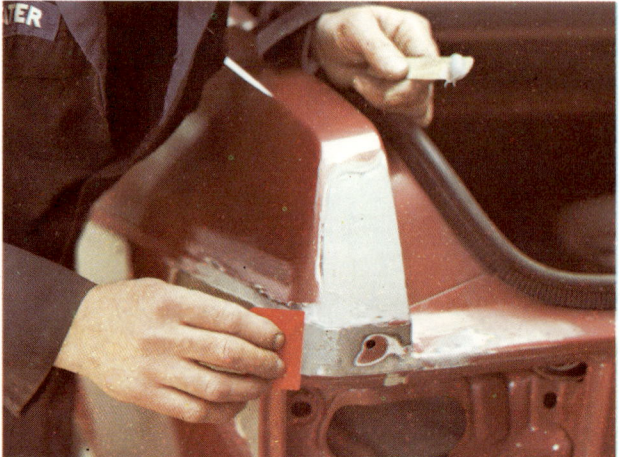

... applying the filler. Filler should be applied with a flexible applicator, as shown, for best results: the wooden spatula being used for confined areas. Apply thin layers of filler at 20-minute intervals, until the surface of the filler is slightly proud of the surrounding bodywork

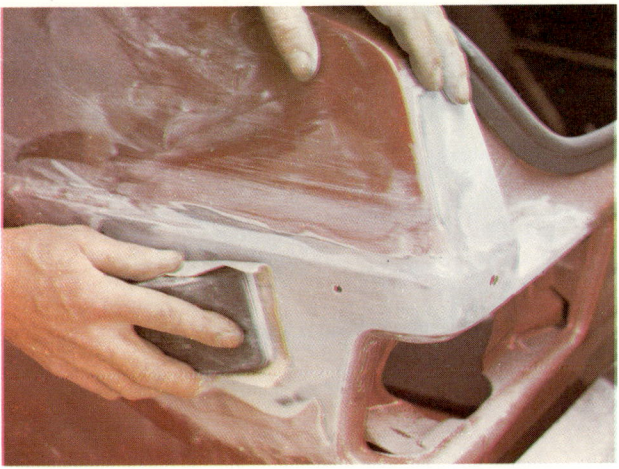

Initial shaping can be done with a Surform plane or Dreadnought file. Then, using progressively finer grades of wet-and-dry paper, wrapped around a sanding block, and copious amounts of clean water, rub-down the filler until really smooth and flat. Again, feather the edges of adjoining paintwork

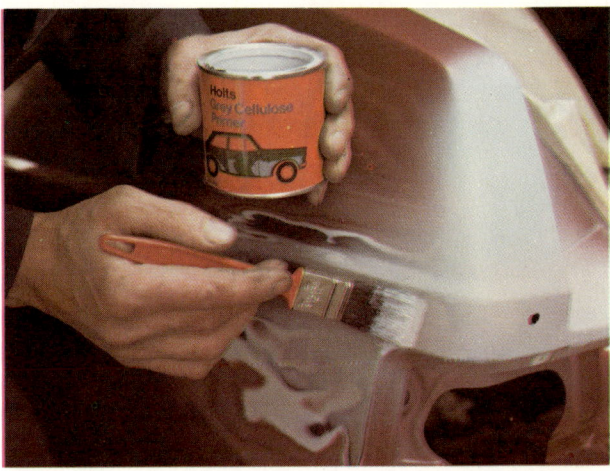

The whole repair area can now be sprayed or brush-painted with primer. If spraying, ensure adjoining areas are protected from over-spray. Note that at least one-inch of the surrounding sound paintwork should be coated with primer. Primer has a 'thick' consistency, so will fill small imperfections

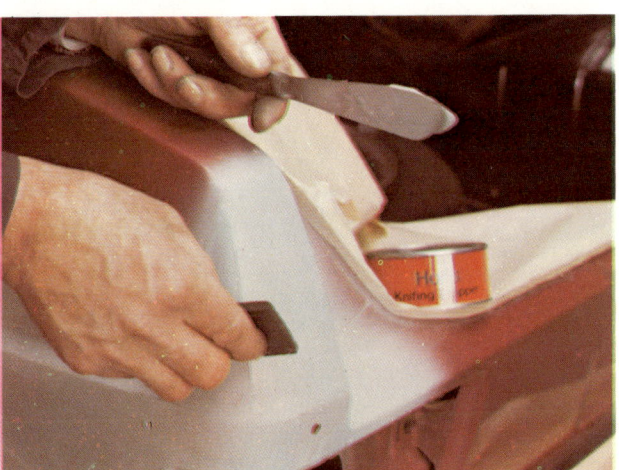

Again, using plenty of water, rub down the primer with a fine grade of wet-and-dry paper (400 grade is probably best) until it is really smooth and well blended into the surrounding paint-work. Any remaining imperfections can now be filled by carefully applied knifing stopper paste

When the stopper has hardened, rub-down the repair area again before applying the final coat of primer. Before rubbing-down this last coat of primer, ensure the repair area is blemish-free - use more stopper if necessary. To ensure that the surface of the primer is really smooth use some finishing compound

The top coat can now be applied. When working out of doors, pick a dry, warm and wind-free day. Ensure surrounding areas are protected from over-spray. Agitate the aerosol thoroughly, then spray the centre of the repair area, working outwards with a circular motion. Apply the paint as several thin coats.

After a period of about two-weeks, which the paint needs to harden fully, the surface of the repaired area can be 'cut' with a mild cutting compound prior to wax polishing. When carrying out bodywork repairs, remember that the quality of the finished job is proportional to the time and effort expended

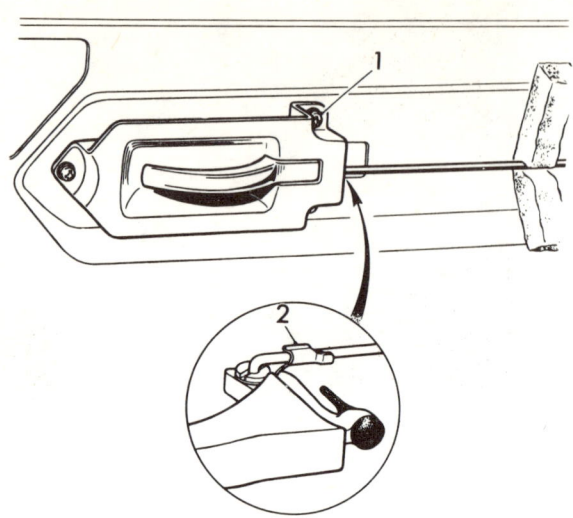

FIG. 12.6. DOOR INTERNAL HANDLE AND REMOTE CONTROL LINKAGE

1 Handle retaining screw   2 Linkage clip

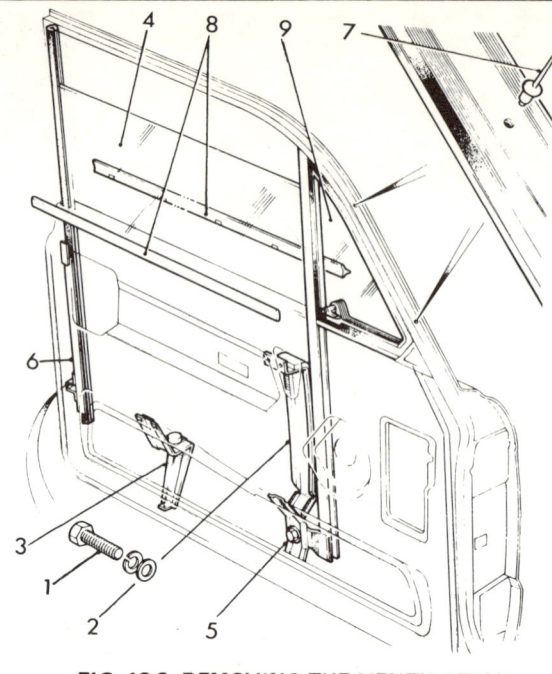

FIG. 12.8. REMOVING THE VENTILATION WINDOW

1	Vertical channel bolt	6	Vertical channel
2	Stiffener	7	Rivets (2)
3	Glass bottom stop	8	Rubber seals
4	Window glass	9	Ventilation window
5	Bolt		

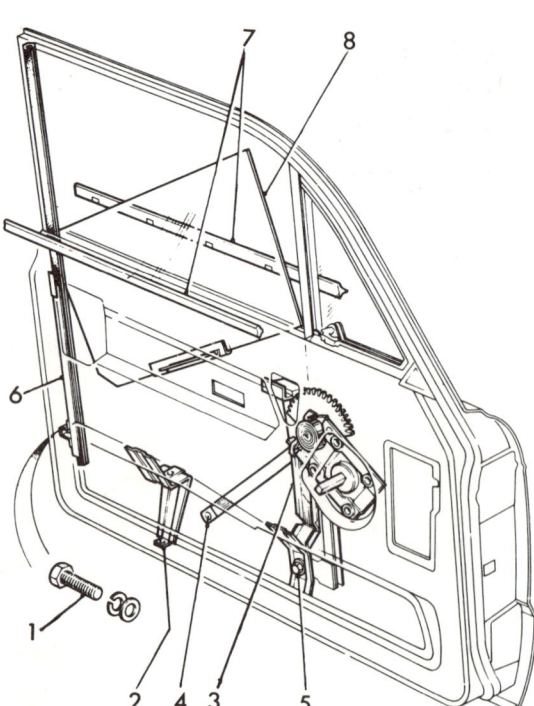

FIG. 12.7. REMOVING WINDOW GLASS AND WINDER MECHANISM

1	Vertical channel bolt	5	Bolt
2	Glass bottom stop	6	Vertical channel
3	Stiffener	7	Rubber seals
4	Regulator arm	8	Window glass

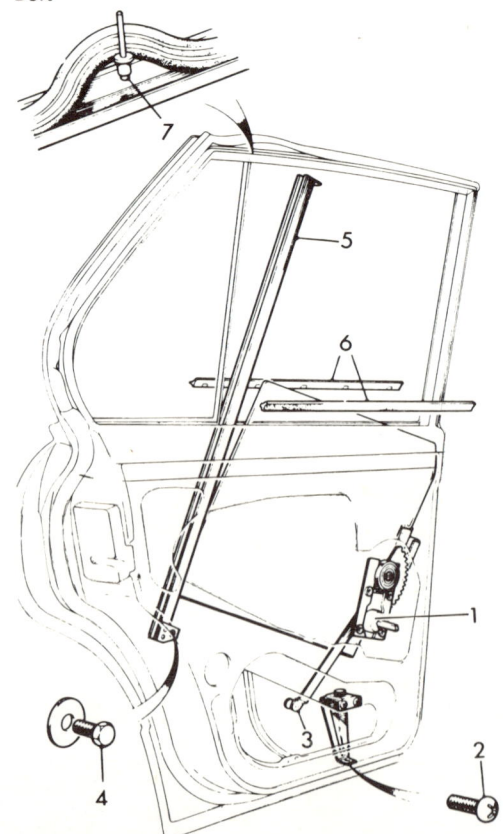

FIG. 12.9. REAR WINDOW COMPONENTS

1	Winder mechanism	5	Vertical channel
2	Screw	6	Rubber seals
3	Regulator arm	7	Rivet
4	Bolt		

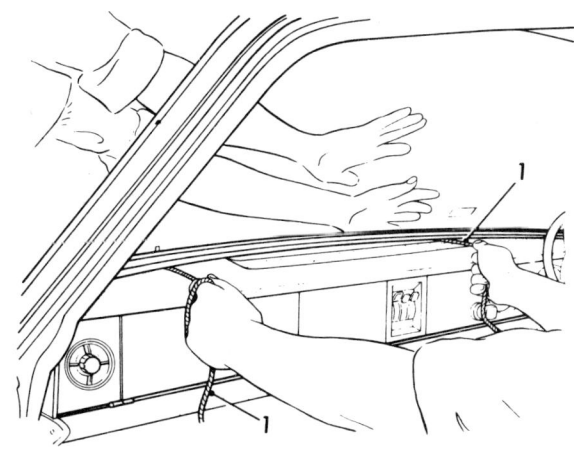

FIG. 12.10. FITTING A NEW WINDSCREEN

1   Cord

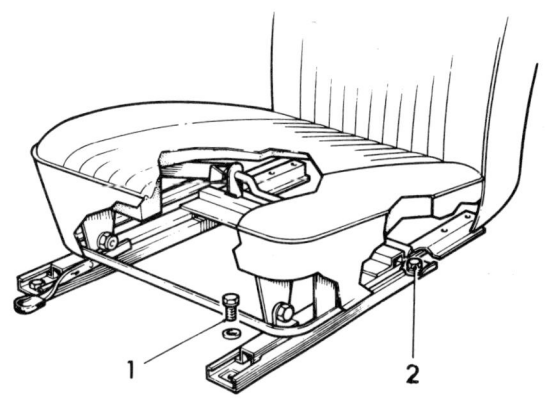

FIG. 12.11. FRONT SEAT CHANNEL BOLTS

1   Front bolt   2   Rear bolt

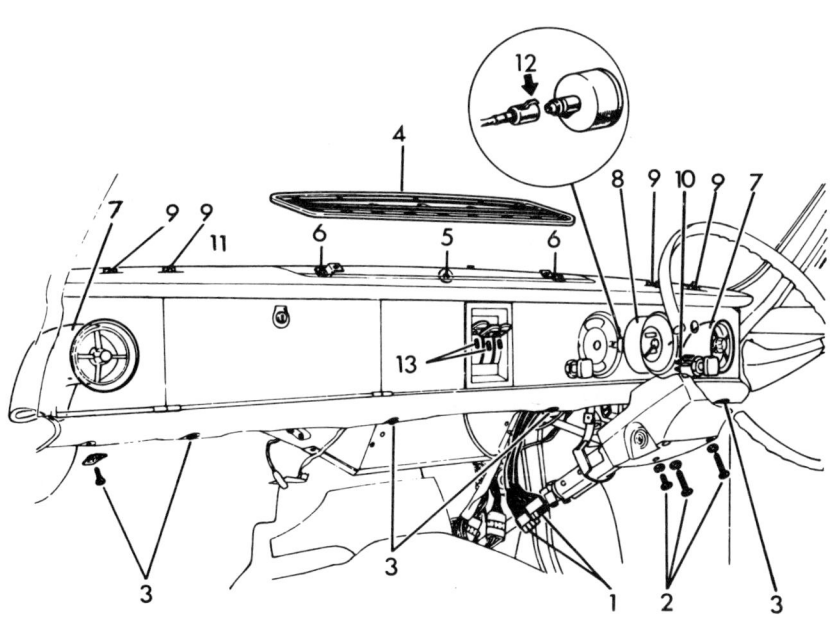

FIG. 12.12. FACIA PANEL SECURING POINTS

1 Wiring harness connectors	5 Centre screw	8 Speedometer	11 Studs
2 Nacelle screws	6 Brackets and retaining	9 Upper securing nuts	12 Disconnection point for
3 Lower fixing screws	screws	10 Windscreen wiper and	speedometer cable
4 Demister grille	7 Vent hoses	washer control	13 Switch grub screws

until the clearance is correct. Tighten the screws and check that the door closes properly without lifting or dropping and that on the road it does not rattle.

14 Windscreen glass - removal and replacement

1   If you are unfortunate enough to have a windscreen shatter, fitting a replacement windscreen is one of the few jobs that the average owner is advised to leave to a body repair specialist. For the owner who wishes to do the job himself, however, the following instructions should be followed:

2   Switch on the ignition and operate the wipers. Switch off the wipers to ensure they are in the rest position. Switch off the ignition.

3   Remove the windscreen wiper arms by prising them off with a screwdriver blade.

4   Using a piece of tapered hardwood, break the seelastik seal around the outside of the windscreen sealing rubber.

5   An assistant must now be obtained and he should be prepared to catch the glass as it is released from the aperture.

6   Sit in the passenger's seat and, with one foot placed on the windscreen glass and a soft pad interposed between the shoe and the glass carefully push the glass out. Ensure the foot is protected in case the glass breaks and your foot goes through. A wellington boot is considered a good safeguard.

7   Carefully pull the weatherstrip and finisher strip from the glass and inspect for signs of stretching or perishing. If evident, a new weatherstrip or finisher should be obtained.

8   Clean the glass, weatherstrip and aperture with petrol or white spirit to remove all old sealing compound from the windscreen aperture edge.

9   Fit the weatherstrip to the windscreen with the joint at the bottom. Seal the rubber to the glass with seelastik. Insert the finisher at this stage as it is easier to do now than when the weatherstrip is back in the aperture.

10 Insert a thick cord, longer than the perimeter of the glass, into the inner channel of the rubber strip in such a manner that the ends protrude from the bottom edge of the weatherstrip.

11 Smear some soapy water solution to the flange of the windscreen aperture. Position the windscreen centrally on the aperture after passing the ends of the cord through into the car.

12 The services of an assistant should be obtained again, this time to maintain a steady pressure on the outside of the glass. The ends of the cord may now be pulled so as to bring the lip of the weatherstrip over the body flange.

13 Make quite sure that the lip is firmly pushed down behind the facia. To obtain a good seating, it may be necessary to strike the outside of the weatherstrip with a rubber faced hammer.

14 Completely withdraw the cord and then seal the weatherstrip to body joint with Sealstik. Remove surplus sealing compound with a cloth moistened in petrol or white spirit. Do not allow any excess cleaning liquid to seep into the joint and destroy the seal.

15 Front and rear seat - removal and refitting

Front seat

1   Move the front seat forwards as far as it will go and remove the bolt from the rear of each channel.

2   Push the seat fully rearwards and remove one bolt from the front of each channel.

3   The front seat may now be lifted away complete with side channels.

4   Refitting is the reverse sequence to removal. To ensure smooth operation of the seat in its channels, apply a little grease to each channel.

Rear seat

1   Lift the front of the rear seat cushion up by about two inches (50 mm) until it is clear of its retaining clip. Draw the cushion forwards and lift away from inside the car.

2   To remove the rear seat squab, undo and remove the two

bolts located in the centre of the lower edge and lift the squab from its two hooks.

3   Refitting is the reverse sequence to removal.

16 Facia panel - removal and refitting

1   For safety reasons disconnect the battery earth terminal.

2   Remove the three screws and washers securing the two halves of the steering column nacelles.

3   Using an electrician's screwdriver, depress the pin securing the choke control knob and withdraw the knob. Unscrew the choke control securing bezel.

4   Release the two water pipes from the rear of the screen washer pump. Note which pipe is connected to its associated nozzle.

5   Working from under the dash panel, detach the speedometer cable from the rear of the instrument by depressing the connector button.

6   Carefully pull the heater control knobs from their operating levers after removing the grub screws.

7   Make a note of the connection at the rear of the two multi connectors located below the right hand end of the facia and disconnect them.

8   Make a note of the cable connections at the various snap connectors and then detach all these cables.

9   Undo and remove the five screws and "fix" nuts that secure the bottom of the facia to the support rail.

10 Remove the six screws securing the demister grille.

11 Remove the one centre screw and washer below the grille.

12 Release the two brackets and their retaining screws also located beneath the grille.

13 Undo and remove the four nuts (two each end of the facia on the upper surface).

14 Pull the hoses off the vents.

15 Insert a hooked tool under the front lip of the facia and lift the studs out of the closed holes whilst the facia is pulled clear.

16 Refitting the facia is the reverse sequence to removal.

17 Parcel shelf - removal and refitting

1   Before removing or refitting the parcel shelf ensure that the air distribution lever is in the OFF position.

2   Remove the trim board by prising it off the clips that secure it.

3   Unscrew the Phillips screws that retain the finisher frame.

4   At the extremities of the parcel shelf, remove the four screws, washers, nuts and cap nuts that secure the shelf to the end brackets.

5   Remove the two bolts and washers, and the two screws, washers and nuts that secure the parcel tray to the parcel tray support tube.

6   Release the two nuts and washers from the bolts that protrude through the brackets either side of the air vent and withdraw the bolts.

7   Remove the two screws that secure the parcel shelf to the metal strap on the right hand side behind the steering column. Withdraw the strap and washers.

8   Ease the parcel shelf clear, carefully watching for any hook-ups with odd cables.

9   Replacement is the reverse of removal: ensure the air distribution lever is in the OFF position.

18 Heater unit and fan motor - removal and replacement

1   Refer to Chapter 2, Section 2 and drain the cooling system.

2   Refer to Section 16 of this Chapter and remove the facia panel.

3   Undo and remove the five bolts securing the facia support rail and the two bolts at the steering column support bracket and lift away the support rail.

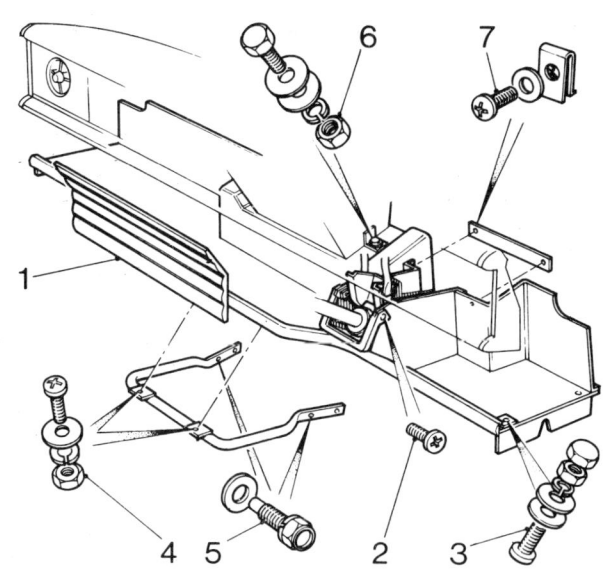

FIG. 12.13. PARCEL SHELF SECURING POINTS

1 Trim board
2 Finisher frame screws
3 End bolts and cap nuts
4 Support tube screws and nuts
5 Support tube bolts
6 Air vent bracket bolts and nuts
7 Strap screws, washers and clips

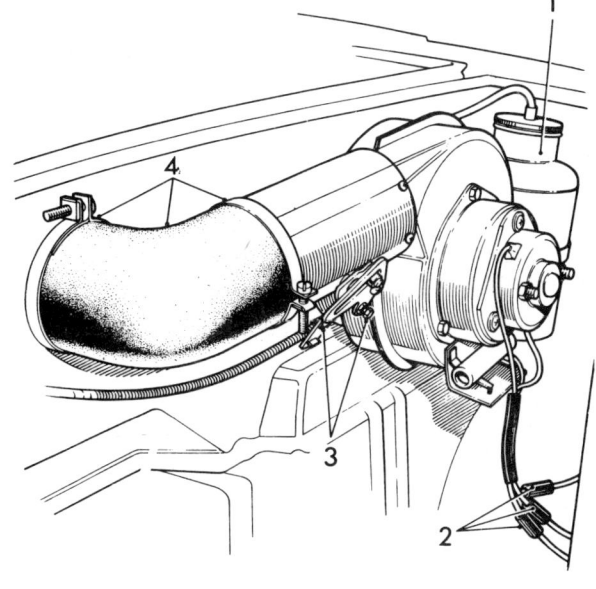

FIG. 12.15. FAN MOTOR, FLAP VALVE AND DUCTING HOSE

1 Windscreen washer bottle
2 Motor leads
3 Flap valve lever and trunnion bolt
4 Hose and clips

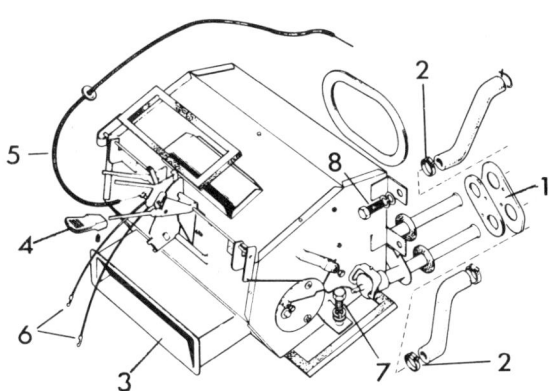

FIG. 12.14. HEATER UNIT DISCONNECTION POINTS

1 Bulkhead gaskets
2 Hose clips
3 Rear gasket
4 Switch knob
5 Control cable
6 Motor leads
7 Bottom bracket bolts
8 Rear bracket bolts

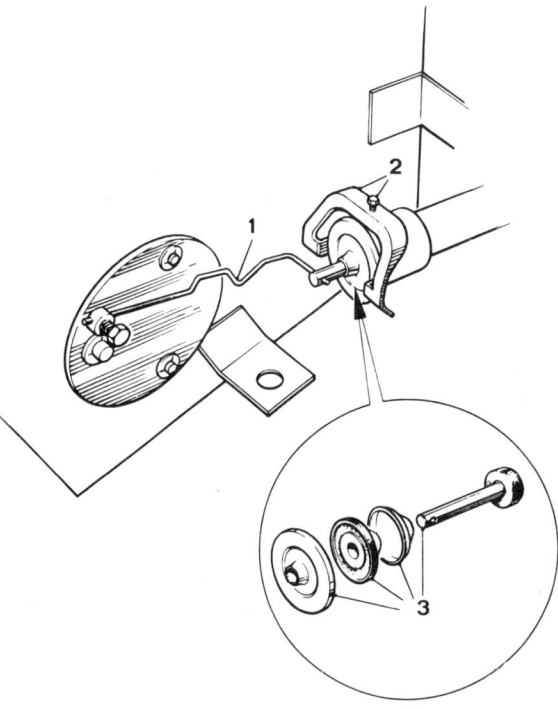

FIG. 12.16. HEATER WATER VALVE LOCATION

1 Control rod
2 Retainer and screw
3 Valve components

4   Place a container of approximately 1 pint capacity under the heater metal pipes and remove the heater hoses.
5   Disconnect the control cable from the central heat control lever, also disconnect the two leads from the central lever.
6   Remove the two bolts that secure the unit frame to the parcel shelf and then remove the four bolts that secure the back of the heater unit to the bulkhead.
7   The heater unit may now be lifted away from inside the car but care must be taken to ensure no water left in the heater matrix flows out onto the carpeting or seats. For safety place some polythene sheeting on the floor to catch any water spilled.
8   If it is necessary to remove the heater blower motor, note the cable connections to the motor and disconnect the cables from their connectors. Then remove the screen washer bottle.
9   Slacken the trunnion bolt and detach the air control cable from the air valve.
10 Slacken the two clips and ease off the moulded plastic air hose.
11 Undo the three bolts securing the blower motor to the bulkhead and lift away the blower assembly. Note that the earth cable is connected to the lower of the two mounting bolts.
12 In both cases, refitting is the reverse sequence to removal. Refer to Chapter 2, and refill the cooling system. Seelastik should be used to seal the fan motor to the bulkhead. Before refitting the control cable, ensure the central control lever is in the OFF position and the fan motor flap lever is positioned fully to the left.

19 Heater air flow control cable - removal and refitting

1   Slacken the trunnion on the blower flap lever and detach the cable.
2   Detach the inner cable from the fan switch and pull the cable assembly clear.
3   To refit, reverse the removal instructions, ensuring the fan switch is in the OFF position and the fan motor flap lever is positioned fully to the left.

20 Heater water valve - removal and replacement

1   Detach the control rod from the locating hole in the end of the valve stem.
2   Slacken the screw that secures the valve retainer on the shoulder of the valve; withdraw the retainer and valve.
3   Replace in the reverse manner to removal, ensuring the control rod is positioned to allow free movement of the valve.

21 Heater fan motor switch - removal and replacement

1   Remove the three grub screws securing the control knobs and pull off the knobs.
2   Next, remove the escutcheon by releasing the two bolts, nuts and washers that secure it to the facia.
3   Unhook the control cable from the switch and disconnect the two leads: it is best to note the connection points of the leads before removal, rather than have confusion when refitting.
4   Remove the two screws that secure the switch and lift it out of the panel.
5   Replace in the reverse manner to removal.

22 Bonnet lock - removal and refitting

1   Open the bonnet and support it on its stay.
2   Slacken the nut and detach the release cable from the trunnion located at the lock lever, loosen the pinch bolt.
3   Detach the release cable and its clip from the bonnet lock.
4   Undo and remove the three bolts, plain and spring washers securing the bonnet lock. Lift away the bonnet lock.
5   Undo and remove the two nuts, plain and shakeproof washers that secure the catch assembly to the underside of the bonnet.
6   Detach the return spring and catch assembly.
7   Refitting is the reverse sequence to removal.
8   Carefully lower the bonnet and check the alignment of the catch with the lock hole. If misaligned slacken the fixing bolts and move the assembly slightly. Retighten the fixing bolts.
9   Close the bonnet and check its alignment with the body wing panels. If necessary reposition the catch assembly.
10 The bonnet must contact the rubber stops. To adjust the position of the stops, remove the screws and place packing beneath the stops until the bonnet will close sufficiently to just compress the stops, thus eliminating any rattle.
11 Lubricate all moving parts and finally check the bonnet release operation.

23 Bonnet lock control cable - removal and refitting

1   Open the bonnet and support on its stay.
2   Slacken the nut and detach the release cable from the trunnion located at the lock lever. Loosen the pinch bolt.
3   Detach the release cable and its clip from the bonnet lock.
4   Remove the screw that secures each combined rubber buffer and cable clip to the wing valance. Lift away the two rubber clips.
5   Undo and remove the nut and shakeproof washer that secures the outer cable to the body side bracket mounted below the facia panel.
6   Carefully withdraw the control cable assembly through the body grommet.
7   Refitting is the reverse sequence to removal. It is however, necessary to adjust the inner cable. Push the release knob in fully and make sure that the lock release lever is not pre-loaded by the release cable.
8   There must be a minimum movement of 0.5 in (12.7 mm) prior to the release of the bonnet. To adjust, slacken the cable trunnion nut and re-adjust the cable so that the bonnet is released within 0.5 to 2.0 in (12.7 to 50.8 mm) of cable movement.

24 Bonnet - removal and refitting

1   Open the bonnet and hold open using the bonnet stay. To act as a datum for refitting, mark the position of the hinges using a soft pencil.
2   Remove the split pin, washers and clevis pin that retain the bonnet stay.
3   With the help of an assistant to take the weight of the bonnet, remove the four bolts, spring and plain washers that secure the hinges.
4   Carefully lift the bonnet up and over the front of the car and place somewhere safe where it will not be scratched or damaged.
5   Refitting the bonnet is the reverse sequence to removal. Any adjustment necessary can be made at the hinges.

25 Boot lid - removal and refitting

1   It is recommended that a blanket be placed under the top side of the lid and spread over the wing panels to act as a precaution against scratching of the paintwork during removal or refitting
2   For safety reasons disconnect the battery earth terminal. Also detach the wires leading to the lid from the top left hand corner of the luggage compartment.
3   With the help of an assistant to take the weight of the boot lid, remove the four securing bolts.
4   Should it be necessary to remove the hinges, disconnect the lead from the boot light switch and pull it clear of the hinge.
5   Remove the single nut, bolt and washers from the inside of the left hand hinge.
6   Finally remove the four nuts and washers and lift away the

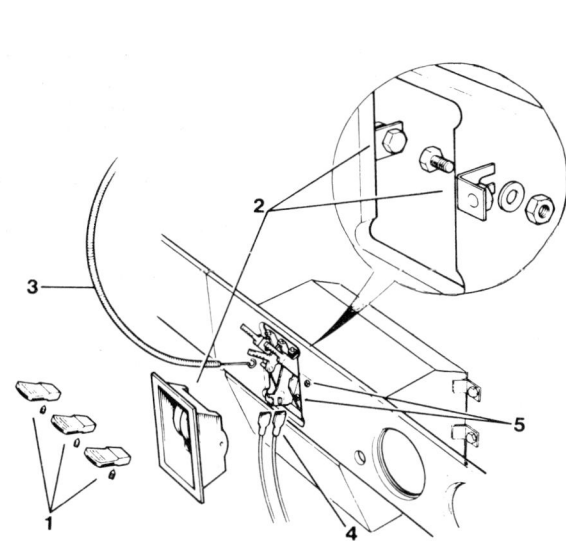

FIG. 12.17. REMOVING FAN MOTOR SWITCH

1 Control knobs and grub screws
2 Escutcheon and locating bolts
3 Control cable
4 Motor leads
5 Switch screws

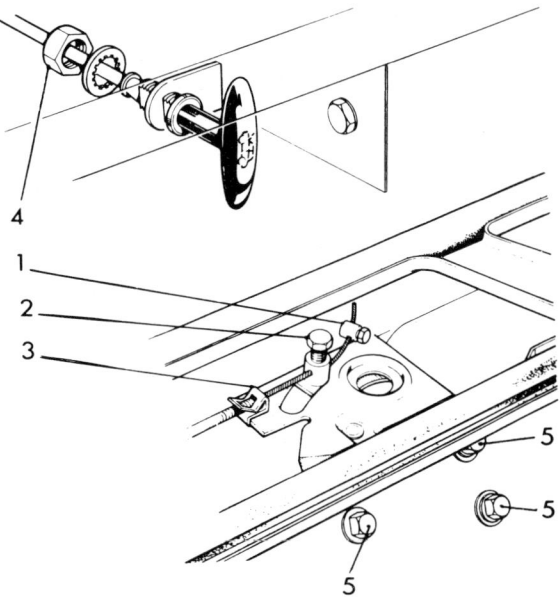

FIG. 12.18. BONNET LOCK AND RELEASE CABLE

1 Trunnion
2 Cable locking bolt
3 Clip
4 Handle securing nut
5 Lock-retaining bolts

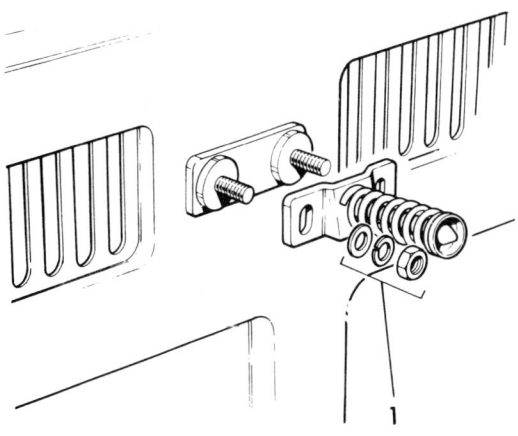

FIG. 12.19. BONNET CATCH AND SPRING

1 Retaining nut and washers

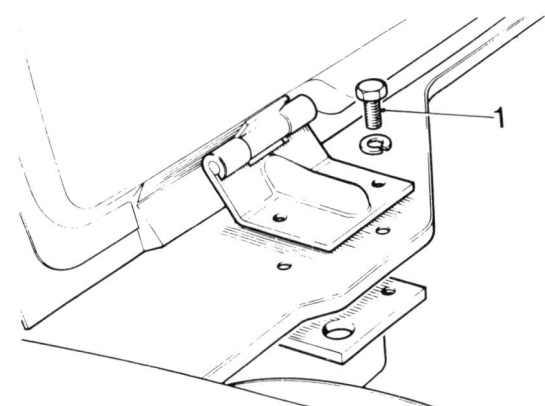

FIG. 12.20. BONNET HINGES

1 Securing bolts

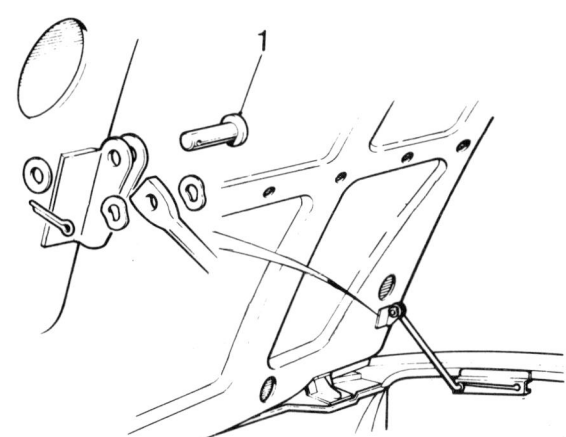

FIG. 12.21. BONNET STAY

1 Clevis pin

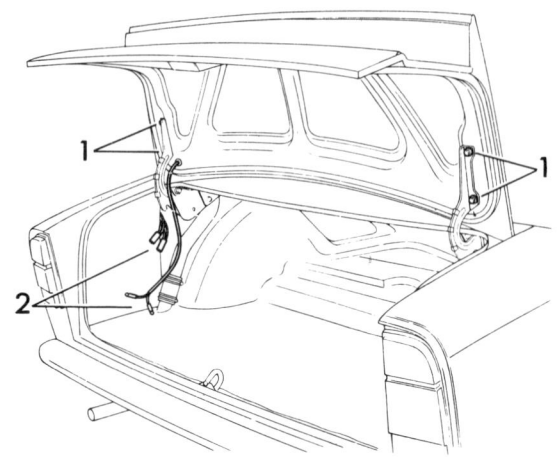

FIG. 12.22. REMOVING THE BOOT LID

1 Hinge bolts   2 Cable connectors

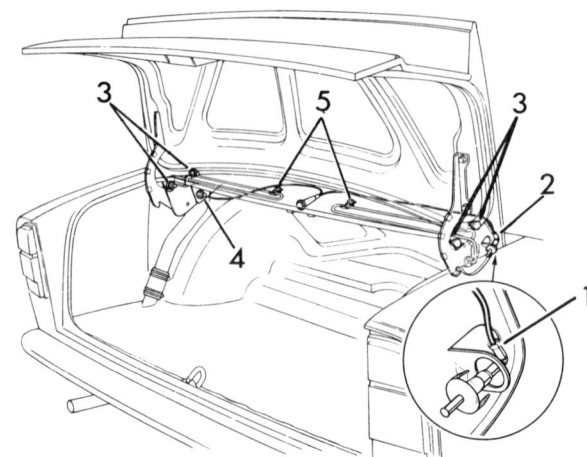

FIG. 12.23. REMOVING THE BOOT LID HINGES

1 Close-up of boot light   3 Hinge bolts
   switch   4 Single bolt on left-hand
2 Boot light switch location   hinge
                                5 Torsion bar

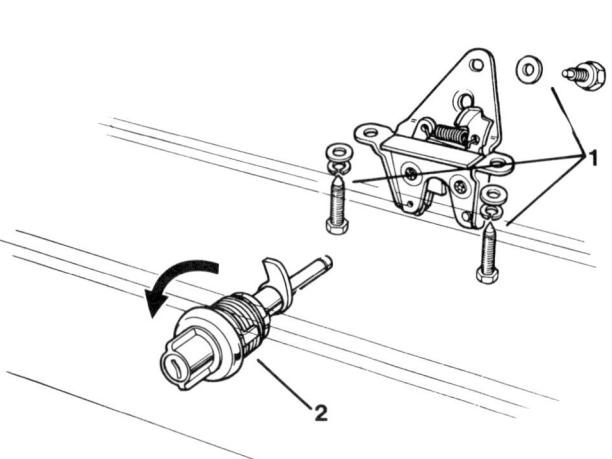

**FIG. 12.24. BOOT LOCK COMPONENTS
(WILMOTT BREEDEN)**

1 Latch retaining bolts   2 Lock

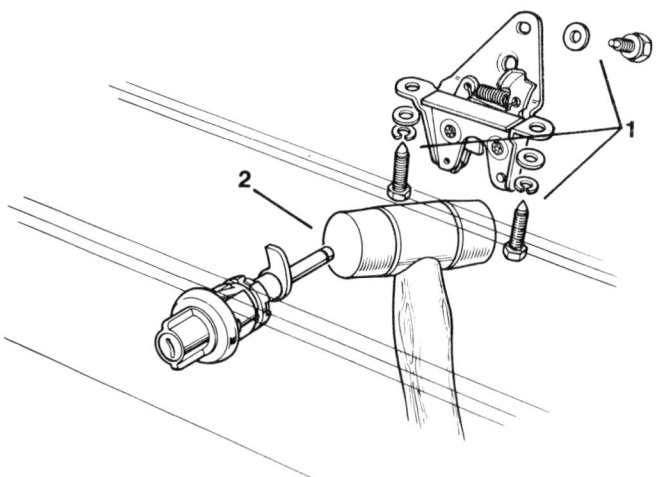

**FIG. 12.25. BOOT LOCK COMPONENTS
(C. E. MARSHALL)**

1 Latch bolts   2 Using mallet
                                     to remove lock

hinge and torsion bar assemblies.
7 Refitting is the reverse sequence to removal.

---

26 Boot lid locks - removal and refitting

   Two different types of boot lid lock are fitted : Wilmott
Breeden or C.E.Marshall. They are fully interchangeable although
the removal and refitting operations vary slightly.
1 Open the boot lid, and remove the three bolts complete with
spring and plain washers. Lift off the latch.
(rotation of arrow) and withdraw the lock assembly and sealing
ring. Refit in the reverse order.
3 C.E. Marshall : Disengage the retaining spring by tapping the
end of the spindle lightly with a wooden mallet. Withdraw the
lock. When refitting, locate the lock in the aperture slots and
press firmly to engage the retaining spring.

---

27 Bumpers and mounting brackets - removal and refitting

   Front
1 Undo and remove the two bolts, nuts, washers and spacers
from each end of the bumper.
2 Lift away the front bumper assembly.
3 Undo and remove the nuts, bolts and washers securing each
bracket to the bumper.
4 Refitting is the reverse sequence of removal. Clean the area of
the body where the bracket fits and rub down any evidence of
corrosion. Apply two good coats of anti-corrosive paint before
refitting the brackets.

   Rear
   The sequence for removing the rear bumper is basically
indentical to that for the front bumper.

Chapter 13 Supplement

Introduction 1
Specifications 2
Exhaust system and manifolds 3
    General description
    Exhaust system – removal and refitting
    Exhaust system sections – removal and refitting
    Exhaust downpipe flange joint – removal and refitting
    Inlet and exhaust manifolds and gasket – removal and refitting
Ignition system 4
    Lucas 45D4 distributor – dismantling
    Lucas 45D4 distributor – inspection and repair
    Lucas 45D4 distributor – reassembly
    Ignition coil and ballast resistor wire – general description
Gearbox (single rail) 5
    General description
    Gearbox (single rail) – removal and refitting
    Gearbox (single rail) – dismantling
    Gearbox (single rail) – examination
    Input shaft (single rail gearbox) – dismantling and reassembly
    Mainshaft (single rail gearbox) – dismantling and reassembly
    Gearbox (single rail) – reassembly
Propeller shaft 6
    General description
    Propeller shaft – removal and refitting
    Centre bearing – removal and refitting
Braking system 7
    Rear brake shoes (self-adjusting) – inspection, removal and refitting

Rear brake wheel cylinder (self-adjusting) – removal, inspection, overhaul and reassembly
Electrical system 8
    Windscreen wiper motor (Lucas) – removal, overhaul and refitting
    Master light switch – removal and refitting
    Door light switch – removal and refitting
    Luggage compartment illumination switch – removal and refitting
    Oil pressure switch – removal and refitting
    Windscreen wiper/washer switch – removal and refitting
    Heated rear window switch – removal and refitting
    Brake stop lamp switch – removal and refitting
    Hazard warning switch (later models only) – removal and refitting
    Temperature and fuel gauges (later models) – removal and refitting
    Roof lamp (later models) – removal and refitting
    Windscreen washer pump (early models) – removal and refitting
    Windscreen washer jets (early models) – removal and refitting
    Windscreen washer reservoir (early models) – removal and refitting
    Windscreen washer system (later models)
    Windscreen washer switch (Toledo) – removal and refitting
    Windscreen washer pump and reservoir – removal and refitting
    Windscreen washer pump – overhaul
    Windscreen washer/wiper switch (Dolomite) – removal and refitting

1 Introduction

Modifications and/or additions to the Triumph Toledo, which was first introduced in August 1970, have been essentially of a minor nature.

In March 1975 the two-door Saloon was discontinued, and in April of the same year the four door Saloon was fitted with a single-rail gearbox which is similar to that currently used on the

Triumph TR7. The four-door Saloon continued until February 1976, when it was renamed the Dolomite 1300cc.

This supplement is intended to cover any modifications and/or additions between the introductory vehicles of 1970 and the later Dolomite 1300cc. Each Section of this Chapter relates to one of the other 12 Chapters in this book.

It can be assumed that any component or procedure not mentioned specifically in this Supplement remains as described in the relevant Section of Chapters 1 to 12 of this manual.

2   Specifications

The specifications listed here are revised or supplementary to those given at the beginning of the first twelve Chapters of this manual. The original specifications apply unless alternative figures are quoted here

Engine

General
Maximum power (1972 onwards) . . . .   58 bhp net at 5,500 rev/min

Valve data
Valve head diameters (from engine numbers DG25001,
DM5001 and DS5001)*:
    Inlet:
        Up to engine no. DH55700 . . . .   1·437 to 1·443 in (36·45 to 36·65 mm)
        From engine no. DH55701 . . . .   1·375 to 1·385 in (34·92 to 35·18 mm)
    Exhaust . . . .   1·168 to 1·172 in (29·66 to 29·76 mm)

        Valve head diameters up to these engine numbers are as specified in Chapter 1

Valve stem-to-guide clearance:
    Inlet valve from engine No. DH55701 . . . .   0·0007 to 0·0023 in (0·018 to 0·058 mm)

Valve springs
Type A:*
    Internal diameter . . . .   0·795 in (20·193 mm)
    Working coils 3¼
    Length at 27 to 30 lbf (12·25 to 13·61 kgf) load . . . .   1·316 in (34·54 mm)
    Free length . . . .   1·61 in (40·9 mm)
    Solid length . . . .   0·93 in (23·6 mm)
Type B:**
    Internal diameter . . . .   0·795 in (20·193 mm)
    Working coils 3½
    Length at 105 to 115 lbf (47·3 to 52·2 kgf) load . . . .   1·074 in (27·28 mm)
    Free length . . . .   1·590 in (40·4 mm)
    Solid length . . . .   0·96 in (24·4 mm)
Type C:***
    Internal diameter . . . .   0·795 in (20·193 mm)
    Working coils 3¾
    Length at 123 to 133 lbf (55·8 to 60·3 kgf) load . . . .   0·989 in (25·1 mm)
    Free length . . . .   1·520 in (38·6 mm)
    Solid length . . . .   0·875 in (22·2 mm)

        Type A fitted to 1300 cc engines up to engine no. DG25001 with the exception of engines within the following three groups: DG10731 to 10750, DG10786 to 10909 and DG11116 to 11622

        ** Type B fitted to 1300 cc engines up to engine no. DM5001 and DS5001*

        *** Type C fitted to 1300 cc engines from engine no. DG25001 onwards and Dolomite*

Fuel system

Carburettor
Type, from engines nos. DG25001, DM5001, DS5001 . . . . .   SU HS4E
Needle size, between engines nos. DG25001 and DHI,
DM5001 and DM10001, & DS5001 and DS10001 . . . .   AAW
Needle size, from engine nos. DHI, DM10001 and DS10001,
up to DH55700, including Dolomite . . . .   ABF or ABQ
Needle size, from engine no. DG55701 onwards . . . .   ABT

Ignition system

Distributor
Type, between engine nos. DG2500H or L, and DG42825 . . .   Lucas 25D4
Lucas part number   41381
Ignition timing (static) . . . .   10° BTDC
Advance at 2800 rpm (distributor speed) . . . .   7° to 9°
        1900 rpm (distributor speed) . . . .   6·5° to 8·5°
        1400 rpm (distributor speed) . . . .   5° to 7°
        800 rpm (distributor speed) . . . .   3° to 5°

600 rpm (distributor speed)	$0 \cdot 5°$ to $2 \cdot 5°$
Below 450 rpm (distributor speed)	No advance to occur
Type, from engine no. DH42826, including Dolomite	Lucas 45D4
Lucas part number	24085
Dwell angle	$51° \pm 5°$
Open angle	$39° \pm 5°$
Ignition timing (static)	$10°$ BTDC
Advance at 2800 rpm (distributor speed)	$7°$ to $9°$
1900 rpm (distributor speed)	$7°$ to $9°$
1400 rpm (distributor speed)	$5 \cdot 5°$ to $7 \cdot 5°$
800 rpm (distributor speed)	$3 \cdot 5°$ to $5 \cdot 5°$
600 rpm (distributor speed)	$1 \cdot 5°$ to $3 \cdot 5°$
Below 450 rpm (distributor speed)	No advance to occur

Ignition coil

Type, later models, including Dolomite	Lucas 15C6 or 15P6
Lucas part number	45243
Primary winding resistance	$1 \cdot 30$ to $1 \cdot 5$ ohms

Ballast resistor wire, later models including Dolomite

Resistance	$1 \cdot 3$ to $1 \cdot 5$ ohms
Length of wire	63 in (160 cm)

Spark plugs, later models including Dolomite

Type	Champion N12Y
Gap	$0 \cdot 025$ in (0·64 mm)

Gearbox (single rail type), April 1975 onwards

Oil capacity . . . .   1·5 Imp pints (1·8 US pints, 0·85 litres)

Oil type . . . .   SAE 90EP

Torque wrench settings

	lbf ft	kgf m
Clutch housing-to-gearbox case	32	4·4
Clutch housing-to-cylinder block	20	2·8
Clutch housing-to-rear engine plate	20	2·8
Flange-to-mainshaft	120	16·6
Selector shaft-to-forks	10	1·4
Sump coupling plate-to-clutch housing	37	5·1
Top cover-to—gearbox case	10	1·4

Propeller shaft (commission nos. ADG25393/ADF27622 onwards, including Dolomite)

Type . . . .   Two-piece tubular with centre bearing

Torque wrench settings

	lbf ft	kgf m
Centre bearing mounting bolts	22	3·0
Flange retaining bolt nuts	28	3·8

Electrical system

Windscreen wiper motor

Type (commission no. ADF100001 onwards, including Dolomite)	Lucas 15W
Running current after 60 seconds from cold, linkage arm disconnected:	
Normal speed	1·5 amp
High speed	2·0 amp
Armature endfloat	0·002 to 0·008 in (0·05 to 0·20 mm)
Brush length:	
New	0·250 in (6 mm)
Minimum permissible	0·125 in (3 mm)

Suspension and steering

Steering geometry

	Unladen condition	Laden condition (4 up)
Type A:*		
Camber angle	$\frac{1}{2}°$ positive $\pm 1°$	$\frac{3}{4}°$ negative $\pm \frac{3}{4}°$
Castor angle	$2\frac{1}{4}° \pm 1°$	$2\frac{3}{4}° \pm \frac{1}{2}°$
King pin inclination	$6\frac{1}{2}° \pm 1°$	$7\frac{3}{4}° \pm \frac{3}{4}°$
Type B:**		
Camber angle	$1\frac{1}{4}°$ positive $\pm 1°$	$\frac{1}{2}°$ positive $\pm \frac{3}{4}°$

Castor angle	$2\frac{1}{4}° \pm 1°$	$2\frac{3}{4}° \pm \frac{1}{2}°$
King pin inclination	$5\frac{3}{4}° \pm 1°$	$6\frac{1}{2}° \pm \frac{3}{4}°$
Type C:***		
Camber angle	$1°$ positive $\pm 1°$	$\frac{1}{4}°$ positive $\pm \frac{3}{4}°$
Castor angle	$2\frac{1}{4}° \pm 1°$	$2\frac{3}{4}° \pm \frac{1}{2}°$
King pin inclination	$5\frac{3}{4}° \pm 1°$	$6\frac{1}{2}° \pm \frac{3}{4}°$

Type A used up to commission nos. ADG11512 and ADS648 and Dolomite
**Type B used from commission nos. ADG11512 and ADS648*
***Type C from commission nos. ADH1 and ADF50001*

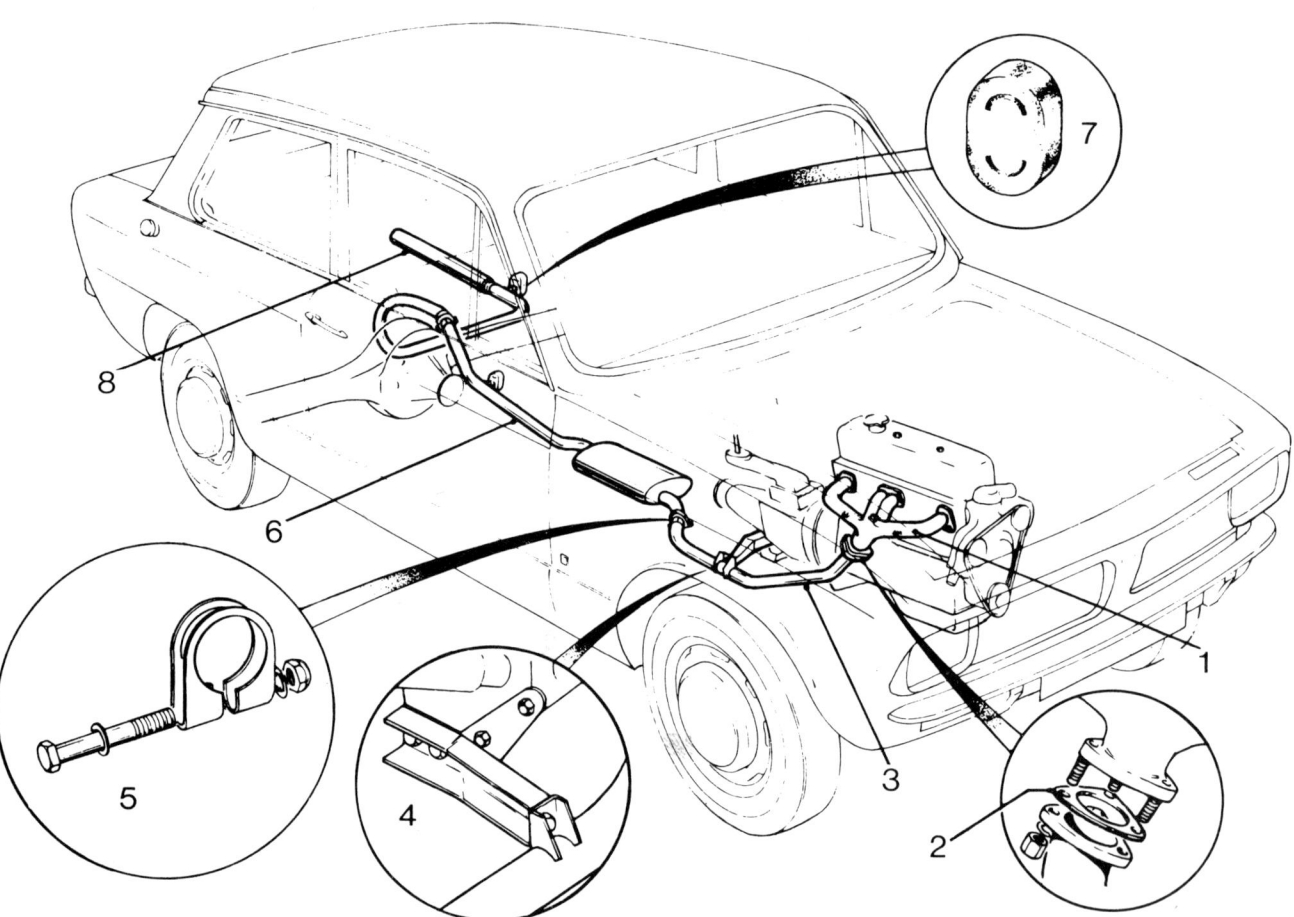

Fig. 13.1 Exhaust system components (late Toledo shown)

1 *Exhaust manifold*	3 *Exhaust front downpipe*	6 *Intermediate pipe and silencer*	8 *Tailpipe and silencer assembly*
2 *Downpipe flange and gasket*	4 *Front pipe support bracket*	7 *Exhaust mounting*	
	5 *Inter-pipe clamp*		

---

3 Exhaust system and manifolds

General description

1   A three-section exhaust system is fitted to both Toledo and Dolomite models, comprising a front downpipe attached to the exhaust manifold by three nuts and a gasket, an intermediate silencer assembly, and a rear silencer assembly.

2   The rear silencer assembly on all Dolomite and early Toledo models includes a conventional silencer box, but late Toledo models are fitted with an expansion tube type silencer.

3   Both inlet and exhaust manifolds are attached to the cylinder head by studs and nuts, and a gasket is used at the flange joint.

Exhaust system – removal and refitting

4   Jack up the rear of the car and support it adequately with axle-stands; to provide room for manoeuvring the tailpipe, it is better to support the body and allow the rear axle to drop to its lowest position.

5   Chock the front wheels.

6   Unscrew and release the clamp securing the intermediate section to the tailpipe, and prise the tailpipe rubber mounting from the bracket.

7   Remove the tailpipe rearwards; if it is rusted to the intermediate section, tap around the joint with a hammer to release it.

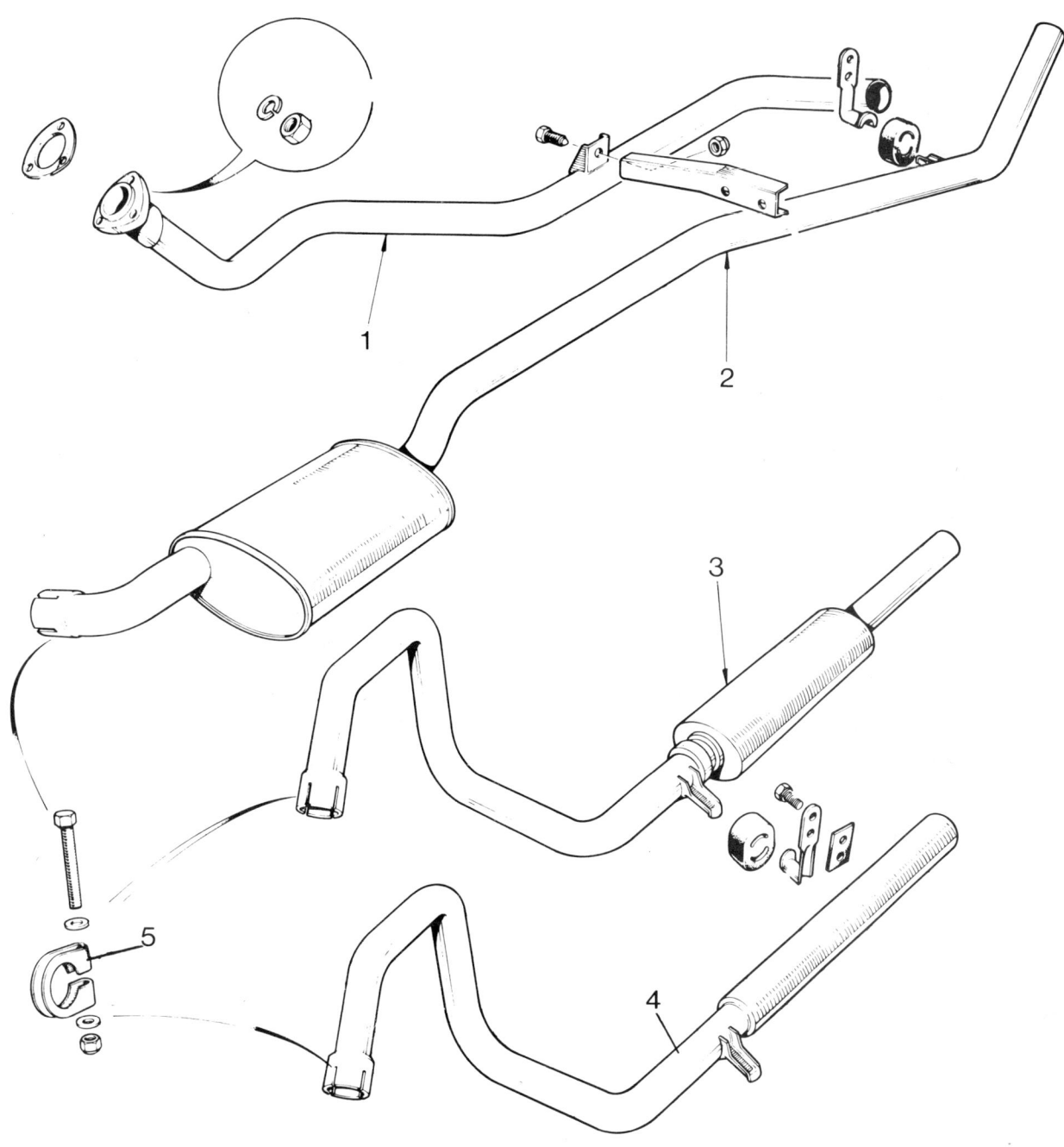

Fig. 13.2 Alternative Toledo exhaust systems

1 *Front downpipe*
2 *Intermediate pipe*

3 *Early tailpipe and silencer assembly*

4 *Late tailpipe and silencer assembly*

5 *Connecting bracket*

8   Prise the intermediate section rubber mounting from its bracket, and unscrew and remove the front downpipe support bracket nut and bolt.
9   Unscrew and remove the three nuts securing the downpipe to the exhaust manifold and remove the throttle spring plate, if fitted.
10 Withdraw the exhaust system being careful not to damage the manifold studs, and remove it from beneath the car.

11 Refitting the exhaust system is a reversal of the removal procedure but the following additional points should be noted:

   (a) *Always fit a new downpipe-to-manifold gasket.*
   (b) *Check the rubber mountings for deterioration and renew them if necessary.*
   (c) *Before finally tightening the joint clamps and manifold joint, make sure that the system is correctly aligned and*

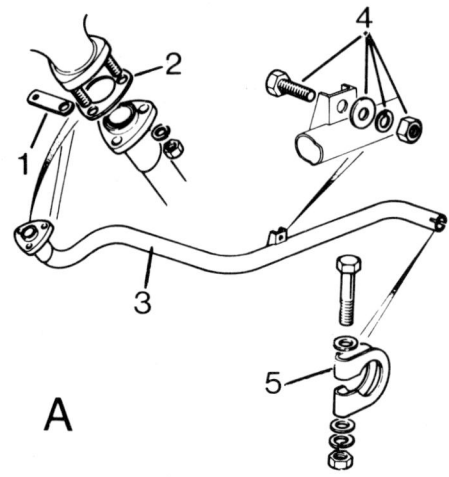

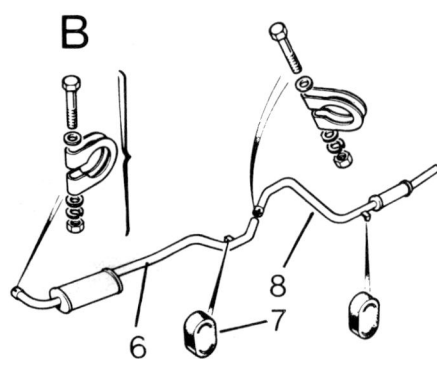

Fig. 13.3 Exhaust system components (Dolomite)

1 *Throttle spring plate*
2 *Flange gasket*
3 *Front downpipe*
4 *Front support bracket*
5 *Inter-pipe clamp*
6 *Intermediate pipe*
7 *Rubber mounting*
8 *Tailpipe assembly*

is not stressed in any way.
(d) *Do not overtighten the clamps or they will be distorted.*
(e) *When fitted, lower the car to the ground, start the engine, and check that all the joints are leak-proof.*

Exhaust system sections – removal and refitting

12 Each section of the exhaust system can be removed separately without the need to remove the complete assembly.
13 To remove the front downpipe, simply release it from the intermediate section, the manifold, and the support bracket; the rear mountings are sufficiently flexible to allow the downpipe to be moved rearwards off the manifold studs.
14 To remove the intermediate section, it will be necessary to detach the tailpipe as described in paragraphs 6 and 7, then release it from the front downpipe and support mounting.
15 Removal of the tailpipe is described in paragraphs 6 and 7.
16 Refitting of the exhaust system sections is a direct reversal of the removal procedure but reference should be made to paragraph 11.

Exhaust downpipe flange joint – removal and refitting

17 Unscrew and remove the three nuts retaining the downpipe flange to the exhaust manifold and remove the throttle spring plate, if fitted.
18 Release the front downpipe from the support bracket; carefully lower the downpipe and remove the flange joint.
19 Refitting the joint is a reversal of the removal procedure.

Inlet and exhaust manifolds and gasket – removal and refitting

20 Disconnect the battery negative terminal.
21 On models fitted with a water-cooled inlet manifold, partially drain the cooling system as described in Chapter 2, then disconnect the three water hoses.
22 Remove the carburettor as described in Chapter 3.
23 Loosen the clip securing the brake vacuum hose (when fitted) to the inlet manifold, and carefully pull the hose clear.
24 Prise the crankcase breather hose from the rocker cover.
25 Unscrew and remove the nuts, spring washers, and clamps securing the inlet manifold to the cylinder head. At this stage, the inlet manifold on late Toledo models may be lifted away from the cylinder head.
26 Unscrew and remove the three nuts and washers securing the exhaust front downpipe to the exhaust manifold and remove the throttle spring plate, if fitted.
27 Unscrew and remove the remaining nuts, and spring washers securing the exhaust manifold to the cylinder head.
28 Carefully withdraw the inlet and exhaust manifolds, or exhaust manifolds (late Toledo), from the cylinder head and downpipe, and remove the flange gasket.
29 Remove the gasket from the cylinder head.
30 If required, the inlet manifold may be separated from the exhaust manifold (all models except late Toledo), by unscrewing and removing the nut and washer.
31 Refitting the manifolds and gasket is a reversal of the removal procedure but the following additional points should be noted:

(a) *Always thoroughly clean the faces of the cylinder head and manifolds.*
(b) *Fit a new manifold gasket, flat side towards the cylinder head, and a new downpipe gasket.*
(c) *Adjust the throttle and choke cables as described in Chapter 3.*
(d) *Refill the cooling system as necessary by referring to Chapter 2.*
(e) *Start the engine, and check the exhaust joints at the manifold and downpipe for leakage.*

---

4   Ignition system

Lucas 45D4 distributor – dismantling

1   Spring back the cap retaining clips and remove the cap.
2   Pull off the rotor arm and extract the felt pad from the cam.
3   Remove the two vacuum unit retaining screws, tilt the unit to disengage the link from the plate then remove the unit.
4   Push the low tension lead and its grommet into the distributor body.
5   Remove the screw which retains the baseplate.
6   Carefully lever the slotted segment of the baseplate from its retaining groove then lift out the baseplate assembly.
7   Drive out the drive dog parallel retaining pin then remove the dog and thrust washer.
8   Draw out the shaft assembly, steel washer and spacer.
9   Push the moving contact spring inwards and detach the electrical connector from the spring loop.
10   Remove the screw to release the earthing lead and the capacitor (condenser).
11   Remove the single screw and lift out the contact set.

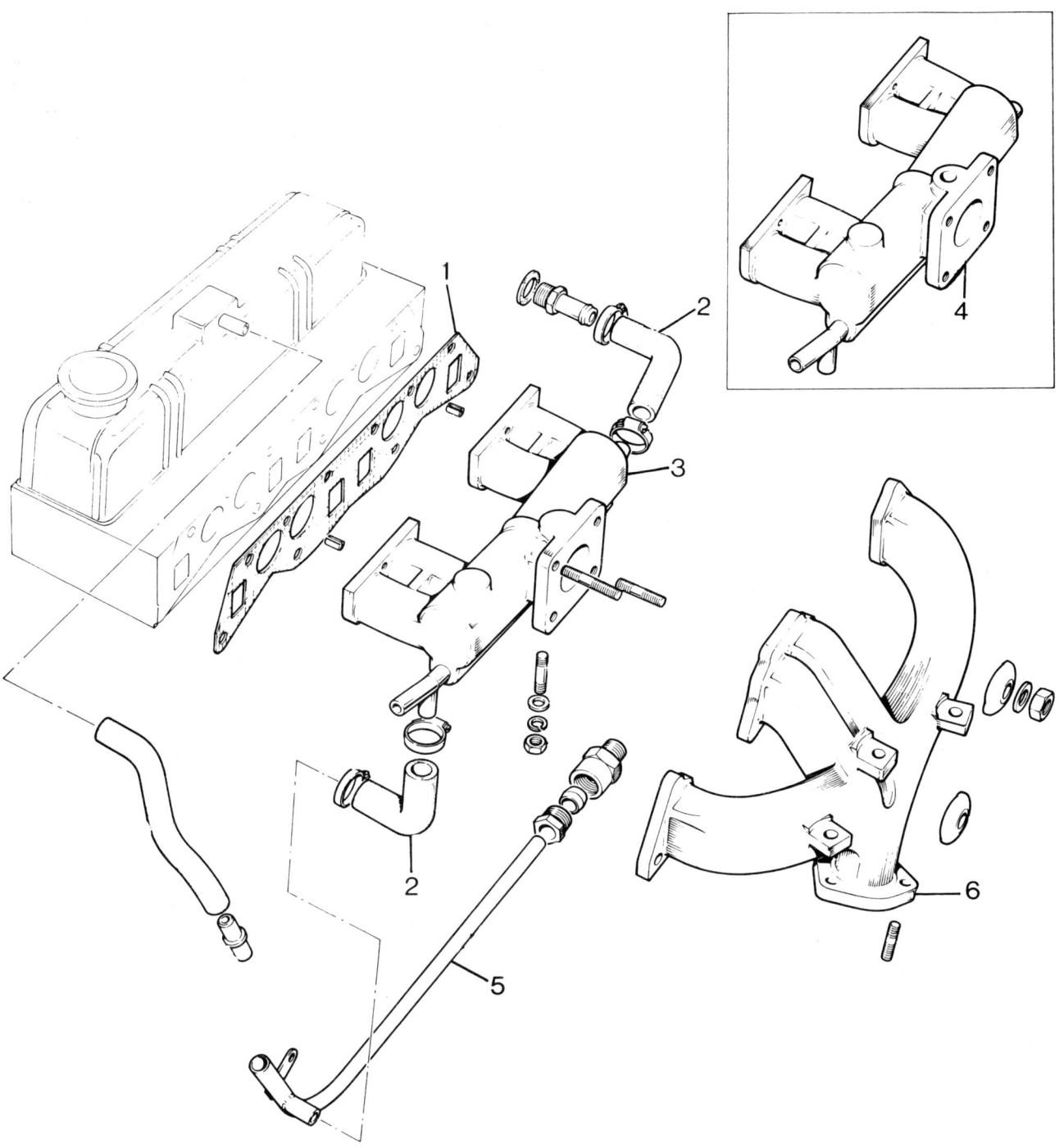

Fig. 13.4 Exhaust and inlet manifold components

1 *Manifold gasket*	3 *Inlet manifold*	*brake servo*	6 *Exhaust manifold*
2 *Inlet manifold water hoses*	4 *Inlet manifold for use with*	5 *Breather pipe*	

Lucas 45D4 distributor – inspection and repair

12 Thoroughly wash all the mechanical parts in petrol and wipe them dry using a lint-free cloth.

13 Check the contact breaker points, as described in Chapter 4, Section 3. Check the distributor cap for signs of tracking, indicated by a thin black line between the segments. Replace the cap if evident.

14 If the metal portion of the rotor arm is badly burned or loose, renew the arm. If slightly burnt, clean the arm with a fine file. Check that the carbon brush moves freely in the centre of the distributor cover.

15 Do not dismantle the advance mechanism beyond removal

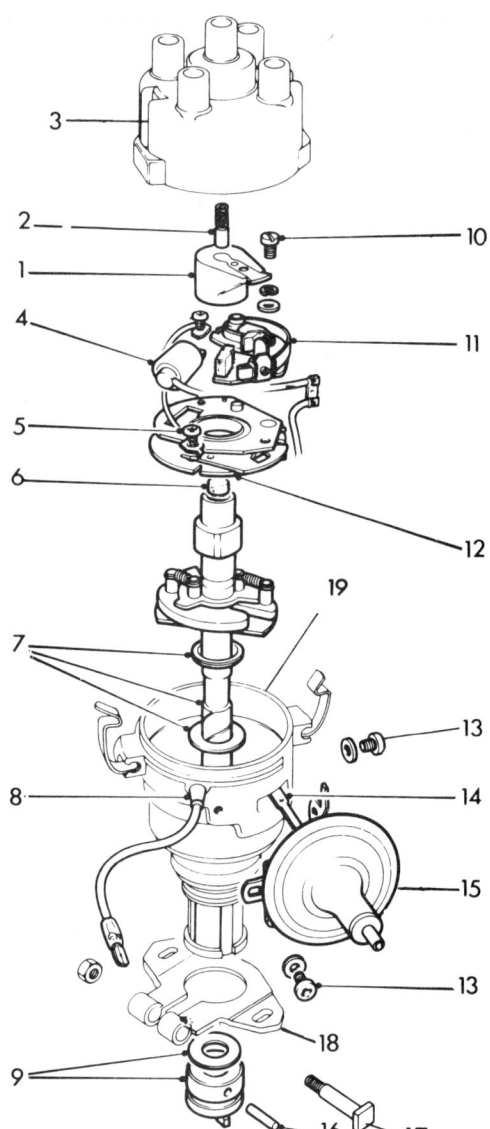

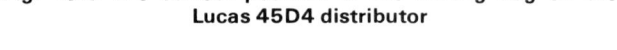

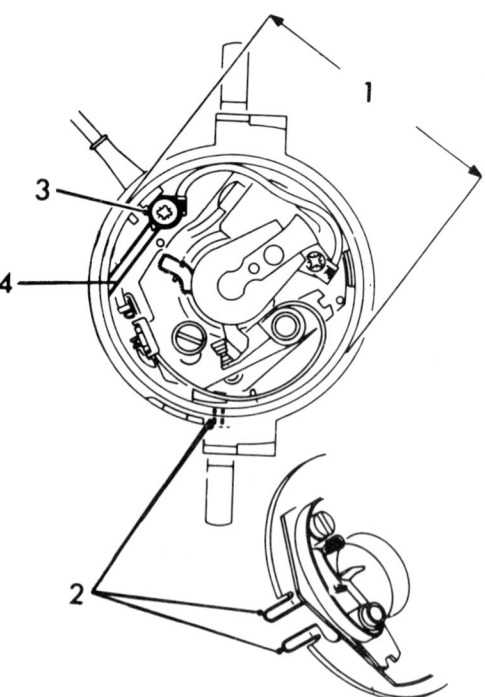

Fig. 13.6 The correct position of the driving dog on the Lucas 45D4 distributor

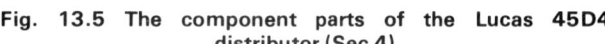

Fig. 13.5 The component parts of the Lucas 45D4 distributor (Sec 4)

1 Rotor	10 Contact set securing
2 Carbon brush and spring	screw
3 Cap	11 Contact set
4 Condenser (capacitor)	12 Baseplate
5 Baseplate securing screw	13 Vacuum unit retaining
6 Felt pad	screws and washers
7 Shaft assembly with steel	14 Vacuum unit link
washer and spacer	15 Vacuum unit
8 Low tension lead and	16 Parallel pin
grommet	17 Pinch bolt and nut
9 Drive dog and thrust	18 Lock plate
washer	19 Distributor body

Fig. 13.7 Installing the Lucas 45D4 distributor baseplate (Sec 4)

1 Dimension across distributor cap register
2 Downward pointing prongs on baseplate
3 Earth lead
4 Slot in baseplate

of the control springs. If any of the moving parts, or the cam, are worn or damaged, a replacement shaft assembly must be obtained.

16 Check the fit of the shaft in its bearing. If excessive play exists, a replacement distributor must be obtained.

17 Check the baseplate assembly. If the spring between the plates is damaged, or the plates do not move freely, a replacement assembly must be obtained.

Lucas 45D4 distributor – reassembly

18 The reassembly procedure is essentially the reverse of the removal procedure. However, the following points must be noted:

(a) A trace of a general purpose grease or petroleum-jelly (Vaseline) should be applied to the contact pivot post.

(b) Lubricate the spacer and steel washer with a molybdenum disulphite dry lubricant such as Rocol MP (Molypad) before fitting them on the shaft.

(c) Install the thrust-washer with the pipe towards the drive dog.

(d) Fit the drive dog so that the driving tongues are parallel with the rotor arm electrode and to the left of its centreline (see Fig. 13.6). If a new shaft has been used, it must be drilled through the hole in the dog. Whilst drilling, push the shaft from the cam end, pressing the drive dog and washer against the body shank.

(e) Secure the pin in the drive dog by means of a centre-punch. If the shaft is new, tap the drive end to flatten the washer pip to ensure correct end-float.

(f) Position the baseplate assembly so that the two downward-pointing prongs can straddle the screw hole below the cap clip. Press the plate into the body to engage it in the undercut.

(g) Accurately measure the dimension across the distributor cap register on the body at right angles to the slot in the baseplate. Position the earth lead, then fit and tighten the baseplate securing screw. Measure the dimension across the cap register again; if this is not at least 0.06 in (0.15 mm) greater than that first measured, the baseplate assembly must be renewed.

(h) Check that the baseplate prongs still straddle the screw hole. Refit the vacuum unit, engaging the operating arm with the pin of the moving plate.

(j) Set the contact points gap to the specified figure.

Ignition coil and ballast resistor wire – general description

19 Ignition coils fitted to early models had a separate ballast resistor mounted under the rear coil mounting screw. Later models still include a ballast resistor, but in the form of a wire built into the harness between two crimped joints.

20 The system is designed to assist engine starting under adverse conditions. During normal operation the resistor wire, positioned in series in the normal supply to the ignition coil, causes a voltage drop in the circuit so that the 12 volt supply from the ignition switch may be employed to power the nominally rated 6 volt ignition coil.

21 During engine starting, the resistor wire is bypassed and the battery voltage (reduced from 12 volts by the starter motor load) is applied to the coil direct from the starter solenoid. This slight voltage overload provides an increased high tension voltage at the spark plugs.

---

5 Gearbox (single rail)

General description

1 The single rail gearbox, which is fitted to all models from April 1975 onwards, is identified by the gearbox number which is prefixed with the letters DN.

2 Aptly named single rail, gear selection is achieved by the

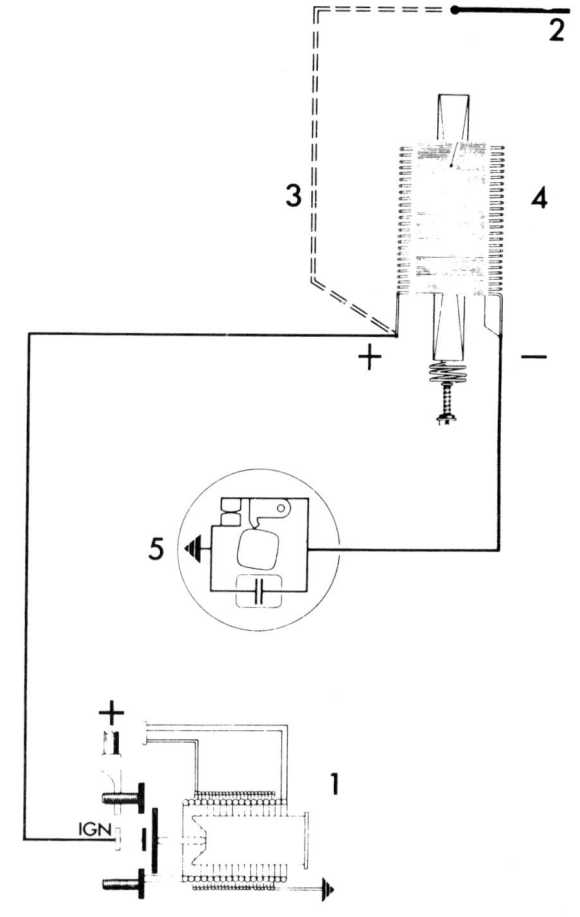

Fig. 13.8 The ballast resistor wire in the ignition system (Sec 4)

1 Starter solenoid
2 Normal ignition supply
3 Ballast resistor wire
4 Ignition coil (6 volt)
5 Distributor

use of one selector shaft, as opposed to three shafts on the early model gearbox.

3 The gear lever is mounted on the extension housing and operates the selector mechanism in the gearbox by the previously mentioned selector shaft. When the gear change lever is moved sideways the shaft is rotated so that the pins in the gearbox end of the shaft locate in the appropriate selector fork. Forward or rearward movement of the gear change lever moves the selector fork, which in turn moves the synchromesh unit outer sleeve until the gear is firmly engaged. When reverse gear is selected, a pin on the selector shaft engages with a lever and this in turn moves the reverse idler gear into mesh with the laygear reverse gear and mainshaft. The direction of rotation of the mainshaft is thereby reversed.

4 The gearbox input shaft is splined and it is onto these splines that the clutch driven plate is located. The gearbox end of the input shaft is in constant mesh with the laygear cluster, and the gears formed on the laygear are in constant mesh with the gears on the mainshaft with theexception of the reverse gear. The gears on the mainshaft are able to rotate freely which means that when the neutral position is selected the mainshaft does not rotate.

5 When the gear change lever moves the synchromesh unit

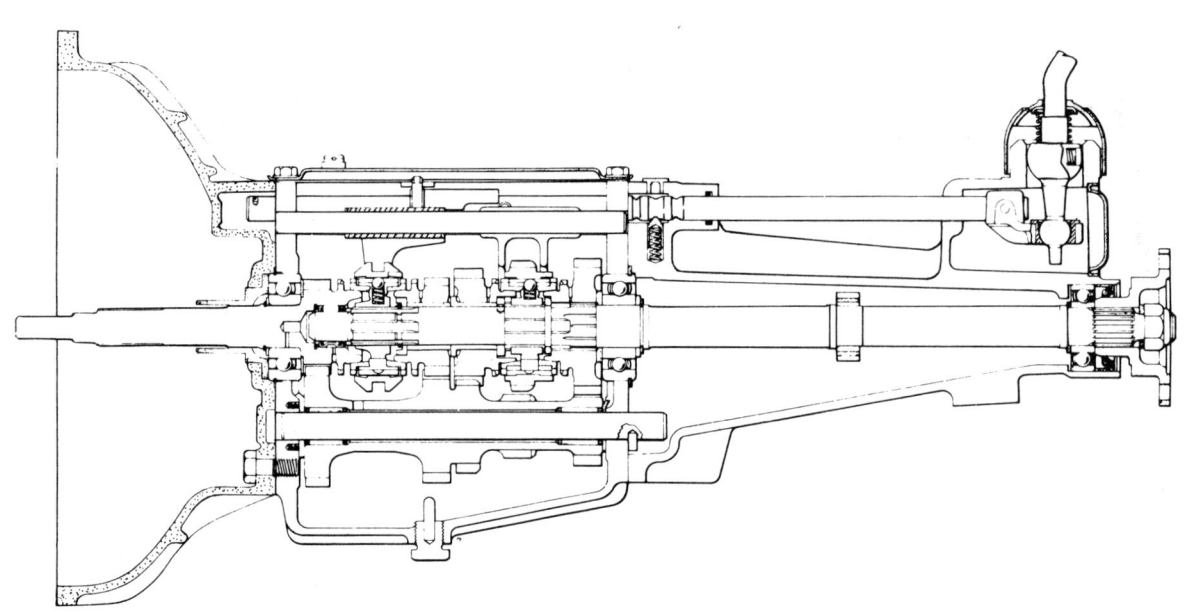

Fig. 13.9 A sectional view of the single rail gearbox (Sec 5)

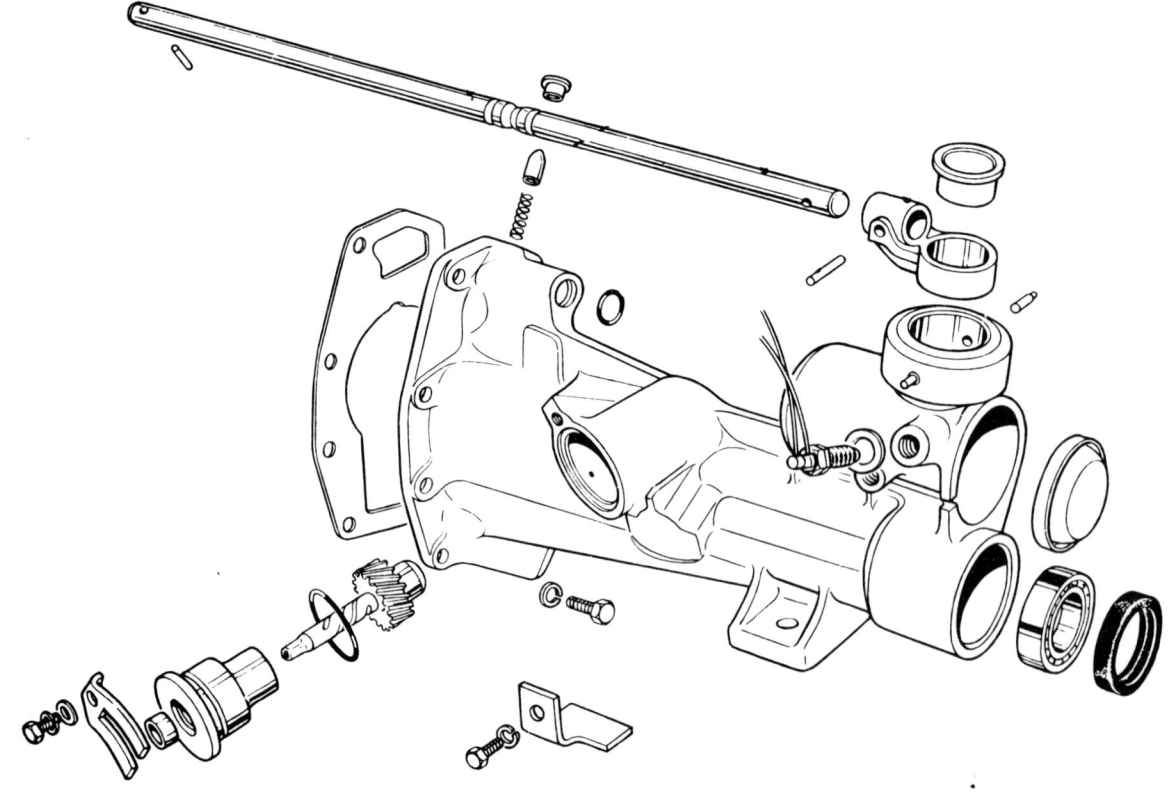

Fig. 13.10 The gearbox rear extension parts (Sec 5)

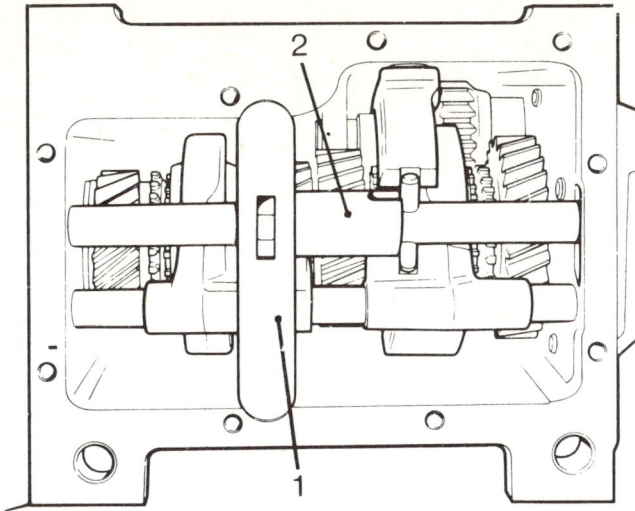

Fig. 13.11 The interlock spool plate (1) and selector spool (2)

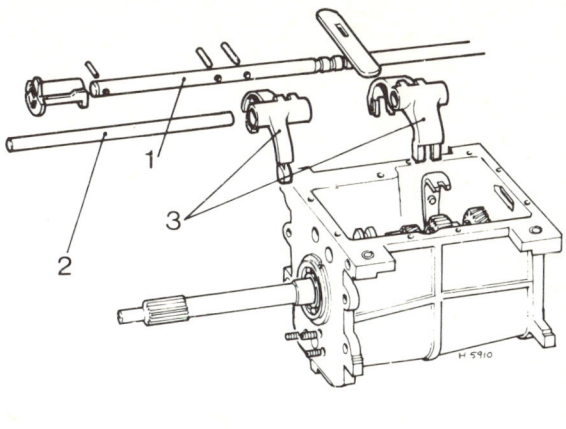

Fig. 13.12 The selectors and associated parts

1 Gear selector shaft
2 Selector fork shaft
3 Selector forks

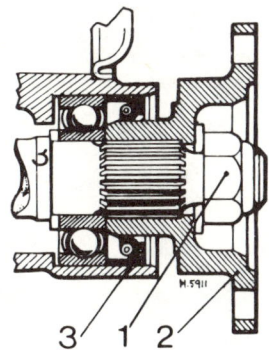

Fig. 13.13 The mainshaft flange and oil seal

1 Nut
2 Flange
3 Oil seal

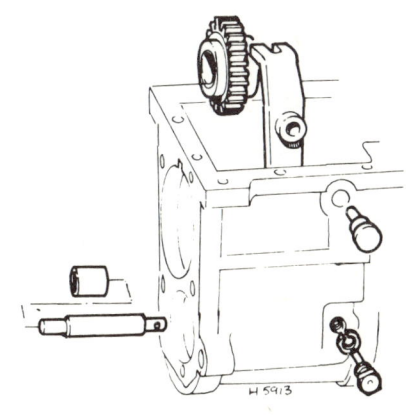

Fig. 13.14 Reverse gear and associated parts

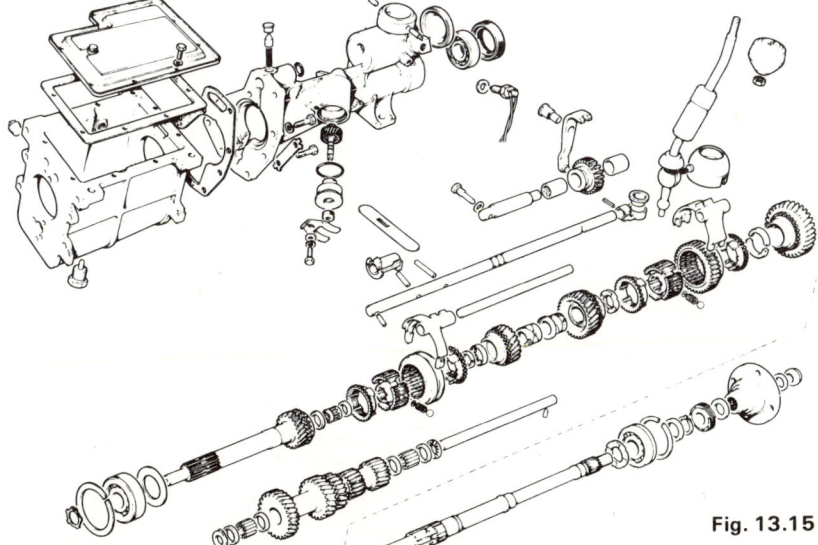

Fig. 13.15 An exploded view of the gearbox parts

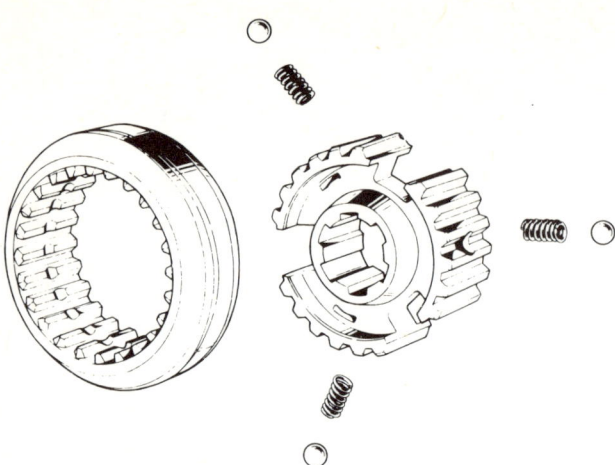

Fig. 13.16 An exploded view of a synchro assembly

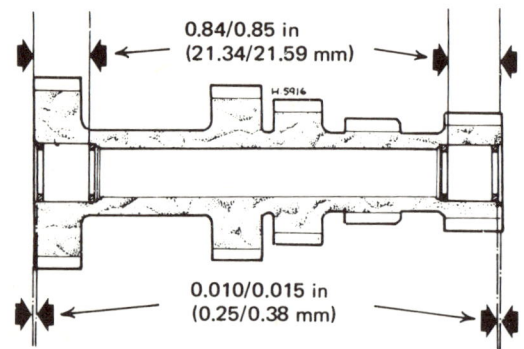

0.84/0.85 in
(21.34/21.59 mm)

0.010/0.015 in
(0.25/0.38 mm)

Fig. 13.17 Installation depth for needle roller retaining rings in laygear

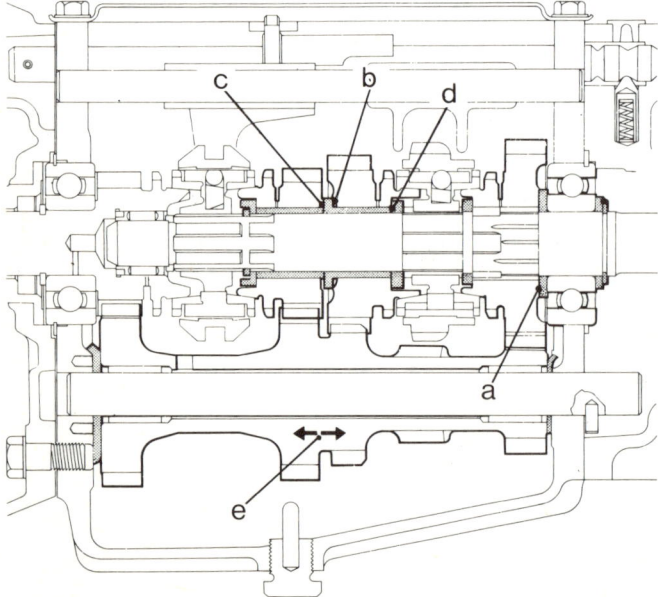

Fig. 13.18 Setting dimensions for mainshaft and laygear

a *1st gear endfloat*
b *2nd gear endfloat on bush*
c *3rd gear endfloat on bush*

d *2nd and 3rd gear bush clearances*
e *Laygear endfloat*

outer sleeve via the selector fork, the synchromesh cup first moves and friction, caused by the conical surfaces meeting, takes up initial rotational movement until the mainshaft and gear are both rotating at the same speed. This condition achieved, the sleeve is able to slide over the dog teeth of the selected gear and thereby giving a firm drive. The synchromesh unit inner hub is splined to the mainshaft and because the outer sleeve is splined to the inner hub engine torque is passed to the mainshaft and propeller shaft.

Gearbox (single rail) – removal and refitting

6   The gearbox can be removed in unit with the engine, as described in Chapter 1 or, alternatively, as a separate entity. This latter method is relatively straightforward and should be used if only the gearbox or clutch requires attention. Removal and refitting of the gearbox is fully described in Chapter 6, Section 2.

7   In the case of the single rail gearbox, the rear extension and the selector mechanism can only receive attention after removal of the gearbox. The gear lever is removed, as an assembly, by releasing the bayonet cap. Take care not to lose the nylon plunger and the anti-rattle spring.

Gearbox (single rail) – dismantling

8   Before commencing to dismantle the gearbox, clean the exterior with a water-soluble solvent. This will make the gearbox more easy to handle, and possibly prevent dirt from contaminating the internal parts. Drain the gearbox oil, then refit the plug.

9   Remove the clutch release bearing and lever as described in Chapter 5.

10   Remove the bolts and washers, and withdraw the bellhousing. *Note that a copper washer is used for the lowermost bolt, whereas the others have spring washers.*

11   Remove the three layshaft preload springs, and the bellhousing gasket.

12   Remove the gearbox top cover and the interlock spool plate.

13   Support the gearbox in a vice with the jaws firmly clamping the drain plug.

14   Remove the reverse lamp switch.

15   Drive out the roll pin from the selector rod.

16   Release the speedometer cable clamp plate and remove the pinion housing.

17   Pass a long bolt through the mainshaft flange so that it can wedge against the rear extension housing, then unscrew the flange nut and washer.

18   Pull off the mainshaft flange.

19   Move the gear selector to engage reverse gear; ensure that the selector shaft pins clear the interlock spool and selector forks.

20   Remove the bolts and spring washers, and detach the exhaust bracket and rear extension. Ensure that the selector pins do not foul, and that the layshaft does not move.

21   Lift out the interlock spool, then remove the rear extension gasket.

22   Remove the distance washer from the end of the mainshaft.

23   Slide the gear selector shaft off the rear extension rearwards to contact the blanking plug, then gently push out the plug using the shaft.

24   Slide the shaft rearwards, then drive out the rollpin securing the yoke. Withdraw the yoke.

25   Push the selector shaft forwards, keeping the rollpin hole horizontal to prevent the plunger from trapping the shaft.

26   Remove the shaft. Take out the nylon plug, plunger, spring and O-ring.

27   Remove the selector shaft and forks from the gearbox.

28   Using a round bar of suitable diameter, (eg, an old layshaft), drive out the layshaft and allow the laygear cluster to fall to the bottom of the gearbox.

29   Using a suitable small drift, drive the input shaft and bearing forwards out of the gearbox. Ensure that load is applied to the outer race only. If the caged needle bearing has remained

on the mainshaft spigot, remove this also.

30 Remove the bolt and spring washer, then withdraw the reverse idler gear spindle. Remove the spacer and reverse idler gear.

31 Release the circlip securing the bearing to the mainshaft.

32 Carefully tap off the speedometer gear.

33 Tap the mainshaft rearwards a little so that two large screwdrivers can be used behind the bearing circlip to lever the bearing out.

34 With the bearing removed from the mainshaft shoulder, lift the mainshaft out of the top of the gearbox. Collect the circlip, selective washer, bearing and thrust washer as this is being done.

35 Remove the laygear and thrust washers from the casing.

36 Remove the reverse operating lever.

37 Remove the 25 needle rollers from each end of the laygear. The retaining rings need not be removed unless renewal is found to be necessary.

Gearbox (single rail) – examination

38 The gearbox has been stripped, presumably, because of wear or malfunction, possibly excessive noise, ineffective synchromesh or failure to stay in a selected gear. The cause of most gearbox ailments is failure of the ball bearings on the input or mainshaft, and wear on the syncho rings, both the cup surfaces and dogs. The nose of the mainshaft which runs in the needle roller bearing in the input shaft is also subject to wear. This can prove very expensive as the mainshaft would need replacement, and this represents about 20% of the total cost of a new gearbox.

39 Examine the teeth of all gears for signs of uneven or excessive wear and, of course, chipping. If a gear on the mainshaft requires replacement check that the corresponding laygear is not equally damaged. If it is the whole laygear may need replacing also.

40 All gears should be a good running fit on the shaft with no signs of rocking. The hubs should not be a sloppy fit on the splines.

41 Selector forks should be examined for signs of wear or ridging on the faces which are in contact with the operating sleeve.

42 Check for wear on the selector rod and interlock spool.

43 The ball bearings may not be obviously worn but if one has gone to the trouble of dismantling the gearbox it would be shortsighted not to renew them. The same applies to the four synchronizer rings although for these the mainshaft has to be completely dismantled for the new ones to be fitted.

44 Examine the bush in the reverse idler gear for wear. If any is found, press out the old bush, and then press in a new one so that it is flush with the boss opposite the collar of the operating lever. Ream the bush to a diameter of 0.6585/0.6592 in (16.7279/16.8011 mm).

45 If worn, the reverse lever pivot pin can be pressed out of the casing and a new one inserted.

46 It is recommended that new oil seals are fitted in the input shaft guide counterbore of the clutch bellhousing and in the rear extension. These should be fitted with the lips towards the gearbox. **Note**: *If the rear extension bearing is to be renewed, this should be done before the oil seal is refitted.*

47 Before finally deciding to dismantle the mainshaft and replace parts, it is advisable to make enquiries regarding the availability of parts and their cost. It may still be worth considering an exchange gearbox even at this stage. You should reassemble the old gearbox before exchanging it.

Input shaft (single rail gearbox) – dismantling and reassembly

48 Place the input shaft in a vice, splined end upwards, and with a pair of circlip pliers, remove the circlip which retains the ball bearing in place.

49 With the bearing resting on top of the open jaws of the vice and splined end upwards, tap the shaft through the bearing with a soft faced hammer. **Note**: *The offset circlip groove in the outer track of the bearing is towards the front of the input shaft.*

50 Lift away the oil flinger.

51 Remove the caged needle roller bearing from the centre of the rear of the input shaft if it is still in place.

52 Remove the circlip from the old bearing outer track and transfer it to the new bearing.

53 Refit the oil flinger and with the aid of a block of wood and vice tap the bearing into place. Make sure it is the right way round.

54 Finally refit the bearing retaining circlip.

Mainshaft (single rail gearbox) – dismantling and reassembly

55 Remove the 1st gear (and thrust washer if not already removed) from the rear of the mainshaft (photo).

56 Remove the 1st gear synchro cup followed by the two split collars (photos).

57 Remove the 3rd/4th synchro hub and sleeve assembly from the front end of the mainshaft, followed by the 3rd gear synchro cup (photos).

58 Carefully prise open the ends of the retaining circlip then lever off the 3rd gear bush, thrust washer and circlip (photo).

59 Remove the 2nd gear and bush, followed by the selective washer and synchro cup (photos).

60 Using a small magnet, extract the selective washer locating ball from the mainshaft drilling.

61 Withdraw the 1st/2nd synchro hub and sleeve assembly (photo).

62 Index mark the sleeve and synchro hub assemblies of the 1st/2nd and 3rd/4th gears to ensure assembly in their original locations. Separate the sleeves from the hubs, ensuring that the three balls and springs are not lost. **Note**: *In some cases shims may be fitted below the springs.*

63 Clean all the parts in petrol or paraffin, and dry them with a lint-free cloth.

64 Reassemble the synchro assemblies ensuring that the teeth of the outer members are adjacent to the longer boss of the synchro hub. Where shims were previously fitted, refit them.

65 Check that a load of 19 to 27 lbf (8.7 to 12.2 kgf) is required to shift the 1st/2nd sleeve in either direction, and a load of 19 to 21 lbf (8.7 to 9.5 kgf) is required to shift the 3rd/4th sleeve. Add or remove shims to obtain this requirement.

66 The mainshaft can now be assembled following the reverse of the removal procedure. **Note**: *The second gear bush flange and the rim of the 3rd gear thrust washer are towards the front of the gearbox.* When installing the retaining circlip, ensure that the inclined end faces forwards and the clip aligns with the edge of the mainshaft spline. Ensure that the larger boss of the 3rd gear synchro assembly is towards the front of the gearbox. During the assembly procedure, the following clearances must be checked:

(a) 1st gear endfloat measured between the split collar and thrust washer, should be 0.004 to 0.013 in (0.0102 to 0.33 mm). Renew the split collars and/or thrust washer as necessary.

(b) 2nd gear endfloat on the bush should be 0.002 in (0.051 mm). Renew the flanged bush if necessary.

(c) 3rd gear endfloat on the bush should be 0.002 in (0.051 mm). Renew the flanged bush if necessary.

(d) 2nd and 3rd gear bushes should have a clearance of 0 to 0.006 in (0 to 0.15 mm). If adjustment is required obtain a new selective washer; these are available in steps of 0.003 in (0.076 mm).

Gearbox (single rail) – reassembly

67 Using a general purpose grease to hold them in position, fit the needle rollers into each end of the layshaft, and put the outer retaining ring in position (photo).

68 Locate the laygear thrust washers in the casing with their respective tabs in the casing slots.

69 Hold the laygear in position and check for an endfloat of 0.007 to 0.015 in (0.178 to 0.381 mm). If necessary, obtain

5.55 Removing the 1st gear

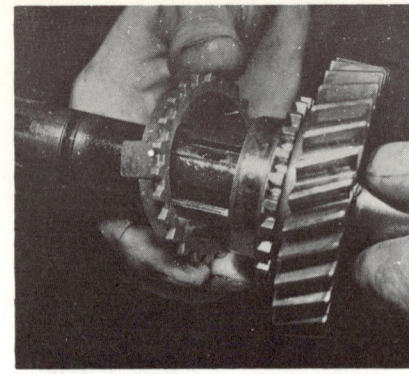

5.56A Removing the synchro cup ...

5.56B ... and split collars

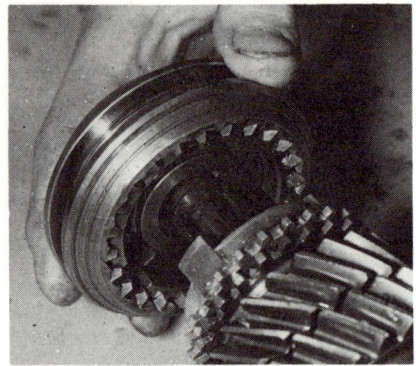

5.57A Removing the 3rd/4th synchro hub and sleeve assembly...

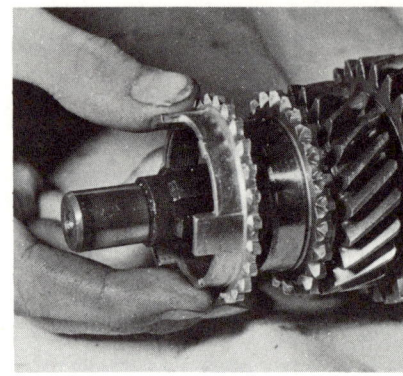

5.57B ... followed by the synchro cup

5.58 3rd gear being removed after circlip and thrust washer have been removed

5.59A Removing the 2nd gear ...

5.59B ... 2nd gear bush ...

5.59C ... selective washer ...

5.59D ... and synchro cup

5.61 Removing the 1st/2nd synchro hub and sleeve assembly ...

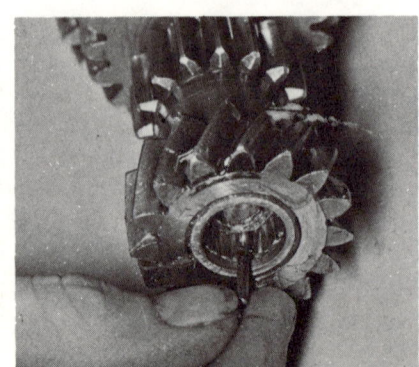

5.67 Installing the needle rollers

5.71 Fitting the mainshaft

5.72 Fitting the casing rear bearing onto the mainshaft

5.73A Supporting the mainshaft with a metal bar ...

5.73B ... as the bearing is driven into position

5.77 Fitting the input shaft

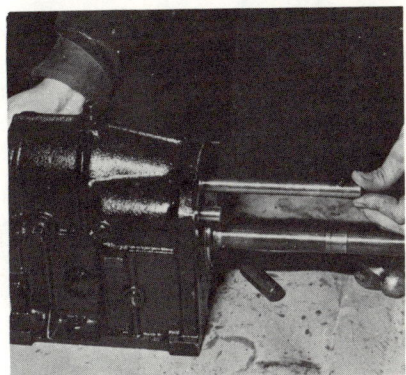
5.78A Installing the layshaft

5.78B Note that the pin aligns with the groove

5.80A Fitting the 3rd/4th selector fork

5.80B Fitting the 1st/2nd selector fork

5.80C Inserting the shaft through the forks

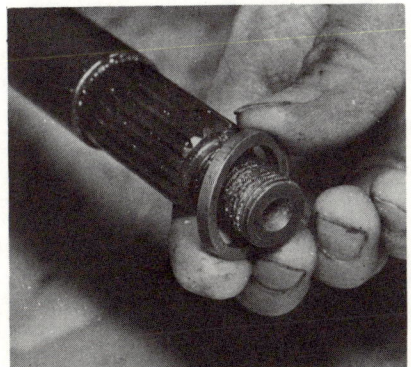
5.82A Fitting the distance washer

5.82B Fitting the interlock spool to the selector rail

5.85 Fitting the roll pin to the selector rail

5.91A Fitting the interlock spool plate

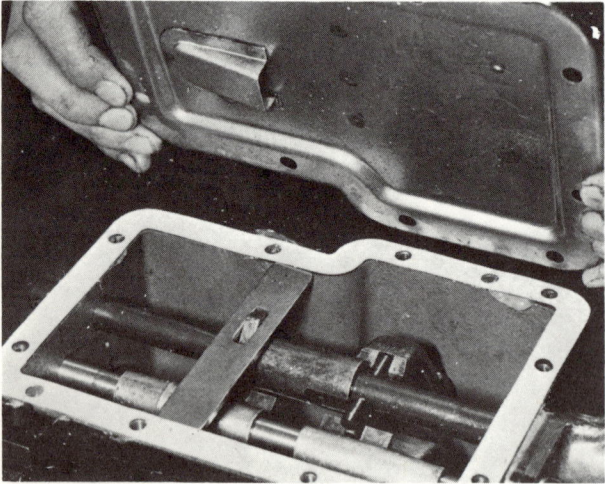

5.91B Positioning the top cover on a new gasket

new thrust washers to achieve this dimension.

70 Take out the laygear and insert the dummy layshaft used when dismantling. Place the laygear assembly into the casing again so that the large gear is towards the front.

71 Tilt the assembled mainshaft into the casing, then place reverse gear in the bottom of the casing and fit the reverse operating lever (photo).

72 Fit the circlip to the casing rear bearing, then slide the bearing onto the mainshaft (photo).

73 Whilst supporting the front of the mainshaft with a suitable metal bar, drive the rear bearing into position in the casing and on the mainshaft. A suitable size metal tube can be used, but apply loads to the bearing inner race only (photo).

74 Ensure that the bearing is fully home then fit a washer and selective circlip so that mainshaft endfloat does not exceed 0.002 in (0.051 mm). Circlips are available in 0.003 in (0.076 mm) steps.

75 Fit the speedometer gear so that it contacts the shoulder on the mainshaft.

76 Fit the needle roller bearing and rings to the mainshaft spigot.

77 Fit the 4th gear synchro cup on the input shaft, then push the input shaft into engagement with the mainshaft so that the bearing circlip contacts the front face of the casing (photo).

78 Push in the layshaft, at the same time driving out the dummy shaft (photos).

79 Fit the reverse gear, shaft and spacer.

80 Fit the selector forks and shaft, followed by the selector mechanism. This is basically the reverse of the removal procedure as described in paragraphs 23 to 26 (photos). Also refer to Fig. 13.11.

81 Ensure that the mating faces are clean, then position a new gasket on the rear face of the casing.

82 Fit the distance washer to the mainshaft then offer up the rear extension, guiding the selector rail into position. Do not forget to fit the selector interlock spool (photos).

83 Fit the bolts and washers, together with the exhaust bracket and lockplate.

84 Smear some gearbox oil around the oil seal lip and drive flange surface, then install the flange, washer and nut. Tighten the nut to the specified torque whilst preventing the flange from turning.

85 Fit the rollpin to the front end of the selector rail so that it is positioned centrally (photo).

86 Refit the speedometer drive pinion using a new O-ring.

87 Fit the reverse light switch.

88 Fit the three layshaft thrust springs.

89 Fit the clutch housing gasket, clutch housing, release fork and bearing, following the reverse of the removal procedure. Take care that the input shaft splines do not damage the oil seal.

90 Fit the gearbox drain plug, and top up to the level plug hole using the specified type of gear oil. Fit the filler/level plug.

91 Fit the spool interlock plate, a new gasket and the top cover (photos).

6 Propeller shaft

General description

1 The propeller shaft fitted to early Triumph Toledos, (up to commission numbers ADG 25392 for two door vehicles and ADF 27621 for four door vehicles), has the splined sliding yoke mounted in the front section of the propeller shaft attached to the gearbox output flange, and is fully described in Chapter 7 of this manual.

2 Vehicles produced after these commission numbers are of a modified design, with the splined sliding yoke mounted in the rear section of the propeller shaft, and attached to the axle companion flange.

3 The front and rear sections of the propeller shaft are joined together by means of a male spline on the front section, and a female spline on the rear section. A modified type of centre

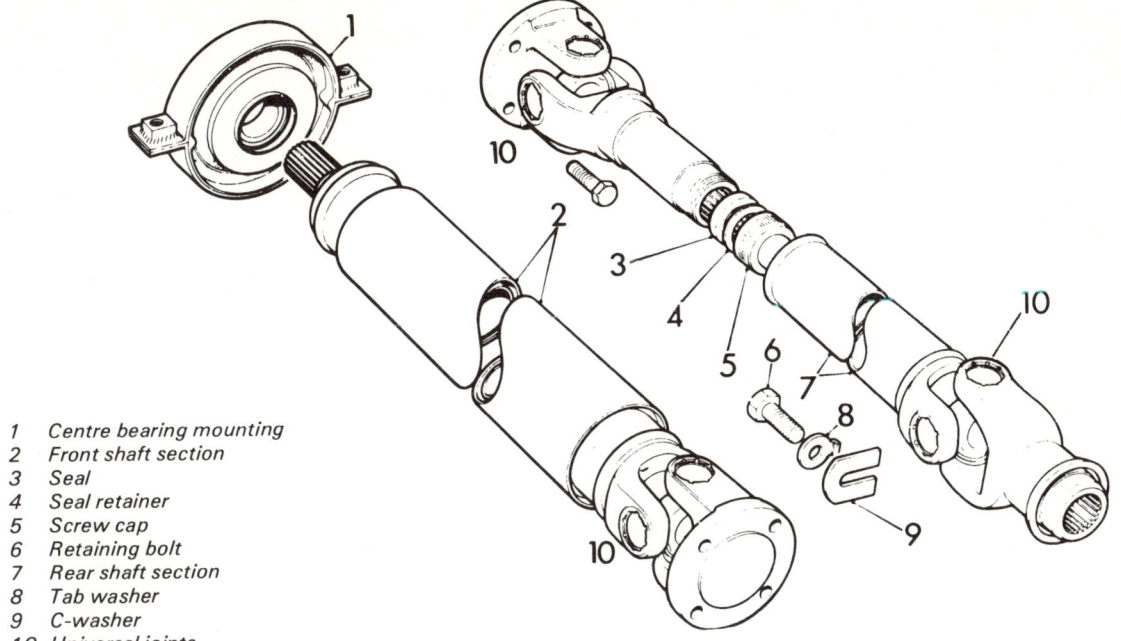

1 Centre bearing mounting
2 Front shaft section
3 Seal
4 Seal retainer
5 Screw cap
6 Retaining bolt
7 Rear shaft section
8 Tab washer
9 C-washer
10 Universal joints

Fig. 13.19 Front and rear sections of the propeller shaft

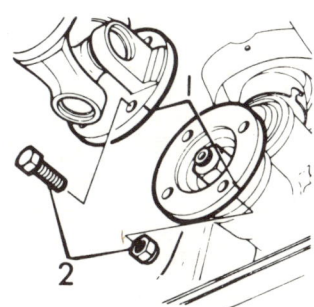

Fig. 13.20 The propeller shaft attachments

1 Front/rear propeller shaft
   and gearbox/rear axle
   flanges
2 Securing bolt and locknut

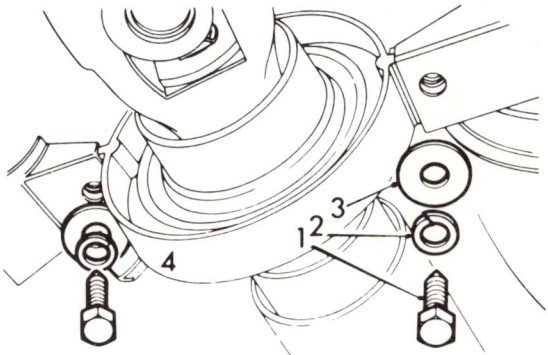

Fig. 13.21 The centre bearing attachments

1 Bolt   3 Plain washer
2 Spring washer   4 Centre bearing assembly

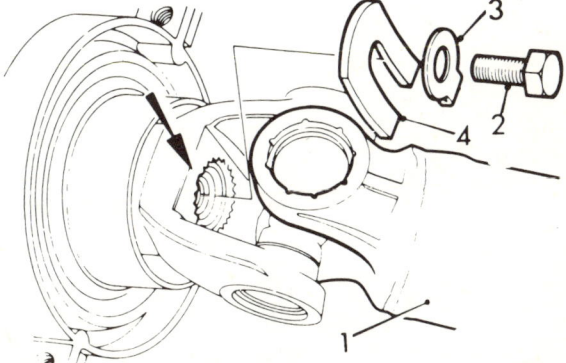

Fig. 13.22 Rear propeller shaft section to centre bearing attachment

1 Rear propeller shaft section   3 Lockwasher
2 Bolt   4 C-washer

bearing mounting supports the joined sections of the shaft, mid-way between the two flange ends.

4 The universal joints are identical to those used on early vehicles and are fully described in Chapter 7.

Propeller shaft – removal and refitting

5 Jack-up the rear of the vehicle and support on firmly based axle-stands. Alternatively, position the rear of the vehicle on a ramp or over an inspection pit. Chock the front wheels.

6 The propeller shaft is carefully balanced to fine limits and it is important that it is refitted in exactly the same position prior to its removal. Scratch marks on the gearbox, differential pinion and propeller shaft drive flanges for correct re-alignment when refitting.

7 Support the weight of the front section of the propeller shaft. Undo and remove the four gearbox drive flange nuts and bolts (Fig. 13.20).

8 Support the weight of the rear section of the propeller shaft. Undo and remove the four axle companion flange nuts and

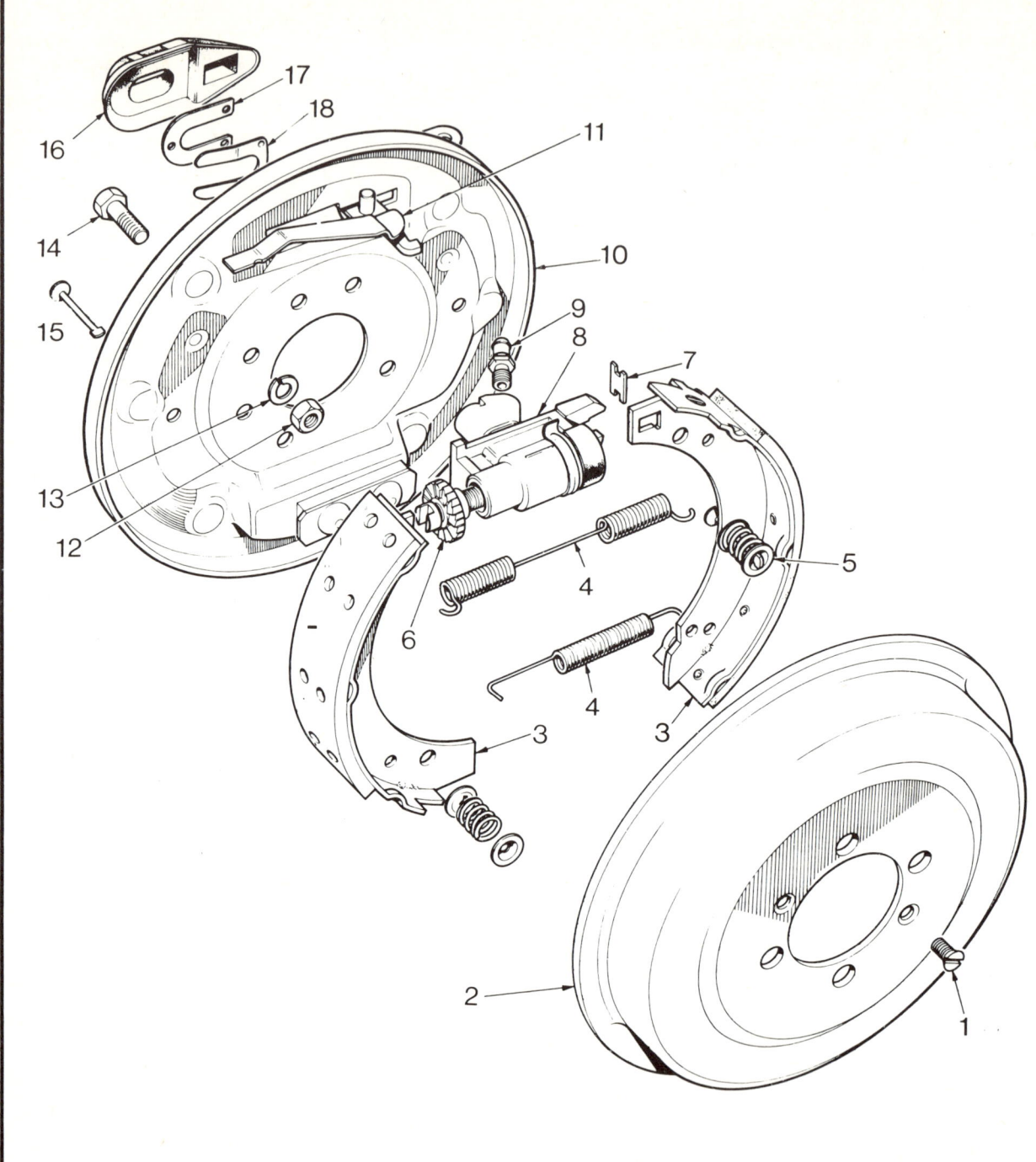

Fig. 13.23 The component parts of the rear wheel brake assembly

1	Countersunk screw	11	Handbrake lever
2	Brake drum	12	Nut
3	Brake shoes	13	Washer
4	Shoe return springs	14	Bolt
5	Steady pin assembly	15	Steady pin
6	Adjuster	16	Rubber boot
7	Plate support	17	Wheel cylinder retaining plate
8	Wheel cylinder		
9	Bleed nipple	18	Wheel cylinder retaining plate
10	Backplate		

bolts.

9   Undo and remove the two bolts, spring and plain washers that retain the centre bearing mounting to the body brackets (Fig. 13.21).

10 Lift away the propeller shaft assembly, together with the centre mounting assembly, from the underside of the vehicle.

11 To separate the two halves of the propeller shaft assembly, first bend back the locking washer tab, then undo and remove the retaining bolt. Lift away the C-washer and tab washer (Fig. 13.22).

12 Draw the front propeller shaft section away from the rear propeller shaft section universal joint splines.

13 Reconnection and refitting the two sections of the shaft is the reverse sequence to removal, but the following additional points should be noted:

> a) Ensure that the mating marks scratched on the propeller shaft, gearbox and differential pinion flanges are lined up.
> b) Tighten the centre bearing mounting bolts to a torque wrench setting of 22 lbf ft (3.0 kgf m).
> c) Tighten the front and rear flange retaining nuts to a torque wrench setting of 28 lbf ft (3.8 kgf m).

Centre bearing – removal and refitting

14 Remove the propeller shaft assembly as previously described in this Section. Separate the two halves.

15 Using a universal puller and a suitable thrust block (a suitable size bolt will do) draw the centre bearing from the end of the front section of the propeller shaft.

16 To fit a new bearing simply drive it into position using a piece of suitable diameter metal tube.

17 Reconnect and refit the propeller shaft assembly, following the reverse sequence to removal.

---

7   Braking system

Rear brake shoes (self-adjusting) – inspection, removal and refitting

1   Chock the front wheels then raise the relevant road wheel. Support the car on an axle-stand to prevent accidents. Release the handbrake.

2   Remove the road wheel, then take out the counter-sunk-head screws which are used to secure the brake drum and remove the drum. This may require tapping outwards around its periphery using a soft-faced mallet whilst it is being rotated.

3   The brake linings should be renewed if they are so worn that the rivet heads are flush with the surface of the lining. If bonded linings are fitted they must be renewed when the lining material has worn down to $\frac{1}{16}$ in (1.6 mm) at its thinnest point.

4   To remove the brake shoes, first spring the self adjuster operating lever on the underside of the wheel cylinder clear of the ratchet wheel.

5   Now rotate the ratchet wheel as far as possible, to release the brake adjustment.

6   Remove the brake shoe steady cups, springs and pins.

7   Release the leading shoe (ie, the one operated by the wheel cylinder piston) from the anchor plate at the top and then from the wheel cylinder at the bottom.

8   Repeat the procedure for the trailing shoe.

9   Disconnect the shoe return springs and pull the brake shoes completely away; be careful that the wheel cylinder piston does not come out. Strong rubber bands can be used to hold the pistons in place. On no account should the brake pedal be depressed whilst the brake shoes and drums are off.

10 Thoroughly clean all traces of dust from the shoes, backplates and brake drums using a stiff brush. The use of compressed air is not recommended, and care must be taken not to inhale any dust. Brake dust can cause judder or squeal and, therefore, it is important to clean out the brakes thoroughly.

11 Check that the piston is free in its cylinder, that the dust covers are undamaged and in position, and that there are no hydraulic fluid leaks. Ensure that the handbrake lever assembly is free and also that the brake adjuster operates correctly. Unscrew the adjuster fully, clean the threads then smear them with a little high melting point brake grease and refit them. Adjust the ratchet wheel so that the adjuster spindle is fully into the wheel cylinder recess, and ensure that the brake shoe locating slot is vertical.

12 Prior to reassembly smear a little high melting point brake grease on to the sliding surfaces of the backplate. Check that the wheel cylinder is free to move in the slot in the backplate (If it is found that the wheel cylinder is not free to move it should be removed as described in paragraphs 22 to 34).

13 Taking great care that no grease or dirt is allowed to contact the brake lining material, arrange the shoes in the manner in which they will be offered up to the backplate.

14 Engage the upper spring ends in the webs of the shoes, with the spring fitted inboard (behind the web).

15 Offer both shoes up to the backplate and engage the ends of the shoes in the anchor plate.

16 Fit the lower spring ends in the webs of the shoes, with the spring fitted inboard.

17 Engage the leading shoe in the handbrake operating lever, ensuring that the lever pad is properly located in the shoe web.

18 Now fit the trailing shoe into the slot in the adjuster spindle.

19 Refit the brake shoe steady pins, springs and cups.

20 Centralize the brake shoes then refit the brake drum and road wheel.

21 Lower the car to the ground and operate the handbrake lever several times to adjust the position of the shoes. It will not normally be necessary to bleed the brakes unless any fluid has escaped from the system during the time when the brake shoes were removed.

Rear brake wheel cylinder (self-adjusting) – removal, inspection, overhaul and reassembly

22 Remove the brake drum and shoes as described previously. Clean the rear of the backplate using a stiff brush. Place a quantity of rag under the backplate or a tray to catch any hydraulic fluid that may issue from the open pipe or wheel cylinder.

23 Place a piece of polythene under the reservoir cap and screw down the cap tightly. Carefully detach the hydraulic pipe from the rear of the wheel cylinder. The left-hand cylinder has only the feed pipe connected, while the right-hand cylinder has a feed pipe and a transfer pipe connected. Also disconnect the handbrake cable from the handbrake lever assembly at the rear

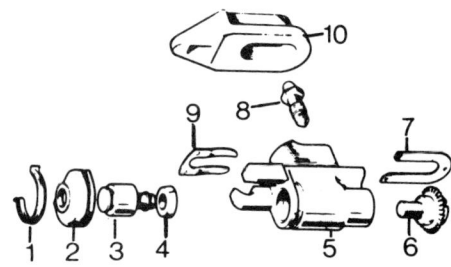

Fig. 13.24 The component parts of the rear wheel cylinder

1	Clip	6	Adjuster
2	Rubber boot	7	Retaining plate
3	Piston	8	Bleed nipple
4	Piston seal	9	Retaining plate
5	Wheel cylinder	10	Rubber boot

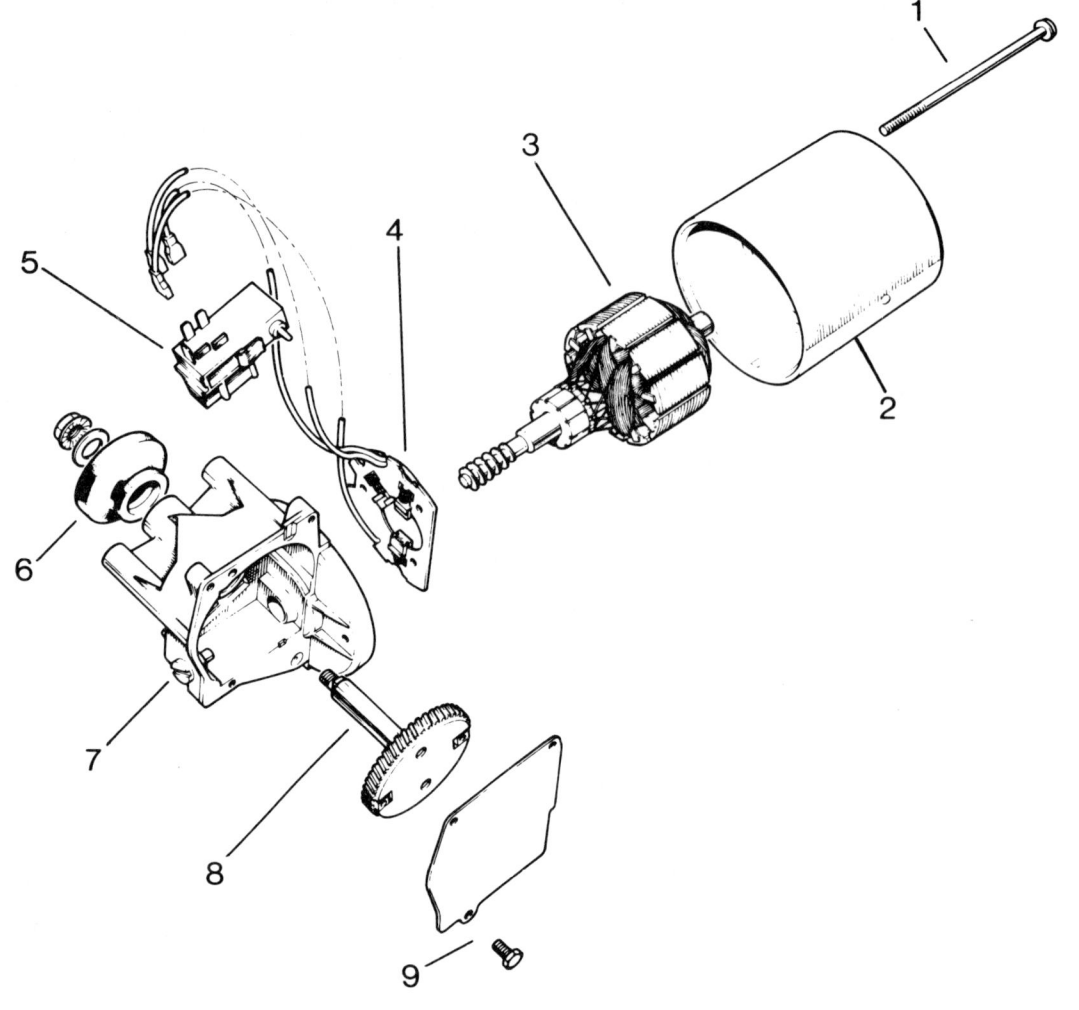

Fig. 13.25 The windscreen wiper motor parts

1 Through-bolt
2 Cover
3 Armature

4 Brush assembly
5 Limit switch
6 Rubber seal

7 Gearbox
8 Shaft

9 Gearbox cover and screw

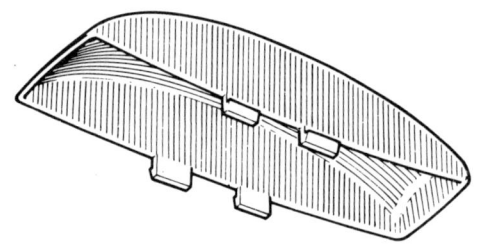

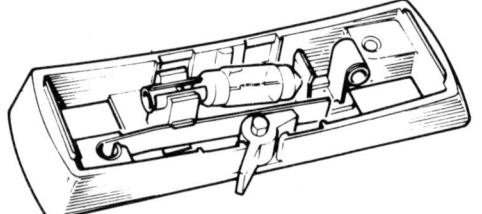

Fig. 13.26 A later type roof lamp

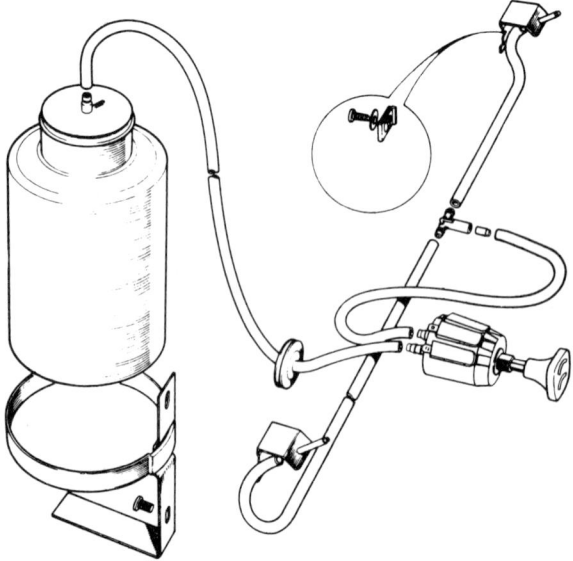

Fig. 13.27 The component parts of the windscreen washer system (early vehicles)

of the backplate by removing the split pin and extracting the clevis pin noting that the head is uppermost. Remove the rubber boot.

24 Using a wide bladed screwdriver separate the horseshoe clip and wheel cylinder retaining spring plate and carefully pull the horseshoe clip towards the front of the car.

25 Withdraw the handbrake assembly from the wheel cylinder, followed by the spring plate and shaped distance washer which is held in position by a retaining spring. Carefully pull the wheel cylinder assembly from the hub side of the brake backplate.

26 Ease off the spring clip, remove the dust boot and withdraw the piston from the cylinder. Remove the piston seal using a non-metal pointed rod, or fingers. Do not use a metal screwdriver as this could scratch the piston.

27 Inspect the inside of the cylinder for score marks. If any are found the cylinder and piston will require renewal. **Note**: *If the wheel cylinder requires renewal ensure that the replacement is the same diameter as originally fitted.*

28 If the cylinder is sound, remove the self adjuster spindle and ratchet wheel. Clean the parts and smear a little high melting point brake grease onto the screw threads. Thoroughly clean the cylinder interior using hydraulic fluid and a lint-free cloth.

29 Regardless of the condition of the old rubber seal, fit a new one. Wet assemble it to the piston, and the piston to the cylinder, using brake fluid. Fit a new rubber dust cover and spring clip. Refit the adjuster.

30 Using high melting point brake grease, smear the backplate where the wheel cylinder slides and then refit the wheel cylinder to the backplate with the adjuster ratchet wheel facing towards the front of the car.

31 Screw the adjuster back fully and ensure that the slot is vertical then replace the handbrake lever assembly, not forgetting the shaped distance washer and its retaining spring. Install the spring plate with the open end towards the front of the car, and with the dimples towards the differential. Fit the horseshoe clip from the front of the cylinder, ensuring the holes in the end engage with the dimples on the spring plate. Check that the cylinder is free to float in the backplate.

32 Refit the rubber cover, connect the hydraulic pipe to the wheel cylinder and the handbrake cable to the handbrake lever. Refit the clevis pin with the head uppermost, and lock using a new split pin.

33 Refit the brake shoes, drum and road wheel, then adjust the brakes by pulling the handbrake on, and off, several times.

34 Now remove the polythene from the master cylinder reservoir and bleed the brakes as described in Chapter 9, Section 2.

8 Electrical system

Windscreen wiper motor (Lucas) – removal, overhaul and refitting

1 Disconnect the battery earth lead.
2 Remove the nut that secures the motor shaft to the crank; withdraw the crank and collect the shaft washer.
3 Remove the screws and bolts that secure the motor to the support bracket.
4 Lift off the motor and disconnect the electrical leads.
5 Recover the six washers and three spacers.
6 Remove the rubber seal at the drive end.
7 Remove the gearbox cover (three screws).
8 Ensure that there are no burrs on the drive end of the shaft, then withdraw it complete with the dished washer.
9 Remove the thrust screw on the casing, complete with locknut (if fitted).
10 Remove the cover through-bolts, carefully withdraw the cover about 0.2 in (5 mm) then continue withdrawing, allowing the brushes to drop clear of the commutator.
11 Pull the armature out of the cover then remove the brush assembly (three screws).
12 The limit switch can be removed from the brush assembly

by turning the former to release the spring clip.

13 Examine the armature worm and gear for excessive wear on the teeth, renewing the parts as necessary. In view of the expense of renewing an armature for wear alone, a certain amount of wear can be tolerated. Also, if the armature requires repair for any reason it is worthwhile considering a replacement wiper motor.

14 Remove any dust with a brush or compressed air jet. Do not allow any liquid cleaner into contact with the field coils.

15 Inspect the commutator for signs of burning or pitting, and if evident, clean with a little fine glass paper. Wash away any dust with petrol.

16 Examine the brushes for wear and general condition, renewing as necessary. The minimum permissible brush length is 0.125 in (3 mm).

17 Check for wear in the bearings and renew if necessary.

Note: *The following lubricants (or suitable equivalents) will be required during reassembly*

Shell Turbo 41 oil
Ragosine Listate grease

18 Lubricate the cover bearing, and saturate the felt washer with Shell Turbo 41 oil.
19 Fit the armature into the cover against the permanent magnetic pull.

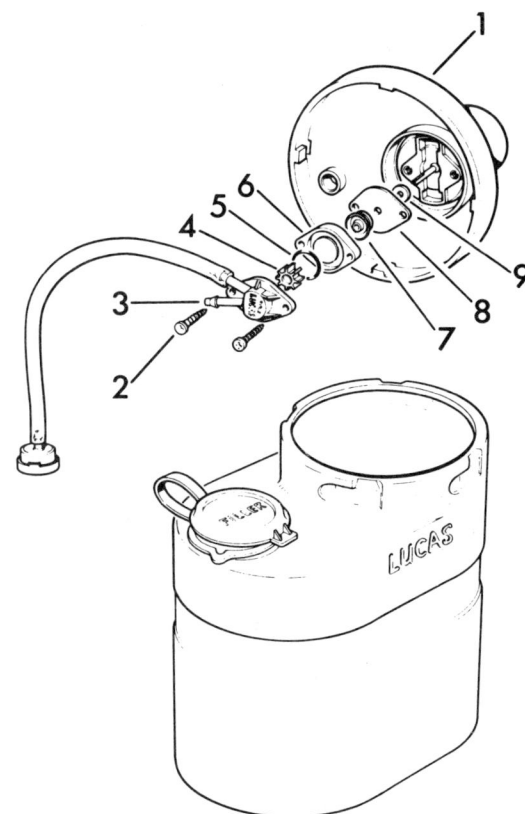

Fig. 13.28 The windscreen washer component parts (electrical type)

1 Cover	6 Seal housing
2 Screws	7 Seal
3 Pump housing	8 Plate
4 Rotor	9 Rubber disc
5 O-ring	

20 Refit the limit switch to the brush assembly, then fit the latter (three screws).
21 Lubricate the self-aligning bearing with Shell Turbo 41 oil then fit the armature through the brush plate and cover. Take care to lift the brushes on the commutator, and ensure that they are not contaminated with oil.
22 Turn the cover to align the two markings then fit the through-bolts.
23 Fit the thrust screw (and locknut, if applicable).
24 Where a non-adjustable (no locknut) screw is used, check for 0.002 to 0.008 in (0.05 to 0.2 mm) endfloat and adjust either by shims beneath the screw head (if the gap is too small) or by turning the required amount off the end of the screw using a lathe. Where a screw and locknut are fitted, screw inwards until resistance is felt then screw out again $\frac{1}{4}$ turn and tighten the locknut.
25 Lubricate the gearbox brushes with Shell Turbo 41 oil.
26 Lubricate the final gear cam with Ragosine Listate grease, fit the dished washer with the concave surface towards the final gear then insert the shaft.
27 Pack Ragosine Listate grease around the worm gear and final gear then refit the cover (three screws).
28 Finally, refit or renew the rubber seal.
29 The assembly can now be refitted to the car in the reverse order to removal. Note the different sized washers for the mounting bolts to accomodate the shank diameter and smaller thread diameter.

Master light switch – removal and refitting
30 Disconnect the battery earth lead.
31 Locate the hole in the underside of the knob. Insert a suitable probe into the hole, and while depressing, pull the knob from the shaft.
32 Using a suitable tool, slacken and unscrew the bezel.
33 Withdraw the switch from the facia and manoeuvre it into a viable position.
34 Note the wire connections and disconnect them.
35 Refitting is a reversal of the removal procedure.

Door light switch – removal and refitting
36 Open the appropriate door and remove the single screw retaining the switch.
37 Withdraw the switch and disconnect the terminal end.
38 Refitting is the reversal of the removal procedure.

Luggage compartment illumination switch – removal and refitting
39 Open the luggage compartment lid and locate the switch mounted on the right-hand hinge assembly.
40 Pull the switch from the bracket and disconnect the terminal end.
41 Refitting is the reverse of removal but ensure that a good electrical contact exists between the switch and the body.

Oil pressure switch – removal and refitting
42 Locate the oil pressure switch on the left-hand side of the engine block. Disconnect the Lucar connector.
43 Unscrew the switch from the engine block.
44 To refit, screw the switch into the block and tighten to a torque wrench setting of 11 to 14 lbf ft (1.5 to 2.0 kgf m).
Note: *The oil pressure switch thread is tapered and no attempt should be made to seat the switch shoulder.*
45 Reconnect the Lucar connector.

Windscreen wiper/washer switch – removal and refitting
46 Early vehicles were fitted with a manually operated washer system whilst later models have an electrically operated washer system. The removal and refitting procedure described in Chapter 10, Section 29, still applies, but disconnect four Lucar connectors. In the later type switch there are obviously no water pipe connections.

Heated rear window switch – removal and refitting
47 Removal and refitting of this switch is identical to the master light switch, described earlier in this Section.

Brake stop lamp switch – removal and refitting
48 Disconnect the battery earth lead.
49 Locate the switch adjacent to the brake pedal arm above the steering column.
50 Disconnect the two Lucar connectors.
51 Slacken the large hexagon nut.
52 Unscrew the switch from the nut and remove it from the vehicle. The nut and washer may remain in position retained by the spring-loaded brake pedal arm.
53 Refitting is a reversal of the removal procedure but the following points should be noted:

  a) *Do not overtighten the nut on the plastic threads of the switch.*
  b) *The setting distance between the face (brake pedal side) of the switch bracket to the brake pedal should be 0.60 in (15.24 mm) with the brake pedal in its released position.*
  c) *Switch on the ignition and check for satisfactory function of the switch on completion.*

Hazard warning switch (later models) – removal and refitting
54 Unscrew the switch pull and remove the illumination bulb.
55 Release the switch from the back of the instrument panel.
56 To refit, reverse the removal procedure.

Temperature and fuel gauges (later models) – removal and refitting
57 Removal of these instruments is as described in Chapter 10, Section 33 but, instead of removing the trim board, the speedometer will have to be removed. Removal of the speedometer is described in Chapter 10, Section 34.

Roof lamp (later models) – removal and refitting
58 Disconnect the battery earth lead.
59 Gently squeeze the lens adjacent to the clip projections and remove the lens.
60 Carefully pull out the festoon bulb.
61 Disconnect the two terminal ends.
62 Remove the two retaining screws and lift away the lamp base.
63 Refitting is a straightforward reversal of the removal procedure, but ensure that the earth tag is positioned under the appropriate screw head.

Windscreen washer pump (early models) – removal and refitting
64 The windscreen washer pump is an integral part of the windscreen wiper switch. Removal and refitting is described in Chapter 10, Section 29.

Windscreen washer jets (early models) – removal and refitting
65 Open the bonnet and locate the washer jets which are secured to the vehicle by screws and washers.
66 Unscrew the appropriate jet and pull off the water pipe.
67 Refitting is a reversal of removal procedure, but check to ensure that the water jet passes unobstructed through a bonnet air intake louvre. If necessary, adjust the aim of the jet by slight bending of the jet tube bracket, or alternatively, slacken the jet retaining screws and reposition the jet.

Windscreen washer reservoir (early models) – removal and refitting
68 Removal of the reservoir is carried out by unscrewing the top, placing it to one side, and lifting it from the carrier.
69 The carrier can be removed by removing the two retaining screws.

70 Refitting of the carrier and reservoir is a reversal of the removal procedure.

Windscreen washer system (later models)
71 The windscreen washer system fitted to later models uses the original jets, but is operated electrically from the dash-mounted switch. A larger reservoir is fitted to house the pump and its associated parts.

Windscreen washer switch (Toledo) — removal and refitting
72 The operating switch is an integral part of the windscreen wiper switch. Removal and refitting is described in paragraph 46.

Windscreen washer pump and reservoir — removal and refitting
73 Rotate the reservoir cover anti-clockwise to release the bayonet fitting.
74 Pull off the outlet pipe and withdraw it from the cover. Disconnect the two Lucar connectors.
75 Manoeuvre the reservoir upwards from the carrier.
76 Refitting of the pump and reservoir is a reversal of the removal procedure, but to ensure that the pump motor runs in the correct direction, the connections must be as follows:

   Light green/black wire to positive terminal

   Black wire to negative terminal

Windscreen washer pump — overhaul
77 No replacement parts for the pump are available but dismantling for cleaning can be carried out as described below.
78 Rotate the cover anticlockwise to release the bayonet fitting, then lift the cover off.
79 Remove the pump housing (two screws).
80 Withdraw the rotor and drive plate, lift out the O-ring then remove the seal housing.
81 Withdraw the seal from the motor shaft then remove the plate.
82 Finally, withdraw the small rubber disc from the motor shaft.
83 Clean all parts using warm water and detergent. Carefully scrape off any stubborn deposits with a penknife.
84 Reassemble in the reverse order to dismantling.

Windscreen washer/wiper switch (Dolomite) — removal and refitting
85 Disconnect the battery earth lead.
86 Remove the steering column assembly as described in Chapter 11, Section 17.
87 Remove the two screws retaining the switch. Disconnect the switch from the wiring harness.
88 Refitting is a reversal of the removal procedure.

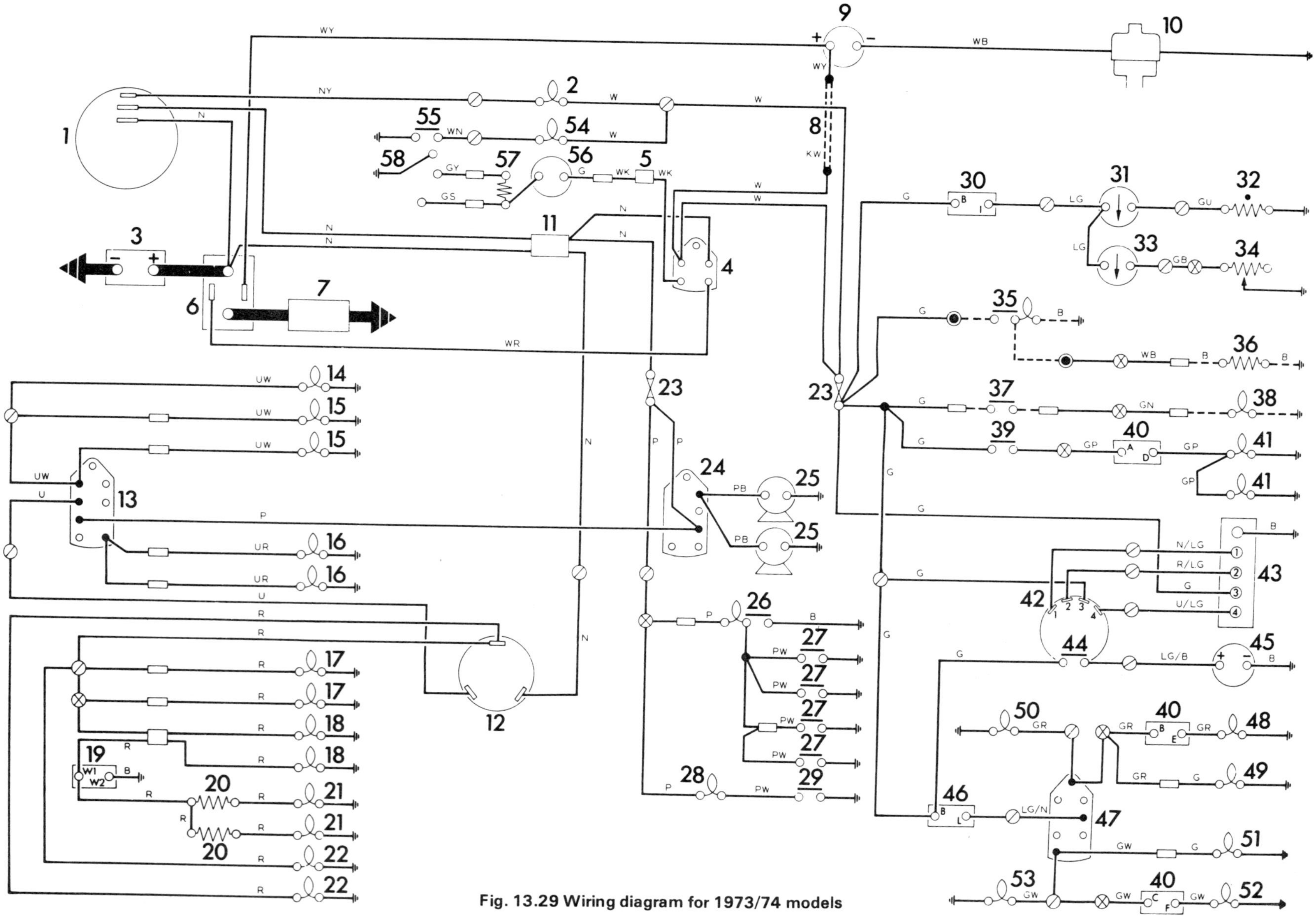

Fig. 13.29 Wiring diagram for 1973/74 models

Fig. 13.29 Key to wiring diagram for 1973/74 models

1 Alternator
2 Ignition warning light
3 Battery
4 Ignition/starter switch
5 Radio supply
6 Starter solenoid
7 Starter motor
8 Ballast resistor wire
9 Ignition coil
10 Ignition distributor
11 Connector
12 Master light switch
13 Main/dip/flash switch
14 Main beam warning light
15 Main beam
16 Dip beam
17 Front parking lamp
18 Plate illumination lamp
19 Night dimming relay winding
20 Tail lamp resistor

21 Tail lamp
22 Instrument illumination
23 Fuse
24 Horn switch
25 Horn
26 Roof lamp
27 Door switch
28 Luggage boot lamp
29 Luggage boot lamp switch
30 Voltage stabilizer
31 Temperature indicator
32 Temperature transmitter
33 Fuel indicator
34 Fuel transmitter
35 Heated backlight switch (when fitted)
36 Heated backlight (when fitted)
37 Reverse lamp switch (when fitted)
38 Reverse lamp (when fitted)
39 Stop lamp switch

40 Night dimming relay contacts
41 Stop lamp
42 Windscreen wiper switch
43 Windscreen wiper motor
44 Windscreen washer switch
45 Windscreen washer pump
46 Turn signal flasher unit
47 Turn signal switch
48 LH rear flasher lamp
49 LH front flasher lamp
50 LH turn signal warning light
51 RH front flasher lamp
52 RH rear flasher lamp
53 RH turn signal warning light
54 Oil pressure warning light
55 Oil pressure switch
56 Heater motor
57 Heater resistor
58 Heater switch

Colour Code:

B Black
G Green
K Pink
LG Light green

N Brown
O Orange
P Purple
R Red

S Slate
U Blue
W White
Y Yellow

200

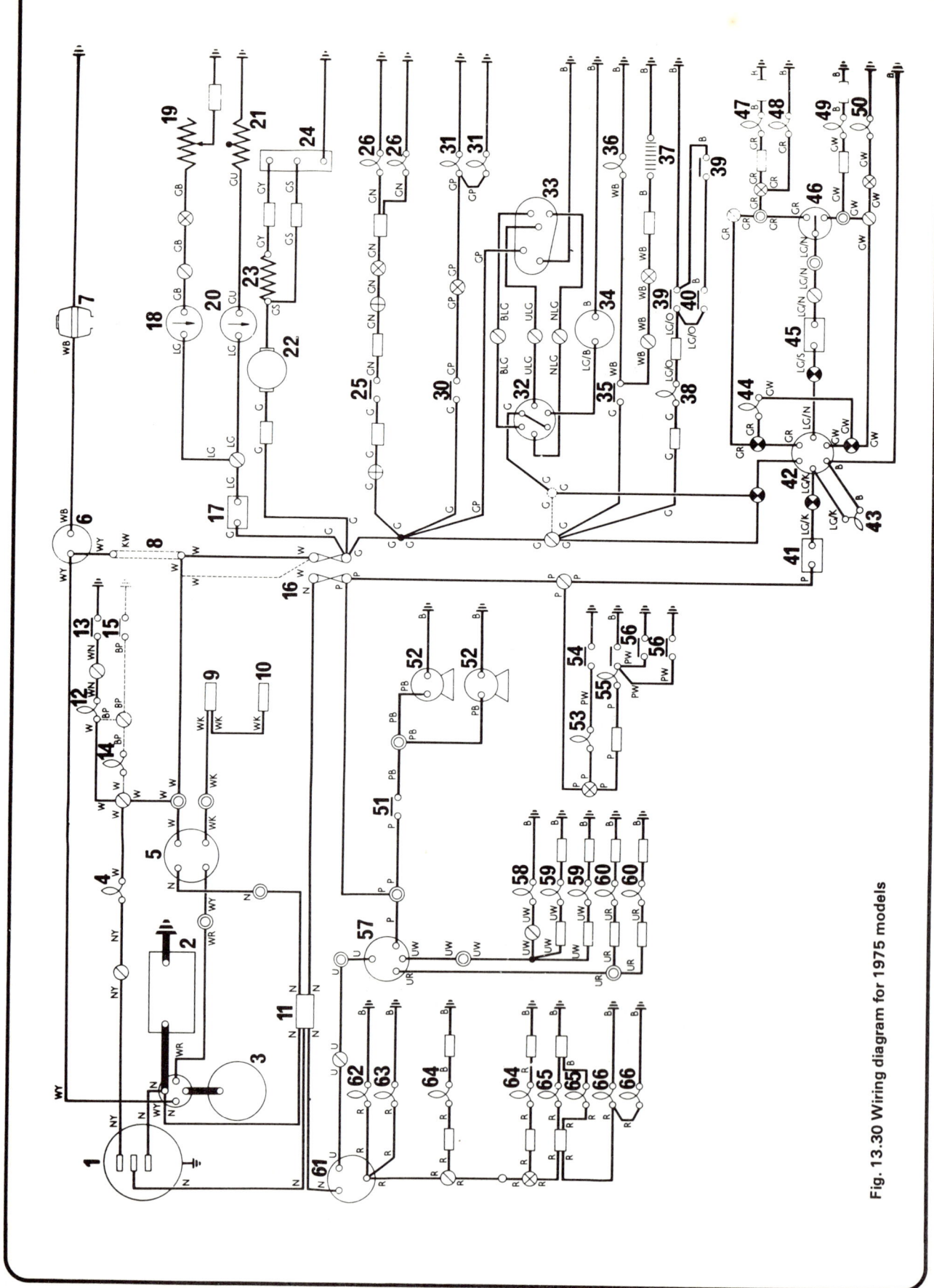

Fig. 13.30 Wiring diagram for 1975 models

Fig. 13.30 Key to wiring diagram for 1975 models

1 Alternator
2 Battery
3 Starter motor
4 Ignition warning light
5 Ignition/starter switch
6 Ignition coil
7 Ignition distributor
8 Ballast resistor wire
9 Radio supply
10 Alternative heater supply
11 Battery lead connector
12 Oil pressure warning light
13 Oil pressure switch
14 Brake failure warning light‡
15 Brake failure switch‡
16 Fusebox
17 Voltage stabilizer
18 Fuel indicator
19 Fuel tank unit
20 Temperature indicator
21 Temperature transmitter

22 Heater motor
23 Heater resistor
24 Heater switch
25 Reverse lamp switch
26 Reverse lamp
30 Stop lamp switch
31 Stop lamp
32 Windscreen wiper/washer switch
33 Windscreen wiper motor
34 Windscreen washer pump
35 Heated backlight switch
36 Heated backlight warning light
37 Heated backlight
38 Seat belt warning light
39 Seat belt switch
40 Seat sensor switch
41 Hazard flasher unit
42 Hazard flasher switch
43 Hazard flasher warning light
44 Direction indicator warning light
45 Direction indicator flasher unit

46 Direction indicator switch
47 Front direction indicator lamp (LH)
48 Rear direction indicator lamp (LH)
49 Rear direction indicator lamp (RH)
50 Front direction indicator lamp (RH)
51 Horn switch
52 Horn
53 Luggage compartment lamp
54 Luggage compartment switch
55 Courtesy lamp
56 Door switch
57 Headlamp selector switch
58 Main beam warning light
59 Main beam filament
60 Dip beam filament
61 Master lighting switch
62 Speedometer illumination
63 Instrument illumination
64 Front parking lamp
65 Plate illumination lamp
66 Tail lamp

‡ Where fitted

Colour Code

B	Black	N	Brown	S	Slate
G	Green	O	Orange	U	Blue
K	Pink	P	Purple	W	White
LG	Light green	R	Red	Y	Yellow

202

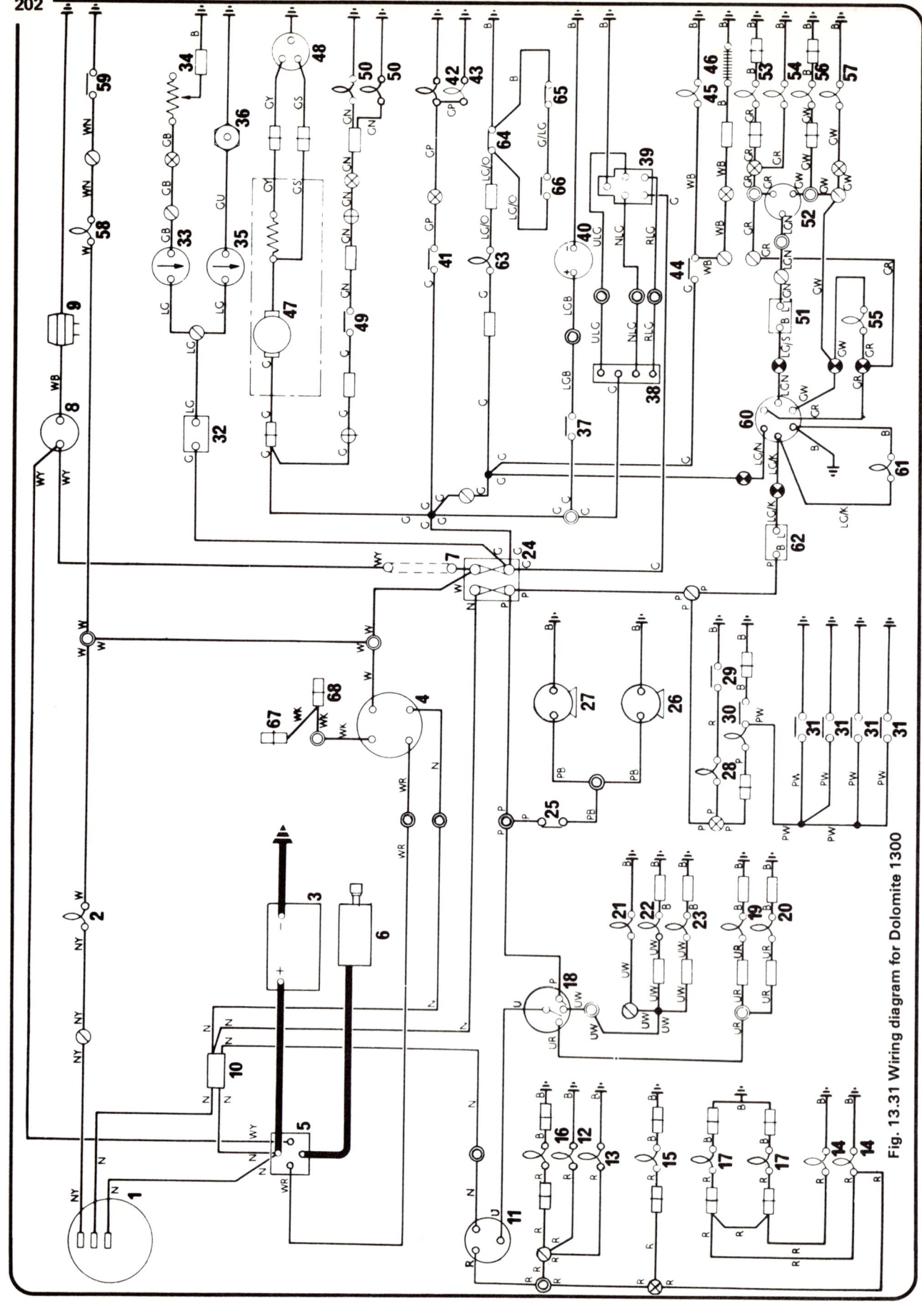

Fig. 13.31 Wiring diagram for Dolomite 1300

Fig. 13.31 Key to wiring diagram for Dolomite 1300

1 Alternator
2 Ignition warning light
3 Battery
4 Ignition/starter switch
5 Starter solenoid
6 Starter motor
7 Ballast resistor wire
8 Ignition coil
9 Ignition distributor
10 Connector
11 Master light switch
12 2-in-1 instrument illumination
13 Speedometer illumination
14 LH and RH tail lamps
15 LH front side lamp
16 RH front side lamp
17 Number plate illumination lamps
18 Main/dip/flash switch
19 LH dip beam
20 RH dip beam
21 Main beam warning light
22 LH main beam
23 RH main beam

24 Fusebox
25 Horn-push switch
26 Horn LH
27 Horn RH
28 Luggage boot light
29 Luggage boot light switch
30 Interior light switch
31 Door switches
32 Voltage stabilizer
33 Fuel indicator
34 Fuel tank unit
35 Temperature indicator
36 Temperature transmitter
37 Windscreen washer switch
38 Windscreen wiper switch
39 Windscreen wiper motor
40 Windscreen washer pump
41 Stop lamp switch
42 LH stop lamp
43 RH stop lamp
44 Heated backlight switch
45 Heated backlight warning light
46 Heated backlight

47 Heater motor
48 Heater switch
49 Reverse lamp switch
50 Reverse lamps
51 Turn signal flasher unit
52 Turn signal switch
53 LH front flasher lamp
54 LH rear flasher lamp
55 Indicator warning light
56 RH front flasher lamp
57 RH rear flasher lamp
58 Oil pressure warning light
59 Oil pressure switch
60 Hazard switch
61 Hazard warning light
62 Hazard unit
63 Seat belt warning light
64 Driver's belt switch
65 Passenger belt switch
66 Seat sensor switch
67 Radio supply
68 'Aux' heater feed

Colour code

B	Black	U	Blue	W	White
G	Green	Y	Yellow	P	Purple
O	Orange	LG	Light green	K	Pink
N	Brown	R	Red	S	Slate

Index

A

Air cleaner – 50
Alternator – dismantling, overhaul and reassembly – 129
    drive belt adjustment – 129
    functional check – 126
    general description – 125
    remove and refit – 129
Anti-freeze mixture – 48

B

Battery – charging – 125
    electrolyte replenishment – 125
    maintenance and inspection – 124
    removal and replacement – 124
Big end bearing – examination and renovation – 27
    removal – 25
Bodywork and underframe – general description – 161
    maintenance – 161, 163
    repairs – 163
    repair sequence – 166, 167
Bonnet – 172
Boot – 172, 174
Braking system – adjustment – 108
    bleeding – 108
    brake pedal – 118
    disc brakes – description – 118
    fault diagnosis – 122
    flexible hose – 108
    front brake shoes – 110
    front brake wheel cylinder – 116
    front disc brake caliper – 119, 121
    front disc brake caliper pad – 118
    general description – 108
    handbrake – 116
    master cylinder – 112, 114, 121
    rear brake shoes – 110, 193
    rear brake wheel cylinder – 115, 193
    servo unit – 121
    specifications – 107
    stop light switch – 118
    torque wrench settings – 107
Bumpers – 174

C

Camshaft – examination and renovation – 28
    removal – 24
    replacement – 32
Carburettor – adjustment and tuning – 58
    description – 54
    dismantling and reassembly – 54

    examination and repair – 54
    float chamber flooding – 58
    float chamber fuel level adjustment – 58
    float needle sticking – 58
    jet centering – 58
    needle replacement – 58
    piston sticking – 55
    removal and refitting – 54
    water or dirt in – 58
Choke cable – 60
Clutch – bleeding – 74
    faults – 80
    master cylinder – 75, 77
    pedal – 78
    release mechanism – 78
    removal, inspection and replacement – 77
    slave cylinder – 75
Clutch and actuating mechanism – general description – 74
    specifications – 74
    torque wrench settings – 74
Condenser – 66
Connecting rod – removal – 25
Connecting rod to crankshaft – reassembly – 32
Contact breaker points – adjustment – 66
    removal and replacement – 66
Cooling system – draining – 43
    expansion tank – 43
    fault diagnosis – 49
    filling – 43
    flushing – 43
    general description – 42
    specifications – 42
    torque wrench settings – 42
Crankcase ventilation system – 27
Crankshaft – examination and renovation – 27
    housing replacement – 38
    rear seal replacement – 38
    removal – 25
    replacement – 30
Cylinder bores – examination and renovation – 28
Cylinder head – decarbonisation – 30
    removal – 20
    replacement – 36

D

Decarbonisation – 30
Distributor – dismantling – 68
    inspection and repair – 68
    lubrication – 66

reassembly – 68
removal – 68
replacement – 38, 68
Distributor drive – removal – 25
replacement – 38
Door – front – 163, 164
rattles – 163
rear – 164
striker plate – 164

E

Electrical system – fault diagnosis – 142
flasher circuit – 134
general description – 124
ignition/starter switch – 136
light bulbs – 136
specifications – 123, 177
steering column combination switch – 136
temperature and fuel gauge – 138
voltage stabiliser – 136
wiring diagrams – 140, 198
Engine – ancillary components removal – 20
dismantling – 18
end plate removal – 25
end plate replacement – 38
examination and renovation – 27
fails to start – 71
fault diagnosis – 41
final assembly – 40
general description – 13
major operations – 15
misfires – 77
reassembly – 30
removal – 15
replacement – 40
specifications – 11, 176
start up after overhaul – 40
torque wrench settings – 13
Exhaust system and manifolds
general description – 178
removal and refitting – 178

F

Facia panel – 170
Fan belt – adjustment – 48
removal and replacement – 49
Fault diagnosis – braking system – 122
clutch – 80
cooling system – 49
electrical system – 142
engine – 41
fuel system and carburation – 63
gearbox – 97
ignition system – 71
steering – 160
suspension – 160
Flywheel – examination and renovation – 29
removal – 25
replacement – 38
Flywheel starter ring – 29
Front hub bearings – 146
Fuel gauge – 138
Fuel pipe lines – 60
Fuel pump – description – 50
dismantling, overhaul and reassembly – 51
removal and replacement – 51
testing – 51
Fuel system and carburation – fault diagnosis – 63
general description – 50
specifications – 50, 176
Fuel tank – cleaning – 60
removal and replacement – 60
sender unit – 60

Fuses – 136

G

Gearbox – cover extension – 94
dismantling – 83, 186
examination and renovation – 88, 187
fault diagnosis – 97
general description – 81, 183
input shaft – 88
mainshaft – 85
rear extension – 96
rear oil seal – 94
reassembly – 90, 187
removal and replacement – 83, 186
specifications – 81, 177
top cover – 94
torque wrench settings – 81
Gudgeon pin – removal – 25

H

Headlights – beam adjustment – 134
removal and replacement – 134
Heater – 170, 172
Horns – 134

I

Ignition system – ballast resistor – 68, 183
coil – 68
dismantling – 180
fault diagnosis – 71
general description – 64
inspection and repair – 181
reassembly – 183
specifications – 64, 183
timing – 69
torque wrench settings – 64

L

Lubricants – recommended – 7
Lubrication system – 27

M

Main bearing – examination and renovation – 27
removal – 25

O

Oil filter – 27
Oil pressure relief valve – 27
Oil pump – examination and renovation – 29
removal and dismantling – 27
replacement – 38

P

Parcel shelf – 170
Piston/connecting rod – reassembly – 32
Piston rings – examination and renovation – 28
renewal – 25
replacement – 32
Pistons – examination and renovation – 28
removal – 25
replacement – 32
Propeller shaft – centre bearing – 100, 193
general description – 98, 190
removal and replacement – 98, 191
specifications – 98, 175

R

Radiator – 43
Rear axle – bearings – 101
differential assembly – 104
general description – 101
half shafts – 101

oil seals – 101
    pinion oil seal –104
    removal and replacement – 104
    specifications – 101
    torque wrench settings – 101
Rear hub assembly – 152
Rocker arm/valve – adjustment – 38
Rocker assembly – dismantling – 23
    examination and renovation – 29
    reassembly – 36

S

Seats – 170
Spare parts – ordering – 8
Spark plugs – 70
    colour chart – 73
Specifications – braking system – 107
    clutch and actuating mechanism – 74
    cooling system – 42
    electrical system – 124
    engine – 11
    fuel system and carburation – 50
    gearbox – 81
    ignition system – 64
    propeller shaft – 98
    rear axle – 101
    steering – 144
    suspension – 144
    universal joints – 98
Speedometer – 138
Starter motor – dismantling and reassembly – 130
    general description – 129
    inertia drive – 130
    removal and replacement – 130
    testing on engine – 129
Steering – arm – 152
    column – 159
    fault diagnosis – 160
    general description – 145
    front wheel alignment – 160
    front wheel camber – 160
    outer ball joint assembly – 160
    rack and pinion – 154, 156
    rear wheel alignment – 160
    specifications – 144
    torque wrench settings – 145
    wheel – 154
    wheel intermediate shaft – 159
Sump – examination and renovation – 30
    removal – 25
    replacement – 38
Suspension – fault diagnosis – 160
    general description – 145
    front lower wishbone arm – 149

    front spring and damper – 147
    front upper wishbone arms – 149
    front vertical link upper ball joint – 149
    radius rod – 154
    rear arm – 154
    rear damper – 153
    specifications – 144, 177
    torque wrench settings – 145

T

Tappets – examination and renovation – 29
    reassembly – 36
Temperature gauge – 48, 138
Thermostat – 45
Throttle pedal and cable – 60
Timing chain tensioner – examination and renovation – 29
    removal – 27
    replacement – 27, 32
Timing cover and gears – replacement – 32
Timing cover, gears and chain – removal – 23
Timing gears and chain – examination and renovation – 28
Torque wrench settings – braking system – 107
    clutch and actuating mechanism – 74
    cooling system – 42
    engine – 13
    gearbox – 81
    ignition system – 64
    rear axle – 101
    steering – 145
    suspension – 145
Tyre pressures – 144

U

Universal joints – dismantling and fitting new bearings – 100
    general description – 98
    inspection and repair – 100
    specifications – 98

V

Valve guides – examination and renovation – 30
Valves – adjustment – 38
    examination and renovation – 28
    reassembly – 36
    removal – 23

W

Water pump – dismantling and reassembly – 48
    removal and replacement – 45
Windscreen – 170
Windscreen wiper – arms – 130
    mechanism – 130, 132
    motor – 132, 195
    switch – 136, 196
    washer – 196

Printed by
Haynes Publishing Group
Sparkford Yeovil Somerset
England